Tableau Your Data!

Fast and Easy Visual Analysis
with Tableau Software®

Daniel G. Murray and
the InterWorks BI Team

WILEY

Tableau Your Data!: Fast and Easy Visual Analysis with Tableau Software®

Published by
John Wiley & Sons, Inc.
10475 Crosspoint Boulevard
Indianapolis, IN 46256
www.wiley.com

Copyright © 2013 by John Wiley & Sons, Inc., Indianapolis, Indiana

Published simultaneously in Canada

ISBN: 978-1-118-61204-0
ISBN: 978-1-118-61219-4 (ebk)
ISBN: 978-1-118-83946-1 (ebk)
Manufactured in the United States of America

10 9 8 7 6 5 4 3 2 1

For general information on our other products and services please contact our Customer Care Department within the United States at (877) 762-2974, outside the United States at (317) 572-3993 or fax (317) 572-4002.

Wiley also publishes its books in a variety of electronic formats and by print-on-demand. Not all content that is available in standard print versions of this book may appear or be packaged in all book formats. If you have purchased a version of this book that did not include media that is referenced by or accompanies a standard print version, you may request this media by visiting http://booksupport. wiley.com. For more information about Wiley products, visit us at www.wiley.com.

Library of Congress Control Number: 2013948016

To my wife, Linda, and my children, Erin and Hannah, for your understanding during the months I was "away" writing at home. And to my parents, Mike and Joan, who instilled the desire to learn.

About the Author

Daniel G. Murray has over 30 years of professional experience. Dan has seen firsthand the technical revolution in data that lead to the creation of Tableau Software. Prior to starting the InterWorks Tableau/BI practice in 2008, he held a variety of increasingly responsible roles in finance, accounting, sales, and operations for a mid-sized global manufacturing company serving the heavy industry and construction markets. During the late 1990s his employer acquired over 50 companies. Dan's role in 2006 as a CFO/CIO lead to an assignment to integrate and create a global reporting environment. Uninspired by the high cost and complicated products available from traditional vendors, Dan discovered Tableau Software through data visualization expert Stephen Few. Less than one month after downloading a trial license of Tableau Software, Dan and his team were able to successfully create a reporting platform for less than 15 percent of the cost, and in 1/10th the time that traditional vendors had quoted. At this point it was apparent that everyone needed Tableau—they just didn't know it yet.

Within months after speaking at Tableau's first customer conference, Dan went to friend and Founder of InterWorks Inc., Behfar Jahanshahi, to convince him to allow Dan to form a boutique consulting team focusing on providing the best practices of data visualization and reporting using Tableau Software and any emerging or popular database.

InterWorks, Inc. is now the premier Gold Professional Consulting Partner for Tableau Software with clients all over the world and over 35 Tableau consultants providing data visualization, database, and hardware expertise to many of the most significant organizations spanning business, education, and government.

Dan is a 1982 graduate of Purdue University's Krannert School of Business. He and his family live in the metro Atlanta area.

Credits

Executive Editor
Robert Elliott

Project Editor
Ed Connor

Senior Production Editor
Kathleen Wisor

Copy Editor
Caroline Johnson

Editorial Manager
Mary Beth Wakefield

Freelancer Editorial Manager
Rosemarie Graham

Associate Director of Marketing
David Mayhew

Marketing Manager
Ashley Zurcher

Business Manager
Amy Knies

Vice President and Executive Group Publisher
Richard Swadley

Associate Publisher
Jim Minatel

Project Coordinator, Cover
Katie Crocker

Compositor
Maureen Forys, Happenstance Type-O-Rama

Proofreader
Nancy Carrasco

Indexer
Johnna VanHoose Dinse

Cover Image
Courtesy of Dan Murray

Cover Designer
Ryan Sneed

Acknowledgments

This book is the product of years of experience and the collective effort of many different InterWorks team members. Writing a book requires a little more effort than a tweet or a blog post. Many different people provided technical feedback and inspiration.

Brian Bickell and Eric Shiarla contributed initial drafts of the chapters related to Tableau Server. Kate Treadwell provided a section and examples related to Tableau's `tabcmd` and `tabadmin` command line functionality. Significant portions of Chapter 2 were provided by UK team members Mel Stephenson, Rob Austin, and James Austin.

Creating function references in Appendix A was a team effort, but Mike Roberts was instrumental in collecting and organizing all of the examples, and also contributing a lot of original example material. Ben Bausili, Josh Davis, Tim Costello, and Matthew Miller from the North American team provided code examples. Jeroen Spanjers, Alastair Young, and Darren Evans of the UK Team also contributed excellent reference material.

Several Tableau Software employees were instrumental in providing technical feedback. I especially want to thank Molly Monsey for the many hours she spent reviewing initial drafts and coordinating other subject area experts within Tableau. François Ajenstat provided guidance during several phases of the book's development—thank you Francois for your enthusiasm and wonderful perspective! Dan Huff and Lee Gray provided detailed technical feedback and advice on the chapters that related to Tableau Server. Russell Christopher gave critique on Tableau's dashboard features and feedback on my ideas related to best practices. All of your contributions improved the content. Any mistakes that have made it into the final release are entirely my own.

Case studies and advice were contributed by clients and friends: Andy Kriebel of Facebook; Paul Lisborg of Newnan Utilities; John Hoover of Norfolk Southern; Gregory Lewandowski, Rob Higgins, and Paul Laza of Cisco; Tim Kuhn of the ACT .org; and Ted Curran of Carnegie Mellon University. Tableau Zen Master Jonathan Drummey of the Southern Maine Medical Center contributed an interesting case study, which came from Jonathan's amazing mind and with no assistance from InterWorks. A former client and current friend, Adrian Abarca, contributed an interesting study of Tableau use for human resource analysis. Most of all I want to thank Brian McKinsey, my old boss and President of Blastrac, Inc., for tasking me to figure out a way to globalize our reporting schema; and Elaine Hillyer, a friend and co-worker, who provided a lot of solutions during our first Tableau project. That initial project literally changed my life.

Finally, a big thank you to the first believer in the idea for a consulting practice focused on Tableau and for supporting this book—Behfar Jahanshahi, CEO and Founder of InterWorks, Inc. Without his early "faith"—it wouldn't have happened. Thank you all!

Contents

    Saving Time and Improving Formatting 177
        Double-Click Fields to Build Faster 177
        Reduce Clicks using the Right-Mouse Button Drag 179
        Quick Copy Fields with Control-Drag. 179
        Replace Fields by Dropping the New Field on Top 180
        Right-Click to Edit or Format Anything 181
        Editing or Removing Titles from Axis Headings. 181
        Speed Up Your Presentation Page Views 182
        A Faster Way to Access Field Menu Options 183
    Improving Appearance to Convey Meaning
        More Precisely 184
        Changing the Appearance of Dates 184
        Formatting Tooltip Content. 185
        *Change the Order of Color Expressed in Charts to
            Compare Related Values more Easily* 185
        *Exposing a Header in a One-Column Crosstab to
            Add Meaning and Save Space* 186
        *Unpacking a Packaged Workbook
            File (.twbx)* 187
        Make a Parameterized Axis Label 187
        Using Continuous Quick Filters for Ranges of Values 188
        Create Your Own Custom Date Hierarchy 189
        Assemble Your Own Custom Fields. 190
        Let Tableau Build Your Actions 191
        Formatting Table Calculation Results 192
        When to Use Floating Objects in Dashboards 195
    Customizing Shapes, Colors,
        Fonts, and Images 196
        Customizing Shapes 196
        Customizing Colors 198
        Customizing Fonts 199
        Customizing Images in Dashboards. 200
    Advanced Chart Types 201
        Bar in Bar Chart 201
        Box Plots 202
        Pareto Charts. 204
        Sparklines 207
        Bullet Graphs 208

Foreword

Tableau was founded with a simple mission: to help people see and understand their data. More than ten years later, we're pursuing that same mission. We've been fortunate to build a talented team of people who deeply believe in serving that mission. Just as importantly, we've collaborated with hundreds of thousands of people working for our 13,500+ customer accounts worldwide.

Tableau Desktop and Tableau Server, which are the focus of this book, put the power of data into the hands of those people who inspired us from the beginning. We've designed our software to be flexible and capable enough to help a single person answer questions from a spreadsheet, or to enable thousands of people across an enterprise to execute complex queries against massive databases.

Tableau can help you answer questions with data. We hear stories daily about how people use Tableau to help increase sales, streamline operations, improve customer service, manage investments, assess quality and safety, study and treat diseases, pursue academic research, address environmental problems, and improve education.

My hope is that this book can accelerate your adoption of Tableau.

CHRISTIAN CHABOT
CEO, CO-FOUNDER AND CHAIRMAN
TABLEAU SOFTWARE

Introduction

Tableau Software started ten years ago as a desktop application, but as the tool has matured it has become popular in the enterprise and is being used in "Big Data" environments. The *enterprise* means any type of significant organization—a global business or non-profit, such as a large university, small college or hospitals, banks, retailers, or internet-based data companies that have accumulated massive data sets. Or, this might refer to a small business with only a few employees. A short list of the types of organizations using Tableau should include:

- Multi-national financial institutions
- Federal Government
- International police organizations
- The military
- Government intelligence organizations
- Media companies
- Financial institutions
- Hospitals
- Book publishers
- Internet-based business (with Big Data)
- Insurance companies
- Non-profit entities
- Manufacturing and Distribution companies
- Education (universities, colleges, charter schools, public schools)
- Law firms
- Consulting firms
- Retailers
- Consumer products' companies
- Accounting firms
- Consulting firms

Any person who needs to see and understand data is a candidate for using Tableau Software.

Tableau does a good job listening to their customers and partners. They've improved the speed, security, and added more visualization types to Tableau's capabilities.

Today, many large enterprises use Tableau because they find it increases user adoption rates. It also allows business users to create their own reports with relative ease—reducing the report backlog that accumulates within information technology departments. Smaller enterprises are using Tableau because it provides a low-cost way to turn data into useful information.

OVERVIEW OF THE BOOK AND TECHNOLOGY

This book aims to provide an introduction to Tableau in the context of the needs of enterprises—large and small. With every Tableau deployment, there are several user constituencies—report designers, who are responsible for performing analysis and creating reports; information technology team members, responsible for managing Tableau Server and maintaining good data governance; and the information consumers who use the output and may want to do their own report creation.

This book's goal is to provide each group with a basic introduction to Tableau's Desktop and Server environments, while also providing best practice recommendations that encompass novice, intermediate, and advanced use of the software.

HOW THIS BOOK IS ORGANIZED

There are four distinct sections. Part I (Chapters 1-8) covers the basics related to Tableau Desktop and then progresses to more advanced topics, including best practices for building dashboards that will be understandable to end users, load quickly, and be responsive to query requests made by information consumers.

Part II (Chapters 9-11) focuses on Tableau Server, mostly from the perspective of a technology manager responsible for installing, securing, and maintaining the Tableau Server environment.

Part III (Chapter 12) includes case studies from clients and experienced users who have deployed Tableau and are actively using it effectively. These short stories provide a glimpse into how other people are using Tableau and will provide grist for your brainstorming related to your own project.

Part IV (Appendices A, B, C, D)—Appendix A includes a detailed function reference, sorted alphabetically, that includes every function with example code and brief explanations. The intent is to provide a quick reference if you need to refresh your memory about the syntax of a function. One to three examples for most of the functions are provided. The goal of the function reference is to give you an easy way to refresh your memory regarding infrequently-used functions or help you learn about a function you've never used. Other supplemental material related to preparing data for analysis is presented in Appendix B, and Appendix C provides a brief introduction to the book's InterWorks book website. A glossary of technical terms is provided in Appendix D.

WHO SHOULD READ THIS BOOK

This book is intended to introduce new users to the features that Tableau Desktop has to offer from the perspective of someone who needs to create a new analysis or do reporting. It is also intended for staff responsible for installing, deploying, and maintaining Tableau Server.

The chapters related to Tableau Server are more technical because the subject matter assumes that you have a grasp of server terminology and security.

You can read the book sequentially from start to finish. Or, you can skip around and read about a topic of particular interest. Each chapter builds on the previous material, but if you've already mastered the basics of connecting and using the Desktop, you can skip any chapter related to Tableau Desktop and focus on topics of interest.

TOOLS YOU WILL NEED

You can read the book without having Tableau Software installed on your computer, but you'll get a lot more from the material if you follow the examples yourself. Tableau provides free trials of the software. Alternatively, you can download Tableau Public for free, indefinitely—all of the book examples related to Tableau Desktop should work on Tableau Public.

WHAT'S ON THE INTERWORKS BOOK WEBSITE?

Tableau constantly updates the Desktop and Server products with multiple maintenance releases and at least one major product release every 12 to 15 months. The InterWorks book website (`http://tableauyourdata.com`) includes articles related to the releases, sample files related to the book's examples, and will also include examples related to new capabilities added to the product as

Tableau makes them available. The InterWorks team actively tests new Tableau products, so the companion website may also include demonstrations of new visualization types or techniques before they become available publically.

Wiley also has a website dedicated to the book that you can find at:

`www.wiley.com/go/tableauyourdata`

SUMMARY

Tableau lowers the technical bar for accessing data from many different data-sources. This book should allow you to advance your technical ability and enable you to save time deploying Tableau in your enterprise by making better decisions, earlier in your deployment.

PART I

DESKTOP

In this part

CHAPTER 1

Creating Visual Analytics with Tableau Desktop

Data graphics should draw the viewer's attention to the sense and substance of the data, not to something else.

EDWARD R. TUFTE[1]

The seeds for Tableau were planted in the early 1970s when IBM invented Structured Query Language (SQL) and later in 1981 when the spreadsheet became the killer application of the personal computer. Data creation and analysis fundamentally changed for the better. Our ability to create and store data increased exponentially.

The business information (BI) industry was created with this wave; each vendor providing a product "stack" based on some variant of SQL. The pioneering companies invented foundational technologies and developed sound methods for collecting and storing data. Recently, a new generation of NOSQL[2] (Not Only SQL) databases are enabling web properties like Facebook to mine massive, multi-petabyte[3] data streams.

Deploying these systems can take years. Data today resides in many different proprietary databases and may also need to be collected from external sources. The traditional leaders in the BI industry have created reporting tools that focus on rendering data from their proprietary products. Performing analysis and building reports with these tools requires technical expertise and time. The people with the technical chops to master them are product specialists that don't always know the best way to present the information.

The scale, velocity, and scope of data today demands reporting tools that deploy quickly. They must be suitable for non-technical users to master. They should connect to a wide variety of datasources. And, the tools need to guide us to use the best techniques known for rendering the data into information.

THE SHORTCOMINGS OF TRADITIONAL INFORMATION ANALYSIS

Entities are having difficulty getting widespread usage of traditional BI tools. A recent study by the Business Application Research Center (BARC, 2009) reported adoption rates are surprisingly low.[4]

In any given BI using organization just over 8 percent of employees are actually using BI tools. Even in industries that have aggressively adopted BI tools (e.g., wholesales, banking, and retail), usage barely exceeds 11 percent.

NIGEL PENDSE, BARC

In other words, 92 percent of the people that have traditional BI tools—don't use them. The BARC Survey noted these causes:

- The tools are too difficult to learn and use.
- Technical experts were needed to create reports.
- The turnaround time for reports is too long.

Companies that have invested millions of dollars in BI systems are using spreadsheets for data analysis and reporting. When BI system reports are received, traditional tools often employ inappropriate visualization methods. Stephen Few has written several books that illuminate the problem and provides examples of data visualization techniques that adhere to best practices. Stephen also provides examples of inappropriate visualizations provided by legacy vendor tools.[5] It turns out that the skills required to design and build database products are different from the skills needed to create dashboards that effectively communicate. The BARC study clearly indicates that this IT-centric control model has failed to deliver compelling answers that attract users.

People want to make informed decisions with reliable information. They need timely reports that present the evidence to support their decisions. They want to connect with a variety of datasources, and they don't know the best ways to visualize data. Ideally, the tool used should automatically present the information using the best practices.

THE BUSINESS CASE FOR VISUAL ANALYSIS

Whether the entity seeks profits or engages in non-profit activities, all enterprises use data to monitor operations and perform analysis. Insights gleaned from the reports and analysis are then used to maintain efficiency, pursue opportunity, and prevent negative outcomes. Supporting this infrastructure (from the perspective of the information consumer) are three kinds of data.

THREE KINDS OF DATA THAT EXIST IN EVERY ENTITY

Reports, analysis, and ad hoc discovery are used to express three basics kinds of data.

Known Data (type 1)

Encompassed in daily, weekly, and monthly reports that are used for monitoring activity, these reports provide the basic context used to inform discussion and frame questions. Type 1 reports aren't intended to answer questions. Their purpose is to provide visibility of operations.

Data You Know You Need to Know (type 2)

Once patterns and outliers emerge in type 1 data the question that naturally follows is: Why is this happening? People need to understand the cause of the outliers so that action can be taken. Traditional reporting tools provide a good framework to answer this type of query as long as the question is anticipated in the design of the report.

Data You Don't Know You Need to Know (type 3)

By interacting with data in real-time while using appropriate visual analytics, Tableau provides the possibility of seeing patterns and outliers that are not visible in type 1 and type 2 reports. The process of interacting with granular data yields different questions that can lead to new actionable insights. Software that enables quick-iterative analysis and reporting is becoming a necessary element of effective business information systems.

Distributing type 1 reports in a timely manner is important, but speed in the design and build stage of type 1 reports is also important when a new type 1 report is created. To effectively enable type 2 and 3 analyses the reporting tool must adapt quickly to ad hoc queries and present the data in intuitively understandable ways.

HOW VISUAL ANALYTICS IMPROVES DECISION-MAKING

Rendering data accurately with appropriate visual analytics reduces the time required to achieve understanding. Review the following examples to see how visual analytics can reduce the time to insight. The goal of these reports is to provide sales analysis by region, product category, and product sub-category.

Figure 1-1 presents data using a grid of numbers (crosstab) and pie charts. Crosstabs are useful for finding specific values. Pie Charts are intended to show one-to-many comparisons of dimensions. The pie charts compare sales by product sub-category.

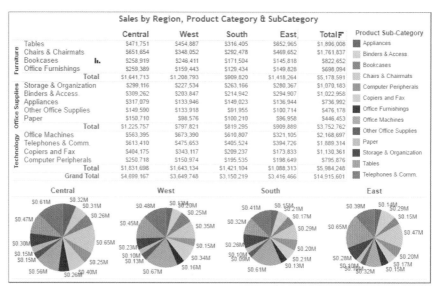

FIGURE 1-1 *Sales Mix Analysis using a crosstab and pie charts*

Crosstabs are not the most effective way to make one-to-many comparisons or identify outliers. Pie charts are commonly used for comparisons but are one of the least effective ways to compare values across dimensions. It is difficult to make precise comparisons especially between slices, and even more so when there are many slices.

Figure 1-2 employs a bar chart and heat map to convey the same information. Bar charts provide a better means for comparing product sub-categories. The heat map on the right provides total sales for each category. The gray scale color range highlights the high and low selling product sub-categories. The color encoding in the bar chart provides additional information on profit ratio. Reference lines in the bar chart display the average sales for all product sub-categories within each region.

Clearly the bar chart and heat map communicate the sales values more quickly while adding profit ratio information with the use of color. The reference lines within each region and product category provide average sales values. One could argue that the bar chart doesn't communicate the details available in the crosstab, but in Figure 1-3 those details and more are provided via Tooltips that pop out when you point your mouse at a mark.

Appropriate visual analytics improve decision-making by making it easier to see summary trends and outliers without sacrificing desired details by making those details available on demand.

FIGURE 1-2 *Sales Mix Analysis using a bar chart and heat map*

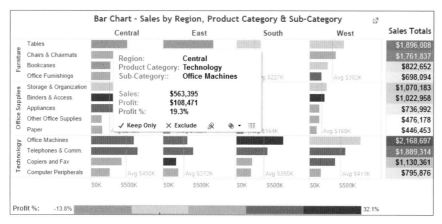

FIGURE 1-3 *Adding labels and Tooltips*

TURNING DATA INTO INFORMATION WITH VISUAL ANALYTICS

Data that is overly summarized loses its ability to inform. When it's too detailed, rapid interpretation of the data is compromised. Visual analytics bridges this gap by providing the right style of data visualization and detail for the situational need. The ideal analysis and reporting tool should possess the following attributes:

- Simplicity—Be easy for non-technical users to master.
- Connectivity—Seamlessly connect to a large variety of datasources.
- Visual Competence—Provide appropriate graphics by default.
- Sharing—Facilitate sharing of insight.
- Scale—Handle large data sets.

Traditional BI reporting solutions aren't adapted for the variety of datasources available today. Analysis and reporting can't occur in these tools until the architecture is created within the proprietary product stack. Tableau Software was designed to address these needs.

THE TABLEAU SOFTWARE ECOSYSTEM

Tableau's product line includes desktop design and analysis tools for creating and consuming data. For larger deployments, Tableau Server permits information consumers to access reports in a secure environment without the need to load software. Reports are consumed in Tableau Server via a web browser. Tableau Server also enables reports to be consumed on iOS or Android tablet computers. Tableau Public is a free tool that facilitates sharing public data on the web via blogs or webpages. For those that want a hosted solution, Tableau Public Premium is a fee-based service that uses the same technology as Tableau Public in a private consumption environment.

TABLEAU DESKTOP AND TABLEAU READER

Desktop is the design tool for creating visual analytics and dashboards. There are two versions: Personal Edition and Professional Edition. Professional Edition is more popular because it connects to a wider variety of datasources than Personal Edition. Less common datasources can be accessed via the Open Database Connectivity (ODBC) standard.

Tableau Desktop

Table 1-1 displays the available connections arranged by the type of datasource. Personal Edition only connects to local files.

TABLE 1-1 Datasources Accessible to Tableau Desktop

LOCAL FILES	RELATIONAL DATABASES	ANALYTIC DATABASES	DATA APPLIANCES	DATA CUBES	NOSQL DATASOURCES	WEB SERVICES APIS	OTHER
Microsoft Excel	Firebird	Actian Vectorwise	IBM Netezza	Oracle Essbase	Cloudera Hadoop	Google Analytics	ODBC
Microsoft Access	IBM DB2	EMC Greenplum	Teradata	Microsoft Analysis Services	Hortonworks Hadoop Hive	Google Big Query	
Text files (txt, csv)	Microsoft SQL Server	ParAccel	SAP Hana	Microsoft PowerPivot	MapR Hadoop Hive	ODATA	
Import from Workbook (tbm)	MySQL	SAP Sybase IQ			DataStax Enterprise	Salesforce	
Tableau Data Extract (tds)	Oracle	HP Vertica				Windows Azure Marketplace Datamarket	
	PostgreSQL	Aster Database				Amazon Redshift	
	Progress OpenEdge						
	SAP NetWeaver Business Warehouse						
	SAP Sybase ASE						

Tableau Desktop is licensed by a named-user. Tableau allows you to reassign licenses and also permits you to install Tableau Desktop on multiple computers so long as the named-user is the only person with access to them.

Tableau Reader

Tableau also permits you to share content with another desktop tool. Tableau Reader is a free version that allows users to consume Tableau Desktop reports without the need for a paid license. The only requirement is that the Tableau report be saved as a packaged workbook.

File Types

You can save and share data using a variety of different file types. The differences between each file type relates to the amount and type of information being stored in the file. Table 1-2 summarizes different Tableau file types.

TABLE 1-2 Tableau File Types

FILE TYPE (FILE EXTENSION)	SIZE	USE CASE	INCLUDES
Tableau Workbook (twb)	Small	Tableau's default way to save work.	Information to visualize data. No source data.
Tableau Datasource (tds)	Small	Accessing frequently-used datasources.	Server address, password, and other metadata related to the datasource.
Tableau Bookmark (tbm)	Normally small	Sharing worksheets from one workbook to another.	Information to visualize the datasource if the source workbook is a packaged workbook.
Tableau Data Extract (tde)	Potentially large	Improves performance. Enables more functions.	Source data as filtered and aggregated during extract.
Tableau Packaged Workbook (twbx)	Potentially large	Sharing with Tableau Reader or those without access to the source data.	Extracted data and workbook information to build visualizations.

When you save your work in desktop the default save method creates a workbook (twb) file. If you need to share your work with people that don't have a Tableau Desktop license or don't have access to the datasource you can save your work as a packaged workbook (twbx) by using the Save As option when saving your file.

Tableau Datasources (tds) are useful when you frequently connect to a particular datasource or you have edited the metadata associated with that datasource in some way (renaming or grouping fields for example). Using saved datasources reduces the time required to connect to the data.

Tableau Bookmarks (tbm) allow you to share a single worksheet from your workbook with others. To create a bookmark file, access the main file menu window/bookmark/create bookmark option.

Tableau Data Extracts (tde) leverage Tableau's proprietary data engine. When you create an extract your data is compressed. If your datasource is from a file (Excel, Access, text) Data Extracts add formula functions that don't exist in those sources—including count distinct and median. If you are publishing workbooks via Tableau Server, Data Extracts provide an effective way to separate the analytical load Tableau generates from your source database.

Tableau Server

If you produce a large number of workbooks that have to be updated regularly or you have a large number of people consuming your work, Tableau Server will save you time. Server allows people to view and interact with your work via a web browser. Server will also automatically refresh data extracts that have been published to Tableau Server.

Server is licensed in two ways: by named-user or by core licensing. Named-user licensing makes sense in smaller deployments when fewer than 150 people need access to Tableau Reports. In larger deployments with dynamic access requirements, core licensing is more cost-effective and reduces administrative time because the license is defined by the number of cores in your database server's processor.

Tableau Server provides enhanced security and permits users to customize their access to reports within boundaries defined by the server administrator. Tableau Server's interface provides users with tools for finding, organizing, and commenting on reports. Server enables users to create subscriptions that provide e-mail notification when updated reports are published. It also provides administrators with the ability to monitor access and monitor system performance. Details regarding installation, access, and administration will be covered in Chapters 9 and 10.

Tableau Public

Tableau Public is a free hosted web service that can be used to publish Tableau Reports on the web. Commonly used content management systems like WordPress, Tumblr, and Typepad are supported. Tableau's licensed desktop editions can also publish content to Tableau Public. Tableau also offers a free Public desktop edition for creating and publishing reports. Tableau Public has the following limitations:

- Tableau Desktop only connects to Microsoft Access, Excel, or text files.
- Your work can only be saved to Tableau's public Server.
- Storage space on Tableau Public is limited to 50 megabytes per named-user.

- Datasource size is limited to 100,000 records.
- Workbooks saved on Tableau Public can be viewed and downloaded by anyone.

For these reasons Tableau Public is an ideal way for hobbyists and bloggers to create and share interactive visualizations on the web. But, it is not a substitute for full desktop or server licensing.

Tableau Public Premium

The premium edition is a fee-based service that permits subscribers to protect the confidentiality of their data by blocking the ability for information consumers to download source workbook files. Subscriber fees are based on the customized record limits and storage limits. For entities that do not have the resources or desire to manage their own instance of Tableau Server, Tableau Public Premium offers a cost effective way to share proprietary data over the web and maintain security over the source data set used to create the visualizations.

Recommended Hardware Configuration

Tableau provides minimum hardware specifications on their website, which are presented below. Analysts that build reports should have better equipment. More internal memory will have a significant positive effect on speed.

Install 4 to 8 megabytes of internal memory for the best performance. Tableau's rendering engine will take advantage of modern graphics cards as well. Solid-state disk drives outperform physical hard disks. But, don't outfit your Report-building analysts with state-of-the-art equipment if the majority of your user base is using 4 year-old junk. What performs well on a well-appointed computer may not be as enjoyable an experience on a dated system.

Tableau Desktop

- Microsoft Windows 7, Vista, XP, Server 2008, Server 2003 (on x86 or x64 chipsets), or Microsoft Windows 8.
- 32-bit or 64-bit versions of Windows.
- Minimum of an Intel Pentium 4 or AMD Opteron processor.
- 250 megabytes minimum free disk space.
- 32-bit color depth recommended.
- Note: Internet Explorer is not supported.

At the time of this writing (January 2013) Tableau does not support Apple operating systems. Many people successfully use Apple products to run Tableau by running a virtual Windows environment on their laptop. Apple's Boot Camp provides a means to run Windows on a MacBook. Other commercial products such as VMware Fusion or Parallels Desktop can be used to run Tableau on a MacBook as well.

Tableau is believed to be planning a desktop Mac OSX version, but there have been no official statements from the company regarding release dates.

Tableau Server

- Microsoft Windows Server 2008, 2008R2, 2003 SP1, or higher; Windows 7 or x86 or x64 chipsets; or Microsoft Windows 8
- 32-bit or 64-bit version of Windows
- Minimum of a Pentium 4 or AMD Opteron processor
- 32-bit color depth recommended
- Internet Protocol version 4 (IPv4)

Very Small Deployments (proof of concepts, initial evaluations, 1-2 users)

- Dual-core 2.0 GHz or higher minimum recommended CPU
- 4.0 gigabytes minimum system memory
- 2.5 gigabytes minimum free disk space

Small Deployments (less than 25 users)

- Quad-core, 2.0 GHz or higher minimum recommended CPU
- 8 gigabytes minimum system memory
- 5 gigabytes minimum free disk space

Medium Deployments (less than 100 users)

- Two Quad-core, 2.0 GHz or higher minimum recommended CPU
- 32 gigabytes minimum system memory
- 50 gigabytes minimum free disk space

Large Enterprise Deployments

Many factors affect the sizing and configuration of hardware for large enterprise deployments. The number of concurrent users, demand patterns, and network infrastructure must all be considered. Server licenses can be deployed over multiple hardware boxes to ensure good response times. You should consult your Tableau representative for configuration options.

INTRODUCING THE TABLEAU DESKTOP WORKSPACE

In this section you will learn about Tableau's workspace controls. This chapter is intended as a supplement (not a replacement) to Tableau's excellent online manual.

USING THE WORKSPACE CONTROLS EFFECTIVELY

If you are accustomed to working with spreadsheets or other analysis tools, learning Tableau's desktop environment will be a breeze. If you have no familiarity with database terminology or spreadsheets you can still be effectively using Tableau within a few hours.

THE START PAGE AND DATA CONNECTION PAGE

Open Tableau and you'll be presented with the start page displayed in Figure 1-4. Notice the small tabs in the upper-right side of the screen. The Home button with the orange house icon should be highlighted.

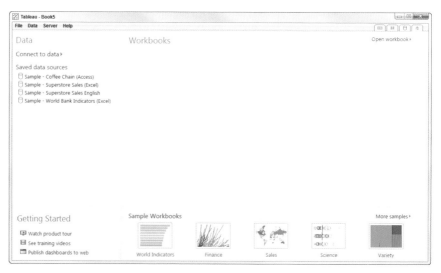

FIGURE 1-4 *Tableau start page*

On the left side, the data window presents connection options. If you click on Connect to Data you'll be taken to the data connection workspace. You can also access this page by clicking on the hard disk icon tab next to the Start button.

If you need to connect to one of the datasources listed in the On a Server section, you must to go to Tableau's website and download a connector for the desired database. Downloading a connector requires less than a minute if you have a decent web connection. There is no limit to the number of data connection drivers you can install, but some vendors require that you validate a valid license to their software before downloading their connector.

On the right side of the Connect to Data page you will see saved data connections. Tableau provides four as sample data for learning. Any other connections you have saved (.tds files) are displayed there as well.

Return to the Home button and look at the Workbooks area in the start page. The Workbooks area saves the last nine workbooks you've opened. If you want to keep a workbook there that you use frequently, hover over the workbook image and click on the push pin. That will prevent the workbook from being cycled out of view. Figure 1-5 displays a workbook related to this chapter that I want to keep on my start page.

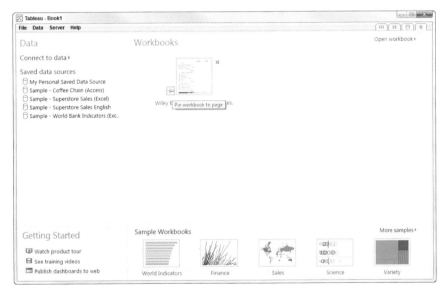

FIGURE 1-5 *Pin a workbook to the start page*

To remove saved workbooks from the start page click on the red X that appears when you hover over the workbook's image. At the bottom of the start page, the Getting Started area provides links to training videos and promotional materials. The sample workbook area provides links to sample workbooks containing excellent example material. Clicking on More Samples takes you to Tableau's visual gallery on the web with even more example workbooks.

Multiple Worksheet Page

There are two more workspace icons in the start page. The one with four gray boxes aligned in a square displays all of the worksheets in the workbook. There is a workbook with all the examples for this chapter that you can see in Figure 1-6 containing 18 different worksheets. This is the "slide-deck" view—it looks like PowerPoint's slide sorter view.

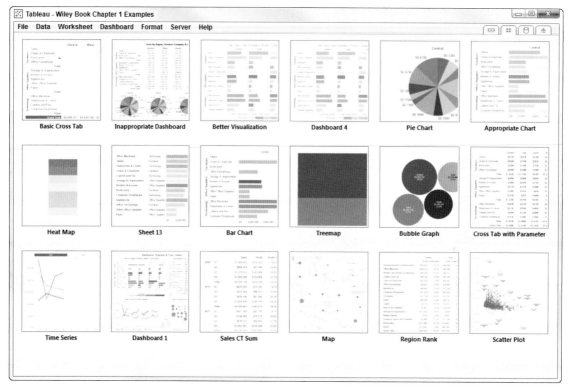

FIGURE 1-6 *Multiple worksheet display*

You can reorder worksheet tabs by dragging them to the desired position. Double-clicking will open that worksheet. If you have to give a presentation using a workbook with many worksheets, and you want the transitions from worksheet to worksheet to instantly appear, right-click while pointing anywhere in the page and select the (Refresh All Thumbnail) option. This will cause Tableau to update every view in the workbook and will make transitions to new worksheets appear instantly. This is particularly helpful if your datasource contains large files.

Tableau Workspace

Clicking on the far left icon (with three squares) displays the Tableau Worksheet page and exposes the contents of the worksheet tab selected at the bottom of the screen. When you connect to a new datasource this is also the default workspace view. Go to the home page and select the Sample - Superstore Subset (Excel) spreadsheet file. You just opened a connection to a saved datasource and should have a blank worksheet open.

There are many ways you can open a workspace page; for example, if you display Tableau's icon on your desktop and you have a datasource displayed on your desktop. Dragging any datasource icon and dropping it on the Tableau icon opens Tableau's worksheet page for the selected datasource. Keep in mind that you can open as many connections as you want in Tableau by going to the start page or data connection page and selecting a new connection. Figure 1-7 is worksheet-connected to the Sample-Superstore Sales-Excel data set used to create scatter plots.

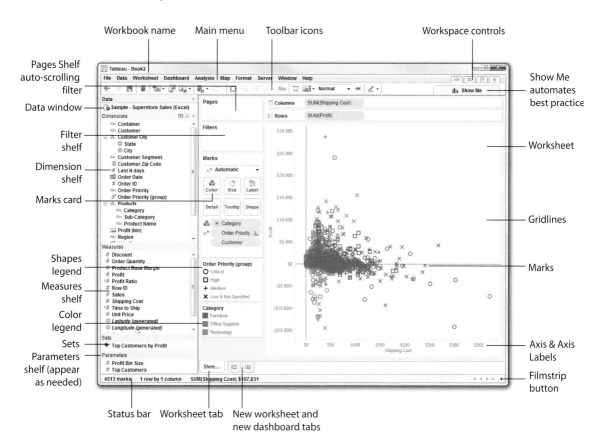

FIGURE 1-7 *Worksheet page*

The annotations in Figure 1-7 are the specifics that are covered in the remainder of this chapter.

WHAT YOU NEED TO KNOW ABOUT THE MENU

As Tableau Desktop has matured, the desktop menu has become less important. There has been a migration of features away from the main menu closer to the work in the worksheet, near marks, and in Tooltips. This section will focus on features that are still accessed via the main menu.

File Menu

Like any Windows program the file menu contains Open, Save, and Save As functions. The most frequently used feature found in this menu is the Print to pdf option. This allows you to export your worksheet or dashboard in pdf form. If you can't remember where Tableau places files, or you want to change the default file-save location, use the repository location option to review and change it. A fast way to create a packaged workbook is available from the export packaged workbook option. Saving your workbook this way eliminates a couple of clicks versus the more commonly used file/save as method.

Data Menu

The Paste Data option is handy in a couple of ways. You can use this if you find some interesting tabular data on a website that you want to analyze with Tableau. Highlight and copy the data from the website, then use the Paste Data option to input it into Tableau. Once pasted, Tableau will copy the data from the Windows clipboard and add a datasource in the data window. The Edit Relationships menu option is used in data blending. This menu option is necessary if the field names in two different datasources are not identical. It allows you to specifically define the related fields. Details related to data blending will be covered in Chapter 2.

Worksheet Menu

Several frequently used features exist in this menu. The Export option allows you to export your worksheet as an image, an Excel crosstab, or in Access database file format. The Duplicate as Crosstab option creates a crosstab version of the worksheet and places it in a new worksheet. Figure 1-8 is the output from the Describe Sheet Menu option.

Dashboard Menu

The Action Menu is a very useful feature that is reached from both the Dashboard Menu and the Worksheet Menu. Chapter 8 covers the three types of actions in detail.

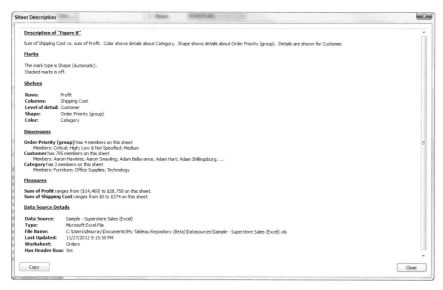

FIGURE 1-8 *Describe worksheet output*

Analysis Menu

As your skills advance you'll venture to this menu to access the aggregate measures and stack marks options. These switches allow you to adjust default Tableau behaviors that are useful if you need to build non-standard chart types. You'll build an example in Chapter 7 that requires the use of these options. The Create Calculated Field and Edit Calculated Field options are used to make new dimensions or measures that don't exist in your datasource.

Map Menu

The Map Menu option is used to alter the base map color scheme between normal (water is color blue), gray (water is white) or dark (land is black, water gray). The other menu options all relate in some way to replacing Tableau's standard maps with other map sources. You can also import geocoding for custom locations using the geocoding menu. All these options will be covered in detail in Chapter 5.

Format Menu

You may not use this menu very often because pointing at anything and right-clicking gets you to a context-specific formatting menu more quickly. On rare occasions you may need to alter the cell size in a worksheet. Do that from the Cell Size menu. If you don't like the default workbook theme use the Workbook Theme menu to select one of the other two options.

Server Menu

Use this menu if you need to login and publish work to Tableau Server. If you are doing a little dashboard building for fun or for a blog post, use the Tableau Public menu. To use this you must sign-up for a free Tableau Public account. The section on options in Chapter 10 for securing reports will describe how to use the menu option to create user filters. This provides row-level security by using a dimension to filter out data from view.

Window Menu

If you have a large workbook with many worksheets and you want to share one of the worksheets with someone else, use the bookmark menu to create a bookmark file (tbm).

Help Menu

The top section of this menu includes menu options that access Tableau's on-line manual, training videos, and sample workbooks. If you need to find your product key the Manage Product Key menu option will display it. Finally, if you have a slow loading dashboard—or one that doesn't filter quickly—the Start Performance Recording activates Tableau's performance analysis tool. Then actuate some filters to generate activity. When completed, go back to the menu and turn off the performance recorder. Tableau will create another workbook that contains performance metrics related to the source workbook. Performance tuning will be covered in detail later in Chapter 8 on dashboard design, and in Chapter 9 in the section on server performance turning.

LEVERAGING TOOLBAR ICONS

The toolbar displayed in Figure 1-9 makes the most commonly needed functions readily accessible.

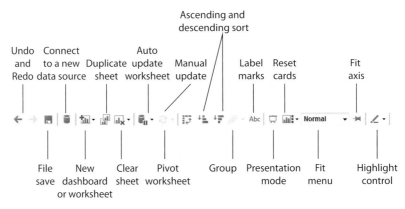

FIGURE 1-9 *Worksheet toolbar*

Tableau keeps an unlimited audit trail of every click made since the beginning of each session. The undo/redo arrows allow you to scroll backward or forward in time—infinitely. If you make a mistake and don't know exactly how to fix it, click the Undo button and go back in time until your error is removed. Use the Save button frequently because Tableau does not have an auto save feature. The new Dashboard/Worksheet button is one of the ways you can add a new page to your workbook.

The Duplicate Sheet button allows you to add an exact copy of a worksheet or dashboard page you're currently in, to a new page. This is useful if you're experimenting and don't want to break your current view.

Using the Auto and Manual Update buttons is useful if you have a particularly large data set that requires a few seconds to generate visuals when you drag elements into the worksheet. Suspending Auto Update allows you to place elements without delay and then run the update after you've finished.

Quickly sort your worksheet by clicking the Ascending or Descending Sort buttons. The toolbar that looks like a paper clip allows you to multi-select marks in the worksheet and group them together. The Label Mark button turns toggles labeling of marks on and off.

Presentation mode is turned on or off using the small icon that looks like an upside-down television set or a projector screen. This option hides or un-hides the design shelves. Use this if you are giving a presentation and want to use Tableau as your presentation slide deck.

The reset cards icon provides a menu that allows you to turn on and off screen elements that provide additional information. Caption provides a text description of items that comprise your worksheet. Summary adds statistical details about your visualization.

The fit menu allows you to control how Tableau fills the screen with the visualization. You can fit the entire view in the available space or stretch it vertically or horizontally. The default normal fit uses only the space needed by the visualization. If it is too large for the screen, scrollbars will appear. If it doesn't require the entire screen, gray space will result.

The push pin fixes the axis of your view. Use this if you want to zoom into any chart and hold the view. This is particularly useful on maps. Chapter 5 covers map options in detail.

The highlight control enables comparison by highlighting selected combinations of dimensions. This is useful in many charts but you will find it to be very helpful when highlighting marks in scatter plots.

THE DATA WINDOW, DATA TYPES, AND AGGREGATION

When you connect Tableau to a datasource it is expressed in the data window. You can connect to as many different datasources as you want in a single workbook. The small icons associated with data connections provide additional details about the nature of the connection. Figure 1-10 shows a workbook with three different data connections.

Two cans with an arrow means the connection is an active data extract.

Blue highlight means the fields from this datasource are being displayed in the dimensions and measures shelf.

The blue check mark indicates this data connection is active in this worksheet.

The **Dimensions** shelf contains filtering and sorting elements, text, dates, or geographic fields.

The **Dimensions** shelf contains numbers that you may want to use in formulas.

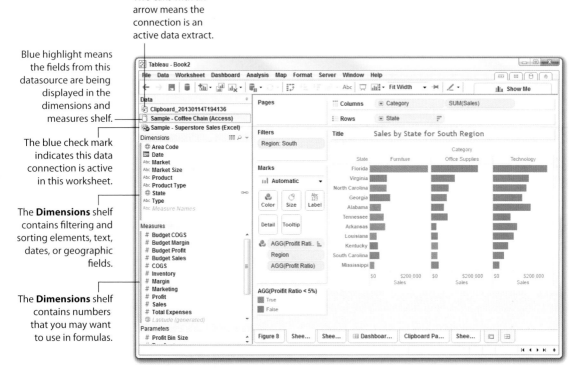

FIGURE 1-10 *Data shelf*

There are subtle visual clues regarding the exact state of each connection. The blue check circle next to the superstore data connection indicates that is the active connection in the worksheet. So, the bar chart in the worksheet was created using dimensions and measures from that datasource. The coffee chain data connection is a direct connection that is indicated by the icon of the single can. Also note the blue highlighting. Those datasource fields are currently displayed on the dimensions and measures shelves. The clipboard datasource at the top of the data window was cut and pasted into Tableau. It is also a data extract indicated by the icon displaying two cans with an arrow.

When you create data connections, Tableau will evaluate the fields and place them on the dimensions and measures shelves automatically. Tableau normally gets most of the fields placed correctly. If something is incorrectly placed, simply drag the field to the correct location. Errors occur sometimes when numbers are used to depict dimensions. For example, if you connect to a spreadsheet that contains customer identification numbers, that field may be placed into the measures shelf. It is important to get those fields properly placed. Dragging a customer identification number from the measures shelf into the worksheet would result in the field being summed. Properly placed on the dimensions shelf, the customer identification number would behave like a dimension and be expressed in a column or row the same way category and state are expressed in Figure 1-10.

Data Types

Tableau expresses fields and assigns data types automatically. If the data type is assigned by the datasource, Tableau will use that data type. If the datasource doesn't specifically assign a data type, Tableau will assign one. Tableau supports the following data types:

- Text values
- Date values
- Date and time values
- Numerical values
- Geographic values (latitude and longitude used for maps)
- Boolean values (true/false conditions)

Look at Figure 1-10 and focus on the icons next to the fields in the dimensions and measures shelves. These icons denote specific data types. Small globes are geographic features; calendars are dates. A calendar with a clock is a date/time field. Numeric values have pound signs, and text fields are denoted by "abc" icons. Boolean fields have "T/F" icons. Explore Tableau's manual for more examples.

Aggregation

It is often useful to look at numeric values using different aggregations. Tableau supports many different aggregation types including:

- Sum
- Average
- Median

- Count

- Count Distinct

- Minimum

- Maximum

- Standard Deviation

- Standard Deviation of a Population

- Variance

- Variance of a Population

- Attribute (ATTR)

- Dimension

If you aren't a statistician or database expert, refer to Tableau's manual for detailed definitions of these aggregate types. Adding fields into your visualization results in default aggregations being displayed. Tableau allows you to change the default aggregation or just alter the aggregation level for a specific view. To change the default aggregation, right-click on that field inside the data shelf and change its default by selecting the menu option (default properties/aggregation). You can also change the aggregation of a field for a specific use in a worksheet. Figure 1-11 provides an example. By right-clicking on the SUM (Sales) pill and selecting the Measure (SUM) menu option, you can select any of the aggregations highlighted.

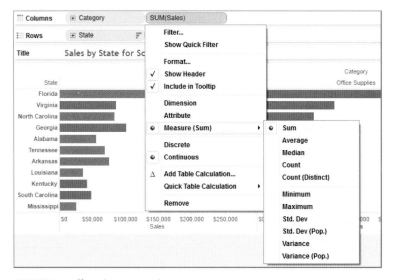

FIGURE 1-11 *Changing aggregation*

The datasource used in Figure 1-11 is a data extract of an Excel spreadsheet. It is important to understand that if you relied on a direct connection to Excel, the median and count (distinct) aggregations would not be available. Excel, Access, and text files do not natively support these aggregate types. Tableau's extract engine does.

A Word about Dimension and Attribute

Most aggregates involve mathematical concepts comprehensible to most people. Even if you don't understand specifically what standard deviation is, you probably appreciate that it has something to do with variation of data within a set of numbers—not so with the dimension and attribute aggregations. The best way to explain these aggregates is to provide examples of them being used. Refer to the aggregate function definitions and examples in Appendix A—Understanding and Using Tableau Functions.

BUILDING VISUALIZATIONS WITH THE ROW AND COLUMN SHELVES

Row and column shelves are used to express data in your worksheet. Dimensions and measures can be displayed in any order or either shelf. Figure 1-12 is a basic time series chart that shows sales trends by year and then quarter.

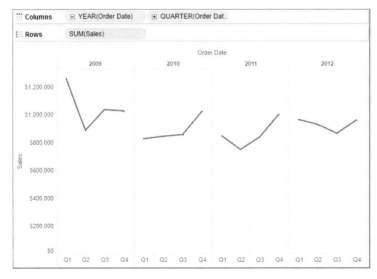

FIGURE 1-12 *Time series by year, quarter*

The time series has breaks in the line because time is discretely broken down by year and then quarter. Figure 1-13 displays the same data, rearranging time by showing quarter first and then year, making it easier to see how sales changed in each quarter.

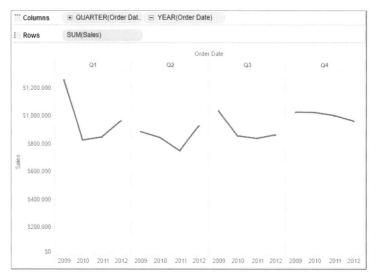

FIGURE 1-13 *Time series by quarter, year*

Placing the year pill to the right of the quarter pill altered the context of the view by making it easier to compare the sales trends within each quarter over time.

NUMBER OF RECORDS, MEASURE VALUES, AND MEASURE NAMES

Tableau automatically adds three fields to every data set. Number of records is a calculated value that sums the rows in the datasource. Note that field icons preceded by an equals sign are calculated values. Measure names and measure values are special fields that allow you to display multiple measures on a single axis. Figure 1-14 was created by double-clicking on the measure names field and selecting the swap button on the toolbar to change the orientation of the chart.

When measure values are deployed, a new shelf appears that holds the pills for every measure in the data set. Selecting measure names and measure values will automatically display all of the measures in your datasource with their corresponding descriptions. You can use the measure names pill to filter out specific values by right-clicking in the pill and de-selecting measures you no longer want to display on the axis.

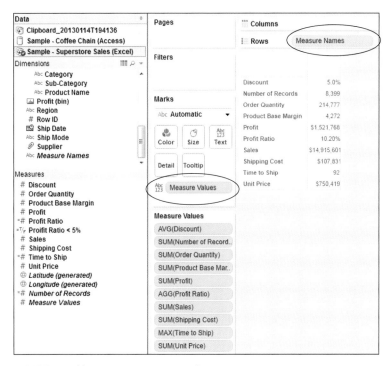

FIGURE 1-14 *Measure names, measure values*

UNDERSTANDING COLOR IN ICONS AND PILLS

Have you noticed the color of the pills placed on shelves is either green or blue? Look at Figures 1-12 and 1-14 again. Can you guess what those colors mean? Most people think blue pills are dimensions and green pills are measures. That's a good guess but the right answer is more subtle. Figure 1-15 displays the time series without any breaks between the years. Notice that there is only one pill on the color shelf and it is green.

Green denotes continuous and blue measures discrete. When a time dimension pill is green the data is displayed using an unbroken, continuous line. In Figure 1-12 the time dimension pills are blue. Time buckets are displayed discretely by year and then quarter. Measures aren't always continuous either. Histograms convert normally continuous measures into discrete dimensions.

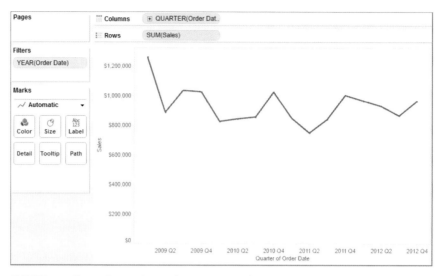

FIGURE 1-15 *Time series: continuous date*

USING THE VIEW CARDS TO IDENTIFY TRENDS AND OUTLIERS

The Marks Card is the primary means for using color, size, shape, position, and text to express dimensions and measures in visualizations.

The Marks Card and Buttons

Tableau applies color, shape, and size to visualizations using the view cards. The view cards also enable filtering, labeling, and provide a way for you to add details on demand that are not visible in your chart. Visual details are added to the chart by placing field pills on the desired mark type.

- Color—Expresses discrete or continuous values
- Size—Expresses discrete or continuous values
- Label—One or more fields can be expressed as label on marks
- Detail—Disaggregates the marks plotted
- Tooltip/Tooltips—Makes fields available to Tooltips without disaggregating data
- Shape—Expresses discrete or continuous fields

Multiple fields can be placed on the color, label, detail, and Tooltip buttons. Figure 1-16 displays a scatter plot with color, shape, and size all being utilized to visualize a comparison of profit and shipping cost.

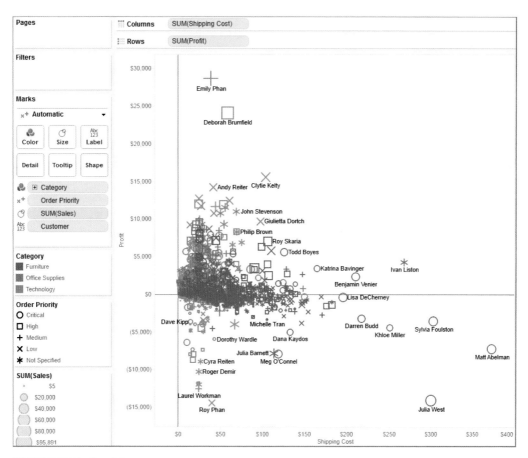

FIGURE 1-16 *Scatter plot*

The column shelf in Figure 1-16 contains shipping expense, making that measure plot horizontally across the page. Profit, on the row shelf, is displayed vertically. Color is being used to depict product category, shape shows order priority, and the size of the marks provides information on sales. This scatter plot is displaying three measures and three dimensions while displaying the outliers in a way that makes them stand out. Notice the customer names display only when they don't overlap. All of the visual styles were applied by dropping individual fields on the desired marks card buttons. You can also alter the way each field in the marks card is used by pointing at the small icons to the left of each pill, clicking your left mouse button, and selecting another option.

The Pages Shelf

Any field placed on the pages shelf generates an auto-scrolling filter. Use it to create animated visualizations in Tableau Desktop. In Figure 1-17 you see that when a field is placed on the pages shelf another supporting shelf appears directly under it that contains a manual field selector and auto-scrolling controls providing forward/pause/stop, control over scrolling speed, and a show history check box.

Checking the show history box exposes a menu that provides different options to control the way history is displayed and how many marks will be displayed while the filter increments through whatever field has been placed on the shelf. For example, if a date field is placed on the pages shelf, the pages shelf filter can automatically increment through each month contained in the data set.

FIGURE 1-17 *Pages Shelf and Show History Menu*

Trails are lines that connect marks sequentially as scrolling occurs. Selections made in the show section of the menu enable you to control whether marks, trails, or both marks and trails are displayed as the auto filter increments. The marks section provides controls over the color and fade of the marks. The trails section provides color and line style controls for the trails.

Auto-scrolling filters are not supported in Tableau Server, but they can be consumed via Tableau Reader or Tableau Desktop.

Filter Shelf

Any field placed on the filter shelf enables a filter for that dimension or field. The style of filter control is dependent on whether the field is continuous or discrete. If you want to expose a filter in the worksheet, right-click on any pill used anywhere in the workspace and select the menu option Show Quick Filter.

HOW THE STATUS BAR HELPS YOU UNDERSTAND VISUALIZATIONS

The status bar appears in the lower left of the worksheet. It provides basic metrics about the number of marks displayed in your visualization. The map visualization in Figure 1-18 demonstrates the value of the status bar.

The map in Figure 1-18 plots pie charts that show sales by city and product category. Notice the status bar at the bottom left of the worksheet indicating 3,624 marks are in view. The total sales value of the marks is $14,915,601. Each slice in the pies counts as a mark. The status will change if a mark or groups of marks are selected in the worksheet, reflecting the count and value of the selection.

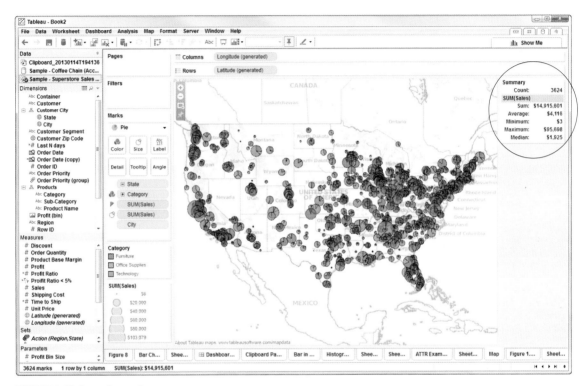

FIGURE 1-18 *Status bar and summary*

The larger summary card in the upper right is optional. You can enable it by using the toolbar highlighted in yellow, and then selecting summary.

SAVING TIME BY USING THE SHOW ME BUTTON

Using the Show Me button allows you to build visualizations very quickly. If you can decide on the combination of dimensions and measures you want to analyze, Show Me will build your visualization for you. It will place all of the pills on shelves automatically. See how the map in Figure 1-18 can be re-created using the Show Me button in Figure 1-19.

You may want to use sales by category and city on the map. To visualize them, multi-select those fields and click the Show Me button. The screen should look like Figure 1-19.

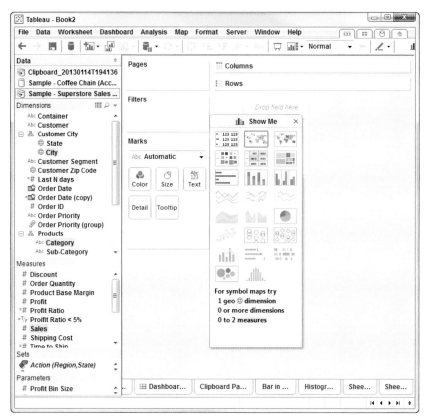

FIGURE 1-19 *Building a map with Show Me*

Show Me can be dragged to any location on your desktop. The text at the bottom provides additional feedback on the combination of dimensions and measures that should be selected in order for chart type to be available. Other highlighted chart styles are also supported by the selections of measures and dimensions. The charts that are grayed-out are not available. Note that the time series charts are all gray because a date dimension hasn't been selected.

The map in Figure 1-18 was created by selecting the map highlighted by Show Me. Leaving the Show Me button open allows you to quickly pick many different chart styles and see the results. Show Me is a time-saver and a great way to see how different pill placements can affect the appearance of your visualization.

Now that you've got a basic introduction to the desktop workspace, in Chapter 2: Connecting to Your Data you will learn a variety of ways you can connect to data and the different kinds of datasources you can connect to using Tableau Desktop.

NOTES

1. Tufte, Edward R. *The Visual Display of Quantitative Information*. Cheshire, CT: Graphics, 2001. Print. Page 91.

2. NOSQL (Not Only SQL), Margaret Rouse, "Essential Guide, Big Data Applications: Real-World Strategies for Managing Big Data," SearchDataManagement, October 5, 2011, `http:// searchdatamanagement.techtarget.com/definition/ NoSQL-Not-Only-SQL`.

3. Petabyte scale data, Andrew Ryan for Facebook Engineering "Under the Hood: Hadoop Distributed Filesystem reliability with Namenode and Avatarnote," `https://www.facebook.com/notes/ facebook-engineering/under-the-hood-hadoop- distributed-filesystem-reliability-with-namenode-and- avata/10150888759153920`.

4. BARC 2009, The Data Warehouse Institute, TDWI, Stephen Swoyer, "Report Debunks Business Intelligence Usage Myth," `http://tdwi.org/ Articles/2009/05/20/Report-Debunks-BI-Usage-Myth.aspx?Page=1`.

5. Few, Stephen. *Information Dashboard Design: The Effective Visual Communication of Data*. O'Reilly Media, Inc., 2006. Print. Page 4.

CHAPTER 2

Connecting to Your Data

I think a manager's world is not black and white. It's a world filled with uncertainties and dilemmas. The sort of thing that would leave any neophyte moaning, "What the Hell is this."

GORDON MACKENZIE[1]

It would be nice if all the data you needed to access resided in one place, but it doesn't. Your data is scattered over multiple databases, text files, spreadsheets, and public services. Connecting to a wide variety of datasources directly, Tableau makes it much easier to analyze data residing in different places. Currently there are thirty-three different database connectors available with more being added every year. You can analyze spreadsheets, public data tools, analytic databases, Hadoop, and a large variety of general-purpose databases as well as data cubes.

HOW TO CONNECT TO YOUR DATA

When you open Tableau you are taken to the home page where you can easily select from previous workbooks, sample workbooks, and saved data-sources. You can also connect to new datasources by selecting Connect to Data. Figure 2-1 displays the screen.

The option In a File is for connecting to locally stored data or file based data. Tableau Personal edition can only access Excel, Access, and text files (txt, csv). You can also import from datasources stored in other workbooks.

The options, listed beneath On a Server, link to data stored in a database, data cube, or a cloud service. Although all of these databases have very different ways of storing and looking up data, the pop-up window is very user friendly and requires little or no understanding of the underlying technology. Most of these databases will require you to install a driver particular to each tool. Installation normally requires a few minutes and you can find all the connectors at: http://www.tableausoftware.com/support/drivers.

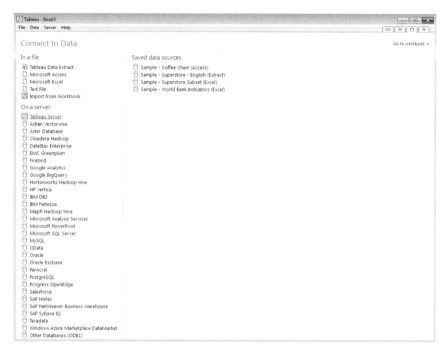

FIGURE 2–1 *Connect to data screen*

If your database isn't listed try the other database connector (ODBC) that utilizes the Open Database Connectivity standard. You will also see a list of saved datasources on the right. Saving datasources that you use frequently saves time. I'll explain how to save a datasource in the Tableau DataSource Files section later in this chapter.

Saved datasource files (.tds) are found on your computer's hard disk in the datasources directory under the My Tableau repository. If you are logged into Tableau Server you may also see saved datasources on your server's repository.

CONNECTING TO DESKTOP SOURCES

If you click on one of the desktop source options under the In a File list you will get a directory window to select the desired file. Once you have chosen your file you will be taken to the Connection Options window. There are small differences in the connection dialog depending on the datasource you are connecting to but the menus are self-explanatory. Figure 2-2 shows the connection window with the Superstore sample spreadsheet being the file that is being accessed.

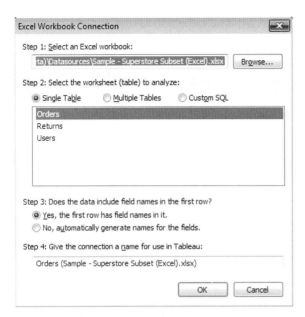

FIGURE 2-2 *The connection window*

There are three tabs in the spreadsheet file. Tableau interprets these tabs the same way it views different tables in a database. The same is true of text files stored within the same folder. If the tabs contain related information, Tableau can join these just like it can join tables in a database. Joining options are the same regardless of the file or database type. Join options will be covered in the Joining Database Tables with Tableau section later in this chapter.

Once you have selected and customized your data connection, you will be taken to the second Data Connection window where you must decide whether or not to create an extract. There are advantages to extracting the data into Tableau's data engine, particularly when you are using Excel, Access, or text files as your datasource. The nuances of data extracts will be covered in The Advantages of a Data Extract section later in the chapter as well. Clicking the OK button creates the connection and opens the workbook authoring environment.

CONNECTING TO DATABASE SOURCES

Databases have an additional level of security—requiring you to enter a server name and user credentials to access the data. The username and password you enter are assigned in the database, meaning the security credentials and the amount of access granted are controlled by the database—not Tableau. Figure 2–3 shows the connection window to a MySQL database.

FIGURE 2–3 *Database connection window*

The remaining steps in the connection window guide you through the process of selecting the database, database tables, and defining the joins between the tables in the datasource. The final step is to decide whether you want to directly connect to the data or to extract data from the database into Tableau's data engine. Following these steps completes the process of connecting to a database.

CONNECTING TO PUBLIC DATASOURCES

The increasing quantity and variety of data available via the Internet falls into three categories:

- Public domain data sets
- Commercial data services
- Cloud database platforms

For example, the United States Census provides free data via the Internet. The World Bank provides a variety of data, and many other government public data repositories have sprouted all over the world. This data can be accessed by downloading files and then connecting Tableau to those files.

There are also a growing number of commercial datasources. At this time Tableau provides connectors to several, including:

- Google Analytics
- Google Big Query
- Amazon Redshift
- Salesforce
- Open Data Protocol (ODATA)
- Windows Azure Marketplace

The Google Analytics connector can be used to create customized click stream analysis of web pages. Google Big Query and Amazon Redshift connectors allow you to leverage the computing capacity of Google and Amazon. Both are designed to allow you to purchase petabyte-scale database processing capacity for a fee. There is also a connector for the popular cloud-based CRM tool—Salesforce. Microsoft supplies data over the web via the Windows Azure Marketplace and ODATA. Tableau's own free cloud service—Tableau Public—allows you to create and share your workbooks and dashboards on the web. Figure 2–4 shows an example dashboard published on Tableau Public that was created for and embedded in a blog post.

Tableau Public is a great way to embed live/interactive dashboards on the web. Be careful not to publish proprietary data there as it is available to everyone without restriction.

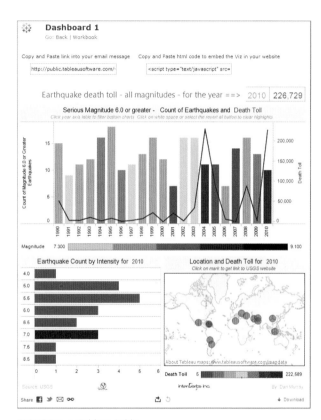

FIGURE 2–4 *Tableau Public*

WHAT ARE GENERATED VALUES?

Tableau has built-in fields that make difficult tasks easier. These are found on the left side of the screen at the bottom of the dimensions list and the bottom of the measures list. When you perform an operation (such as double-clicking on a geographic field) these Tableau generated fields are automatically added to the design window. Generated values include:

- Measure Names and Measure Values
- Longitude and Latitude
- Number of Records

Measure Names, Measure Values, and Number of Records are always present. If your dimensions include standard geographic place names, Tableau will also automatically generate center-point geocodes.

MEASURE NAMES AND MEASURE VALUES

Measure Names and Measure Values can be used to quickly express all the different measures in your data set or to express multiple measures on a single axis.

In Figure 2–5 you can see that two measures are shown, SUM (Profit) and SUM (Sales). These are shown as separate columns in the same bar chart. The generated value, Measure Names, is used in the column shelf to separate the bars. Measure Names is also used on the marks card to distinguish color and on the filters shelf to limit the number of measures shown in the view. Measure Values contains the data and this is shown as rows as you would expect from this type of bar chart.

The side-by-side bar chart in Figure 2–5 was created by multi-selecting one dimension Container and two measures Profit and Sales. Using the Show Me button, the side-by-side bar chart was selected. Tableau automatically applied Measure Names to the column shelf and separated the two measures being plotted on the horizontal axis. The Measure Names Quick Filter was exposed by right-clicking on the Measure Names dimension on the Filter Shelf. Other measures can be added to the axis using the Quick Filter.

The view could also be created by dragging Container to the column shelf, dragging the Sales Measure to the row shelf, then dragging Profit on to the left axis and dropping the measure when a light green ruler appears. The Measure Names and Measure Values pills will automatically appear when the second measure is placed on the vertical axis.

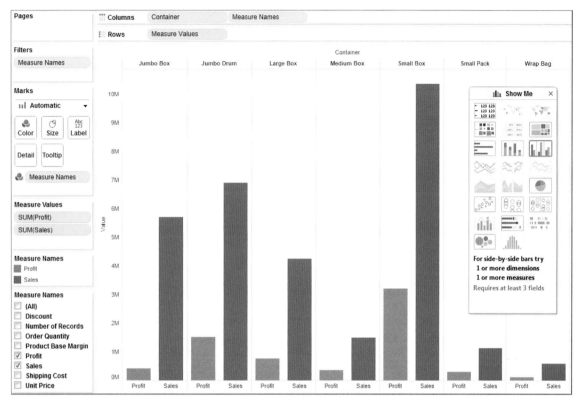

FIGURE 2-5 *Measure values bar chart*

TABLEAU GEOCODING

If your data includes standard geographic fields like country, state, province, city, or postal codes—denoted by a small globe icon—Tableau will automatically generate the longitude and latitude values for the center points of each geographic entity displayed in your visualization. If for some reason Tableau doesn't recognize a geographic dimension, you can change the geographic role of the field by right-clicking on the field and selecting the appropriate geographic role. Figure 2–6 shows a map created using country, state, and city, then using Show Me to display the symbol map.

The Map Option menu seen on the left was exposed from the map menu, Map Option Selection. The marks in the map were styled from the Color button—changing the color transparency and adding a black border. Overlapping clusters of marks are easier to see. Hovering over any mark exposes the Tooltip that includes the geographic entities exposed in the marks card. The summary card was exposed in the view so that you can see that 1,726 marks are plotted.

If Tableau failed to recognize any location, a small gray pill would appear in the lower right of the map. Clicking on that pill would expose a menu that would help you identify and correct the geocoding. Chapter 5 will cover Tableau's mapping capabilities in detail.

FIGURE 2–6 *Longitude and latitude generated measures*

NUMBER OF RECORDS

The final generated value provided is a calculated field near the bottom of the measures shelf called Number of Records. Any icon that includes an equals sign denotes a calculated field. The number of records calculation formula includes only the number one. This is how Tableau generates record counts. The bar chart in Figure 2–7 displays the record count for each customer segment and grand total.

Number of Records helps you understand the row count in your data set. It is particularly helpful when you begin to join other tables. Monitoring how the record count changes helps you understand data quality issues or design challenges that you may need to address.

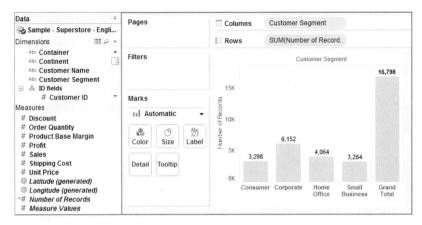

FIGURE 2–7 *Number of records*

KNOWING WHEN TO USE A DIRECT CONNECTION OR A DATA EXTRACT

Direct connections allow you to work with live data. When you extract data you import some or all of your data into Tableau's data engine. This is true in Tableau Desktop and Server. Which connection method is the best to use? There is no straightforward answer. It is entirely dependent on your situation, requirements, and network resources.

THE FLEXIBILITY OF DIRECT CONNECTIONS

Connecting to your datasource with a direct connection means you are always visualizing the most up-to-date facts. If your database is being updated in real-time you only need to refresh the Tableau visualization via the F5 function key or by right-clicking on the datasource in the data window and selecting the Refresh option.

If you connect to massive data, the visualization is very dense, or your data is in a high-performance enterprise-class database; you may get faster response time with a direct connection. Choosing a direct connection doesn't preclude the possibility of extracting the data later. You can also swap from an extract to a live connection by right-clicking the datasource and un-checking the Use Extract option.

THE ADVANTAGES OF A DATA EXTRACT

Data extracts don't have the advantage of real-time updating that a direct connection provides, but using Tableau's data engine provides a number of benefits:

- Performance improvement
- Additional functions
- Data portability

Performance Improvement

Perhaps your primary database is already heavily loaded with requests. Using Tableau's data engine enables you to split the load from your primary database server to the Tableau Server. Tableau's extract may be updated daily, weekly, or monthly during off-peak hours. Tableau's Server can also refresh extracts incrementally and in time intervals as low as fifteen minutes. In many cases, the small time consumed during the data extract update is more than offset by the performance gains.

There are several options available for creating an extract. First, you can aggregate the extract, which will roll up rows so that only the aggregation and fields used are updated for the visible dimensions and measures. Aggregating for Visible Dimensions when performing a data extract will reduce the amount of data that Tableau is importing. The appropriate level of fidelity is provided but the size of the extract file is significantly reduced—making the extract file more portable but also improving security.

Extracting incrementally also speeds refresh time because Tableau isn't updating the entire extract file. It is adding only new records. To do incremental extracts you must specify a field to use as the index; Tableau will only refresh the row if the index has changed, so you need to be aware that changes to a row of data that don't change the index field will be excluded from the update.

Another way to speed extracts is to apply filters when extracting the data. If the analysis doesn't require your entire data set you can filter the extract to include only the records required. If you have a very large data set you will rarely need to extract the entire contents of the database. For example, your database may include ten years of historical data but you may only require one year of history.

Once you have created an extract you may append another file. This may be a great alternative to custom SQL if you are considering a table UNION. This technique might be useful if you need to combine monthly data that is stored in separate tables.

Additional Functions

If your datasource is from a file (Excel, Access, text), doing an extract will add calculation functions (median and count distinct) that are not supported by the datasource.

Data Portability

Extracts can be saved locally and used when the connection to your datasource is not available. A direct connection doesn't work if you don't have access to your datasource via a local network or the Internet. Perhaps you need to supply a dashboard to an executive that will be flying to a remote location. Providing that person with a data extract (.tde) file provides that person with a fully-functional, high-performance, datasource. Data extract files are also compressed and are normally much smaller than the host system database tables.

In enterprise environments, data governance is an important consideration. If you distribute many data extract files to field staff, keep in mind that you should consider the security of those files. Appropriate safeguards should be in place (non-disclosure agreements) before you provide these files to traveling or remote staff. Consider restricting what the extract includes via filters and aggregating to visible dimensions.

USING TABLEAU'S FILE TYPES EFFECTIVELY

Tableau provides flexible options for the sharing of data and design metadata. This is accomplished through a variety of file types:

- Tableau Workbook (.twb)
- Tableau Packaged Workbook (.twbx)
- Tableau Datasource (.tds)
- Tableau Bookmark (.twb)
- Tableau Data Extract (.tde)

You should see many of these files in your My Tableau repository folder which is normally located in My Documents. Data extract (.tde) files were covered in the previous section. Next you will see how the other file types can be used.

TABLEAU WORKBOOK FILES

Tableau Workbook files (.twb) are the main file type created by Tableau to save your entire workbook. These are normally small files because the only data they contain is the metadata related to your connection and the pill placements for rendering the views and dashboards in the workbook. What is not saved is the underlying data from the datasource.

To clarify: A .twb file does not contain any of the actual data from the database. It contains the definition of how you wish to display data. This means workbook files will normally be very small. But, if you want to share the workbook with other people you need to be certain that they have access rights to the database or that you also provide the datasource with the workbook.

TABLEAU PACKAGED WORKBOOKS

If you want to share a workbook with a colleague that doesn't have access to the datasource used to create the workbook, you can still share the file by saving it as a packaged workbook. People without a license to Tableau Server or Tableau Desktop can also access packaged workbooks using Tableau Reader.

Packaged workbooks (.twbx) bundle the data and metadata into a single file. If you later need to access the original datasource file contained within the packaged workbook, point at the file, right-click, and select the Unpackage menu option.

TABLEAU DATASOURCE FILES

Changes made within your data window (the left side of your workbook) alter the metadata of your connection. Grouping, sets, aliased names, field-type changes, and any other modifications made in your workbook are part of the metadata. Can you share just the metadata with others? The answer is yes. This is done by creating a Tableau Datasource (.tds) file.

A Tableau datasource file defines where the source data is, how to connect to it, what fieldnames have been changed, and other changes applied in the dimensions and measures shelves. Datasource files can be saved locally or published to Tableau Server. This is particularly helpful if you work in a large enterprise. Perhaps you have a small number of database experts that understand your database schema well. They can create the connection, define table joins, group or rename fields, and then publish the datasource file for less experienced staff to use as a starting point.

To create a datasource file right-click on the filename in your data window, then select the Add To Saved datasources option. Datasource files are placed in the My Tableau repository/datasource folder. Additionally, files placed in that folder are automatically displayed as saved data connections on Tableau's home and connection tabs. Alternatively, you can publish datasource files to Tableau Server and share them with other staff. The best part about this option—changes made to the datasource file are automatically propagated to other people using that connection!

TABLEAU BOOKMARK FILES

What if you have a massive workbook (with many worksheets) and you want to share one worksheet only with a colleague? This is done by using a bookmark (.tbm) file. Bookmark files save the data and metadata related to a worksheet within your workbook—including the connection and calculated fields.

To create a bookmark file go to the Windows menu bar and look for the Bookmark menu option and select Create Bookmark.

The bookmark will become visible when a new Tableau session is started. The file will appear in the Windows menu. Opening the bookmark file will initiate the connection and add it to the workbook. Tableau bookmark files are stored in your Tableau Repository in the Bookmarks folder.

JOINING DATABASE TABLES WITH TABLEAU

Most Tableau users aren't database experts. This section introduces a fundamental database concept—joining tables. Seldom will your datasource include every bit of information you need in a single table. Even if you normally connect to Excel it may be advantageous to use related data from more than one tab. As long as the data resides in a single spreadsheet or database and each table includes unique identifiers that tie the tables or tabs together, you can perform joins of these tables within Tableau. These identifiers are called Key Records.

Database joins can be complex, but the basic principle is to bring together related information in your view. In Tableau, you can define joins when you make your initial data connection or add them later. This example will use the Orders and Return tabs (tables) from the Superstore sample data set. Figure 2–8 shows portions of both tables. The Orders table includes billing information. The Returns tab includes the smaller returned order table.

Start by connecting to the spreadsheet as you would if you were going to connect to one table. In the Connection Menu under Step 2, select Multiple Tables and click the Add Table button to expose the Add Table menu. Then select the Returns table as you see in Figure 2-9.

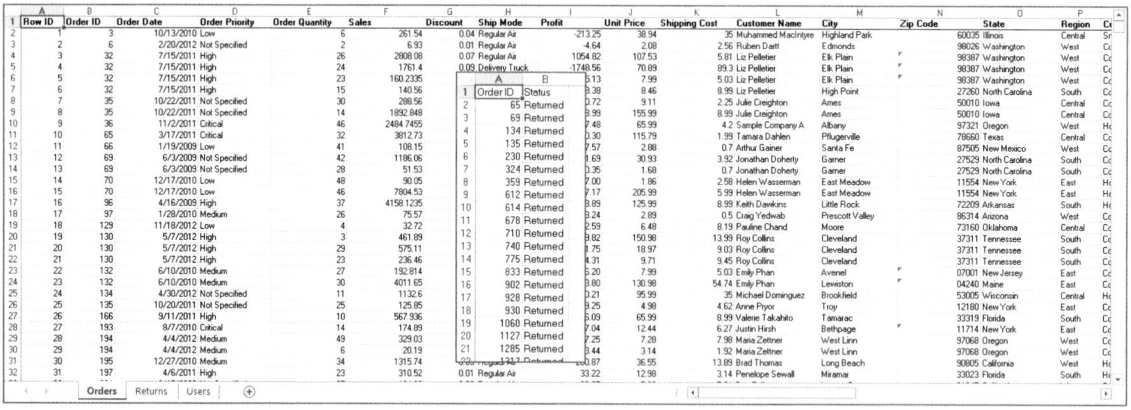

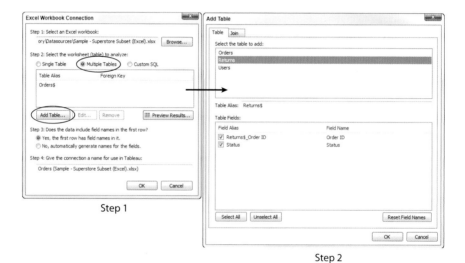

FIGURE 2-8 *Superstore orders and return tables*

FIGURE 2-9 *Joining multiple tables*

While in the Add Table menu, ensure that the Returns table is highlighted and click the Join button. This will expose the menu in which you define the join type as you see in Figure 2–10.

In the example, you see that the Left outer join type has been selected. If you preview the results you will see that the join will result in 9,426. Following these steps results in a left outer join between the Orders and Returns tables.

Keep in mind that you can also join additional tables later just by pointing at the datasource on your data shelf, right-clicking, and selecting the Edit Tables option. Using different join types can result in different record counts so it is important that you understand the different join types.

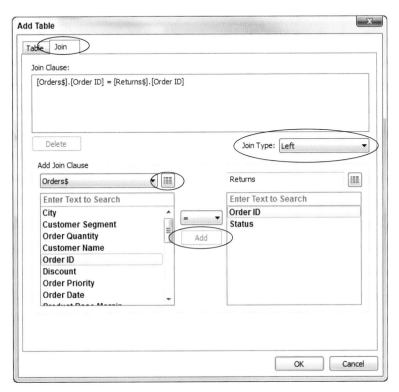

FIGURE 2–10 *Joining tables in Tableau*

THE DEFAULT INNER JOIN

When you join two tables together Tableau will default to the inner join type. Figure 2–11 shows a Venn diagram that illustrates the inner join.

Using an inner join returns only records that match in both the left and right tables. In the Superstore example this join type returns only ninety-eight records. It is a good practice when you join tables to know how many records there are in each table. If you're working with a spreadsheet you can look at each tab and note the total row counts in each. Remember to deduct the header from your row totals. Alternatively, as you are doing the join, utilize the preview buttons to check the row counts.

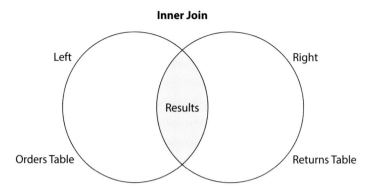

FIGURE 2–11 *The Inner join*

When you complete the join you can also drag the record count field into the view to see how many total records are available. You can have more than one join clause to ensure that the correct results are returned. If you're a database expert this won't present any challenge. If you are like many Tableau users you are probably not accustomed to creating joins. If you run into problems, ask for help from a database expert.

THE LEFT AND RIGHT JOIN TYPES

Tableau provides two other join types via point and click options in the Join menu. These join types give priority to either the left table or the right in the set returned.

Pick the primary table first. In the previous example, the primary table is the Orders table so it is considered the left table. The new table added in the join is the Returns table on the right. Selecting left gives priority to the original table. Selecting right gives priority to the new table. But what does it mean? Figure 2–12 shows a Venn diagram of the left outer join type.

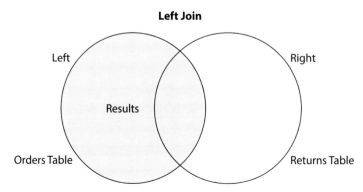

FIGURE 2–12 *The Left outer join*

In the example, the left join returns every record in the orders table plus the matching records in the returns table. Earlier you saw that join generated over nine thousand records being returned. The right join gives priority to the right returns table as you see in Figure 2–13.

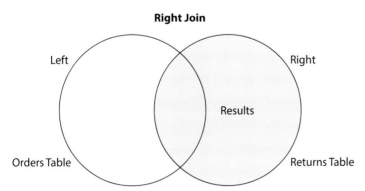

FIGURE 2–13 *The Right outer join*

Since there are fewer rows in the returns table the number of records will drop significantly and only include details from matching records in orders. If you preview results when using left and right joins you may see a lot of null fields in yellow. Or, if you check the record counts and place the key record that you use in the join on your row shelf, you will see the word null appear whenever a record exists in the primary table that is missing in the joined table.

In Superstore, a right join would result in 1,673 records being returned, but only 98 of those records will be matched to the orders table. The remaining 1,573 records will return null. These are the order records in the order table that have no matching record in the returns table.

CUSTOMIZING TABLEAU'S JOIN SCRIPT

So far all of the joins we've covered have been enabled via point and click menus. There may be times when your data needs require something other than the inner, left, or right outer join types. You may need to ask very specific questions of your data, and sometimes providing the answers might require a customized join.

For those of you who have never written any SQL statements before, this may seem daunting. There are ways to edit Tableau's default connection script to minimize manual coding. Using the same Superstore data, what if you needed to analyze the earliest sales date by customer, but generalize that analysis by year? One possible way to express this is shown in Figure 2–14.

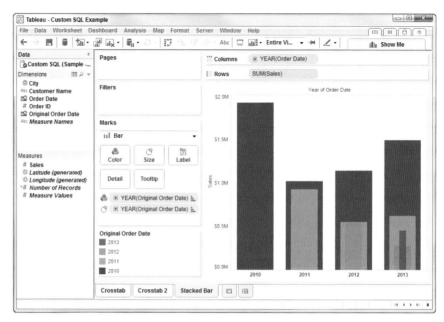

FIGURE 2–14 *Earliest initial sales over time*

The bar-in-bar chart shown in Figure 2–14 uses color to indicate the sales year in which customers purchased from the Superstore for the first time. The horizontal axis shows all sales by year. The dark gray bar denotes sales to customers who made their first purchase in 2010. The orange bar aggregates sales for customers who first purchased in 2012. Notice that the connection in the data window says Custom SQL. The data is coming from the Superstore data set, but the number of fields available has been restricted. Also, there is a dimension field called Original Order Date that does not exist in the Superstore data set. This was created by customizing the connection script.

You can let Tableau do some of the work by connecting to Superstore as you normally would, and then editing Tableau's generated connection script. Figure 2–15 shows the related menus.

Don't try writing your SQL statements using the tiny space available in the workbook connection window. Instead, look at the small "…" button that is located in the Step 2 selections to the right of the Custom SQL radio button. Click on that to expose a more spacious editing window and manually edit the connection script there. Alternatively you can copy the script into any text editor (Notepad or Notepad ++), make revisions, and paste the completed code back into Tableau. Figure 2–16 shows a larger view of Tableau's custom SQL window.

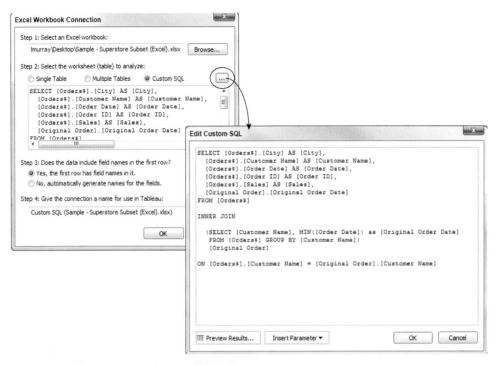

FIGURE 2-15   *The connection and custom SQL windows*

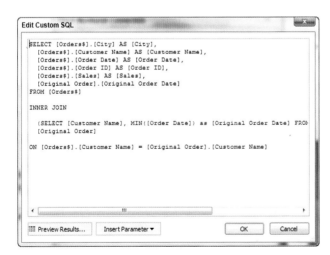

FIGURE 2-16   *Editing the connection script*

The top select statement is the script Tableau generated. Removing the lines related to fields that are not needed removes those fields from the result that is returned to Tableau. The customized script starts with the inner join statement and continues to the end. If you are interested in learning more about SQL scripting, refer to the reading references on the book's website.

BLENDING DIFFERENT DATASOURCES IN A SINGLE WORKSHEET

Wouldn't it be wonderful if all the data you needed to create your analysis always resided in a single database? Many times this isn't the situation. If you need to use data from more than one datasource, Tableau provides a solution that does not require building a middle-layer data repository. As long as the disparate datasources have at least one common field, Tableau facilitates using both sources via data blending.

WHEN TO USE BLENDING VS. JOINS

If your data does reside in a single source, it is always more desirable to use a join versus a data blend. In the last section you saw that Tableau provides plenty of flexibility for creating joins to your datasource. Joins are normally the best option because joins are robust, persist everywhere in your workbook, and are more flexible than blending. However, if your data isn't in one place, blending provides a viable way to quickly create a left-join-like connection between your primary and secondary datasources. Blends are more fragile than joins. They persist only on the worksheet page on which they are created. But blends offer a different kind of flexibility—the ability to alter the primary datasource for each worksheet page.

HOW TO CREATE A DATA BLEND

Creating data blends requires a little planning. If you are going to bring data that doesn't reside in your primary datasource, you have to think about what field(s) you may need in order to achieve the desired result. There are two ways you can create a blend—the automatic method or manually defining the blend.

Automatically-Defined Relationship

The automatic method works well if the field you are employing to create the blend has the same fieldname in both datasources, or if you alias the field names in Tableau so that they match. The Superstore datasource contains geographic sales data. What if you wanted to know what the per capita sales for each state were for the year 2012? The Superstore data set doesn't include population data. But, the United States Census Bureau website has population data. The data in Figure 2–17 was downloaded from the web.

Just two columns of data are included in the table. It is important to note the field description for state. Once again—for automatic blending to work—the field name for the blend must be the same, in Superstore and the census data file. If the fields are not the same you will need to edit the name in the spreadsheet or rename the fields in Tableau so that they match.

To automatically blend the population data with the Superstore data build a view in Tableau that contains the state field. Figure 2–18 shows a view that will work.

Superstore is the primary datasource. The bar chart is filtered for the desired year. The population data is from a completely different datasource, but both datasources include the word State. Automatic blending can now be done by pointing at the population data spreadsheet and dragging it into the worksheet seen in Figure 2–18. Once that is done, the data from the population spreadsheet can be used in the workbook. The visualization in Figure 2–19 uses the blended population data to express sales per hundred thousand population by state.

Look at the data window in the upper left of Figure 2–19. The blue check next to the Superstore datasource indicates that it is the primary datasource. The orange check next to the population data denotes it is the secondary data-source. Since the secondary source is highlighted you see its dimensions and measures fields below. The orange border on the left side of the dimensions and measures shelves confirms that they come from the secondary datasource and the orange link to the right of the State field indicates the field used for the blend. You can also see the State field in Figure 2–18 from the primary datasource.

	A	B
1	**State**	**Poplulation**
2	Alabama	4,822,023
3	Alaska	731,449
4	Arizona	6,553,255
5	Arkansas	2,949,131
6	California	38,041,430
7	Colorado	5,187,582
8	Connecticut	3,590,347
9	Delaware	917,092
10	District of Columbia	632,323
11	Florida	19,317,568
12	Georgia	9,919,945
13	Hawaii	1,392,313
14	Idaho	1,595,728
15	Illinois	12,875,255
16	Indiana	6,537,334
17	Iowa	3,074,186
18	Kansas	2,885,905
19	Kentucky	4,380,415
20	Louisiana	4,601,893
21	Maine	1,329,192
22	Maryland	5,884,563
23	Massachusetts	6,646,144
24	Michigan	9,883,360
25	Minnesota	5,379,139
26	Mississippi	2,984,926
27	Missouri	6,021,988
28	Montana	1,005,141
29	Nebraska	1,855,525
30	Nevada	2,758,931
31	New Hampshire	1,320,718
32	New Jersey	8,864,590
33	New Mexico	2,085,538
34	New York	19,570,261
35	North Carolina	9,752,073

FIGURE 2–17 *Population data*

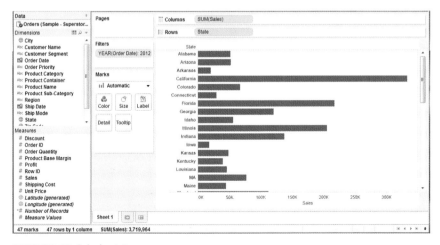

FIGURE 2–18 *Sales by state*

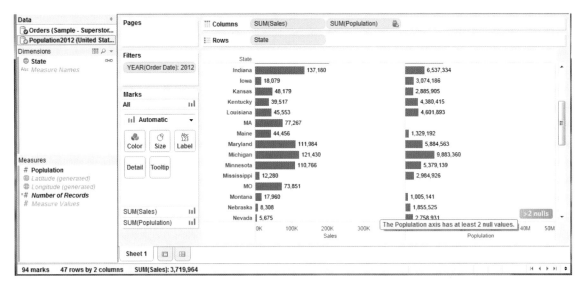

FIGURE 2–19 *Population data blended with Superstore*

A warning—when you perform data blending you must ensure that all of the records you expected to blend actually came into the data set. In Figure 2–19 that is clearly not the case. The states of Massachusetts (MA) and Missouri (MO) didn't come over in the blend because the state names in the census data are not abbreviated. This can be fixed by right-clicking on the abbreviated state label for Missouri and Massachusetts and aliasing full spelling of each state name. After that is done, the population data from those states will be blended as well.

This is an important point with data blending. As the "designer" you must ensure the integrity of the data blend. The whole point in doing this exercise was to use the blended data to calculate per capita sales by state. Figure 2–20 displays the finished blend.

To save space, Figure 2–20 shows only the top seven states by per capita sales. The labels to the right of each bar show the sales per hundred thousand people. The color of each bar encodes the total sales of each state.

Manual Blending

What if your needs are more involved? A scenario that requires a more complicated blend would be the comparison of budget data from a spreadsheet with actual data from a database. Assume that you have defined a budget by product category for each month in the year 2012, and that you want to create

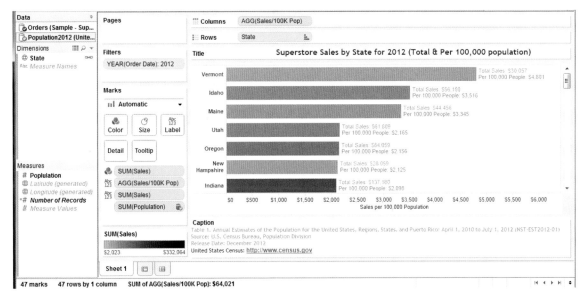

FIGURE 2-20 *Bar chart using blended data*

a visualization that will display the actual and the budgeted sales by month. Building this view will require a blend on the product category and the date field. The steps required are:

1. Connect to both datasources.

2. Use the edit relationship meant to define the blend.

3. Build the visualization.

After connecting to the Superstore data set and the spreadsheet containing budgeted sales, it is possible to define the blend manually. The blending must include both the product category field and a date field. In this example, month and year are used. Figure 2–21 shows a bullet graph that uses the blended Superstore data and budget data.

As you can see in Figure 2–21, actual sales data from the primary datasource (the orders table in Superstore) is displayed as blue or gray bars. Budgeted data from the secondary datasource is plotted using vertical black reference lines for each cell. Notice the two orange links in the dimension shelf for the budget datasource. Both fields are being used in the blend. How do you create a more multi-field blend? Figure 2–22 shows the Edit Relationships menu.

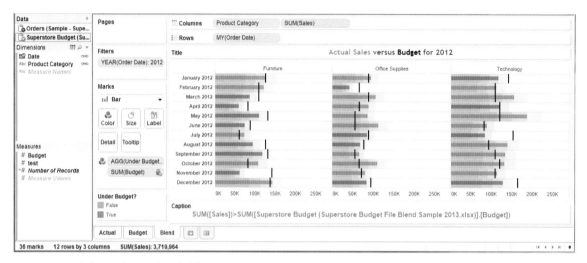

FIGURE 2-21 *Bullet graph using blended data*

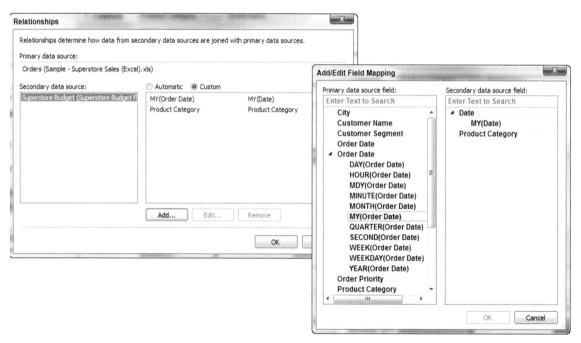

FIGURE 2-22 *The edit relationships menu*

Select the Edit Relationships option from the data menu. This exposes the relationships window. By default, the automatic radio button option will be selected. Product category will appear automatically because that field name exists in both datasources. Since the view contains sales data by month and year for the year 2012, the custom option must be used to select the date field. Figure 2–21 displays the sales by month and year. Clicking the Add button exposes the add/edit field mapping window where the specific data aggregation can be selected from each datasource. Clicking the OK button creates the second link. Confirming that, in the relationship window, finalizes the links for both fields.

Review the pill placements in Figure 2–21 to see where fields were placed to create the chart. The SUM (budget) pill (with the orange check mark on the marks card) was used to create the black reference line. The calculated field used to create the bar colors is displayed in the caption below the graph and is stored in the primary datasource. Gray bars denote items above the budget plan. The gray color gradient behind the sale bars comes from a reference distribution that uses color hue to show sales at 60 percent, 80 percent, 100 percent, and 120 percent of planned sales. For more details on how bullet graphs are created see the "Bullet Graphs" section in Chapter 7.

FACTORS THAT AFFECT THE SPEED OF YOUR DATA CONNECTIONS

There are four areas that affect Tableau's speed:

- The Server hardware, which hosts the database
- The database, which hosts the data
- The network, over which the data is sent
- Your own computer's hardware, which has Tableau Desktop

Like any chain, the weakest link dictates overall performance.

YOUR PERSONAL COMPUTER

Tableau doesn't require high-end equipment to run. But, you will find that more internal memory, a new microprocessor, and a faster hard disk will all contribute to better performance, especially if you are accessing very large data sets. The video card and monitor resolution can contribute to the quality of how Tableau presents the visuals.

Random Access Memory (RAM)

Tableau 8 is a 32-bit application, which means the maximum memory that it can access is four gigabytes. Expanding system RAM beyond this level may not yield any benefit if you are running 32-bit Windows, but if you are running a 64-bit version of Windows you may see a performance boost if you have more RAM.

Processor

A faster processor will help Tableau's performance, but you only really get a chance to change the processor when you buy your computer. Buy the best you can justify and you should be fine.

Disk Access Times

Tableau is not normally a disk intensive program, but having a faster hard disk drive or a solid state drive (SSD) will help Tableau load faster. If you work with very wide and deep data sets that exceed your machine's internal memory capacity, it will slow down and will result in page-swapping to the hard disk drive. In this circumstance a fast hard drive will help performance.

Screen Size

The resolution of your screen will affect the level of detail that you're able to discern. The same visualization on a large, high-resolution screen may provide better insight into your data. If you have a very good monitor, you must consider that other people may be consuming your analysis with equipment that isn't as good. If they have a lower resolution video card, your visualization will not be the same on their computer. Chapter 8 includes tips and tricks that address this issue.

Finally, consider the amount of work you are asking Tableau to do. While it is possible to plot millions of marks in a chart—ask yourself if all those marks add to understanding the data. If you run into performance issues, review the level of detail you're plotting. Using fewer marks in the view may improve the content's value and improve the rendering speed.

YOUR SERVER HARDWARE

The key consideration with regard to the specification of your server hardware is the volume and activity level you anticipate. Is your database currently deployed on the three-year-old production server with thousands of concurrent users? Does your server have other demanding applications running that may cause resource contention?

Tableau can run in the cloud and on servers that have other applications running, but as your deployment expands, it is best to dedicate a server to Tableau. For massive deployments, Tableau core licenses can be divided across multiple servers.

Specifying server hardware is not a one-size-fits-all proposition. Tableau provides guidelines on their website, but each situation is unique and requires some detailed planning. In general, oversizing the hardware a little isn't a bad idea. Tableau normally becomes very popular when it is deployed, so consider the potential for increasing demand and get professional assistance if you are unsure about the Server hardware you should purchase. Chapter 9 covers this topic in more detail.

THE NETWORK

Like any other form of infrastructure (transport, power, water) data networking is a mundane but vital component for the efficient performance of any system. Networking is therefore the responsibility of specialists within your organization, and they can help you identify if there are choke points in your network that slow the performance of Tableau. For all but the very largest organizations, network capacity is seldom a bottleneck.

THE DATABASE

If you are using live connections to your data—as opposed to data extracts— the performance of your database is one of the most significant determining factors of speed.

As more people in your organization use Tableau, it is important to monitor resource load on the Server, the network, and the database. Tuning your database is the responsibility of the database administrator. It is normally helpful if someone from the IT team is directly involved in the early phases of enterprise roll-outs, especially if it is expected that Tableau may create larger or different demands on the database.

If the database administrator understands the type, amount, and timing of the query loads that Tableau may generate—proper planning can ensure that system performance will not be degraded due to inadequately indexed database tables or an overloaded database server.

HOW TO DEAL WITH DATA QUALITY PROBLEMS

Why should you care about the cleanliness of your data? Inaccurate data can lead to bad decisions. Tableau is very good at visualizing data and making it understandable. If your data isn't clean—when you connect Tableau to it, you will see the problem clearly. Fortunately, Tableau provides tools to help you deal with issues that don't require intervention at the database-level to resolve (at least temporarily) unclean data problems. However, the best course of action when you find errors is to report them to the IT person responsible for data quality within the database you are using.

QUICK SOLUTIONS IN TABLEAU

There are several different ways you can correct data problems within Tableau that don't involve changing the source data.

Renaming

Renaming fields in Tableau is done by right-clicking on the field and renaming it. Field member names can be aliased. These changes do not alter the source database. Tableau "remembers" what you renamed without altering the source data.

Grouping

Let's assume that a company name has been entered as all of these: A&M, A & M, A and M, A+M. With Tableau you can Ctrl-Select each of these names and group them—and then create a name alias for the ad hoc grouping. So, all the versions of the name appear as one record in Tableau—A&M. This grouping and name alias will be saved as part of Tableau's metadata.

Aliases

Sometimes the name of something in the database is not a useful term for reporting purposes. For example, everybody on the team enters the customer type as P1, P2, G1, G2 where P2 denotes the size of the customer in annual revenue. For example, "Platinum level 2" could mean that the customer has an annual revenue of $1m to $5m. In Tableau, you can right-click on P2 and alias it with a more meaningful description.

Geographic Errors

Although Tableau has built-in mapping that works very well, there will be occasions when geographic locations are not recognized. Tableau will warn you by placing a small gray pill in the lower right area of your map. Clicking on that pill provides the ability to edit the offending locations or filter them out of view. This is also accessible from Tableau's map menu.

Null Values

When you see the word null appear in a view, that means Tableau can't match the record. You can filter out nulls, group them with non-null members of the set, or correct the join that is causing the null. There are many reasons why a null value could result. If you aren't sure how to correct the null, seek assistance from a qualified technical resource.

CORRECTING YOUR SOURCE DATA

Although it's quick and easy to address data quality issues directly in Tableau, it's important to bear in mind that the changes you have made in Tableau will only benefit those using the same Tableau file. There is no substitute for correcting the underlying data in the datasource. Report errors to the responsible staff quickly and provide them with your Tableau report. Expose the details so that the database is corrected.

In the next chapter you'll learn how to create more nuanced charts that go beyond the basic visualizations provided by the Show Me button by adding more features to your charts in ways that enhance meaning without cluttering your view of the information.

NOTE

1. Mackenzie, Gordon. *Orbiting the Giant Hairball: A Corporate Fool's Guide to Surviving with Grace*. New York: Viking, 1998. Print. Page 88.

CHAPTER 3

Building Your First Visualization

If we have made this our task, then there is no more rational procedure than the method of trial and error—of conjecture and refutation: of boldly proposing theories; of trying our best to show that these are erroneous; and of accepting them tentatively if our critical efforts are unsuccessful.

KARL POPPER[1]

Now that you've learned how to connect Tableau to a variety of datasources you can start building visualizations. In this chapter you will learn about all of the chart types provided by the Show Me button. You will discover how to add trend lines, reference lines, and control the way your data is sorted and filtered. You'll see how creating ad hoc groups, sets, and hierarchies can produce information not available in the datasource. Tableau's discrete and continuous data hierarchies will be explained, and how you can alter Tableau's default date hierarchies by creating your own custom dates.

FAST AND EASY ANALYSIS VIA SHOW ME

Tableau's mission statement is to help you see and understand your data by enabling self-service visual analytics. The software is designed to facilitate analysis for non-technical information consumers. This is the concept behind Tableau's Show Me button. Consider Show Me to be your expert helper. Show Me tells you what chart to use and why. It will also help you create complicated visualizations faster and with less effort. For example, advanced map visualizations are best started via Show Me because Tableau will properly place multiple dimensions and measures pills on the appropriate shelves with a single click. If you know what you want to see, Show Me will get you to your desired destination quickly.

HOW SHOW ME WORKS

Show Me looks at the combination of measures and dimensions you've selected and interprets what chart types display the data most effectively. Most of the examples in this section use the Superstore Sales Excel data set. If you want to follow along, connect to that datasource. Picking order date, sales, and then clicking Show Me will expose the options available for that combination that you see in Figure 3-1.

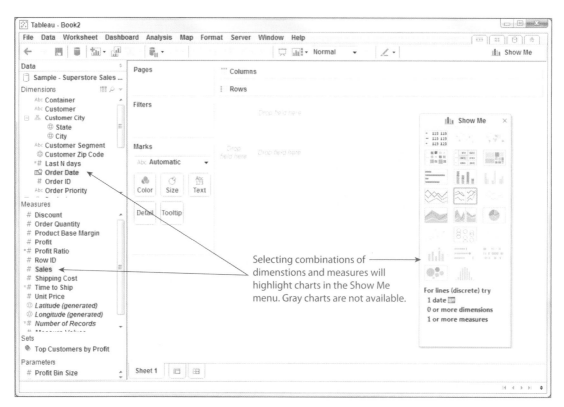

FIGURE 3-1 *Show Me displays chart options*

Tableau recommends a line (discrete) time series chart in Show Me—denoted with a blue outline. At the bottom of the Show Me area you also see additional details regarding requirements needed for building any available chart. The time series chart requires one date, one measure, and zero or more dimensions. Selecting the highlighted chart causes the time series chart in Figure 3-2 to be displayed.

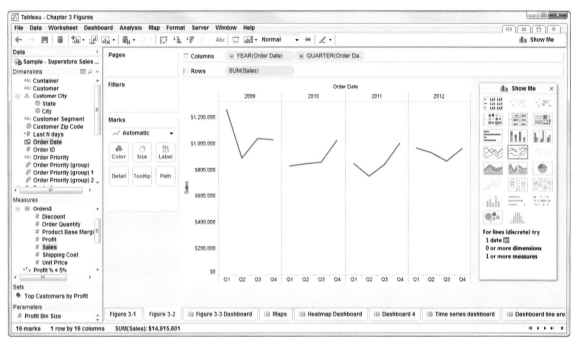

FIGURE 3-2 *Discrete date time series chart*

Pointing at other chart options in the Show Me menu changes the text at the bottom of the menu. This text provides guidance on the combination of data elements required for the chart being considered. Clicking on any of the highlighted Show Me icons alters the visualization in the worksheet.

CHART TYPES PROVIDED BY THE SHOW ME BUTTON

Show Me currently contains twenty-three chart types. Expect to see more charts added to in future releases. Advanced charts are normally variations on the basic pallet of charts you see in Show Me. Now take a look at each chart type provided by Show Me in more detail.

TEXT TABLES (CROSSTABS)

Text tables look like grids of numbers in a spreadsheet. Crosstabs are useful for looking up values. Figure 3-3 shows a standard crosstab on the left.

The text table on the right has been enhanced by adding a Boolean calculation to highlight items with less than five percent profit ratio. Individual cells (marks) that are greater than five percent profit ratio are gray. You will learn how to create calculated values in Chapter 4.

		Text Table (crosstab)				⬈
		Central	East	South	West	All ⊽
Furniture	Tables	471,751	652,965	316,405	454,887	1,896,008
	Chairs & Chairmats	651,654	469,652	292,478	348,052	1,761,837
	Bookcases	258,919	145,818	171,504	246,411	822,652
	Office Furnishings	259,389	149,828	129,434	159,443	698,094
	Total	1,641,713	1,418,264	909,820	1,208,793	5,178,591
Office Supplies	Storage & Org.	299,116	280,367	263,166	227,534	1,070,183
	Binders & Access.	309,262	294,907	214,942	203,847	1,022,958
	Other Office	300,300	197,672	192,165	232,494	922,630
	Appliances	317,079	136,944	149,023	133,946	736,992
	Total	1,225,757	909,889	819,295	797,821	3,752,762
Technology	Office Machines	563,395	321,105	610,807	673,390	2,168,697
	Telephone & Comm.	613,410	394,726	405,524	475,653	1,889,314
	Copiers and Fax	404,175	173,833	209,237	343,117	1,130,361
	Computer Peripherals	250,718	198,649	195,535	150,974	795,876
	Total	1,831,698	1,088,313	1,421,104	1,643,134	5,984,248
	Grand Total	4,699,167	3,416,466	3,150,219	3,649,748	14,915,601

		Text Table (crosstab) with highlight				
		Central	West	East	South	All ⊽
Furniture	Tables	471,751	454,887	652,965	316,405	1,896,008
	Chairs & Chairmats	651,654	348,052	469,652	292,478	1,761,837
	Bookcases	258,919	246,411	145,818	171,504	822,652
	Office Furnishings	259,389	159,443	149,828	129,434	698,094
	Total	1,641,713	1,208,793	1,418,264	909,820	5,178,591
Office Supplies	Storage & Org.	299,116	227,534	280,367	263,166	1,070,183
	Binders & Access.	309,262	203,847	294,907	214,942	1,022,958
	Other Office	300,300	232,494	197,672	192,165	922,630
	Appliances	317,079	133,946	136,944	149,023	736,992
	Total	1,225,757	797,821	909,889	819,295	3,752,762
Technology	Office Machines	563,395	673,390	321,105	610,807	2,168,697
	Telephone & Comm.	613,410	475,653	394,726	405,524	1,889,314
	Copiers and Fax	404,175	343,117	173,833	209,237	1,130,361
	Computer Peripherals	250,718	150,974	198,649	195,535	795,876
	Total	1,831,698	1,643,134	1,088,313	1,421,104	5,984,248
	Grand Total	4,699,167	3,649,748	3,416,466	3,150,219	14,915,601

Profit < 5% ▨ True   ▨ False

FIGURE 3-3 *Text tables (crosstabs)*

MAPS (SYMBOL AND FILLED)

Selecting a field with a small globe icon makes maps available in Show Me. Figure 3-4 shows examples of the two kinds of maps Show Me provides.

Symbol maps are most effective for displaying very granular details, or if you need to show multiple members of a small dimension set. In Figure 3-4 Show Me used pie charts to display product category in the map on the left. In Filled maps it is a good idea to make the marks more transparent and add dark borders because marks tend to cluster around highly populated areas. Using the color button on the marks card to do this makes the individual marks

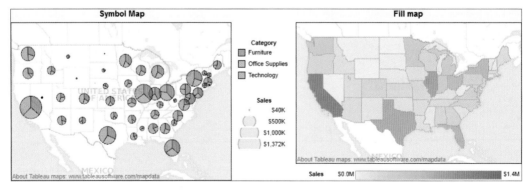

FIGURE 3-4 *Symbol map and filled map*

easier to see. The color and size legends in view are automatically provided by Tableau. Filled maps display a single measure using color within a geographic shape. If you restrict filled maps to smaller geographic areas (state, province) they effectively display more granular areas like county or postal code.

HEAT MAPS, HIGHLIGHT TABLES, TREEMAPS

Comparing granular combinations of dimensions and measures can be done effectively with each of these charts. Heat maps use color and size to compare up to two measures. Highlight tables can display one measure using a color gradient background to differentiate values. Treemaps effectively display larger dimension sets using color and size to display one or more dimensions and up to two measures. Figure 3-5 displays examples of each.

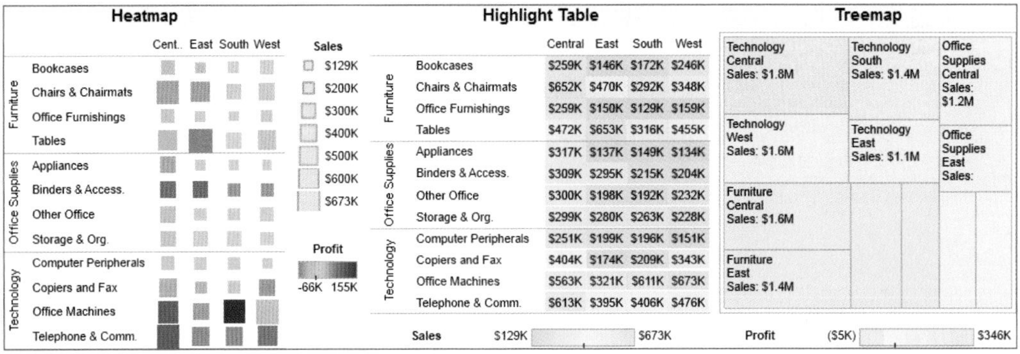

FIGURE 3-5 *Heatmap, highlight table, and treemap*

These charts, and text tables, can also be used to replace Quick Filters on dashboards—providing more information in the same space that a multi-select filter would require.

BAR CHART, STACKED BAR, SIDE-BY-SIDE BARS

These charts facilitate one-to-many comparisons. Figure 3-6 includes examples of each.

Bar charts are the most effective way to compare values across dimensions—their linear nature making precise comparisons easy. Stacked bar charts should not be used when there are many different dimensions because they can be overwhelming if too many colors are plotted in each bar. Side-by-side bars provide another way to compare measures across and dimensions on a single axis.

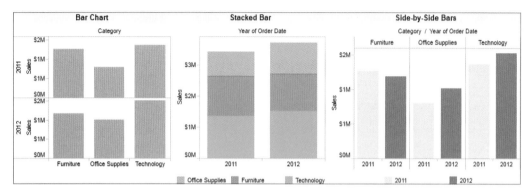

FIGURE 3-6 *Bar chart, stacked bar chart, and side-by-side bar chart*

LINE CHARTS FOR TIME SERIES ANALYSIS

Line charts are the most effective way to display time series data. One variable to consider when presenting time series is the treatment of time as a discrete (bucketed) entity or as a continuous (unbroken) series progression. Discrete line charts place breaks between time units (year, quarter, and month). Most people are familiar with time series charts that are presented in unbroken lines. Figure 3-2 presents a single measure (sales) using a discrete time series. Time is presented discretely by quarters within each year. Figure 3-7 provides three different time series charts that are plotting two measures with a continuous time axis.

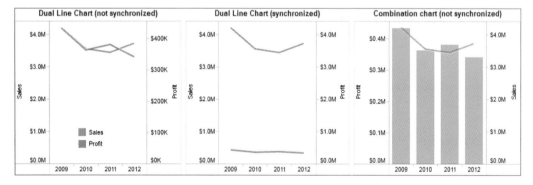

FIGURE 3-7 *Time series presented using continuous time*

The dual line chart presents two measures (sales and profit) using asynchronous axis ranges. Show Me assumes dual axis charts will be used to present values that are dissimilar and plots the marks using different axis ranges. The middle dual line chart, with synchronized axis, provides a better comparison of the relative values of sales and profit. The combination chart, using a bar for profit and line for sales, maintains asynchronous axis ranges, but the use of different mark types accentuates that there are different measures being plotted.

AREA FILL CHARTS AND PIE CHARTS

Figure 3-8 provides a comparison of lines, area fill, and pie charts. Compare the value of each kind of chart for displaying the information. All three charts are plotting the same data using Show Me to create the charts. Which one do you prefer?

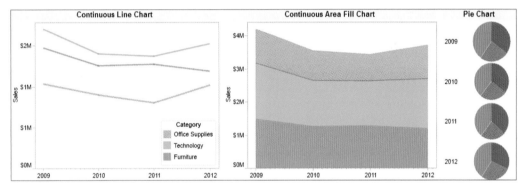

FIGURE 3-8 *Continuous line chart, area fill chart, pie charts*

The line chart facilitates accurate comparison of the relative sales by category. Since the area fill chart plots sales values as bands, it is easy to misinterpret the top band as being the largest value in the set. Area fill charts are best used for plotting a single dimension to avoid misunderstanding. Pie charts should be used for getting a general sense of magnitude and not for precise comparisons. A more effective use of a pie chart and area fill chart is provided in Figure 3-9.

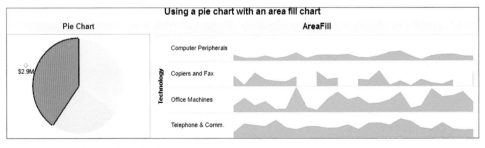

FIGURE 3-9 *Pie chart and area fill chart*

By limiting the area fill chart to one dimension on each axis and using a pie chart with only three slices—the combination of chart types presents the information effectively. The pie chart acts as a filter for the area fill chart in Figure 3-9. If you have limited space and are sure that your pie's slices won't be tiny, pie charts can be used effectively as filters.

SCATTER PLOT, CIRCLE VIEW, AND SIDE-BY-SIDE CIRCLE PLOTS

Enabling analysis of granular data across multiple dimensions, scatter plots, circle views, and side-by-side circles can be used to identify outliers. Figure 3-10 provides an example of each.

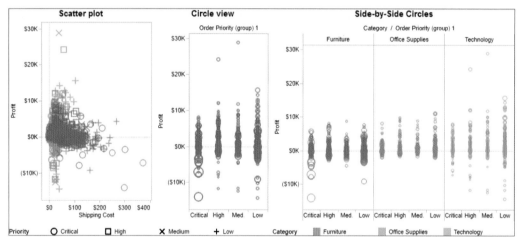

FIGURE 3-10   *Scatter plot, circle view, side-by-side circle view*

All three charts in Figure 3-10 are plotting over four thousand marks in a very small space. The scatter plot uses two axes for comparing profit and shipping cost. Color and shape provide insight into two dimensions. Size isn't being used in the example but could be used for a third measure. The circle view uses one axis to plot a single measure. In both circle plots size is used to denote shipping cost amount. The side-by-side chart provides a more granular breakdown of the product categories.

BULLET GRAPH, PACKED BUBBLE, HISTOGRAM, AND GANTT CHARTS

The last four chart types provided by Show Me are completely different tools. Figure 3-11 shows them together but their uses are very different.

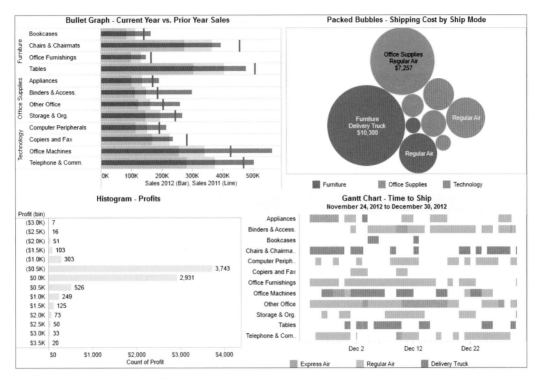

FIGURE 3-11   *The last four Show Me charts*

Bullet graphs are bar charts that include a reference line and reference distribution for each cell in the plot. In the example, current year sales (bars) are compared to prior year sales (red reference lines). The gray color band behind the bar represent sixty and eight percent of the prior year sales. Bullet graphs pack a lot of information into a small space.

Bubble charts offer another way to present one-to-many comparisons by using size and color. They can be interesting to look at but do not allow for very precise comparisons between the different bubbles. For this reason limit the situations that don't require precise visual ranking of the bubbles.

Histograms turn normally continuous measures into discretely-bucketed bins of numeric values. The example histogram breaks down profits into five hundred dollar increments. The bar's length shows the number of orders that fall within the band.

You've probably seen Gantt charts before being used in project planning. The length of each bar color in the example displays a time duration for an activity. These are particularly useful when you want to visualize the timing and duration of events. In the example, the length of the bar is the duration of time required to complete a shipment. The starting position of the bar is the date the order was received.

Using Tableau View Structure to Create New Data when you are new to Tableau and don't completely grasp how each shelf affects your chart's appearance, Show Me will help you build charts without having to understand the mechanics. Show Me helps everyone achieve desirable results quickly, and it helps you gain an understanding of the mechanics of how each shelf and field type can change the appearance of your visualizations.

Once you have a chart in view, you can use that chart structure to add additional information. Two common ways to do this are by adding trend lines or reference lines to your chart. The numbers used to derive trend lines and reference lines can come from the view in Tableau itself and don't necessarily require that the data exist in your datasource.

TREND LINES AND REFERENCE LINES

Visualizing granular data sometimes results in random-looking plots. Trend lines help you interpret the data by fitting a straight or curved line that best represents the pattern contained within detailed data plots. Reference lines provide visual comparisons to benchmark figures, constants, or calculated values that provide insight into marks that don't conform to expected or desired values.

Trend lines help you see patterns in data that are not apparent when looking at your chart of the source data by drawing a line that best fits the values in view. Reference lines allow you to compare the actual plot against targets, or to create statistical analyses of the deviation contained in the plot, or the range of values based on fixed or calculated numbers. Trend lines help you see patterns that can provide predictive value. Reference lines alert you to outliers that may require attention or additional analysis. Figure 3-12 provides examples of a trend line and a reference line.

The chart on the left employs a linear regression line to plot the trend in volatile weekly sales figures. The pattern of sales is volatile—making it difficult to see the overall pattern. The trend isn't very pronounced, but the trend line helps you see that sales are trending down slightly. How reliable is the trend line plot? That question can be answered by pointing at the trend line and reviewing the statistical values displayed or by pointing at the trend line, right-clicking, and selecting Describe Trend Model. Figure 3-13 shows the more detailed description of the trend model statistics.

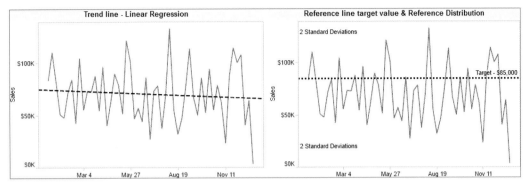

FIGURE 3-12 *Trend line and reference line*

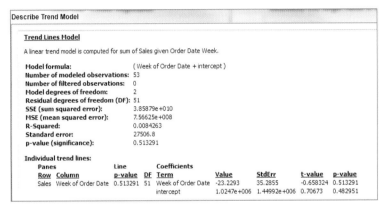

FIGURE 3-13 *Describe the trend model*

Describing the trend model exposes the statistical values that describe the trend line plot. If you are a statistician all the figures will mean something to you. If you aren't a statistics expert, focus on the P-Value and R-Squared figures. They help you evaluate the reliability and predictive value of the trend line plot. If the P-Value is greater than .05, then the trend line doesn't provide much predictive value. R-Squared provides an indicator of how well the line fits the individual marks. The linear regression trend line displayed on the left side of Figure 3-12 clearly doesn't have much predictive value (P-Value is .513291, which implies a confident interval of less than 50 percent), nor does the line fit the marks particularly well. The R-Square value (.008) is very low indicating that the plot doesn't fit the marks very precisely. Tableau does the best job it can fitting the line to the plot, but if the marks are randomly scattered, the R-Squared value will be low. The combination of low P-Value and R-Squared value means that the trend line on the left side of Figure 3-12 does not provide much predictive value.

The chart on the right in Figure 3-12 uses the same data as the chart on the left but this time a reference line has been applied to show the target value of $85,000. A reference distribution has also been calculated to show two standard deviations from the mean value of the plot. Assuming the data is normally distributed—marks outside of that range indicate abnormal variation that would warrant further investigation to determine the cause of the variance.

You don't need to become a statistics expert to use trend lines and reference lines. But, understanding the basics will certainly help you interpret what the plots indicate. A web search will provide more details regarding the mathematics if you are interested.

ADDING TREND LINES AND REFERENCE LINES TO YOUR CHARTS

There are many options available for presenting trend lines and reference lines in Tableau. Take a look below at each in more detail.

FIGURE 3-14 *The trend line options menu*

TREND LINES

Add a trend line to your visualization by right-clicking on the white space in the worksheet and selecting the menu option Trend Lines/Show Trend Lines. This adds a linear regression line to the chart. More trend line options are available if you point at the trend line, right-click, and select Edit Trend Lines. This exposes the trend line menu in Figure 3-14.

The trend line menu provides options for changing the trend line type. If your chart uses color to express a dimension, you can choose to create separate trend lines for each colored line in the view—or not. Selecting Show Confidence Bands adds upper and lower bounding lines based on the variation of the data. If you're applying trend lines in charts like scatter plots, you can also force the trend line to intercept the vertical y-axis at zero.

REFERENCE LINES

There are many different options for reference lines and you can apply more than one reference line to an axis. To add a reference line, right-click on the axis from which you want to apply the reference line. Be careful to point at the white space and not at a title or axis label. Figure 3-15 shows the reference line menu selections used to add the standard deviation reference distribution displayed in the time series plot on the right side of Figure 3-12.

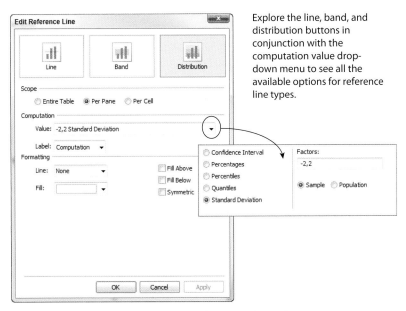

Explore the line, band, and distribution buttons in conjunction with the computation value drop-down menu to see all the available options for reference line types.

FIGURE 3-15 *Reference line menu standard deviation reference lines*

The same chart in Figure 3-12 includes a second reference line that displays a constant. This was added by selecting the reference "line" type to display a manually-entered constant value of $85,000.

Two more reference line examples along with the related reference line menu selections can be seen in Figure 3-16.

The example on the left in Figure 3-16 combines a reference line displaying (median) with reference bands for maximum and minimum values. The chart on the right side of Figure 3-16 uses a reference distribution to plot quintile ranges. Note the use of the Symmetric Color option. Selecting this causes the color bands outside of the widest quintile lines to use the same color hue. If Symmetric Color wasn't selected, the band color would get darker from top to bottom. Alternatively, if the symmetric options were left unchecked and the reverse was selected, the color bands would get lighter from top to bottom.

Applying color fill above or below reference lines calls attention to specific areas of your visualization. Use trend lines and reference lines in moderation. They add insight to your visualizations but too many reference lines can lead to chart clutter and make it more difficult to understand.

FIGURE 3-16 *Reference bands and reference distributions*

WHY THE CONCEPT OF SCOPE IS IMPORTANT

Understanding how the scope in trend line and reference line calculations determines the resulting appearance of the line is important not only for the deriving trend and reference lines, but for understanding how Calculated Values and Table Calculations work in Tableau. We'll cover calculated values in detail in Chapter 4, but the concept of scope (cell, pane, table) that you learn here will help you when you try more advanced calculations later.

Figure 3-17 includes a time series chart on the left that contains two different reference lines and the bullet graph on the right contains a single reference line for each bar (cell) in the view.

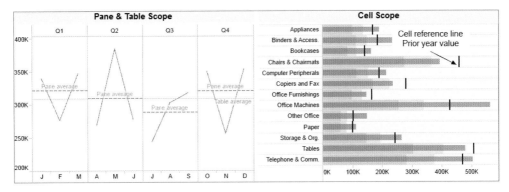

FIGURE 3-17 *Reference lines using entire table, pane and cell*

The time series chart on the left employs discrete dates to create panes by quarter. Tableau outlines the panes using gray lines. The scope that the calculation Tableau uses to create the orange dotted reference line is the table. It shows the average value for the entire table. The scope of the blue dashed line is using the quarter panes to derive that reference line. By coincidence the table average and the pane average lines overlap in the second quarter. In all other quarters in the view, the pane average differs from the average for the entire year (table scope). The bullet graph on the right compares current year values (blue bars) with prior year values plotted using thick black reference lines. Those reference lines are applied using cell scope.

CHANGING THE SCOPE OF TREND LINES

Scope can also be used to change the appearance of trend lines. Figure 3-18 includes examples of trend lines that are applied by pane, and for the entire table.

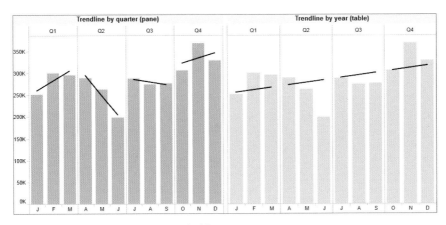

FIGURE 3-18 *Trend lines using pane and table*

Tableau provides four different kinds of trend lines (linear, logarithmic, expo-nential, and polynomial). Most people are accustomed to seeing linear (straight) regression lines in time series data. Polynomial regression provides a more curved line. Increasing the degrees of freedom will make the trend line follow the plot of the individual marks more closely. Logarithmic and exponential regression normally results in curved lines.

Different Trend Line and Axis Types

One reason for using trend lines is predictive analysis. To help you see a pos-sible future condition. The choice of method for calculating trend lines requires some professional judgment and is dependent on the data. People associate the word "exponential" with rapid growth. A real-world example of this is pro-vided by rapid advance of computing power over the past 40 years. Plotting numbers that change drastically and making those figures easy to interpret can be challenging. Figure 3-19 shows three different ways to plot a rapidly changing data set.

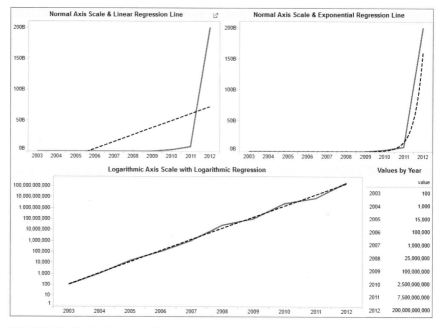

FIGURE 3-19 Rapidly increasing time series

You can tell by looking at the top two time series plots that the values plotted are increasing very rapidly over a ten-year period. These charts use a linear axis scale. In the top left chart a linear trend line is also used to smooth the data.

The top right chart uses an exponential regression line. It's obvious that the exponential trend line fits the data better. The bottom chart utilizes a logarithmic axis scale, which was altered by right-clicking in the white space of the axis and picking the logarithmic scale option. The trend line is also computed using logarithmic regression.

Tableau's logarithmic axis scale makes it easier to compare very different values in the same chart. The logarithmic regression line also makes it easier to see what next year's value might be. If you feel that logarithmic or exponential trend lines might benefit your analysis, you should arm yourself with the technical expertise to explain what the lines mean. As with all statistics, judgment should be applied. History may not repeat.

If you know a friendly statistician, ask them to explain the underlying theory and math. Alternatively, go to Kahn Academy's website `https://www.khanacademy .org/math/probability/regression` and watch the videos related to regression, statistics, and probability. Unless you understand the statistics supporting exponential and logarithmic smoothing, you should stick to what you feel comfortable explaining to your audience.

SORTING DATA IN TABLEAU

Tableau provides basic and advanced sorting methods that are easily accessed through icons or menus. Sorting isn't limited to fields that are visible in the chart—any field in the datasource can be used for sorting.

MANUAL SORTING VIA ICONS

The most basic way to sort is via the icons that appear in the toolbar menu. The toolbar menu sort icons provide ascending and descending sorts. Figure 3-20 shows a bar chart in which a manual sort was applied from the toolbar icon.

Tableau also provides sorting icons near the headings and mark axis. If you don't see an icon, hover your mouse near the area and it will appear. Notice the icon that appears in the sub-category pill on the row shelf? The light gray descending sort icon that appears in that pill provides an indication that a sort has been applied on that sub-category field. Clicking on the sort icon floating over the right-side of the sub-category heading provides ascending and descending sorts using the text of the product category headings. The sort icons that appear over and under the mark (bar) axis provide ascending and descending sorts based on the values displayed by the marks, and also add datasource order sorting.

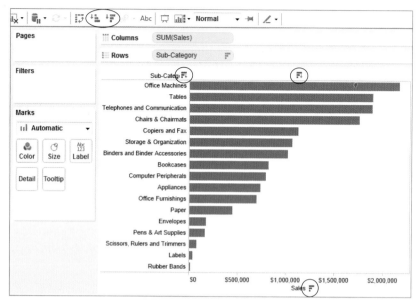

FIGURE 3-20 *Manual sorting applied from the toolbar icon*

It doesn't matter how many levels of hierarchy are added to the view, you can sort on each level. Figure 3-21 includes the category dimension and that pill has been sorted using an ascending sort.

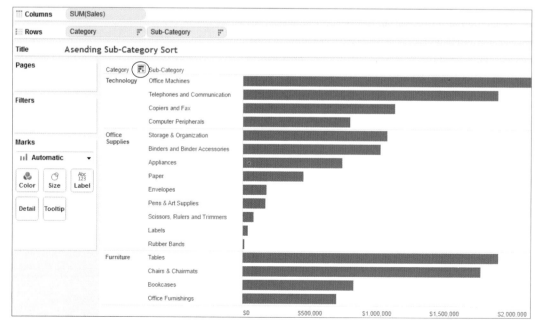

FIGURE 3-21 *Ascending sort by category*

In addition to sorting via the toolbar or the sort icons, you can point at and drag any one of the rows in the display and revise the sort to an arbitrary manual sort. For example, you could change the sort order by dragging computer peripherals to the top of the technology category and defining a new manual sort.

CALCULATED SORTS USING THE SORT MENU

More advanced sorting can be accessed by pointing at a dimension pill, right-clicking, and selecting the Sort option. Figure 3-22 shows the sort menu that displays when you right-click on a dimension pill—in this example the sub-category pill.

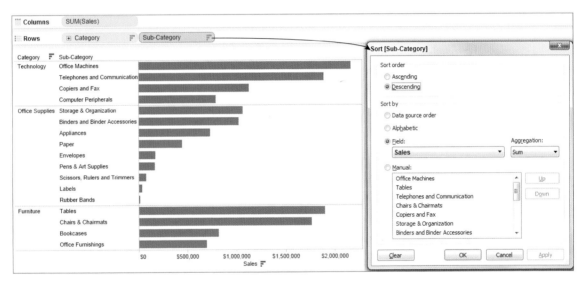

FIGURE 3-22 *Re-sorted computer peripherals and the sort menu*

Tableau's sort menu allows you to more precisely define the default sort method and order. The sort by section includes a drop-down menu that currently displays the sales field using an aggregation of sum. However, it is possible to select any field in the data set and change the aggregation. For example, you could also apply ascending sort by average profit. Leaving the sort menu open and using the apply button at the bottom right side of the menu is useful. You can apply a variety of sort options and see the result. When you decide to keep the sort, click the OK button.

Sorting via Legends

Another useful sort feature is enabled within legends. Figure 3-23 shows two versions of the same bar chart. The left view orders the blue delivery truck dimension on the bottom. The chart on the right shows regular air at the bottom. Reordering the position of the colors displayed within the color legend causes the order of the colors appearing in the bars to change. Reposition the colors within the color legend by pointing at a color, holding down the left mouse button, and dragging the color to the desired position.

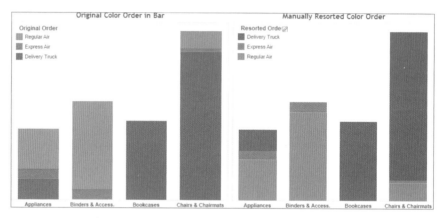

FIGURE 3-23 *Reordering the color in charts*

The ability to reorder colors in a stacked bar chart is important because precise comparisons are most easily made for the color that starts at the zero point on the axis. All of the other colors are not as easily compared because they don't start at the same value.

ENHANCING VIEWS WITH FILTERS, SETS, GROUPS, AND HIERARCHIES

Sorting isn't the only way to arrange data. Creating drill-down hierarchies is easy in Tableau. Perhaps your data includes a dimension set with too many members for convenient viewing. Grouping dimensions within a particular field is available. Interacting with your data may uncover measurement outliers that you would like to save and reuse in other visualizations. That capability is enabled via sets. Even groups of sets can be created on-the-fly.

MAKING HIERARCHIES TO PROVIDE DRILL-DOWN CAPABILITY

Hierarchies provide a way to start with a high-level overview of your data, and then drill down to lower levels of detail on demand. In Figure 3-21 you can see a two-level view of the data that includes product category and then sub-category. That presentation may include more detail than you prefer to see. A hierarchy that combines category and sub-category can address both needs. Figure 3-24 uses a hierarchy to show category first and sub-category on demand.

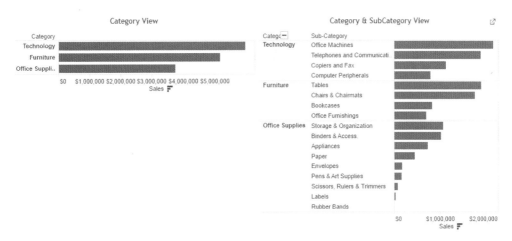

FIGURE 3-24 *Hierarchy using category and sub-category*

The bar chart on the left displays the summary product category. By pointing at the category heading a small plus sign will appear. Clicking on that causes the sub-category level of detail to be exposed. To collapse the hierarchy, point at the category heading again and click on the minus sign. You can create as many levels in your hierarchy as you desire.

Hierarchies are created by pointing at a dimension field and dragging it on top of another field. The order of appearance is defined by dragging the field names contained within the hierarchy icon to the desired position. Figure 3-25 shows the hierarchy icon with category and sub-category. You can change the hierarchy name by pointing at the text to the right of the hierarchy icon and typing **product hierarchy**.

Other fields can be added to the hierarchy by positioning them in the order desired inside the hierarchy grouping on the dimension shelf.

FIGURE 3-25 *Making a custom hierarchy*

CREATING AND USING FILTERS

There are a few different ways to add filtering to your visualization. Dragging any dimension or measure on to the filter shelf provides filtering that is accessible to the designer. Make that filter accessible to more people by turning it into a Quick Filter. This places it on the desktop where it is accessible to anyone—even those reading your report via Tableau Reader or Tableau Server. You can also create conditional filters that operate according to rules you define.

CREATING A FILTER WITH THE FILTER SHELF

In Figure 3-24 the category and sub-category view contains seventeen different rows of data. Suppose you want to hide five of those rows from view. Dragging the sub-category field from the dimension shelf and placing it in the filter shelf exposes the filter menu. Figure 3-26 shows the filtered data with the general tab of the filter menu. The sub-categories that do not have check marks have been filtered out of view.

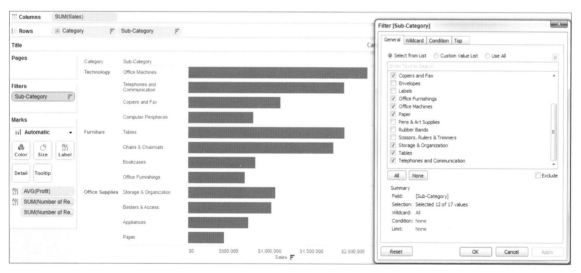

FIGURE 3-26 *Applying a filter via the filter shelf*

Notice that there are three other tabs on the filter menu. The Wildcard tab is typically used to search for text strings to filter. If you want to filter using another field that isn't in your view you can use the Condition tab to select any field in your datasource and filter using that field. The Top tab facilitates building top and bottom filtering or filtering requiring other formula conditions. If you use more than one of the filtering options tabs to define your filter, Tableau applies the conditions defined in each tab in the order the tabs appear from left to right. General conditions will be applied first, then wildcard, then condition, and the top tab conditions last.

Below the general field list to the right of the None button is a check box for the Exclude option. If Exclude is checked, the items that include check marks are filtered out of view. Exclude filters can take a little longer to execute than Include filters, especially if your data set is very large.

Quick Filters

If you want to make the filter available for people that are viewing the report via Tableau Reader or Server you need to expose the filter control on the desktop. To create a Quick Filter, point at and right-click on any pill used on any shelf in your worksheet, then select the Show Quick Filter option. Figure 3-27 includes Quick Filters using the category and sales fields.

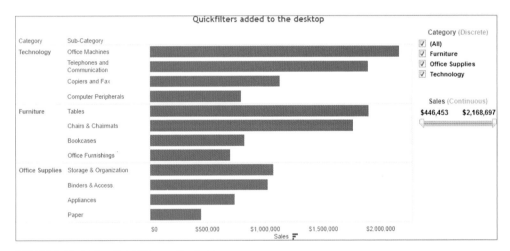

FIGURE 3-27 *Adding Quick Filters to the desktop*

The default Quick Filter styles are dependent on the type of field you apply within the Quick Filter control. In Figure 3-27 the discrete category field results in discrete filter options (furniture, office supplies, technology). Discrete filters are expressed using radio buttons or multi-select boxes. The second Quick Filter for sales (a continuous range of values) is expressed using slider-type filters. Editing the Quick Filter type can be done from inside the Quick Filter itself. Click on the title bar of the filter to expose the available options. Figure 3-28 shows examples of the menus that can be activated from the category and sales Quick Filter title bars.

FIGURE 3-28 *Editing Quick Filter types*

The menu on the left side of Figure 3-28 relates to discrete category filters. The right menu is for the continuous filters. In addition to controlling the filter style you can adjust many other attributes. You can edit the titles of each filter by including the words discrete and continuous and applying a different color to each word and centering the title. The Quick Filter titles in Figure 3-27 have been modified in this way. These are the Quick Filter menus (both continuous and discrete):

- Edit filter—Exposes the main filter menu.

- Clear filter—Removes the Quick Filter.

- Apply to worksheets—Apply the filter to all or selected worksheets.

- Customize—Turn on or off different filter controls.

- Show title—Turn off or on the Quick Filter title.

- Edit title—Modify the text in the Quick Filter title.

- Only relevant values—Turning this on reduces the set members displayed in the filter.

- Include values—Causes selected items in the filter to be included in the view.

■   Exclude values—Causes selected items in the filter to be excluded from view.

■   Hide card—Removes the Quick Filter from view but leaves it on the filter shelf.

These are the Quick Filter menu items that appear only if the Quick Filter is on a dashboard:

■   Floating—If activated, allows the filter to float on top of other worksheet objects.

■   Select layout container—Activates the layout container in the dashboard.

■   Deselect—Removes the layout container selection in the dashboard.

■   Remove from dashboard—Removes the Quick Filter from the dashboard.

The remaining sections of each filter type control the style of Quick Filter. There are seven styles of discrete and three styles of continuous Quick Filter types available. One other feature available directly from the Quick Filter is the ability to control the relevant values displayed directly from the desktop. Figure 3-29 displays a small control (three bars).

This is important when you have several Quick Filters exposed in a view. For example, a hierarchy of Quick Filters might include a filter to select state, then city. Restricting the city filter to include only the relevant values means that if a particular state (Georgia) is selected in the first Quick Filter, the city Quick Filter would only display cities in the state of Georgia. If the city filter didn't apply only relevant values, the filter would contain every city in the United States.

FIGURE 3-29 *Including all or relevant values*

Context Filters

One type of filter that many experienced Tableau users are unaware of is the context filter. Context filters do not only filter the data, they cause Tableau to create a temporary table that contains only the filtered data. For this reason they execute more slowly than a normal filter. Context filters are denoted by a gray-colored pill. They can be useful if you want to work with a subset to achieve a particular result. Don't use a context filter if you plan to alter the filter frequently.

Tableau provides robust filtering. In Chapter 8 on dashboards, you'll learn how to save space on dashboards by making the data act as a filter by using actions to apply filters.

GROUPING DIMENSIONS

When you have a dimension that contains many members and your source data doesn't include a hierarchy structure, grouping can provide summarized views of the data. You can manually group items from headers or multi-select marks in a chart. Tableau also provides a menu option with fuzzy search that will help you group by searching strings in large lists of values. You can even group by selecting marks in a view. If you need to work with data that isn't structured the way you want it, grouping allows you to build that structure within Tableau.

Creating Groups Using Headers

Figure 3-30 includes a bar chart that compares product sub-categories within each product category. The office supplies dimension has too many small members with very low sales values. Grouping the six smallest categories in office supplies into a single (ad hoc) category creates a grouping that is more comparable to the other sub-categories.

There are three ways to group headings. The easiest way is to click on the paper clip icon in the Tooltips that appears when you multi-select the headers. The second way is to right-click after selecting the headings and pick the Group option in the menu. One final option is available via the paper clip icon in the toolbar.

After creating the group, all six members will be combined into a single bar. The name that appears in the heading will be a concatenated list of the individual headings. To rename the combined list heading, right-click while pointing at the new group, choose edit alias, and type in a shorter name. The example group will be called (Other office). Figure 3-31 shows the new group and group name. Now each category includes four members—eliminating the tiny bars seen in Figure 3-30 that are difficult to see and compare.

You can also create groups by selecting marks in the worksheet. This method is a great way to highlight items of interest when you are performing ad hoc analysis. In Figure 3-32 you see a cluster of marks that has been selected.

These marks can be grouped using the paperclip icon inside the Tooltip menu that appears when you point at any of the selected marks.

You can select All Dimensions to create the group. The result is shown in Figure 3-33.

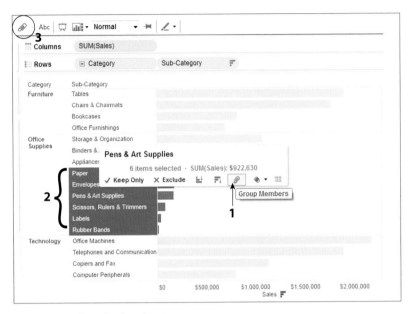

FIGURE 3-30 *Grouping from headers*

FIGURE 3-31 *The ad hoc office group*

Tableau's visual grouping causes the selected marks to be highlighted using a different color than the marks that are not included in the group. These methods work well if you have a small number of members to group or you can easily select the marks that you want to highlight.

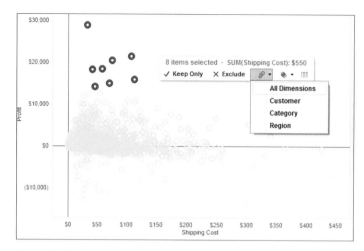

FIGURE 3-32 *Grouping marks using all dimensions*

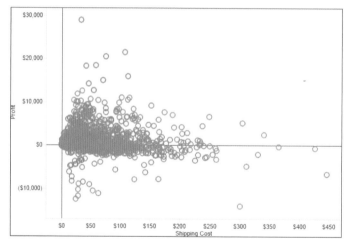

FIGURE 3-33 *Manually selecting a group*

If you have a very large set of dimensions that you need to group, or the grouping must be created using portions of field names—these methods would be
tedious. Tableau provides a more robust way to create groups using fuzzy
search. Figure 3-34 shows another grouping menu that can be accessed by
right-clicking on a specific dimension field within the dimension shelf.

You can also group products by vendor. Figure 3-34 shows a search for all products provided by the vendor Bevis. Using the Find Members search, Tableau executes a string search in all the product names that include that string. After checking to ensure that the group contains the correct information, clicking the Group button will create a new grouping of the products. You can also alias the group name within the menu. After completing all the vendor groups you require, selecting the Include Other check box will generate a group that contains all the other items in the dimension that haven't already been assigned to a vendor group.

Please note that any new group members that are added to your datasource will not automatically appear in any group. You always have to add them manually the first time they appear in the datasource.

Using Sets to Filter for Specific Criteria

Think of sets as special kinds of filters that enable you to share findings made in one worksheet across other worksheets in your workbook. Or, perhaps you want to create an exception report that only displays records that meet specific criteria. Sets can be created several different ways:

- Multi-selecting marks
- Right-clicking on a field in the dimension shelf
- Combining sets on the set shelf

Saving Outliers by Multi-Selecting Marks

Creating a set by selecting marks in a view is fast and intuitive. Figure 3-35 shows a scatter plot that is comparing profit and shipping cost. If you want to create a set that includes low profit items, hold the left mouse button down and draw a box around the marks you want to save. This will automatically open the Tooltips.

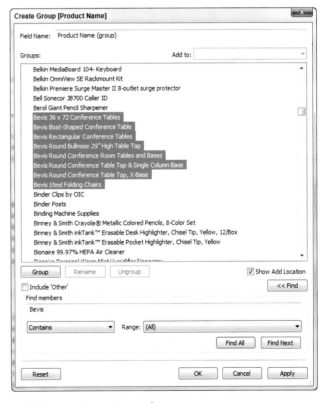

FIGURE 3-34 *Using string search to group*

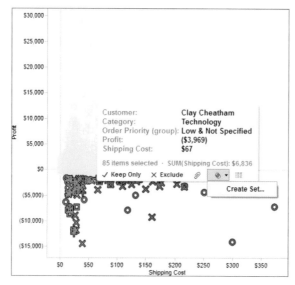

FIGURE 3-35 *Selecting marks to create a set*

Selecting the Create Set menu option exposes the dialog box in Figure 3-36.

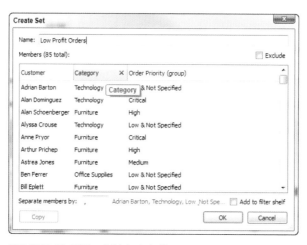

FIGURE 3-36 *Editing fields included in a set*

If you want to exclude a category from the set, hovering the mouse over the category header exposes a red (x) that if selected removes the category field from the set. Similarly, if you want to remove specific records, you could do that by pointing and clicking on the same control appearing in the row. For now, keep all dimensions and measures in this set. In addition, you can rename the set calling it **Low Profit Set**. Clicking the OK button adds a new shelf below the measures shelf that includes this set. You can also use the set in other worksheets within this workbook. Figure 3-37 shows different ways the set could be applied.

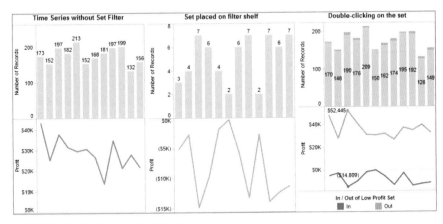

FIGURE 3-37 *Applying sets in different worksheets*

The time series on the left displays record count and profit dollars for one year of sales. By dragging the low profit set to the filter shelf the view will change to reflect only the records included in the set. The middle view in Figure 3-37 shows the result. Notice the record count is much smaller and the profit pane has been filtered as well. Another way you could apply the set filter would be to double-click the low profit orders set on the set shelf. This option produces the visualization on the far right of Figure 3-37. The items that aren't in the low profit set are gray and the low profit orders are blue.

Right-Clicking on a Field in the Dimension Shelf

It is also possible to create a set by right-clicking on a field displayed in the dimension shelf and selecting the Create Set option. This will expose the dialog box in which you can apply filters manually or via calculations.

Combining Multiple Sets to Create a Combination Set

What if you want to create an exception report that only displays records that meet specific criteria? This can be achieved by joining two different sets in combination. You can see this in the following example and then use it to filter a chart. The desired combination set includes only order line detail for sales that are greater than one thousand dollars that have profit ratios of less than three percent. The steps required to create this combination set are:

- Create a concatenated field consisting of order id and row id.

- Make the set for sales greater than $1,000.

- Make the set for profit ratio less than three percent.

- Build a combination set consisting of the intersection of both sets.

- Display the result in a color-encoded bar chart.

Superstore includes information on each order down to each item included in the order. You want to display each order-row that is over one thousand dollars but less than three percent profit ratio. To enable this combination set, create a calculated field that uniquely combines order id and row id. Create a new field called Order-RowID by making a calculated field that concatenates the order id field and row id field. This can be done by using the following formula syntax: [Order ID]+"-"+[Row ID]. You will learn more about calculated values in Chapter 4.

FIGURE 3-38 *Making the sales set*

Make the Set for Sales Over One Thousand Dollars

Figure 3-38 shows how the set dialog box is exposed by right-clicking on the calculated field you just created for the combination of order and row id. On the general tab you will select all records. Using the condition tab you can choose the sales field for the sum of sales exceeding one thousand dollars. Name the set (Sales > $1K) and click the OK button.

Building the Low Profit Set

Next you can create the set that will include only items with a profit ratio of less than three percent. Figure 3-39 shows the condition dialog box exposed after right-clicking on the Order-RowID field and selecting all records from the general tab, then defining the profit ratio limit.

After defining these sets you can now create a combination set. You do this by pointing at the set for sales over one thousand dollars, right-clicking, and selecting the Create Combined Set menu option. Figure 3-40 shows the dialog box that is displayed.

FIGURE 3-39 *The low profit set condition defined*

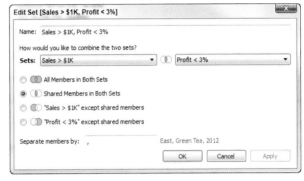

FIGURE 3-40 *Combination set dialog box*

The (Sales > $1K) set is already in the left set drop-down menu. The right drop-down menu was initially empty. Select the (Profit < 3%) set and the Radio button for the shared members option. Then click the OK button. This will generate another filter set that is the combination of the intersection of both sets. Figure 3-41 shows a bar chart that uses the combination set in the view.

Notice that the set option for displaying items in or out of the combination set has been selected. To make this chart easier to view, the color shelf has been edited to display items with profit ratios less than three percent using orange and over three percent using blue. Each bar is labeled with the sum of sales and profit ratio—providing visual confirmation that the data has been properly filtered by the combination set.

HOW TABLEAU USES DATE FIELDS

Tableau recognizes dates that are contained in your source data and allows you to change the level of detail displayed via an auto-generated hierarchy. It is also possible to rearrange date levels by changing the order of date pills on the row or column shelves.

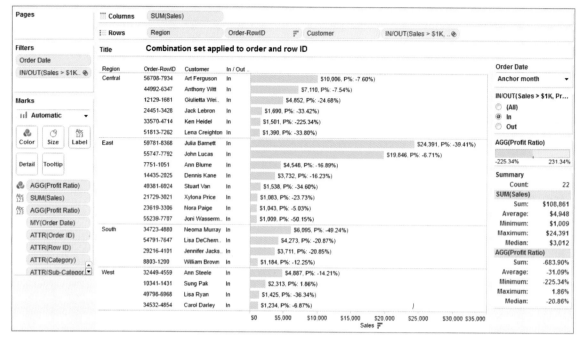

FIGURE 3-41 *Combination filter applied to a bar chart*

Discrete and Continuous Time

You've probably noticed by now that some pills are green and others are blue. Similarly, icons can be in blue or green colors. Most beginners believe blue pills and icons denote dimensions while green pills are used to display measures. While this is frequently the case, the truth is more subtle. Blue pills/icons denote "discrete" fields. Green pills/icons denote "continuous" fields. Dates can be both discrete and continuous. Figure 3-42 shows Tableau's default way of displaying time—as discrete time hierarchy.

You can see that time has been discretely segmented in the time series chart by year. Clicking on the plus sign in the quarter pill would cause the date hierarchy to expand to include months, and panes for each quarter would be exposed. Continuous dates don't discretely bucket time but will cause a drill down to a lower level of detail. Figure 3-43 shows a similar time series chart with continuous time being used and the level of detail being month.

The green pill on the column shelf in Figure 3-43 indicates the level of detail being displayed. Notice that there are no panes in view. Time is continuously displayed as an unbroken line.

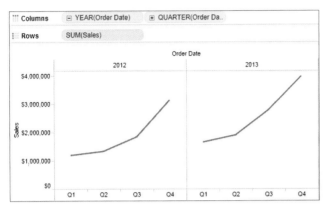

FIGURE 3-42 *Discrete time series*

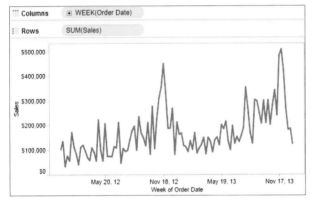

FIGURE 3-43 *Continuous time series*

TABLEAU'S DATE HIERARCHY

Time can be expanded to more granular levels simply by clicking on the plus sign within the date pill. Experiment with this and note that you can rearrange time buckets just by changing the order of the pills by repositioning them. It's also possible to change the level of detail displayed by right-clicking on the date pill. This exposes the menu in Figure 3-44.

The menu includes two different date sections that start with year. The first group provides discrete date parts. The second group provides continuous date values. Figure 3-45 was created by changing the date displayed in Figure 3-42, altering the quarter pill to display month.

FIGURE 3-44 *Changing the date level of detail*

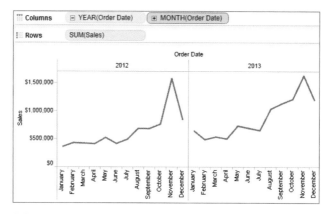

FIGURE 3-45 *Time series displaying discrete year-month*

In Figure 3-44 note the menu option appears twice. The first time it appears is within the discrete date section of the menu. The second time it is in the continuous date section. Explore the menu option in both the discrete and continuous time portions of the menu. The More menu options provide even more granular options for controlling how date and time are presented in your view.

REARRANGING TIME WITH TABLEAU

There are many different date and time combinations that can be displayed. Figure 3-46 rearranges time to display weekday first, then year. Each day is a discrete time bucket. You can also add a reference line by pane that displays the average sales value for each weekday across all four years. This is one of the ways you can leverage discrete time to provide additional information.

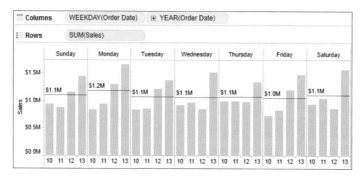

FIGURE 3-46 *Rearranging time and applying a reference line*

If your data supports very granular views of data, Tableau can display details down to the second. This might be particularly useful if you need to analyze click stream data on a website.

CREATING CUSTOMIZED DATE FIELDS

Tableau's date hierarchy is always available. Even people consuming reports via Tableau Reader or Server can expand time. When hovering your mouse pointer over an axis you will see a small plus or minus sign appear. Clicking on those signs expands or contracts the date hierarchy displayed.

Designers with Tableau Desktop can alter Tableau's default date hierarchy by creating custom date fields and then building unique date hierarchies. Making custom date hierarchies requires three steps:

1. Create a custom date.

2. Create the date hierarchy.

3. Use the custom date in your view.

To create a custom date, point at a date field on the dimension shelf and right-click. This will expose a dialog box that provides a means for defining a custom date or time element as you see in Figure 3-47.

Create a custom year date by naming the field "year" and defining the date as a discreet year date part. You can also add another discrete date for month. By dragging the custom month on top of the custom year, you can add a new custom date hierarchy. Figure 3-48 shows the resulting date hierarchy.

FIGURE 3-47 *Creating a custom date*

You can see the custom hierarchy in Figure 3-48 on the dimension shelf. The year and month custom dates are all that will be displayed in this time series chart. In this way you can change how Tableau expands and contracts the dates used in your visualizations.

Tableau's date facility encourages explorations of data over different time slices because it is very easy to use and requires no special skill to master.

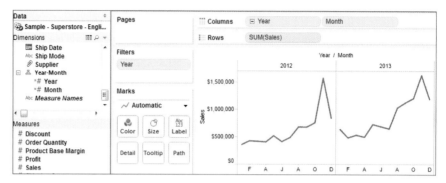

TAMING DATA WITH MEASURE NAMES AND VALUES

Sometimes your data isn't clean and it may not be structured in a way that supports the analysis you need to perform. You might also be looking at a data set for the first time and need to scan it quickly to get a lay of the land. Tableau's measure names and measure values fields help you with all these tasks.

What Are Measure Names and Measure Values?

Measure names and measure values do not exist in your datasource. These fields are generated by Tableau. Measure names hold all of the dimension names in your data set. Measure values hold all of the measures in your data set.

When to Use Measure Names and Measure Values

How can measure names and measure values help you understand new data? One way is by providing a means for you to quickly view all of the dimensions contained in your data set. These fields also allow you to combine multiple measures within a single axis. Figure 3-49 displays all of the measures in Tableau's Superstore data set.

The crosstab in Figure 3-49 was created by double-clicking on measure names on the dimension shelf, swapping the axis, and adding order date on the column shelf. This technique provides a very quick overview of the data. The status bar at the bottom left tells you that there are forty data points and four years of data. Notice that the measure values shelf on the right provides details on the aggregation used to display the information. You can change that by right-clicking on any of those pills and picking another option.

Another way to use measure names and measure values is to tame data that isn't structured in a way that facilitates the analysis you want. Figure 3-50 includes a sales projection in a spreadsheet.

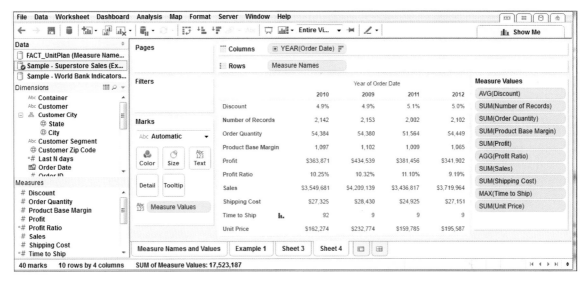

FIGURE 3-49   *Using measure names and measure values*

	A	B	C	D	E	F	G	H	I	J	K	L	M	N
1	Product Code	Product Name	Jan-13	Feb-13	Mar-13	Apr-13	May-13	Jun-13	Jul-13	Aug-13	Sep-13	Oct-13	Nov-13	Dec-13
2	001	Widget 1	100	110	110	105	155	160	150	160	170	160	155	145
3	002	Wangle 2	45	45	50	48	49	52	55	60	70	65	55	50
4	003	Widget 3	25	30	40	50	55	60	60	60	70	70	65	60
5	004	Wangle 1	100	100	105	100	110	110	100	105	115	110	100	90
6	005	Waxel 1	30	30	35	35	35	40	45	45	50	48	45	40

FIGURE 3-50   *Sales forecast in spreadsheet form*

Each product has unit sales projected in columns for each month in the year. Tableau will interpret each column as a separate measure. In a database, this information would be stored in a structure that looks like Figure 3-51.

General-purpose databases normally store data in a row-oriented format. Tableau can connect to both kinds of datasources. If your data is more column-oriented, like Figure 3-50, measure names and measure values provide a means for creating views that wouldn't be supported otherwise. Figure 3-52 shows a time series chart that was built using the spreadsheet datasource.

	A	B	C	D
1	Product Code	Product Name	Month	Unit Forecast
2	001	Widget 1	January-13	100
3	001	Widget 1	February-13	110
4	001	Widget 1	March-13	110
5	001	Widget 1	April-13	105
6	001	Widget 1	May-13	155
7	001	Widget 1	June-13	160
8	001	Widget 1	July-13	150
9	001	Widget 1	August-13	160
10	001	Widget 1	September-13	170
11	001	Widget 1	October-13	160
12	001	Widget 1	November-13	155
13	001	Widget 1	December-13	145
14	002	Wangle 2	January-13	45
15	002	Wangle 2	February-13	45
16	002	Wangle 2	March-13	50
17	002	Wangle 2	April-13	48
18	002	Wangle 2	May-13	49

FIGURE 3-51   *Sales forecast in database form*

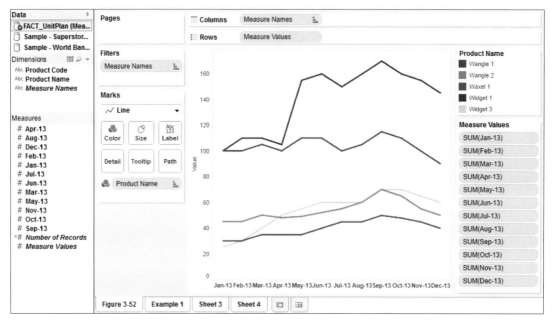

FIGURE 3-52 *Time series using the spreadsheet datasource*

Tableau interprets each column in the spreadsheet as a separate measure. So each column would be treated as a different measure. Measure names and measure values allow you to place multiple measures on a single axis. Even though the data format in the spreadsheet doesn't support that type of view, using measure names and measure values allows you to achieve the desired presentation quickly.

If your datasource was formatted like Figure 3-51 (like a database would store the information), measure names and measure values would not be required to make a time series chart like you see in Figure 3-52. The column and row structure you see in Figure 3-51 directly supports the creation of the view without having to use measure names and measure values because month is contained in a discrete field; product name is a discrete field. Placing the Product name field on the color button within the marks card would express each product with its own color. Placing the month field on the column shelf would put each month in its own column. Using a database structure eliminates the need for the use of measure names and measure values. Unfortunately, you may have to deal with spreadsheet structures and build views. Measure names and measure values help you deal with untidy data structure.

Advanced Uses for Measure Names and Measure Values

Measure names and measure values facilitate more advanced chart types as well. Your spreadsheet should also include unit price and cost information in a separate prices tab that looks like Figure 3-53.

Using Tableau's spreadsheet reshaper tool (see Appendix B), you can change the spreadsheet format to a column-oriented style like Figure 3-51. Then you can join that tab to the prices tab in Figure 3-53 via the product code key record. This will allow you to create calculated values extending sales, cost, and gross margin dollars. Then you can create a time series view of the three measures as you see in Figure 3-54.

	A	B	C
1	Product Code	Price	Cost
2	001	$99.00	$39.62
3	002	$50.00	$22.31
4	003	$60.00	$26.29
5	004	$25.00	$9.85
6	005	$125.00	$52.63

FIGURE 3-53 *Spreadsheet tab with unit price and cost data*

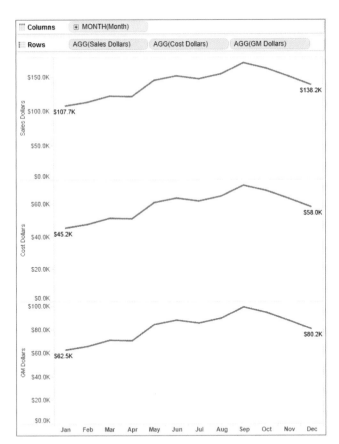

FIGURE 3-54 *Tableau's default time series*

Tableau's default presentation of this information uses a separate axis to display each measure. Using measure names and measure values, you can combine all three measures on a single axis and use color to differentiate the values. Figure 3-55 shows the combined axis time series chart.

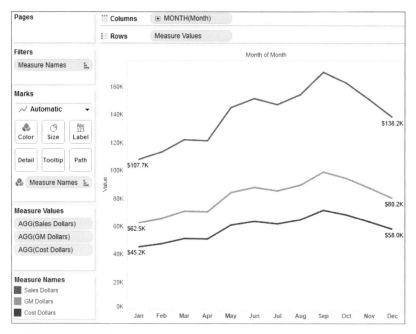

FIGURE 3-55 *Combining multiple measures on one axis*

The combined axis chart in Figure 3-55 can be created a few different ways. Using the view in Figure 3-54 as a starting point, the most intuitive way to combine the measures on one axis is done by dragging each measure to a single axis. Pointing at the cost axis in the upper left makes a green fold mark appear. Pointing at the green fold makes a cross arrow appear. Using the green fold you can drag the cost axis on top of the sales axis.

Repeating the same method, seen in Figure 3-56, you can relocate the gross margin axis so that all three measures are displayed together on a single axis. Note in Figure 3-55 that the row shelf now holds the measure values pill. Measure names are on the marks card for color. The measure values shelf also appears, displaying all three measures. Tableau automatically creates the measure names and measure values pills when a second measure is moved to the same axis. If you are wondering how the labels were made to appear at the beginning and end of each line, explore the label button on the marks card.

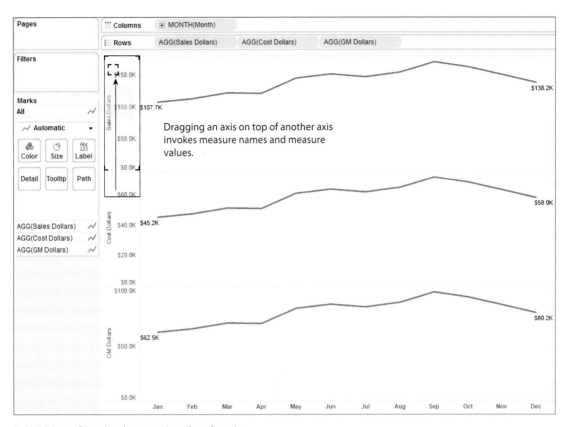

FIGURE 3-56 *Dragging the cost axis to the sales axis*

Measure names and measure values help you understand and present your data set. They help you contend with poorly formatted data, and facilitate creating more advanced chart types. Many beginning and intermediate Tableau users avoid these specific fields because they are unfamiliar. Spend a little time working with them. The added flexibility you discover will be worth the effort.

You've seen all the ways that Tableau's built-in chart types, trend lines, reference lines, groups, sets, sorting, and filtering help you add meaning to your data within Tableau. In the next chapter you'll learn how calculations provide even more flexible ways to add information to your charts and dashboards.

NOTES

1. Popper, Karl R. *Conjectures and Refutations: The Growth of Scientific Knowledge*. London: Routledge, 1989. Print. Page 51.

CHAPTER 4

Creating Calculations to Enhance Your Data

Each new paradigm gives us the opportunity to "see" phenomena that were before as invisible to us as the colors of the sunset to the fog.

BENJAMIN AND ROSAMUND ZANDER[1]

Tableau provides two ways to enhance your data through the creation of new fields that don't exist in your datasource. Tableau also allows you to turn single-purpose dashboards and views into multi-purpose analysis environments though parameter controls. Parameters are formula variables that can be used to provide filter-like controls that allow users to change the measures and dimensions used in a dashboard or worksheet.

In this chapter you will learn how to use calculated values and table calculations to derive facts and dimensions that don't exist in your source data. Tableau's Formula Editing window will be explained as well as the Quick Table Calculation menu, and how to modify Quick Table defaults to address your specific needs.

In the sections at the end of the chapter on parameters, you will learn parameter controls—basic and advanced—so that you can make views that address different needs using the same basic visual design.

Tableau makes formula creation as easy as it can possibly be, but it helps to understand the concept of aggregation, and the functions and operators that are available to use before you start making formulas. For those of you that want to dive deeply into Tableau's functions, Appendix A provides in-depth coverage of every Tableau function, with basic, intermediate and advanced examples.

WHAT IS AGGREGATION?

Aggregation defines how values are expressed. Most Tableau functions are calculated at the database server with only the results being sent to Tableau. If you are familiar with SQL, you will find most of the functions in Tableau are an extension of SQL. Tableau uses the Sum aggregation by default. If the default aggregation isn't what you want, point at the pill of the measure you've placed into the view—right-click, and select a more appropriate aggregation. Supported aggregation types include:

- Sum
- Average
- Median
- Count
- Count Distinct
- Minimum
- Maximum
- Standard Deviation
- Standard Deviation of a Population
- Variance
- Variance of a Population

These are clearly defined in Tableau's online manual. Search the help menu to read more about each of them if you are unfamiliar with the type of aggregation each provides.

COUNT DISTINCT VERSUS COUNT

These functions count records in different ways. Consider a data set that includes 10,000 records with 20 different regions. Performing a Count Distinct on the Region field returns a value of 20. The purpose of Count Distinct is to count the unique instances of a particular item. A Count aggregation of 10,000 records will result with an answer of 10,000 because it counts all records.

Count Distinct is supported by relational database sources but is not supported by Excel, Access, or text files. You can add the ability to create Count Distinct aggregation when accessing those sources by performing a data extract. Tableau's extract files do support Count Distinct aggregation.

MEDIAN

Similarly, Median is not supported by a direct connection from Tableau to Excel, Access, or text files. Performing a data extract will once again give you the ability to compute median values. Using the Superstore data set, Figure 4-1 shows a crosstab displaying all of the different aggregations available for the sales field in the data set.

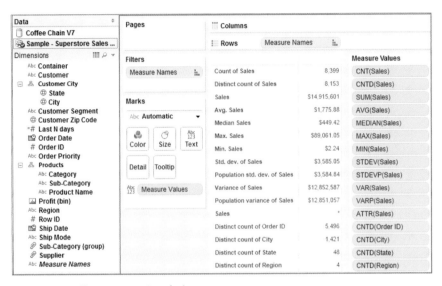

FIGURE 4-1 *Different aggregation of sales*

Notice that the bottom four rows are expressing Count Distinct values for different dimensions. By dragging each of those dimension fields into the crosstab using the right mouse button, the Count Distinct aggregation is expressed for each dimension. As you can see the data set includes over 5,000 different orders; over 1,400 cities; 48 states; and four regions.

DIMENSION VERSUS ATTRIBUTE

Aggregation behavior can be changed by altering the default method by which Tableau expresses dimensions. Figure 4-2 shows a crosstab containing sales by product category and sub-category. A table calculation is being used to display the percent of total sales that each row represents within each product category pane.

By default, Tableau partitions the result by the category dimension. Subtotals have been added by using the main menu option analysis/totals, then showing subtotal and column totals. You can see that in each category pane the amount of sales and percent of sales are totaled within each category pane. But, if the category dimension is changed to an attribute, the category dimension will become a label only and no longer cause the data to be partitioned. Figure 4-3 shows the same data set but with the category field changed to an attribute.

| | Columns | Measure Names | |
| | Rows | ⊟ Category | ⊞ Sub-Category |

Title: Category as a Dimension

Category	Sub-Category	Sales	% of Total Sales along Pane (Down)
	Tables	$1,896,008	36.6%
	Chairs & Chairmats	$1,761,837	34.0%
Furniture	Bookcases	$822,652	15.9%
	Office Furnishings	$698,094	13.5%
	Total	$5,178,591	100.0%
	Storage & Organization	$1,070,183	28.5%
	Binders and Binder Accessories	$1,022,958	27.3%
	Appliances	$736,992	19.6%
	Paper	$446,453	11.9%
Office Supplies	Envelopes	$174,086	4.6%
	Pens & Art Supplies	$167,107	4.5%
	Scissors, Rulers and Trimmers	$80,996	2.2%
	Labels	$38,982	1.0%
	Rubber Bands	$15,007	0.4%
	Total	$3,752,762	100.0%
	Office Machines	$2,168,697	36.2%
	Telephones and Communication	$1,889,314	31.6%
Technology	Copiers and Fax	$1,130,361	18.9%
	Computer Peripherals	$795,876	13.3%
	Total	$5,984,248	100.0%
	Grand Total	$14,915,601	100.0%

FIGURE 4-2 *Product category as a dimension*

| | Columns | Measure Names | |
| | Rows | ATTR(Category) | ⊞ Sub-Category |

Title: Category changed to an Attribute

Category	Sub-Category	Sales	% of Total Sales along Pane (Down)
	Tables	$1,896,008	12.7%
Furniture	Chairs & Chairmats	$1,761,837	11.8%
	Bookcases	$822,652	5.5%
	Office Furnishings	$698,094	4.7%
	Storage & Organization	$1,070,183	7.2%
	Binders and Binder Accessories	$1,022,958	6.9%
	Appliances	$736,992	4.9%
	Paper	$446,453	3.0%
Office Supplies	Envelopes	$174,086	1.2%
	Pens & Art Supplies	$167,107	1.1%
	Scissors, Rulers and Trimmers	$80,996	0.5%
	Labels	$38,982	0.3%
	Rubber Bands	$15,007	0.1%
	Office Machines	$2,168,697	14.5%
	Telephones and Communication	$1,889,314	12.7%
Technology	Copiers and Fax	$1,130,361	7.6%
	Computer Peripherals	$795,876	5.3%
	Grand Total	$14,915,601	100.0%

FIGURE 4-3 *Product category as an attribute*

The view still shows the light gray boundary lines between each category, but because the category dimension has been changed to an attribute, it no longer partitions the view. The sales total reflects the total for the entire crosstab and the percent of total sales is now expressing the percentage of total sales, not the sales within each category. This may appear to be trivial, but as your skills advance and you begin to employ more advanced table calculations you will need to understand how attributes change Tableau's behavior.

WHAT ARE CALCULATED VALUES AND TABLE CALCULATIONS?

Calculated Values and Table Calculations allow you to add new data to your Tableau workbook, but the way you add the data, and where the calculations occur, is different for each method.

Calculated Values are defined by entering a formula into Tableau's formula editing dialog box. For example, if you have gross margin dollars and sales dollars in your source data, you may want to add a new field called Gross Margin Percent by creating a calculated value. The formula to create the gross margin percent is: sum([gross margin dollars])/sum([sales dollars]).

The Sum aggregation function in front of each field name tells the source database what to return to Tableau. Calculated values are normally processed at the datasource. What this means is that the power of your database server is used to do the heavy number crunching, with the database returning only what is needed for Tableau to build the visualization.

Table calculations are created in a different way—using your data visualization as the source for the formula.

Pre-defined Quick Table Calculations remove the need for you to create the formula manually, but these are always processed locally because they rely on the data presented in your view to derive the formula.

Calculated values can also include table calculation functions. These are functions you use in calculated values that are processed locally just like Quick Table calculations.

HOW DO CALCULATED VALUES WORK?

Calculated Values can be used to generate numbers, dates, date-times, or strings. All calculated values require the following elements:

- Functions—including aggregate, number, string, date, type conversion, logical, user, and table calculation types
- Fields—selected from the datasource
- Operators—for math and comparison of values, dates, and text
- Optional elements can be added within the formula dialog box including:
    - Parameters—for creating formula variables that are accessible to information consumers
    - Comments—for documenting formula syntax and notes within the formula dialog box

Start the formula dialog box via the main menu using the Analysis/Created Calculated Field option or by right-clicking on a field. The formula dialog is where you enter the functions, operators, and parameters to create the logic for your formula. Alternatively, right-clicking a field in the dimensions or measures shelves opens the formula dialog box as well, but also includes that field already entered in the formula editing area.

People experienced at writing SQL script or creating spreadsheet formulas normally have very little difficultly learning how to write formulas in Tableau. Those with very little experience writing formulas may need more help. Tableau provides assistance via a real-time formula editor and a help window in the formula editing window, as well as an online manual that is accessible from the editing window.

HOW DO TABLE CALCULATIONS WORK?

Table calculations are derived from the structure of the data included in your visualization, so table calculations are dependent on the source worksheet view contained in your workbook. That means these calculations are always derived locally using your personal computer's processor to return the result.

Understanding exactly how Table Calculations work takes a little time because Table Calculations can change as your visualization is altered. As with any new concept, after you create some Table Calculations you'll get comfortable with how they behave in different situations. Tableau's online manual has a large number of examples that you can view that provide a good basic introduction.

Creating a Table Calculation requires that you have a worksheet with a visualization. A good way to create them is to right-click on a measure pill used in the view to expose the Quick Table Calculation menu. Quick Table Calculations are provided for:

- Running total
- Difference
- Percent difference
- Percent of total
- Moving average
- YTD total
- Compound growth rate
- Year over year growth
- YTD growth

Depending on the view of the data included in your worksheet some of these may be unavailable because your worksheet view doesn't support the calculation. Unavailable calculations will be visible in the menu but will appear grayed-out.

A WORD ON CALCULATIONS AND CUBES

Tableau connects to relational databases, spreadsheets, columnar-analytic databases, data services, and data cubes (multi-dimensional datasources). Data cubes are different from regular database files because they pre-aggregate data and define hierarchies of dimensions in specific ways.

If you need to access pre-aggregated data that is stored in a multi-dimensional datasource, you can still perform calculations using Tableau formulas or create formulas using the standard query language of multi-dimensional databases, Multidimensional Expressions (MDX). The syntax is a bit more complex but MDX also provides the ability to create more complex formulas. If you desire to learn more about options for creating calculations when accessing Data Cubes, refer to Tableau Software's quick start guide Creating Calculated Fields-Cubes. Tableau's behavior when you connect it to a data cube is different because the cube controls aggregation. For example, date fields behave differently because the cube controls date aggregation in specific ways.

USING THE CALCULATION DIALOG BOX TO CREATE CALCULATED VALUES

Calculated Values require that you enter fields, functions, and operators. Tableau strives to make formula creation fast and easy, so it is possible to write formulas with minimal typing. Once you've connected to a datasource, you can create a calculated field from the main menu by selecting Analysis/Create Calculated Field. This example uses the Superstore spreadsheet. Figure 4-4 shows the Calculated Value editing window.

The figure shows a calculation for Profit Ratio that uses two fields from the Superstore file to derive the result. The Name field at the top of Figure 4-4 is where you type the name of your Calculated Value as you want it to appear in the data window of the worksheet. The Formula box is used to write the script for the formula.

You will also see that Tableau color-encodes different elements of formulas so that they are easy to separate visually. Fields are orange, Parameters are purple, and Functions are blue. Notice the example in Figure 4-4 includes comments at the top, color-encoded in green. Comments are useful for documenting sections of complex formulas or for adding basic descriptive information to other analysts that may use your formula in their work. You can add comments anywhere in the formula window by typing two forward slashes (//) in front of the text.

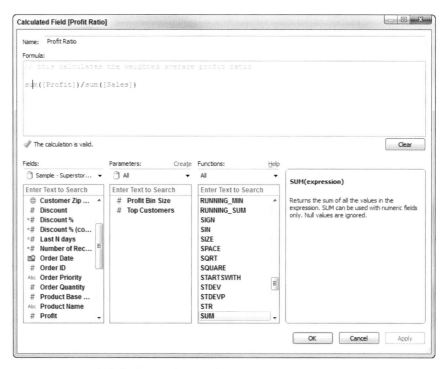

FIGURE 4-4 *Formula dialog box or editing window*

Below the formula window is a green check mark followed by the statement, The Calculation Is Valid. This is the formula editor that will help you correct syntax errors. If you get something wrong a red X will appear. In Figure 4-5, you see this in action.

For example, if the beginning parenthesis is omitted in front of the sales field, clicking on the error message—or in the formula near the crooked red line—will provide more information about the syntax error. Typing in the missing parenthesis will correct the problem. If you are new to writing formulas, or if you are creating a particularly complex formula, Tableau's editor will help you find and correct errors.

Referring to Figure 4-4 again you can see four panes on the bottom half of the window. These panes display the available fields, parameters, and functions. If you have a particular field or function selected, the yellow window at the far right provides a brief description of the field or the formula definition.

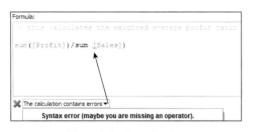

FIGURE 4-5 *The real-time formula editor*

FIELD SELECTION

Looking below the Fields title you will see a filter that allows you to select different datasources (if you have more than one being used in your worksheet), or filter for specific data types available (numbers, text, dates, etc.). Figure 4-6 shows this in action with the Number data types only being displayed below.

If you have many fields in your source data, a high-level field selection filter may not prune the list enough. In Figure 4-4, notice the small boxes below each window that provide a fuzzy String search for a specific field name. Notice that the Parameter and Function windows also provide the same search capability.

You can add fields to your Formula window by typing them manually, pasting them in from a text editor, or by double-clicking on the desired field from the Fields window. If you are new to writing formulas, use the double-click method. Tableau inserts the appropriate syntax automatically. For example, double-clicking on the Profit field in the Fields window will cause the following script to be entered: ([Profit]).

FIGURE 4-6 *Filtering field selections for numbers*

FUNCTION SELECTION

Functions can be added exactly the same way. The filter at the top of the Functions window lets you filter for a function category. To add functions without typing, place your cursor within the location of the formula window where you want the function to be placed and double-click on the desired function name in the function window below. Figure 4-7 shows the function window.

When the Sum function is selected, the yellow help window displays a brief description of the function along with the function syntax. It you want a more detailed definition, selecting the help menu option will take you to Tableau Software's online manual.

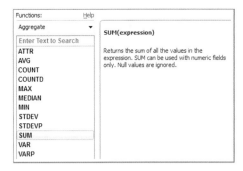

FIGURE 4-7 *Filter the function window*

PARAMETER SELECTION

Parameters are optional elements that allow you to add variables in formulas. Figure 4-4 shows two parameters that are included with the Superstore sample file. Parameters will be covered in detail in the sections on parameters at the end of this chapter.

When you complete editing the formula, don't forget to click the OK button at the bottom because the new field isn't created until you do that. If you get interrupted while writing a very long formula either keep your window open, or copy the script to a text editor and save it. When you resume work, you can paste that script back into the formula window and continue. Once you get comfortable with the formula editor and the available functions, you'll find many ways to leverage Calculated Values.

BUILDING FORMULAS USING TABLE CALCULATIONS

In contrast to Calculated Values, Quick Table calculations use the data in your Visualization to create a formula. Before you can use Quick Table calculations you must first create a worksheet that includes Visualization. Using Superstore again, Figure 4-8 displays a time series of monthly sales on top. The bottom half employs a Quick Table calculation to derive the running total of sales as the year progresses.

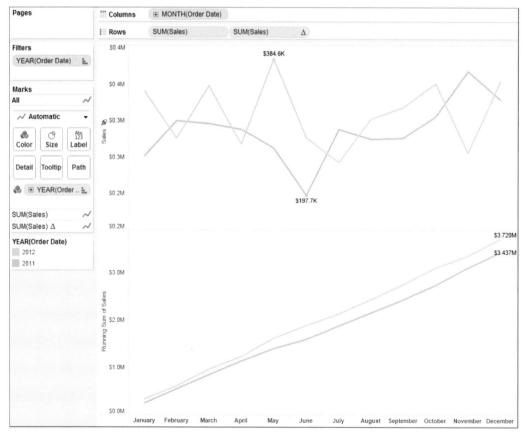

FIGURE 4-8 *Time series using a running sum*

The steps required to build the charts in Figure 4-8 are:

1. Add month to the column shelf.

2. Add sales to the row shelf.

3. Filter order date for the year(s) 2011 and 2012.

4. Add order date to the color marks button.

5. Turn on labeling for min/max values.

The data from the Sales Time-Series chart will serve as the datasource for a quick table calculation that will be used to create the chart in the bottom half of Figure 4-8. That chart displays the Running Sum of Sales for each month within the displayed years. The steps required to add that portion of the view are:

1. Ctrl drag the sales pill on the row shelf to create a duplicate chart.

2. Right-click on the second sales pill.

3. Select Quick Table Calculation—Running Total.

4. Turn on field labels for the line ends and un-check Label Start of Line.

Figure 4-9 shows how right-clicking on the duplicate sales pill exposes the Quick Table Calculation menu.

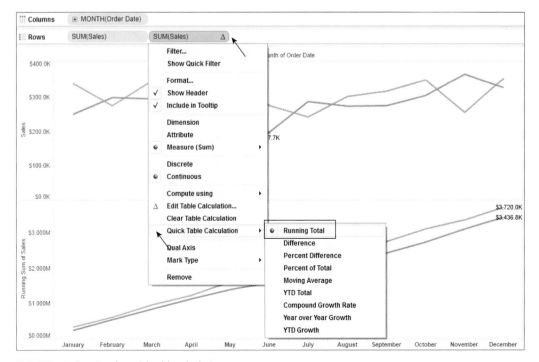

FIGURE 4-9 *Creating the quick table calculation*

Selecting Running Total generates the table calculation that results in the Running Total Time Series chart. The label number format was also formatted to display the results in thousands in the top chart and millions in the lower chart. The total time required to build this chart was less than 60 seconds.

EDITING TABLE CALCULATIONS TO SUIT YOUR PURPOSE

FIGURE 4-10 *The table calculation editing menu*

You can also see in Figure 4-9 that there are many other Quick Table Calculation options available. There is also a menu option called Edit Table Calculation. In fact, the four rows in the menu below Continuous are all used to customize Table Calculations.

Understanding how Table Calculations work takes a little time—playing with the options and looking at the results. Take a close look at the Edit Table Calculation menu option displayed in Figure 4-9.

Table Calculations require selections of the following options:

- Calculation type—as seen in Figure 4-10

- Aggregation method—sum, average, median, (these will change depending on the content of your source)

- Running Along—defines the direction that the calculation travels (Table Across, Table Down, etc)

The Restarting Every option is grayed-out in Figure 4-10 because there are no discrete time or other dimension panes dividing the Time Series. Modifying the Time Series to show time as discrete quarters and months creates quarterly partitions as seen in Figure 4-11.

The bottom Time Series showing the Running Sum of Sales is still using Table Across to calculate the total. Right-clicking on the table calculation (denoted by a small triangle on the right side of the pill) and selecting the Edit Table Calculation Menu exposes the Running Along control. Figure 4-12 shows the Table Calculation editing menu for Running Along and includes more options. Adding the partition for quarter creates quarterly panes that can be used in the Table Calculation.

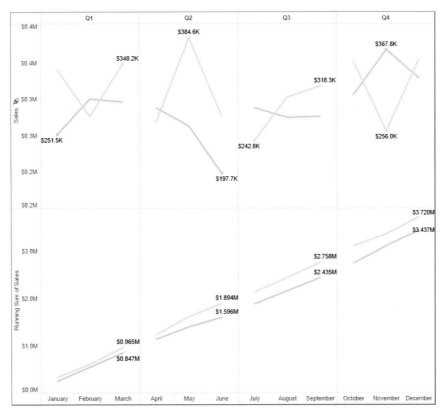

FIGURE 4-11 *Using discrete quarter and month*

Changing the scope of the calculation to Pane Across causes the Running Sum calculation to reset every quarter (pane). Figure 4-13 reflects the revised scope in the lower pane. As you see, the running totals restart at the beginning of each quarter.

FIGURE 4-12 *Changing table calculation scope*

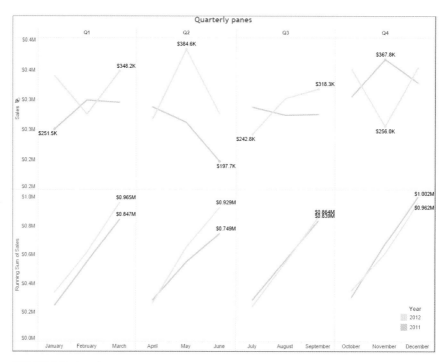

FIGURE 4-13 *Running sum set to pane across*

UNDERSTANDING TABLE CALCULATION BEHAVIOR

Learning exactly how Table Calculations behave in different Visualizations takes a little time. The best way to learn is to build a crosstab report, then start playing with different options to see the results. Tableau's online manual provides many different examples. Figure 4-14 shows Percent of Total table calculations using all of the different standard Running Along scope options.

Notice that in this example the example for the Table scope returns exactly the same result as the Table Down Then Across scope. Also, the Cell scope is calculating the mark value of itself, resulting in 100 percent in every cell. Depending on the structure of your view it is not uncommon for different scope options to return the same values. In general, adding more dimensions to your view will increase the number of available options provided by Table Calculations. Experiment with different Visualization styles and Table Calculations. With practice you'll be able to anticipate how they behave in different situations.

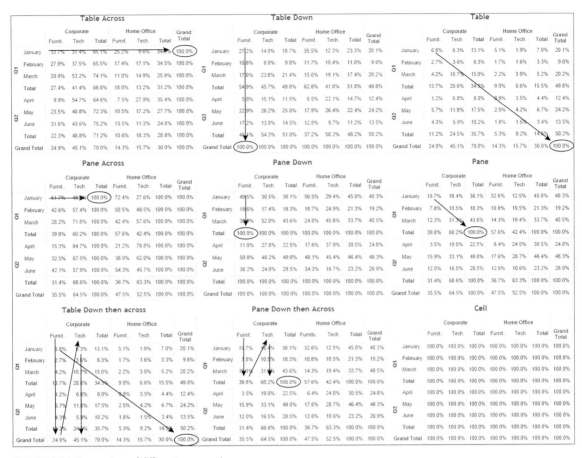

FIGURE 4-14 *Comparison of different scope options*

CUSTOMIZING TABLE CALCULATIONS

Quick Table Calculations don't normally result in Calculated Values appearing on the Measures shelf, so what if you want to use the result returned by a Quick Table Calculation on another worksheet? Is that possible? Table Calculation Functions enable you do to this.

Refer to Figure 4-8. The Quick Table Calculation was used generating a Running Sum of Sales chart at the bottom. To create a Calculated Value using that Table Calculation as the source requires just a couple of steps. Right-clicking on the Table Calculation pill used in that chart exposes the Table Calculation dialog box. Figure 4-15 shows how to convert the Quick Table Calculation into a Calculated Value that is reusable in another worksheet.

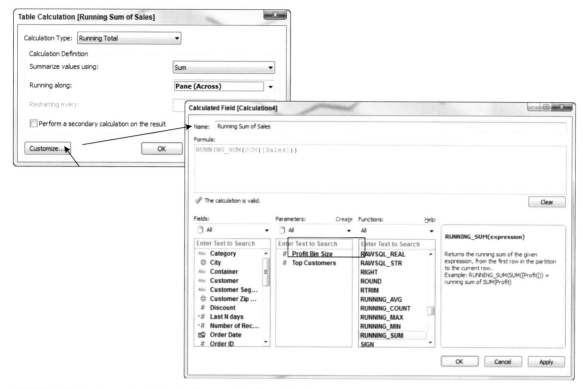

FIGURE 4-15 *Creating a calculated value from a quick table calculation*

Clicking the Customize button causes the Calculated Value editing window to open with the formula already completed. Notice the formula employs a Table Calculation Function Running Sum and the Sum aggregation function together to create a new Calculated Value. The Name field is used to type in the name that will appear on the Measures shelf when the OK button is clicked. Now this table calculation can be reused in a new worksheet. Figure 4-16 shows one possible way that it could be deployed.

In this worksheet all four years are displayed using the customized Running Sum of Sales measure. Notice the new measure highlighted in green on the Measures shelf. The Row shelf displays the new measure as a Table Calculation.

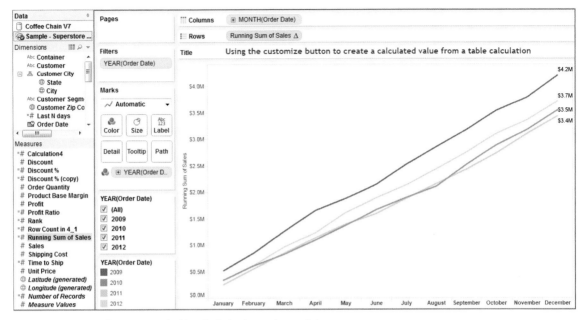

FIGURE 4-16 *Using the customized table calculation in another worksheet*

SECONDARY TABLE CALCULATIONS

Secondary Table Calculations allow you to pass the result of an initial Table Calculation to a second Table Calculation. The next example will use some data from the United States Census. The file includes state population figures. In the next example you'll see how a Secondary Table Calculation can be used to enhance the population analysis.

The source spreadsheet is a small list that includes the state name along with the population tally. An initial view of the data shows the population information in a bar chart, sorted by descending population. You can see the result in Figure 4-17.

Each state is placed in order from the largest to smallest in descending order. The population values are also included as labels on each bar. There is nothing wrong with this chart. It was easy to build (requiring less than a minute). How could this be enhanced using Table Calculations? By using a Quick Table Calculation that employs a secondary pass, it will be possible to calculate running total population, and then perform a Secondary Calculation to derive the percentage of the total population represented. Figure 4-18 was created using a two-stage table calculation using Running Sum and then deriving the percent of total in the Second Calculation.

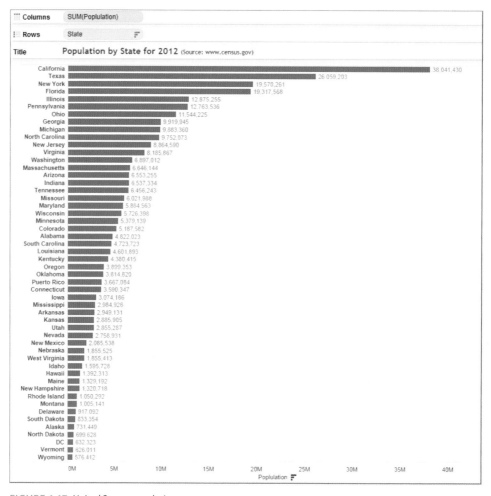

FIGURE 4-17 *United States population*

The Dual Axis chart requires the following items:

- Running Sum of state population
- Percent of total population
- The Index Table Calculation function (to create the state ranking)
- A Boolean calculation to derive the top 10 states (used in bar color)

The Running Sum of state population and percent of total population values will be created using a two-stage table calculation. Figure 4-19 shows the Table Calculation edit menu with the Secondary switch activated.

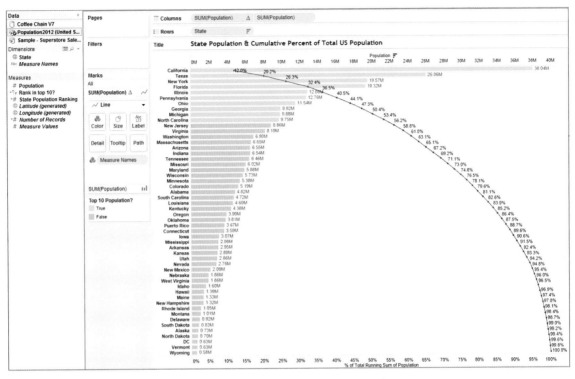

FIGURE 4-18 *Dual axis chart with population and the percent of total cumulative population*

FIGURE 4-19 *Using a secondary table calculation*

The first running total calculation sums the state population along the scope of state. The bar chart is sorted by descending population values so the largest state is first in the table, followed by each lower ranked state in order. The Secondary Calculation uses the percent of total to derive the cumulative percent of total population that each state represents to the total United States population. Clicking the OK button locks in the table calculation. The result is used to create the line chart with the labels displaying the cumulative total population at that row position.

USING TABLE CALCULATION FUNCTIONS

The Index function is a Table Calculation function that counts the position of a row or column in a set. A calculated value called State Population Ranking was created using this function. Figure 4-20 shows the Calculated Value using the Index function.

Creating the Boolean Calculated Value compares the result of the Index to a top 10 ranking value. The resulting Calculated Value is placed on the color shelf for the bar chart to color encode the top 10 states a different color. Figure 4-21 shows the Boolean formula being created.

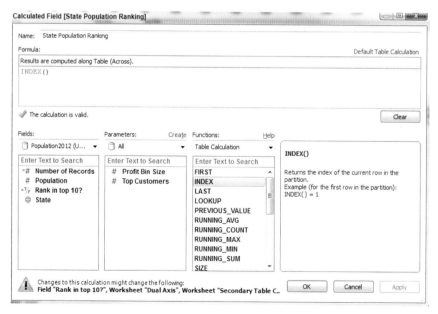

FIGURE 4-20 *Creating a population rank*

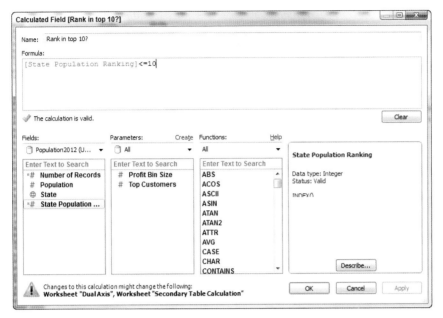

FIGURE 4-21   *Creating the Boolean calculation*

The Boolean formula in Figure 4-21 compares the state population ranking with the number 10 to derive a true-false condition for the top 10 ranked states by population. The resulting Calculated Value is then added to the color button on the Marks card. The resulting color encoding is seen in Figure 4-18.

Using Table Calculations in combination with Calculated Values that employ Table Calculation Functions helps you add more meaning and context to analysis. There really is no limit to the creative ways you can use Calculated Values and Table Calculations to enhance information.

ADDING FLEXIBILITY TO CALCULATIONS WITH PARAMETERS

Parameters empower information consumers to change the content that appears in worksheets and dashboards. Basic parameter controls can be created using embedded options for a limited number of common use cases. Advanced parameters offer the ability to create parameters to address more unique use cases at the expense of a little more time developing the parameter control.

WHAT ARE BASIC PARAMETERS?

Basic parameters are variables that are provided in specific situations that reduce the number of steps required to create a parameter control. Basic Parameters are available to make flexible top or bottom filters for a specified number of items in a set. In histograms, a parameter can be added that allows users to specify the size of each bin. Reference lines include a parameter option that provides a way to make the reference line change based on a user-selectable parameter value. Figure 4-22 shows the three Basic Parameter controls in action.

The histogram on the top of Figure 4-22 displays order counts by the Size of Orders. The Sales Bin parameter allows the end user to change the size of each bin. The Parameter Size Range is from $500 to $10,000. The bullet graph in the lower left of Figure 4-22 compares sales (bars) to prior year sales (black reference lines) for every product name. The data set includes over 1,000 product names.

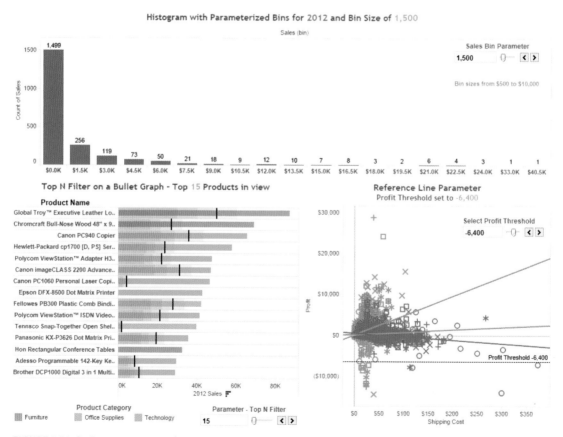

FIGURE 4-22 *Basic parameter controls*

The parameter allows the user to change the number of products displayed through a flexible top down filter. You can see that currently the top 15 products are being displayed. The scatter plot in the lower right includes a reference line called Profit Threshold that allows the user to change the threshold value and change the position of the reference line and the corresponding shading below the line.

All of these are Basic Parameters that are selectable options for these uses. Parameterizing a histogram's bin size is accessed via a right-click on the bin field name that appears in the dimensions shelf. The flexible filter in the bullet graph is accessed by right-clicking on the product name dimension and selecting the Top tab in the filter dialog. The reference line parameter is accessed when adding the reference line by clicking the Value drop-down selector and picking the Create a Parameter Option. Figure 4-23 shows each of the menus.

While Basic Parameters are very easy to create they are also currently limited to the specific use cases you see in Figure 4-23. Top or Bottom Filters, Bin Sizing, or Flexible Reference Lines; if you want to create more advanced parameters, these require a little more effort.

Invoke this menu by right-clicking on the dimension you wish to filter.

Access this parameter menu by right-clicking on the field name of the bin created for a histogram.

To create a parameterized reference line right-click on the axis you want to add the reference line to, and select the create a new parameter option.

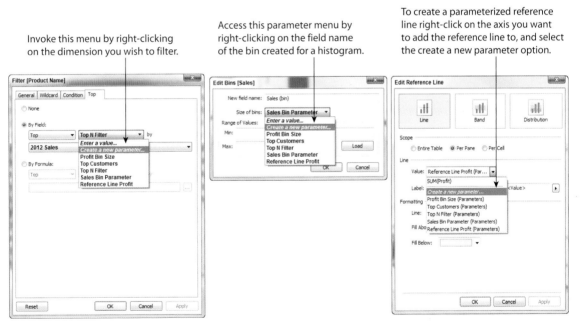

FIGURE 4-23 *Dialog windows for basic parameter creation*

WHAT ARE ADVANCED PARAMETERS?

Advanced Parameters controls are limited only by your imagination. You can create multiple Parameter Controls. Parameter Controls can be chained together to create linked parameters. An entire book could be written on Parameter Controls because they provide programming-like functionality to Visualizations. Creating Advanced Parameter controls requires three or four steps:

1. Create the parameter control.

2. Expose the parameter control on the desktop.

3. Use the parameter in a calculated value (optional).

4. Use the calculated value in the view.

If the parameter is being directly placed in the Visualization, it may be unnecessary to create a Calculated Value. The key point is that whatever the parameter is being used to change (typically a formula variable), that item must be used somehow in the Visualization in order for the Parameter Control to work.

The most popular use cases for Advanced Parameter is that it permits users to change measures or dimensions being displayed in a view. The technique in either case is the same. Figure 4-24 shows a Time Series chart in which a parameter is being used to change the measure plotted.

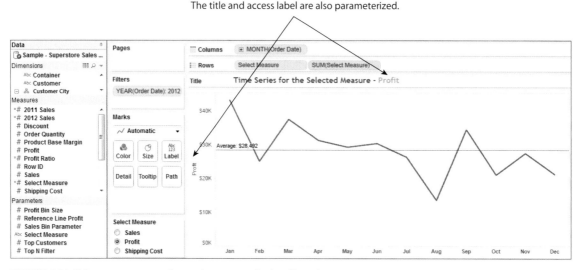

FIGURE 4-24 *Using a parameter to change the measure displayed in a view*

The Parameter Control appears below the Marks card in a radio-button style filter. It allows the user to select three different measures for the time series chart. Currently the view shows profit dollars. Notice that the title of the worksheet includes the parameter, and the axis label also changes.

Adding a Parameter Description to the title bar is done by double-clicking on the title bar and selecting the parameter used in the view. To add the Parameter Name to an axis, drag the parameter from the Parameters shelf to the axis. Then edit the axis and erase the static title. This example also rotated the parameter label and removed the label heading. When a new selection is made from the Parameter Control, the Visualization will change along with the headings and reference line to reflect the selected value.

Creating the Parameter Control

This can be done directly in the Formula Editing window or by right-clicking on blank space in the Dimensions, Measures, or Parameters shelf. Doing that exposes the dialog window that is used to define the parameter as you see in Figure 4-25.

Enter the name of the Parameter as you want it to appear in the control that is placed on the desktop, and then define the data type. Parameters can be numbers (floating decimal point or integers), Strings, Boolean (true/false), and Date or Date and Time values.

The allowable values section is where you define the variables that will contain the Parameter. In Figure 4-24 there is a small list of Measure names defined. While it isn't always desirable, I suggest that for this type of parameter you exactly copy the field names of the Measures. This will make formula creation easier in the next step. However, if you find that the performance of your parameter is not good, use numbers in a series (1,2,3…) as your value names in the parameter definition. It makes creating the formula in the next step a little more difficult; using numbers in the parameter definition will generally result in a more responsible parameter control. This is especially noticeable with larger data sets.

Notice that there is a Display As option. This is used to create a name alias that will

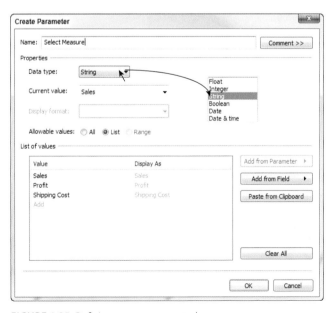

FIGURE 4-25 *Defining a parameter control*

appear instead of the actual field name. The options to the right of the List of Values section are not applicable to this example, but are useful for cases where you might be using values from another Parameter Control or adding members of a particularly large set. To complete the formula definition, click OK and the parameter will appear on the Parameters shelf.

Expose the Parameter in the Workspace

In order for users to access the Parameter Control it needs to be placed on the desktop. To do this, right-click on the Parameter name appearing in the Parameters shelf and select Show Parameter Control. If you access the parameter now, nothing will happen because you haven't used the control yet in a formula or in any other way in the Visualization. This is because the parameter hasn't been used in a formula yet or in any other way in the visualization. The next step is to use this parameter variable in a formula.

Create a Formula That Uses the Parameter Control

In Figure 4-24 the Parameter Control is used to change the Measure being plotted in the Time series. This requires a formula that will link the String values defined in the parameter to measure field names in the datasource. You can see the formula definition in Figure 4-26.

Now the parameter variable comes into play. The formula logic associates the selected parameter string with the related field name. This is why it is a good idea to define the Parameter String names to exactly match the field names you want to associate. It just makes writing the formula easier. But keep in mind that if performance degrades, using sequentially-ordered numeric values in the parameter definition will result in the best performance.

Clicking OK adds the Calculated Value to the Measures shelf with the name Select Measure. It's also a good idea to give your parameter name the same name as the related calculations, especially if you have many parameters defined in the worksheet. This just makes it easier to retrace your work at a later date if you need to modify the Parameter Control to add or delete items.

Use the Calculated Value in the View

Dragging the Select Measures measure to the Row shelf will activate the Parameter Control. Each selection made in the parameter control will trigger changes in the Select Measure formula and will change the measure being displayed in the Time series.

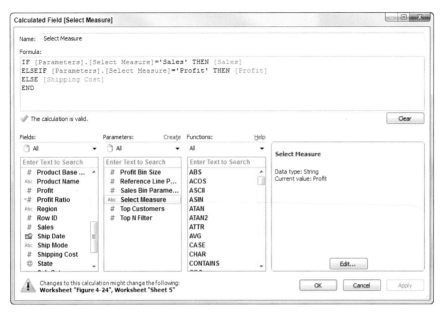

FIGURE 4-26 *Using a parameter in a formula*

Parameters can be used to create multi-purpose Visualizations. There are many different ways that Advanced Parameters can be used. The limit is your imagination. For more examples, go to Tableau Software's website and search for Parameters. You should find many different forum posts that relate to parameters and some training videos.

USING THE FUNCTION REFERENCE APPENDIX

Tableau provides good online documentation of Functions. The user forum on Tableau's website is also quite good. However, many novice users have asked for a more detailed reference for Tableau Functions that provide examples and explain the formula syntax in more detail. That is what you will find in Appendix A.

Functions are listed by function type, alphabetically. Each Function Reference entry provides a short description of the Function; typical use cases; and basic, intermediate, and advanced examples. Hopefully you'll find the Function Reference a useful addition to your tool set. As questions come in, the book's websites, the InterWorks book website and the Wiley companion website, will provide additional tips and tricks related to Functions, Parameters, dashboard building, and other topics that merit an ongoing discussion.

In the next chapter you will learn how Tableau creates geospatial data for mapping. If your data includes country, state, or other standard geographic dimensions, you can easily plot your data in maps.

NOTES

1. Zander, Rosamund Stone, and Benjamin Zander. *The Art of Possibility*. New York: Penguin, 2002. Print. Page 13.

CHAPTER 5

Using Maps to Improve Insight

In our time, when men have looked upon Earth from afar, seeing it as a small, glistening sphere spinning in the black sea of space, it requires a long backward flight of imagination to appreciate earlier perception of Earth. There were visions of wonder and myth, and often they were marvelously wrong.

JOHN WILFORD[1]

People are accustomed to using maps to find places, predict the weather, and see information regarding world events. Seeing your data displayed on a map can provide new insight. Tableau provides three standard map formats. If you don't like the standard maps you can replace them with customized maps provided by web mapping services. Or, if you have spatial data that is too small to fit on a map, you can replace maps with images.

If you have a connection to the web, Tableau's standard maps provide very granular geographic details. Alternatively, if you don't have an available Internet connection, Tableau allows you to change to locally-rendered offline maps, Building Maps Quickly with Show Me.

If your data includes geographic information, you can create a map visualization in less than five seconds by double-clicking on any geographic dimension (denoted by the globe icon), then double-clicking on any measure. When you do this, Tableau will place three pills on the appropriate shelves and present you with a map view of your data with the measures placed at the center of the geographic unit you selected. Tableau provides two different map types for displaying data; symbol maps and filled maps. Symbol maps place marks at specific geographic center points. Filled style maps color-encode the geographic shapes using a measure or dimension to apply the fill. Tableau also provides three map background image styles:

- Normal—Off-white land forms with blue water

- Gray—Gray land forms with white water

- Dark—Dark gray land forms with light gray water

If you do not need to make a clear distinction between land and water forms, you will find that the gray map style places more emphasis on your data. The dark map style can be particularly useful if you have to project maps on an older overhead projector. Try different appearance options by going to the map menu, then selecting Map Options. From there you can change the map style, alter the washout of the map background, or apply map layers. Tableau includes map layers that add more geographic details (base, land cover, roads) and United States census data. If you want to save your map option selections for use later, click the Make Default button at the bottom of the menu.

CREATING A STANDARD MAP VIEW

Take a look at what happens when you want to plot more complex data using the Show Me menu to create a map. Using the Superstore Sales data set, create a map that uses state and product category from the dimensions shelf and sales from the measures shelf. Multi-select the fields and use the Show Me button to pick the symbol map. The resulting map is displayed in Figure 5-1.

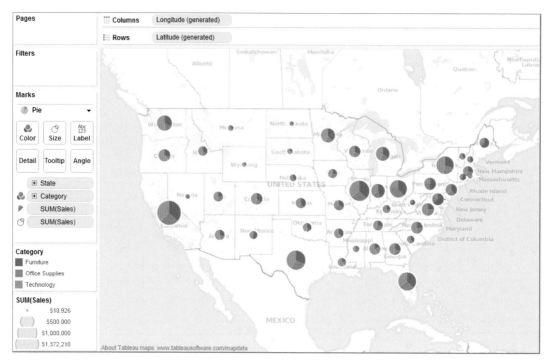

FIGURE 5-1 *Symbol map created using Show Me*

You can see that Tableau placed five pills in various places to create the symbol map. Click on the Show Me menu again and select the filled map. In fact,
double-clicking on any field that Tableau recognizes as a geographic entity
will result in a map being created in which the marks plotted will show the
center-point geocoding of the selected entity—even if you don't select any
other dimensions or measures. This is why you should lean on Show Me to build
maps—it's much faster than manually dragging the fields. When you make that
change, Tableau places category on the row shelf. This results in three maps
being displayed. Each map displays a specific product category. Dragging the
category pill from the row shelf to the filter shelf (then turning that filter into
a Quick Filter) results in the filled map you see in Figure 5-2.

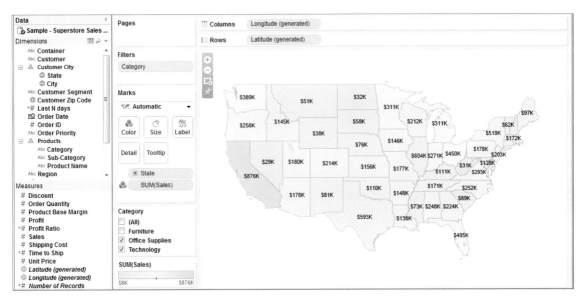

FIGURE 5-2 *Filled map created with Show Me*

Color encoding is used to show the sales values in each state. The sales amount
labels were turned on by clicking on the label button on the marks card and
selecting the show mark labels option. The map's appearance was edited to
remove background images for geographies that have no sales. To edit the
map style, use the main menu option for map and choose the map options
menu. The map options menu is seen in Figure 5-3.

For the filled map in Figure 5-3, the map washout was changed to one hundred percent. This hides map features from view. The areas bordering the United States are blank. If any state lacked sales it would be blank as well. At the top of the background section, the gray map type is selected. There are two other map types: normal and dark. Figure 5-4 shows the differences between normal, gray, and dark backgrounds.

The map options menu in Figure 5-3 also allows you to add more details to the map by adding more map layers. These options allow you to color-encode geographic shapes in the map using state, county, zip code, or census block level of detail. For the United States there are thirty different census data sets related to population, race, occupation, households, and housing. If you want to override Tableau's standard map settings with the new options you've selected, click the Make Default button at the bottom of the menu.

FIGURE 5-3 *Map options menu*

FIGURE 5-4 *Standard map background*

HOW TABLEAU GEOCODES YOUR DATA

Tableau places marks on your map automatically positioning them at the center of the geographic unit displayed. It recognizes a large number of standard geographic entities. The United States is mapped in detail and the geographic detail for international locations is extensive and growing with every version update. Geographic units include:

- Area code
- CBSA/MSA (USA census blocks)
- City
- Congressional District (USA only)
- Country/Region
- County

- State/Province

- Zip Code/Post Code

Locally-stored geographic data is used to place your information on the maps. By default, Tableau uses detailed online maps. If you can't get a web connection, Tableau's offline maps provide you with less detailed map images. Figure 5-5 shows online map examples for San Francisco and New York City.

FIGURE 5-5 *Tableau online map*

Using the gray map style and displaying the streets and highways map layer, Figure 5-5 also includes projected population growth at the zip code level of detail. Zip code boundaries and titles are also displayed. Tableau doesn't include international census data at this time, but international maps do include extensive road details. Figure 5-6 shows four international cities using the normal map style.

Tableau balances the rendering speed of maps with good map details so that you can find relevant reference points. This is accomplished by providing more granular details as you zoom into smaller areas. Providing over two hundred and ninety thousand municipalities recognized globally, detailed map views are available for most locations.

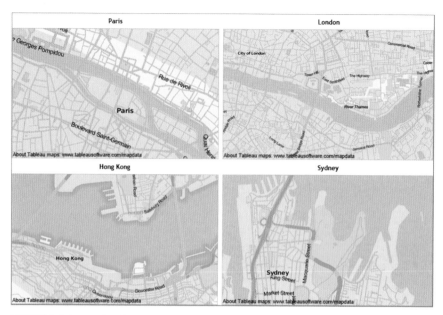

FIGURE 5-6 *International maps*

TYPICAL MAP ERRORS AND HOW TO DEAL WITH THEM

It isn't unusual to have some missing or erroneous data, especially when you are investigating a table for the first time. Fortunately, Tableau helps you identify non-conforming details and make corrections quickly without having to edit the datasource directly. Figure 5-7 shows a filled map. The color encoding of the map displays the relative sales value of each state. You can see that there is something wrong with the view because Missouri is blank. This could be caused if an abbreviation was used for Missouri (MO) if the other state names are not abbreviated.

In the lower right area of the map in Figure 5-7 there is a gray pill that includes the text (1 unknown). This indicates that one geographic record is missing or unrecognized in the data set. Clicking on the pill opens the special values menu that provides three options for dealing with the unknown record:

- Editing the locations (to correct the error)
- Filtering the data (to exclude the record)
- Showing the data at the default position (this means zero)

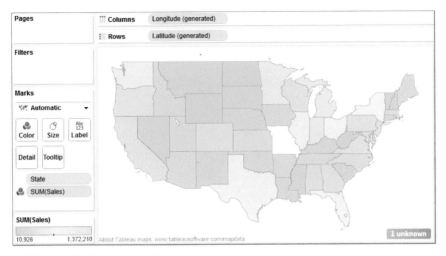

FIGURE 5-7 *Filled map missing data*

Clicking the edit location option exposes the special values menu you see in the upper left area of Figure 5-8.

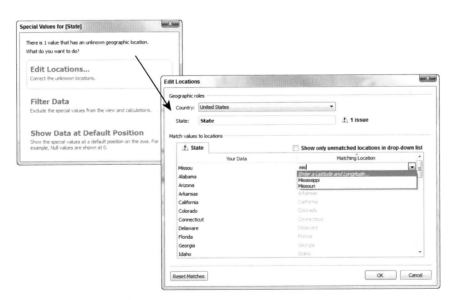

FIGURE 5-8 *Correcting place name errors*

Selecting the Edit Locations option exposes the menu on the right of Figure 5-8. Tableau identified that the state of Missouri is misspelled. This is why there is no color fill for Missouri in the map. Fixing the error is done by typing the correct spelling into the "matching location" area. After typing a few letters, Tableau narrows the list of candidates to Mississippi or Missouri. Selecting Missouri aliases the state name in Tableau with the correct spelling and fixes the problem. The source data set is still wrong but Tableau's name alias will correct the problem in the map. Lock in the change by clicking the OK button. Tableau recognizes different place name variations (abbreviations) and will edit other geographic entities as well (city, county, province, etc.). This ability to quickly identify and correct non-conforming records will save you time and make it easy for you to provide detailed feedback to correct errors in your source data.

PLOTTING YOUR OWN LOCATIONS ON A MAP

It would be impractical for Tableau to monitor and save every possible location in the world. If you have specific places you want to plot on maps that Tableau doesn't automatically recognize, you can enable this using two different methods. You can add the specific longitude and latitude to your source data, or you can import custom geocode lists into Tableau.

ADDING CUSTOM GEOCODING TO YOUR DATASOURCE

You must obtain geographic coordinates in the form of longitude and latitude values that you provide to your data set in order to add custom geocoding to your datasource. There are many free web-based geocoding services that provide this information. My personal favorite is `www.gpsvisualizer.com`. Figure 5-9 shows a list of jazz clubs in the metro New York area that have the necessary latitude/longitude data added.

	A	B	C	E	F	G	H	I	J
1	ID	Venue Name	Type	Address	City	State	Phone	latitude	longitude
2	1	Paramount Center for the Arts	Jazz Played	1008 Brown Street	Peekskill	NY	877-840-0457	41.2899838	-73.9197845
3	2	Metropolitan Museum of Art	Jazz Played	1000 Fifth Avenue	New York	NY	212-535-7710	40.7791544	-73.962697
4	3	Buckingham Hotel	Jazz Played	101 W. 57th St.	New York	NY	212-999-5585	40.7645904	-73.9773501
5	4	Vox Pop Brooklyn	Jazz Played	1022 Cortelyou Road	Brooklyn	NY	718 940 2084	40.63932	-73.967996
6	5	Oceana Hall	Jazz Played	1029 Brighton Beach Ave	Brooklyn	NY	7185136616	40.5783085	-73.9584269
7	6	Oceana Ballroom	Jazz Played	1029 Brighton Beach Ave.	Brooklyn	NY	347-462-2810	40.5783085	-73.9584269
8	7	North Square Lounge	Jazz Played	103 Waverly Place	New York	NY	212-254-1200	40.7325	-73.998692
9	8	Jazz Museum in Harlem	Jazz Played	104 E. 126th Street	New York	NY	212-348-8300	40.80528	-73.938056
10	9	Lansky Lounge & Grill	Jazz Played	104 Norfolk Street	New York	NY	212-677-9489	40.7143528	-74.0059731
11	10	Cafe Sabarsky	Jazz Played	1048 5th Avenue	New York	NY	212-628-6200	40.781219	-73.960228
12	11	Havana - New Hope	Jazz Played	105 South Main Street	New Hope	PA	215-862-1933	40.3616309	-74.9504278

FIGURE 5-9 *Custom location list*

The sample data partially in view in Figure 5-9 includes over five hundred addresses. You can see the coordinates in the far right columns. Using the custom latitude and longitude data allows you to plot each location on its specific address. Figure 5-10 shows the custom plot with a Tooltips exposed displaying additional location details.

FIGURE 5-10 *Dark style map with address detail*

The column and row shelves hold the custom latitude and longitude coordinates that place the marks on the map. The Tooltips were customized to show the street address, phone number and venue information. The dark map style was modified slightly by employing a twenty-five percent washout via the map/map options menu.

IMPORTING CUSTOM GEOCODING INTO TABLEAU

If you go to the trouble to add customized geographic coordinates, wouldn't it be nice to make that available to other people within your organization? This is done by importing the address coordinates directly into Tableau Desktop. After they are imported, the custom locations behave like Tableau's default geographic units. The import file should have the following characteristics:

- Give each location record a unique identifier (key record).

- Save the location file in comma-delimited CSV format.

- Label the coordinate fields Latitude and Longitude (these key words must be used).

It's best not to include a lot of additional dimensional data in these import files. Be sure that you have only one instance of Tableau open when you perform the import. If you want to share this custom data with other people building reports in Tableau, store the list in a shared network directory so that other users can import from the same list as well. Figure 5-11 is an example of a custom geocode table properly formatted for import.

After saving the custom list in comma delimited CSV format, the custom geographic data can be imported into Tableau. Initiate the import using the main menu (map/geocoding/import custom geocoding). A small file will only require a few seconds to load. Large lists can take several minutes. Running the import will create a new data file on your computer within (My Tableau Repository/Local Data). The custom data is stored as a Tableau datasource file (tds) with the same name as the source CSV file that was imported.

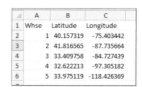

FIGURE 5-11 *Custom geocode table*

USING CUSTOM GEOGRAPHIC UNITS IN A MAP

After importing custom geocodes into Tableau Desktop you can use them with other data files to build maps as long as those files contain the same location key record defined in your data import table. The custom data file used in the rest of this example looks like Figure 5-12.

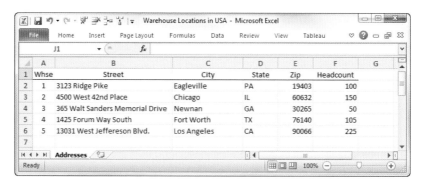

FIGURE 5-12 *Warehouse location table*

Notice that there is no longitude or latitude data in the table shown in Figure 5-12. However, the (Whse) field can be used to link the imported data from the custom geocode table displayed in Figure 5-11. The steps to use custom geocoding in this example are:

- Attach Tableau to a datasource.
- Alter the geographic role of the key records (use the imported custom geography).
- Use the key record in your view to plot the location on a map.

Altering the geographic role of the warehouse location is done by right-clicking on the Whse field, selecting Geographic Role/Whse as you see in Figure 5-13.

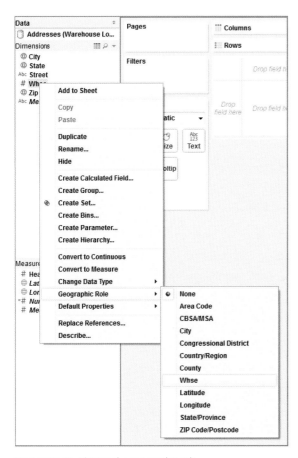

FIGURE 5-13 *Altering the geographic role*

The Whse field icon will change to an icon that is similar to a standard geographic icon but with a small list in front of the globe. Tableau will now recognize the imported geographic data. Figure 5-14 shows a map plot of the custom geocoded warehouse locations.

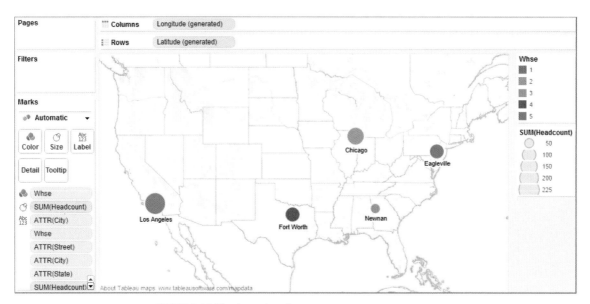

FIGURE 5-14 *Warehouse location map*

Notice that the column and row shelves are using Tableau's (generated) latitude and longitude fields. However, the warehouse marks actually use the imported custom locations to place the marks. Hovering over the Los Angeles location causes a customized Tooltip to appear showing particulars about the warehouse. Zooming in on the Los Angeles location in Figure 5-15, you can see that the mark is more precisely placed than Tableau's standard geocoding can provide. This detail comes from the imported geocodes you saw in Figure 5-12.

The order of the steps for enabling custom geocodes at the beginning of this section isn't the only way to achieve the result. You can import the custom geocoding at any point—even after a map plot is done using standard geographic plotting.

Now that you've learned how to precisely plot any location on a map with custom geocoding, in the next section you'll learn how to replace Tableau.

FIGURE 5-15 *Los Angeles warehouse*

REPLACING TABLEAU'S STANDARD MAPS

Tableau Maps visualizations are special scatter plots that use map images for backgrounds and special measures (longitude and latitude) to plot marks on the map. This implies that you can replace Tableau's standard map images with other image files.

WHY REPLACE TABLEAU'S STANDARD MAPS?

Tableau's dynamic map files are designed to balance high quality graphic details while optimizing map rendering speed. But if standard maps don't provide the detail you require, Tableau makes it easy to replace the standard maps with custom maps provided by map services. With a little more effort you can even use standard image files for map backgrounds.

Using custom maps or building visualizations with custom image backgrounds can enhance understanding and yield new information that wouldn't be visible on a standard map. There could be many reasons you might want to replace Tableau's standard map files. Custom maps can include non-standard geographic units or demographics particular to your organization. Perhaps you have spatial data that isn't large enough to be seen on a standard map. Examples might include warehouse or office layouts, retail planograms, building complexes, circuit board schematics, web pages, or even the human body. Or, the scale of your spatial data might be microscopic.

As long as you can define the vertical (y) and horizontal (x) coordinates within the spatial layout, it is possible to place data points on image files precisely. This process can be trivial—requiring only a few clicks—or require significant effort.

REPLACING TABLEAU'S STANDARD MAPS TO ENHANCE INFORMATION

The easiest way to replace Tableau's standard maps is with a web map service. Tableau can seamlessly integrate maps that adhere to an open source map protocol developed by the Open Geospatial Consortium. Many web mapping services adhere to the Web Mapping Service (WMS) protocol. Replacing Tableau's standard maps with WMS services is easy because the service provides the coordinate dimensions of the map, thereby eliminating the need for you to define the map coordinates. Tableau saves these map imports as Tableau Map Source (tms) files.

Web Mapping Service Pros and Cons

The quality of the map files provided from free services is generally not very good and the rendering speed can be unacceptably slow. If you need map images that are more responsive, investigate paid services. Tableau's maps are created and maintained by San Francisco-based, Urban Mapping. Due to their familiarity with Tableau. Software, Urban Mapping is a good place to start if you have special interactive map needs. Their maps conform to Tile Map Service (TMS) that is used by Tableau. Urban Mapping provides free sample map files upon request. Their map files render more quickly than WMS services found on the Internet. Figure 5-16 compares a standard Tableau map with a custom map provided by Urban Mapping.

FIGURE 5-16 *Standard and custom maps*

The map on the left is a standard Tableau map using the normal map style. The custom map on the right from Urban Mapping includes Chicago bus routes. The bus route map was enabled by copying a Tableau Map Source (tms) file supplied by Urban Mapping to `C:\Program File(x86)\Tableau\Tableau 8.0\Mapsources`. Map files that are placed into that map's sources directory appear as an option within Tableau's map menu. To replace Tableau's standard maps with any map service use the main menu and follow these steps:

1. Click on the map menu.
2. Select background maps/WMS Servers.
3. Input the URL for the map service.
4. Click OK.

Following these steps, the customized map will appear as an option under the map menu/background maps. The name that appears for the custom map in the menu is whatever name you assign when establishing the connection to the map service. The steps required to share a WMS custom map with others Tableau users are:

- Establish the initial connection to the web mapping service.
- Export the connection (creates a tms file).
- Import the tms connection file (the end user).

Figure 5-17 displays a custom map image that came from a web mapping service free of charge.

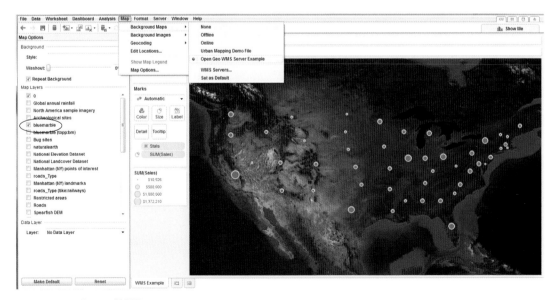

FIGURE 5-17 *Custom (WMS) map*

After entering the URL for the service, the connection name was edited to Open Geo WMS Server Example. This name appears in Figure 5-17 via the map menu. The satellite image layer was added to the view by selecting the "bluemarble" map layer in the map layer menu. At the time of writing Open Geo WMS Server was functional.

Using a web mapping service allows you to customize maps to fit your particular needs. In the next section you'll learn how to import custom image files to build map displays that meet your specific requirements.

USING CUSTOM BACKGROUND IMAGES TO PLOT SPATIAL DATA

If the spatial data you want to plot isn't adequately portrayed on a map you can also use image files as backgrounds. This option offers the advantage of infinite flexibility. But, it requires more effort to implement because you will have to define the image boundary coordinates and the point coordinates for the items you want to place on the image.

WHY ARE NON-STANDARD PLOTS USEFUL?

Analyzing spatial data that's too small to be meaningful on a map may still yield interesting insight. Alternatively, if you know that your audience won't have access to the web, you can import a custom map image that contains specific details that are normally available only using online maps or not at all. For example, if you work in a large office and you want to analyze activity within the office, plotting employee movement over time within that space could help you improve the office layout. Retail merchandise managers are interested in tracking how the placement of products on shelves affect sales. Casino managers might be interested in seeing how the placement of cash machines within the casino affects revenue generation in different wagering areas. The options for spatial analysis in Tableau are limited only by your imagination.

THE STEPS REQUIRED TO BUILD A CUSTOM SPATIAL PLOT

Creating spatial analysis with image files requires additional steps that aren't needed when using images from web mapping services. This is because the boundary coordinates on a map are based on the longitude (y-axis) and latitude (x-axis) of the map. Image files don't have the built-in coordinates that are provided by map services. The steps to use an image for a spatial plot are:

1. Find or create an image file (jpeg or png formats work well).

2. Trim the image to include only the details you need.

3. Define the image boundaries (using any metric you desire).

4. Add point coordinates to your data set.

5. Tweak point coordinates to precisely position marks on the image.

Assume you want to lay out a small office floor plan for use as a background image to map employee movement within the space. The level of precision you can achieve is dependent on your capture system. Figure 5-18 includes a basic floor plan that will be used to create a custom map background.

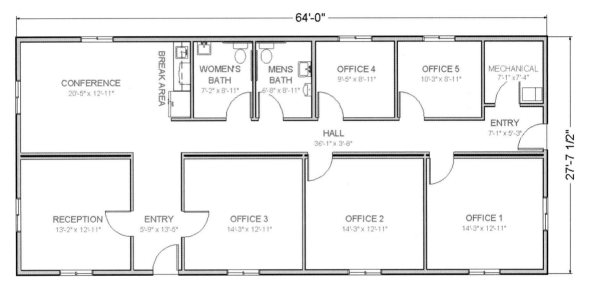

FIGURE 5-18 *Office floor plan image*

You can see Figure 5-18 includes some peripheral areas outside of the floor plan in the image file. These areas are not part of the floor plan. Including areas outside of the floor plan in the image file complicates the image layout later because the dimensions of the office only encompass the office space. For this reason it makes sense to trim the image to include only the actual floor plan image and not the surrounding white space. The example floor plan dimensions are (64'-0" × 27'-7.5"). It makes sense to define the layout coordinates in inches. This will provide for precise placement of marks within each location desired within the office space.

POSITIONING MARKS ON A NON-STANDARD MAP

Positioning the points within images can take a little time. A point coordinate system allowing for at least one position in each room in the floor plan provides the necessary level of detail for this example. Figure 5-19 includes the data set with locations that will need to have point coordinates. The initial estimated point coordinates are in the table.

The goal of this visualization will be to place the marks in a way that won't obscure the place labels that are included in the office layout image. The steps to finish a map of the office plan are:

	A	B	C	D
1	Location	LocID	X	Y
2	Reception	1	120.0	72.0
3	Conference	2	120.0	264.0
4	Womans Bath	3	318.0	300.0
5	Mens Bath	4	330.0	300.0
6	Mechanical	5	720.0	312.0
7	Break Area	6	228.0	300.0
8	Office 1	7	696.0	72.0
9	Office 2	8	576.0	72.0
10	Office 3	9	300.0	72.0
11	Office 4	10	540.0	300.0
12	Office 5	11	648.0	300.0

FIGURE 5-19 *Estimated office point coordinates*

1. Connect to a data set that includes the data in Figure 5-19.

2. Disaggregate the measures (so that each individual office location appears).

3. Add an image of the floor plan from Figure 5-18.

4. Edit the (X-Y) point coordinates to precisely position the marks.

After connecting to the data set, the (X-Y) coordinate measure values should be placed on the column and row shelves. This will result in a scatter plot view with one mark. Tableau will express the sum of the (X-Y) coordinate values. The measures need to be disaggregated to display all of the rows in the data set. This will cause one mark to appear in the view for each location in the floor plan. To do this, de-select the aggregate measure option from the analysis menu. Figure 5-20 shows the view before and after disaggregating the measures.

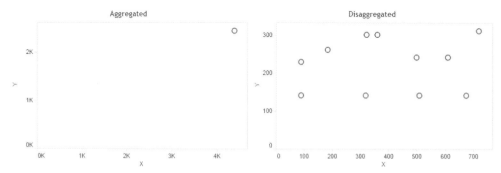

FIGURE 5-20 *Connecting to the data*

Next the background image will be added to the floor plan by accessing the maps/background images menu and setting the boundary coordinates for the background image. Figure 5-21 shows the menus used to enter the coordinates and define how the image will be displayed.

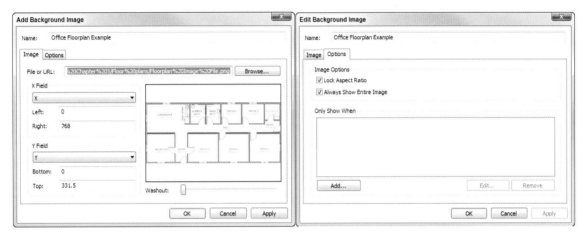

FIGURE 5-21   *Defining the image boundaries*

On the left side of Figure 5-21 you see the map/background images dialog box. Access this menu from the main map menu/background images option. This is where the coordinates for the (X-Y) axis ranges are entered. The values are defined in inches. Selecting the options menu exposes the menu seen on the right of Figure 5-21. The selected options you see on the right of Figure 5-21 ensure that the image will not be distorted if its overall size is changed. Clicking the OK button will add the image to the view seen in Figure 5-22.

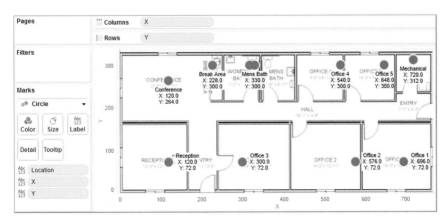

FIGURE 5-22   *Initial floor plan image*

As you can see in Figure 5-22 the initial estimates for the mark coordinates are a little off. A good way to reposition the marks is to open the source file next to your Tableau workbook. (It helps if you have a large monitor or dual monitor setup when you do this.) With the source file opened next to the visualization, enter revised coordinate values in the source file (save it), then refresh the Tableau view by right-clicking on the datasource in Tableau's data window. You will see the position of the mark change. Figure 5-23 shows the final adjusted coordinate layout.

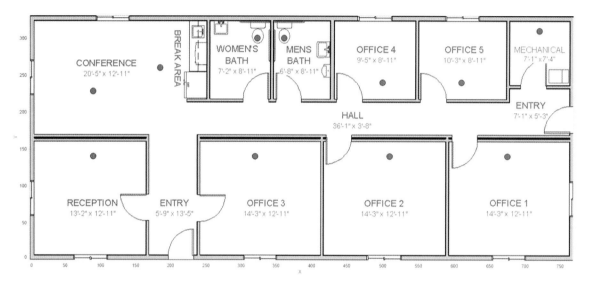

FIGURE 5-23 *Adjusted point coordinates*

See how precisely each mark is placed? The bathroom marks are right on the toilet seats. It normally requires a few tries to get the marks centered exactly because it's largely a trial and error process to position marks precisely on image files. Using point annotation on the marks also helps when you perform this task. With an appropriate capture system, the point coordinate data could be provided by a real-time system that captures staff position with time stamps to create the possibility of making an animated view of staff movement. This technique can be used in many different settings.

PUBLISHING WORKBOOKS WITH NON-STANDARD GEOGRAPHIES

If you use a custom map or image file and share a Tableau workbook file (twb) with other people, you must also share the custom source map file (tms) with them or they won't be able to see the custom map. Alternatively you can distribute the workbook as a Tableau Packaged Workbook file (twbx). Tableau

Packaged workbooks save all your data and any custom (tms) image files together—eliminating the need to provide the (tms) file separately.

SHAPING DATA TO ENABLE POINT-TO-POINT MAPPING

Mapping point-to-point details on maps requires that your data supports plotting and linking each point. Possible use cases for this style of presentation might include delivery truck routes, subway line activity, or city traffic flow. Similar presentations could be made using image files for spatial plots of areas too small for maps. Real-world applications may require automation to collect time-stamped geographic points and could require millions of records. To plot customized points on a map your data must include:

- A unique key record for each location

- Location coordinates (longitude and latitude)

- Other interesting measures or facts related to the data

The next example will map point-to-point travel between two office locations. A line connecting each point will be color-encoded to express the duration in minutes at normal speeds required to traverse each segment between points. Figure 5-24 shows a sample data set with the necessary details.

	A	B	C	D	E	F	G	H
						Elapsed	Seg	
1	Point ID	Location Name	Type	Latitude	Longitude	Time	Duration	Comment
2	1	Stillwater Office	Office	36.105116	-97.104061	0.0	0.0	Starting point in front of the Stillwater office
3	2	Stillwater entrance	Roadpoint	36.105144	-97.104984	0.1	0.1	Turn right on to S. Sangre Road
4	3	OK-51 and S Sangre Rd	Roadpoint	36.11603	-97.105223	1.0	0.9	Turn left on to OK-51
5	4	I-35 Ramp, South	Roadpoint	36.115686	-97.345358	15.0	14.0	Turn right on exit ramp to I-35 South
6	5	I-35 South	Roadpoint	35.812803	-97.416398	35.0	20.0	Continue on I-35 South
7	6	Highway	Roadpoint	35.609447	-97.425155	48.0	13.0	Continue on I-35 South
8	7	Highway	Roadpoint	35.544237	-97.458242	50.0	2.0	Take I-44 West toware Lawton/Amarillo
9	8	Harrison Ave	Roadpoint	35.529691	-97.514078	58.0	8.0	Task the south exit to 1-235 South
10	9	NE 4th Street, OKC	Roadpoint	35.473929	-97.508934	60.0	2.0	Turn right on Harrison Avenue exit
11	10	Walker Avenue, OKC	Roadpoint	35.471846	-97.511866	63.0	3.0	Veer right on 4th Street
12	11	OKC Office	Office	35.472169	-97.520441	65.0	2.0	You have arrive at the InterWorks, Oklahoma City Office

FIGURE 5-24 *Point-to-point details*

The route in Figure 5-24 starts in Stillwater, Oklahoma at point one and finishes in Oklahoma City, Oklahoma at point eleven. If there were multiple records for each location, a combination of the location, the key record, and the time stamp can be used to identify unique points. In that case, the measures would need to be disaggregated (by accessing the analysis menu and de-selecting aggregate measures) so that the plot displays all the different times each location was visited. Since the sample data set includes only one record per location, there is no need to disaggregate the measures to display all the records. Figure 5-25 shows the completed point-to-point plot.

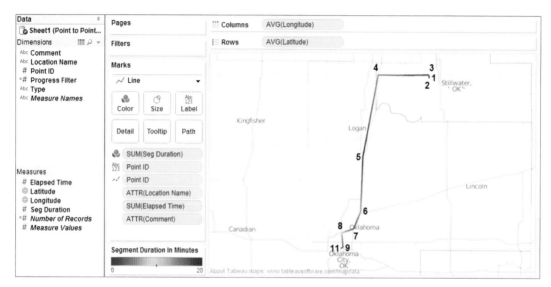

FIGURE 5-25 *Map view of the route*

Notice that the line mark type is selected on the marks card. Point ID defines the order of the route and must be placed in the path button so that the line connects each point in the correct order. Placing the Point ID on the label shelf causes the location point ID number to display in the map as well. The line connecting the route is color encoded by segment time duration.

Since this covers a large area it would be helpful to provide two additional map views that zoom into the local areas surrounding the origin and destination, making more granular street-level detail visible, as in Figure 5-26.

The maps on the right of the dashboard show more road details around the starting and ending points. Pointing at any mark exposes a Tooltip with additional information about the location. The main map view on the left shows the Tooltip related to the end point of the route.

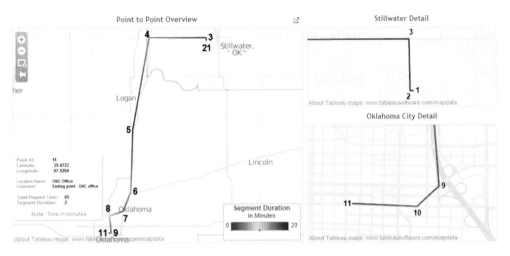

FIGURE 5-26 *Route dashboard*

ANIMATING MAPS USING THE PAGES SHELF OR SLIDER FILTERS

The most convenient way to animate views is to utilize a date/time dimension on the filter shelf (or the pages shelf) to increment time forward and backward. Creating a Quick Filter using a continuous dimension presents the user with a slider-type filter that will work well for animating the view. The pages shelf goes beyond Quick Filters by enabling an auto-incrementing filter. The pages shelf works well in Tableau Desktop and Reader; however, it is not supported in Tableau Server.

The example in Figure 5-25 doesn't include a date/time dimension, but there is a single key record for each point ID. The example map can be animated by placing the Point ID field on the filter shelf. Figure 5-27 shows the Point ID added to the desktop as a continuous slide filter.

The route line now ends at point eight as specified in the Quick Filter. Dragging the slider to the left or right animates the route map manually. Notice that the Point ID pill on the filter shelf is green. This color indicates that the point ID was changed to a continuous dimension. The point ID field was initially a discrete dimension. Using a discrete dimension for the Quick Filter would not facilitate animating the view. The filter was changed from discrete to continuous by right-clicking on the Point ID pill on the filter shelf and selecting continuous.

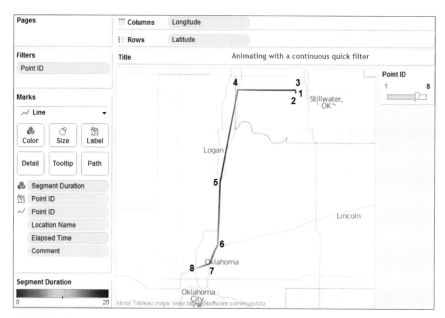

FIGURE 5-27 *Animating a map*

Tableau's standard maps and automatic geocoding should meet your needs most of the time. Through the use of custom geocoding and custom maps you'll be able to create even more detailed geographic analysis. And, by using custom map backgrounds from web services or image files you can fully customize the detail and appearance of map backgrounds.

In the next chapter you'll learn how to use parameter controls to facilitate ad hoc analysis for information for consumers viewing your visualizations through Tableau Reader, Tableau Server, or even in visualizations embedded on websites.

NOTES

1. Wilford, John Noble. *The Mapmakers*. New York: Vintage, 2001. Print. Page 18.

CHAPTER 6

Developing an Ad Hoc Analysis Environment

Any time a bureaucrat (i.e., a custodian of a system) stands between you and something you need or want, your challenge is to help that bureaucrat discover a means, harmonious with the systems, to meet your need.

GORDON MACKENZIE[1]

Tableau core design encourages discovery. In Chapter 2 you learned that Tableau connects to a wide variety of datasources, and this is further extended through data blending from external sources. Chapter 3 introduced the Show Me button; trend lines; reference lines; and how filters, sets, grouping, and hierarchies can be used to present information meaningfully—for facts and dimensions that are included in views.

Webster's Dictionary defines *ad hoc* as follows:

Concerned with a particular end or purpose, formed or used for specific or immediate problems or needs, fashioned from whatever is immediately available.

In this chapter you'll explore three ways Tableau facilitates ad hoc analysis:

- Generating new data with forecasts
- Designing flexible views using parameters
- Changing or creating designs in Tableau Server

Desktop users can create forecasts when viewing time series data, and also get feedback from Tableau on the quality and type of forecasts Tableau generates. Desktop report designers can also build flexibility into views and dashboards using variables called parameters. Parameters allow information consumers to alter views within limits defined by the designer. Most significantly, even staff with Tableau Server licenses can build completely new views or alter existing designs without the need for Tableau Desktop.

GENERATING NEW DATA WITH FORECASTS

Tableau Desktop users can create forecasts with a couple of mouse clicks. The resulting figures can be exported, revised, and possibly added to your datasource—providing a fast and easy way to model the future based on past history.

HOW TABLEAU CREATES FORECASTS

Tableau generates forecasted values by using time-series data that is included in your worksheet. Figure 6-1 shows a time series chart that includes forecasted values.

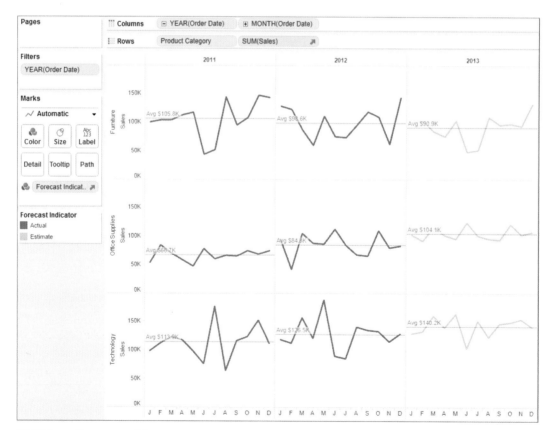

FIGURE 6-1 *Time series with forecast*

Forecasted values are presented in a lighter color than the actual values. The forecast values in Figure 6-1 can be added by right-clicking within the worksheet, and selecting the Forecast/Show Forecast menu option. You can also generate the forecast from the Analysis menu/Forecast option.

Forecasting Options

Tableau can forecast data in a variety of ways and will automatically select what it feels is the best method. If you don't want to accept the default, edit the forecast model by right-clicking on the worksheet and selecting the forecast options menu. Tableau provides the following forecast trend models:

- Trend and season

- Trend only

- Season only

- No trend or season

Depending on the amount and granularity of the historical data, each option will generate different results. Trend and season will generate the most volatile forecast data. The forecast options menu includes several other variables that can be adjusted. You can see the forecast options menu in Figure 6-2.

At the top of Figure 6-2 you can see that by default, Tableau will generate a 12-month forecast, but it is possible to forecast a specific number of periods into the future. The number of periods that Tableau forecasts is dependent on the date range in your view and the data aggregation level presented. The Ignore Last setting allows you to omit incomplete historical data so that it won't skew the forecast results. Checking the Fill In Missing Values With Zeroes box will prevent null values from corrupting the forecast.

Review and Present Forecast Quality Metrics

You can examine the quality of the forecast that Tableau generates by right-clicking within the workspace and selecting the forecast/describe forecast option. Figure 6-3 shows the summary tab.

The summary tab provides details regarding the precision and quality of the forecasted values. You can choose to express forecast precision as number or percentage ranges. Forecast quality is described as poor, OK, or good. Clicking on the Models tab exposes more detailed quality metrics that you see in Figure 6-4.

FIGURE 6-2 *The forecast options menu*

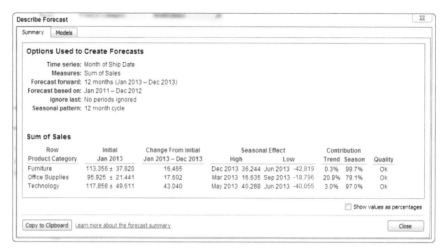

FIGURE 6-3 *Describe forecast summary*

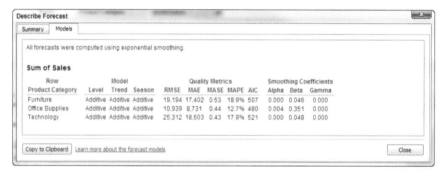

FIGURE 6-4 *Describe forecast model*

Tableau's forecasting model weights recent history more heavily. The statistical models for the different quality metrics presented in Figure 6-4 are defined in detail in the Tableau Desktop manual. The smoothing coefficients for alpha (level smoothing), beta (trend smoothing), and gamma (seasonal smoothing) refer to the amount of smoothing applied. Values closer to one are smoothed less than the lower values. If the value is very close to zero a lot of smoothing was performed.

Adding Quality Metrics to Tooltips in Visualizations

By dragging and dropping the forecasted measure from the measures shelf in the data window to the marks card detail window, this allows you to modify information contained in the Tooltip to include quality and precision metrics. Figure 6-5 shows the placement.

Once sales are dropped into the detail button (Figure 6-5) you can modify the value presented by right-clicking on the pill in the marks card and making a selection as you see in Figure 6-6.

FIGURE 6-5 *Adding sales to detail button*

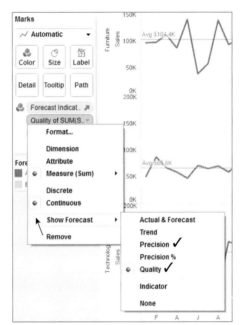

FIGURE 6-6 *Enabling quality metrics*

In Figure 6-6 you see the selection options for adding quality and precision metrics so that they become available for Tooltips in the chart. Each individual selection desired in the view will require another sales measure to be dropped on the details button. In this example, two metrics were added—quality and precision. Figure 6-7 shows the resulting Tooltip.

This Tooltip is exposed to users when they hover their mouse over the mark. Figure 6-7 shows that a Quality of Sales forecast metric and a Precision of Sales forecast metric have been added to the Tooltip. The quality metric range is from zero to 100 (higher numbers mean better quality). The precision metric is expressed as a value range and provides the 95 percent prediction interval for the forecast—a measure of the potential volatility of the forecast value. In this example the value range refers to a sales dollar range of 49,611.

FIGURE 6-7 *Tooltip with quality and precision metrics*

Exporting Forecasts

Exporting Tableau-generated forecasts can be a time-saver for developing more nuanced forecasts. One way to accomplish this might be to duplicate the original view in Figure 6-1 as a crosstab, then export the view using the menu option for worksheet/export/crosstab to Excel. Figure 6-8 shows the resulting spreadsheet values.

Alternatively, it is also possible to go to the menu option Worksheet/Export/ Data to an Access database. Using either method allows you to adjust the forecasted values more specifically and perhaps add those altered figures into your main database in their own field. Tableau's forecasting model isn't intended to replace sophisticated statistical forecasting tools. It provides an easy-to-use way to create forecasts along with quality and precision metrics to access the quality and precision of the resulting estimates.

Creating forecasts in views that you publish to Tableau Server and share with others is one way to stimulate an ad hoc analysis environment for users that only have access to the view via Tableau Server. In the next section you'll learn how to create parameter controls that enable Tableau Server users to change measures and dimensions in views or dashboards.

	A	B	C	D	E	F	G	H
1				Estimate			Actual	
2			Furniture	Office Supplies	Technology	Furniture	Office Supplies	Technology
3		January	102,666	102,326	128,170			
4		February	101,591	91,519	132,001			
5		March	83,837	115,810	159,559			
6		April	74,950	101,429	138,809			
7		May	102,589	95,272	162,800			
8	2013	June	48,032	123,582	102,584			
9		July	51,326	100,568	150,485			
10		August	108,298	95,220	122,150			
11		September	95,236	93,567	145,349			
12		October	97,027	120,540	147,862			
13		November	93,058	102,569	153,228			
14		December	131,741	107,214	139,782			
15		January				99,856	53,332	98,279
16		February				103,530	84,286	112,074
17		March				103,641	69,745	122,650

FIGURE 6-8 *Exported forecast in a spreadsheetw*

PROVIDING SELF-SERVICE AD HOC ANALYSIS WITH PARAMETERS

Parameters allow those consuming reports to change the context of views with Quick-Filter-like controls. Report builders design parameters into views when the report is created in Tableau Desktop. Parameters create a pathway for non-technical consumers to conduct ad hoc analysis by changing what and how facts and dimensions are displayed—within the boundaries of the designer's intended usage. Concerns regarding the efficacy of self-service analysis are minimized because the report designer controls what changes are permitted.

WHAT ARE PARAMETERS?

Parameters are variables that allow users to alter the content of a formula or change a dimension or measure contained in the view. Parameters create a powerful means for changing normally static values into dynamic entities that facilitate ad hoc discovery without the need for changing the design of the view.

HOW CAN PARAMETERS BE USED?

The different ways parameters can be used is limited only by your imagination. Tableau provides some basic parameter controls by building them into different contexts that commonly benefit from the use of a variable. Creative report designers can dream up a myriad of other ways to use this powerful feature by building formula variables that control the facts in view, the dimensions that appear, or the length and granularity of time series data. Anywhere that you can place a field in Tableau Desktop is a potential repository for a parameter control.

BASIC PARAMETER CONTROLS

Parameter controls first appeared in Tableau several years ago, and they have become a popular feature. To make parameters easier for novice users, Tableau created basic parameter types that are built into typical use cases that benefit from variables. These include:

- Reference line parameters
- Bin size parameters (for histograms)
- Ranking parameters (in value comparison views)

The steps required to add basic parameter controls to a view are straightforward provided you know that they exist. Figure 6-9 is a scatter plot that includes basic parameter controls for the vertical and horizontal reference lines.

There are two reference line parameter controls in Figure 6-9 that enable a user to change the location of the reference lines. These variable controls are built into the same dialog box where standard fixed reference lines are created. To create the parameter, right-click on the axis and select Add Reference Line to expose the reference line dialog box, and then in the value box select the Create a New Parameter option. Figure 6-10 shows the added reference dialog box on the left. Selecting the Create a Parameter Option in the value menu exposes the Edit Parameter window on the right of Figure 6-10.

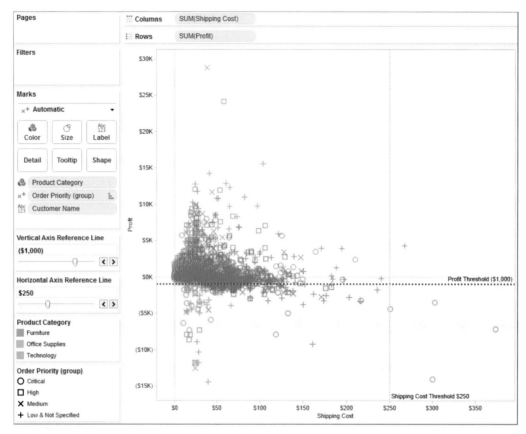

FIGURE 6-9 *Reference line parameters*

The edit parameter window is where you name and define the parameter. A comment field can be used to hold notes describing the parameter. The Properties section is used to define the parameter type. In this example, a floating decimal point value is selected, the display format is currency, and the parameter is defined for a range of values with a specified increment defined by step size. Clicking the OK button adds the parameter control. Refer to Figure 6-9 again and notice that the parameters allow users to move a slider to change the position of the reference lines.

A second basic parameter type is available for making variable bin sizes in histograms. The view seen in Figure 6-11 was initially constructed by selecting the profit field and then picking the histogram chart type from the Show Me menu. This resulted in a bin size of five thousand dollars with a very large concentration of items in only two bins.

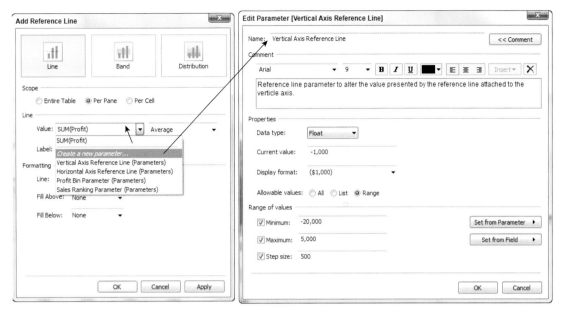

FIGURE 6-10 *Creating a reference line parameter*

Right-clicking on the Profit Bin dimension that Show Me automatically created allows you to select a parameter option for bin size in a manner similar to the last example. By defining a smaller step size for each bin, more granular views of the profit bins can be seen. This is always desirable when viewing histograms. The view seen in Figure 6-12 shows the Profit Bin Parameter set to a smaller value.

The ability to vary bin sizes within histograms can be very useful. As you can see in Figure 6-12 labeling was also added to each bar providing an item count and the total profit or loss expressed in each bin.

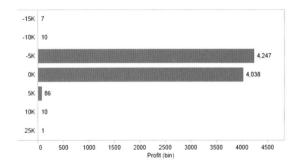

FIGURE 6-11 *A basic histogram*

Another type of basic parameter is built into charts for creating variable sized rank lists. Figure 6-13 shows a bar chart comparing sales values by customer with a year filter. Notice the Parameter Control provides a variable rank list size for the top customers.

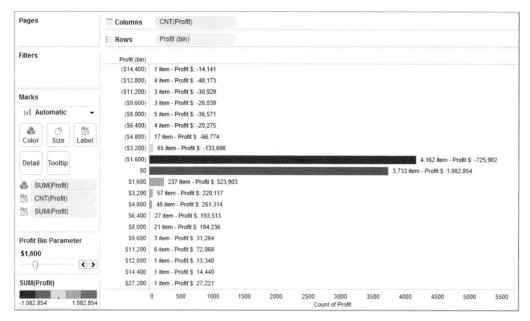

FIGURE 6-12 *Parameterize bins in a histogram*

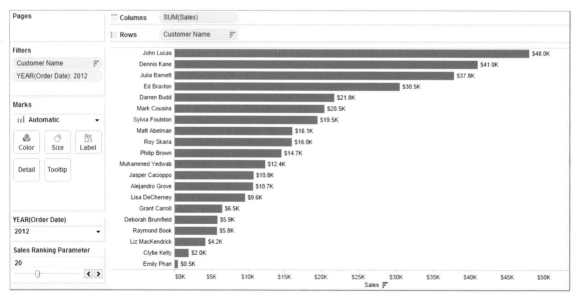

FIGURE 6-13 *A top rank parameter*

In this example the Parameter Control was invoked by right-clicking on the customer name pill on the row shelf, selecting the Top filter tab, and defining the parameter range value for the number of customers you want to display in the bar chart. Figure 6-14 shows the completed top 10 filter. This isn't the only way you can create a flexible rank list, but it is one of the easiest methods.

By placing the sales parameter into the normally static top rank definition dialog box, this creates a flexible rank list. This isn't the only way you can create a flexible rank list, but it is one of the easiest methods.

ADVANCED PARAMETER CONTROLS

More advanced parameter controls can be created that provide greater flexibility. The steps required to create advanced parameters are:

1. Create the parameter control.

2. Expose the parameter control on the desktop.

3. Create a calculated value using the parameter control.

4. Use that calculated value in the view.

Advanced parameters do require a little more effort, but they are easy to build once you become familiar with the process. One of the most common use cases for advanced parameter controls is to permit users to alter the measure being plotted in a view. Figure 6-15 shows a time series chart that is currently displaying sales over time, but with a parameter control that allows the end user to change the measure in view to profit, discount, order quantity, or shipping cost.

FIGURE 6-14 *Quick Filter with Sales Parameter*

The Parameter Control contains strings identifying each different measure. Selecting the Parameter Control's drop-down menu exposes each measure— allowing the user to change the time series chart. Also notice that view contains parameterized headings for both the report title and the axis label. Take a look at the step-by-step creation of the Parameter Control for this example.

Create the Parameter Control

You can create the parameter control from the calculation menu or directly from the Data Shelf by right-clicking within the Dimensions Shelf and selecting the Create Parameter menu option. This exposes the Parameter menu from which you can enter the options you see in Figure 6-16.

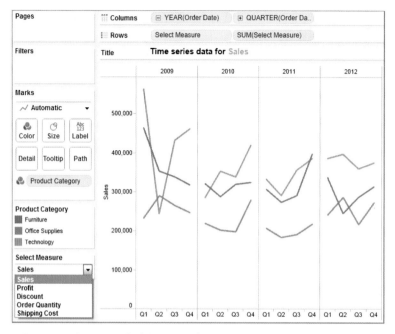

FIGURE 6-15   *A parameterized time series chart*

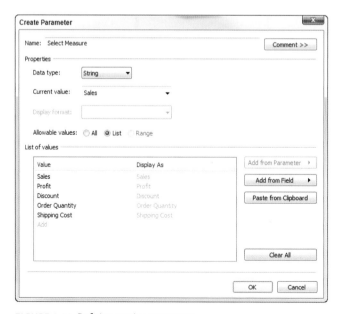

FIGURE 6-16   *Defining a string parameter*

Notice the parameter is named Select Measure, which is what appears in the parameter Quick Filter title. It may seem counter intuitive that the parameter definition is for a String type versus a number. A String is necessary to contain the field names of the measures that will be enabled in the view. This step only defines the filter box that is exposed on the desktop.

Exposing the Parameter Control

To make the Parameter Control available to information consumers it must be exposed to the worksheet. This is done by pointing at the parameter title that appears on the Parameters shelf, right-clicking, and selecting the menu option Show Parameter Control. After this step, the control is available on the desktop to make selections.

Create a Calculated Value Using the Parameter Control

Making a Calculated Value that uses the Parameter Control brings it to life. Figure 6-17 shows the completed Calculated Value.

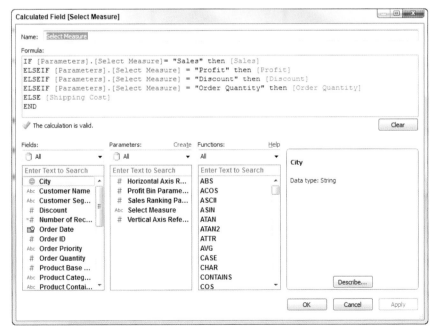

FIGURE 6-17 *Select measure calculated value*

The calculation uses an if/then/else logical statement to evaluate each string contained in the parameter and then associates the selected string with a specific measure field. With the completion of this Calculated Value only one step remains to activate the parameter within the view.

Use the Calculated Value in the View

 Placing the Select Measure calculated value on the row shelf activates the parameter. Figure 6-18 shows the completed view.

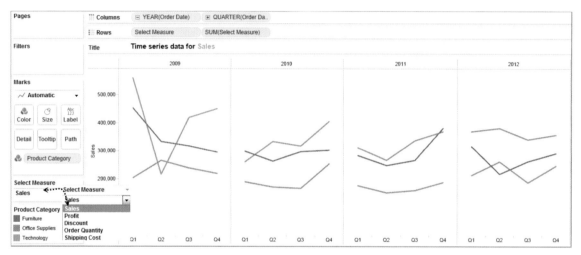

FIGURE 6-18 *A parameterized time series chart*

Adding the Select Measure value to the view connects the Parameter Control to the view and changes what is communicated to the datasource when a different measure is selected within the Parameter Control. The Select Measure filter now allows users to change the measure to any of the items added in the parameter and calculated value. Notice that the report title contains the parameter name. Also, the axis label is variable as well. Enabling these refinements requires a couple of extra steps. First, edit the report title and insert the parameter name into the title block. Then, drag the parameter from the parameter shelf to the axis and add the name variable there as well. By editing the axis label and removing the row heading you can achieve a clean look that flexibly names the report and the axis.

There are many other ways you can use Advanced Parameters but the basic process for all of them follows these four steps. As you gain familiarity with Tableau's calculation functions you will think of many different ways to leverage Advanced Parameter Controls.

EDITING VIEWS IN TABLEAU SERVER

Another way that Tableau enables ad hoc analysis is through a facility called Web Authoring in Tableau Server. This is a very powerful feature released in Tableau Version 8 that allows Tableau Server information consumers to alter and create visualizations from within Tableau Server without the need for anything other than a web browser and access rights to the view.

For this feature to be available the administrator must enable the permission for editing views. When this feature is available the user will find an Edit Menu option in their browser session window. Figure 6-19 shows a typical report window within Tableau Server.

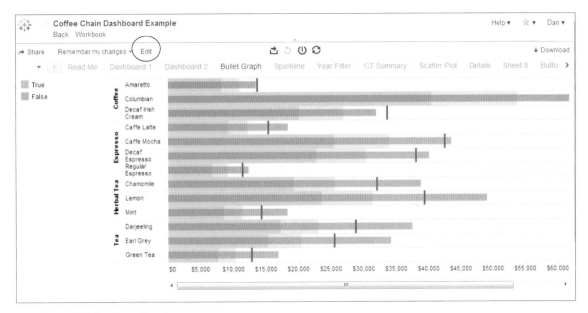

FIGURE 6-19 *Tableau Server bar chart*

Notice the Edit menu option in the upper left-side of the window. This menu option appears in Tableau Server if permissions are set to allow the user to edit views. Selecting the Edit view exposes the data shelf, marks cards, and the row and column shelves. Users can't do everything that a Desktop user can do, but within this specific workbook, they have the ability to edit existing views or create new worksheets and build new views. Figure 6-20 shows the controls that are exposed when editing is turned-on.

FIGURE 6-20 *Tableau Server editing mode*

You can see that a new menu bar appears at the top of Figure 6-20. These controls are optimized to work in the browser and will work when using a tablet computer to access the workbook as well. Full drag and drop capability exists—facilitating true ad hoc analysis for end users in a workbook that is based on data vetted and controlled though the Server administrator.

Tableau's ad hoc analysis capabilities should reduce the workload on the technical resources within your organization and reduce the amount of time required for managers to make new inquiries of your data.

In the next chapter you learn how to bring individual views together in dashboards and how to size, position, and layout dashboards. In addition, you will build interactive features into the dashboard that allow users to filter and highlight the visualization placed into the dashboard workspace.

NOTE

1. Mackenzie, Gordon. *Orbiting the Giant Hairball: A Corporate Fools Guide to Surviving with Grace.* New York: Viking, 1998. Print. Page 139.

CHAPTER 7

Tips, Tricks, and Timesavers

Mastering the basics of building visualizations and dashboards isn't difficult or time-consuming. Most people achieve very good results without having to spend a lot of time learning the nuances of data visualization or mastering more advanced techniques.

In this chapter you will learn timesaving tips for building new views, altering the default formats of fields and axis headers, creating new fields, and customizing the content and appearance of Tooltips. A trick for using legends to change the order in which data is presented in views will also be explained. After learning how to customize shapes, colors, and fonts—useful advanced chart types will be presented that demonstrate how to create more advanced chart types that aren't directly supported using the Show Me menu. The chapter will close by introducing some simple methods for creating subtle behavior in dashboards that will set the table for a more extensive treatment of dashboard-building in Chapter 8.

SAVING TIME AND IMPROVING FORMATTING

There are normally several ways to accomplish desired results in Tableau. Becoming faster at achieving the outcome takes a little practice. Knowing shortcuts that save seconds when you are creating an individual view can add up to hundreds of hours per year. If your team has many people using Tableau, the time-savings can be significant.

DOUBLE-CLICK FIELDS TO BUILD FASTER

Double-click any field to quickly create a view or add it to an existing view. If you are working with a file-based datasource (Excel or Access), you can utilize the measure names and measure values fields to quickly create an overview of an unfamiliar data set. Warning: do not use this technique if you are connecting to a very large database as it may overload your system. Start your analysis by double-clicking on the measure names field. This will result in every measure contained in the data window being displayed as a cross tab—providing a quick view of the facts contained in the data set. Add a time element to see value breakdowns. Figure 7-1 required only three mouse selections to generate.

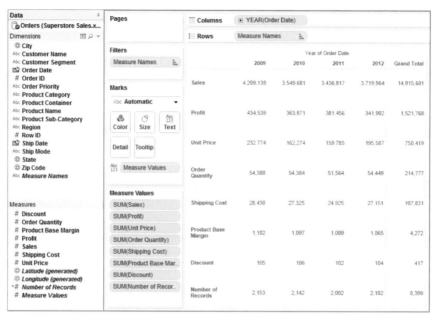

FIGURE 7-1 *Double-click to review the set.*

When you dive into a data set for the first time, knowing measure totals, the number of records in the set, and the breakdown over time helps you tie-out amounts in your views against source data batch totals. Figure 7-1 was created by:

1. Double-clicking Measure Names
2. Clicking the Swap icon
3. Double-clicking Order Date
4. Selecting menu option Analysis/Totals/Show Row Grand Totals

With a little practice you'll be able to create that type of view in under six seconds. When diving into a file-based data set for the first time, it's the fastest way to get some benchmark information.

REDUCE CLICKS USING THE RIGHT-MOUSE BUTTON DRAG

To save time when you want to display dates, numbers, or text, use the right mouse button when you drag fields into a view. Using this method to place the field pills opens a dialog box that gives you access to more presentation options and significantly reduces the number of mouse clicks required to customize the result. Figure 7-2 shows the three different dialog boxes that are provided.

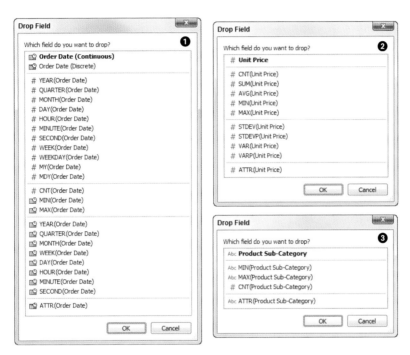

FIGURE 7-2 *Use right-click drag to expose options.*

Option one in Figure 7-2 is the dialog box presented when a date field is placed with a right-click drag. Option two is for measures, and option three is for a non-date dimension. In each case the right-click drag and drop provides direct access to all the available options for expressing time, measure aggregation, and different ways strings can be expressed.

QUICK COPY FIELDS WITH CONTROL-DRAG

Holding the control button down while dragging an active field causes a copy of that pill to be created wherever it's placed. This is particularly helpful if you want to build a table calculation using an active field, or if you want to use a measure or dimension that is expressed in the row or column shelf on the marks card as well.

REPLACE FIELDS BY DROPPING THE NEW FIELD ON TOP

Dropping any measure or dimension on top of a field already expressed in the view will result in that field being replaced with the new selection. This is particularly useful if you are exploring a data set for the first time and want to cycle through a variety of measures using the same view. After creating an initial view and then duplicating that chart, you can use this technique to quickly create a series of charts, each displaying a different measure.

Using Tooltips to drill into details exploring marks within a view generates questions when you find outliers. Figure 7-3 shows how you can use a Tooltip to expose the underlying source data.

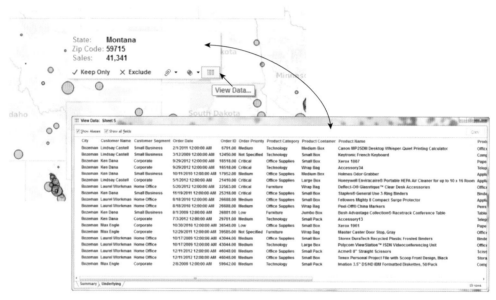

FIGURE 7-3 *Use the Tooltip to expose the data.*

The Tooltip contains a button on the far right that can be used to expose a summary of the mark's make-up, all of the details contained in the data set pertaining to that mark, or selected details. Rearrange columns within the exposed table by dragging them manually. You can also sort the rows by clicking-on any column to toggle between ascending or descending sorts of the data included in the column selected. If the Tooltip doesn't include the details you want to answer your question, this technique will provide access to all of the dimensions and measures available in the source data set.

RIGHT-CLICK TO EDIT OR FORMAT ANYTHING

If you don't like the appearance of any element contained in a view, a quick way to get to the appropriate formatting option menu is to point at the objectionable element, right-click, and select Format. A context-specific formatting menu will appear in place of the data shelf area on the left side of the workspace. Figure 7-4 shows how flexible formatting can be.

	2011					2012					All Years
	Q1	Q2	Q3	Q4	Total	Q1	Q2	Q3	Q4	Total	
Furniture	307,028	273,836	290,886	397,912	1,269,661	337,299	245,445	286,972	313,878	1,183,593	2,453,254
Office Supplies	207,363	183,631	191,405	217,950	800,349	241,281	286,548	217,198	272,870	1,017,897	1,818,246
Technology	333,002	291,116	356,243	386,445	1,366,807	386,387	397,201	359,656	375,229	1,518,474	2,885,281
Grand Total	847,393	748,583	838,533	1,002,307	3,436,817	964,967	929,194	863,826	961,976	3,719,964	7,156,781

FIGURE 7-4 *Right-click formatting*

Special formatting in Figure 7-4 has been applied to rows, columns, panes, totals, and subtotals. Year headers are in a green font. The headings for each quarter, the subtotal heading for each year, and the grand total heading for the column displaying the grand total for both years are colored blue. The "All Years" text was edited from the default "Grand Total" heading text. A custom red color was applied to the year total panes, and a custom black bold font was applied to the column totals at the bottom of the crosstab by applying a custom font to the pane and header of the grand total row. Finally, the red shades were applied to the row banding in the pane and in the header. While there is more than one way to apply these customizations, the easiest way is to point at the screen element, right-click, and Tableau will present the appropriate set of formatting controls on the left-side of the workspace.

EDITING OR REMOVING TITLES FROM AXIS HEADINGS

Sometimes it is desirable to edit axis titles or remove them entirely. This can be done by pointing at the axis (white space or header) and selecting the Edit Axis option. Figure 7-5 shows the menu that is displayed.

Not only does the Edit Axis menu allow you to edit or remove the axis title (without removing the axis header), you can also modify the title or erase the

FIGURE 7-5 *Edit axis menu*

title in the Titles box that you see in Figure 7-5. Later in this chapter you'll see how a range selection can be used to create a Sparkline chart.

SPEED UP YOUR PRESENTATION PAGE VIEWS

Making your presentations truly interactive by replacing static slide decks with interactive visualizations provides a powerful and flexible story. If your Tableau workbook has many different worksheets and dashboards, loading each new worksheet can cause delays as each worksheet or dashboard is materialized. Avoid delay by preloading your dashboard views.

Preloading the views is done by accessing the multiple worksheet view (the PowerPoint slide deck style view) from the tab in the upper right of the screen. Figure 7-6 shows all of the worksheets and dashboards contained within the workbook.

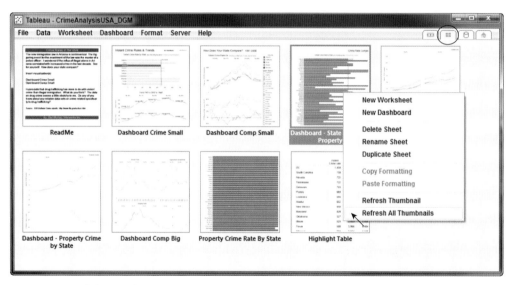

FIGURE 7-6 *Worksheet window*

Right-clicking in the worksheet window exposes a menu option—Refresh All Thumbnails—that triggers Tableau to query the datasource(s) used for all the worksheets and dashboards in the workbook. Now as you run through your presentation, each worksheet and dashboard will be preloaded and will materialize instantly.

You can also trigger a query of all of the datasources via the filmstrip view of worksheets as seen in Figure 7-7.

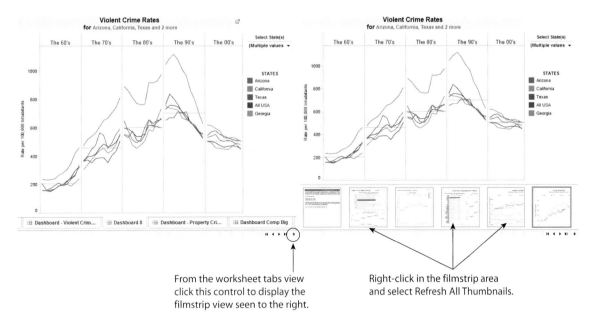

From the worksheet tabs view click this control to display the filmstrip view seen to the right.

Right-click in the filmstrip area and select Refresh All Thumbnails.

FIGURE 7-7 *Filmstrip view*

Turn on the filmstrip view by clicking on the small up and down Show Filmstrip option in the lower right of the worksheet. Trigger the worksheet by right-clicking within the filmstrip sheet area seen on the right-side of Figure 7-7.

A FASTER WAY TO ACCESS FIELD MENU OPTIONS

Hovering over a field pill that is placed anywhere in your worksheet will expose a drop-down arrow located on the right side of the pill. Clicking on the drop-down arrow exposes menu options related to the measure or dimension. Figure 7-8 shows the exposed menu.

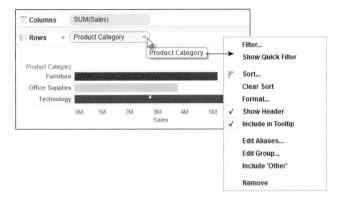

FIGURE 7-8 *Exposing a pill menu*

An easier way to expose the same menu is to point anywhere at the field pill and click the right mouse button. The same menu will be exposed in a way that requires less precise pointing.

IMPROVING APPEARANCE TO CONVEY MEANING MORE PRECISELY

Your dashboard and worksheet designs need to fit in the available space. For this reason, headings, instructions, and details related to your views—conveying the information, while using as little space as possible—is desirable. The techniques are space-efficient without compromising meaning.

CHANGING THE APPEARANCE OF DATES

Alter date formats that appear on an axis by pointing at the date header, right-clicking, and selecting the Format Menu option. This exposes many different date formats—including a custom formatting option as seen in Figure 7-9.

The specific date formatting available will vary depending on the type of date being expressed (continuous or discrete). Continuous dates provide more formatting options than discrete dates.

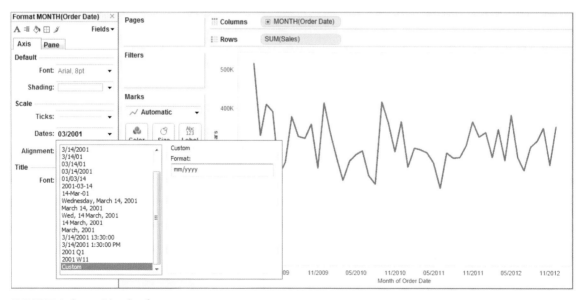

FIGURE 7-9 *Customizing date formats*

FORMATTING TOOLTIP CONTENT

Tooltips in worksheets and dashboards can be improved by adding fields that are not included in the view, formatting text font and color, and adding instructions. Edit your Tooltip from the main menu by selecting Worksheet/Tooltip. Figure 7-10 shows a modified Tootip that uses custom colors, custom font sizes, field name revisions, and explanatory text along with contact information.

FIGURE 7-10 *A customized Tooltip*

Note that any fields included on the marks cards can be added to the Tooltip. Tootips are a space-efficient way to add details on-demand to worksheets and dashboards.

CHANGE THE ORDER OF COLOR EXPRESSED IN CHARTS TO COMPARE RELATED VALUES MORE EASILY

When using colors to express members of dimensions, comparing different members in the set is easier if the item you want to focus on starts at the same point on the axis. Figure 7-11 shows a stacked bar chart that compares the sales mix percentage of product categories in different date aggregations (month, quarter, and year) by using a quick table calculation and color to express the relative sales for each product category.

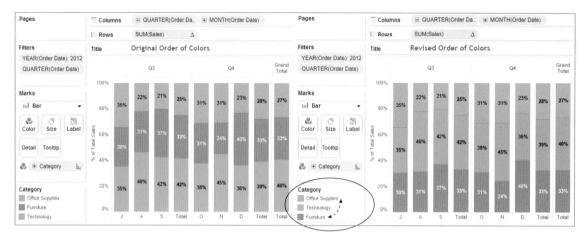

FIGURE 7-11 *Reordering the color legend*

Dragging the Furniture color to the bottom of the color legend as seen on the right of Figure 7-11 enables more precise comparison of the furniture product category.

EXPOSING A HEADER IN A ONE-COLUMN CROSSTAB TO ADD MEANING AND SAVE SPACE

Adding a small crosstab in a dashboard can provide an effective means for triggering a filter action. For this reason you may want to create a very basic crosstab as you see in Figure 7-12.

The chart was created using the Superstore data set. Building Figure 7-12 requires two steps:

1. Double-click on the Region field in the dimensions shelf.
2. Double-click on the Sales field in the measures shelf.

This is fast and easy, but what if you want to add a header directly over the sales values to create a well-labeled crosstab without having to add a worksheet title. Worksheet titles consume additional pixel height, which may take more vertical space than you have available.

At this point there is a row label over the region names in Figure 7-12, but no row header over the sales value. Tableau's default behavior doesn't provide a row label when only one measure is included in the view. To get a header to appear immediately above the sales values, double-click on any other field included on the measures shelf (except for the geocoding measures used for mapping) then point at the column heading of the second measure and right-click to hide the measure. Alternatively, right-click on the Measure Values pill (that automatically appeared on the Marks card when the second measure was added) and filter out the new measure so that the Sales field is the only measure remaining in view. The crosstab should now look like the one in Figure 7-13.

Figure 7-13 presents a very compact view of the sales by region with headers directly above the field values. This crosstab could be placed into a dashboard requiring the same amount of space as a multi-select filter, but providing a little additional data. Another way to build the same crosstab is to use Measure Names and Measure Values directly to build the view by following these steps:

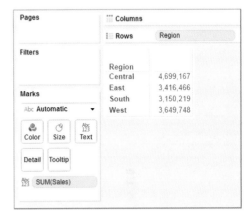

FIGURE 7-12 *One measure crosstab*

1. Double-click on the Region field on the dimensions shelf.

2. Double-click on the Measure Names field on the dimensions shelf.

3. Right-click on the Measure Values pill on the Marks card.

4. Filter-out all of the measures leaving only the Sales selected.

The key understanding in this example is Tableau will not provide a header over the measure when only one measure is in view. You will use a crosstab like this in a dashboard example that you will build in Chapter 8.

UNPACKING A PACKAGED WORKBOOK FILE (.TWBX)

Unpacking a Tableau Packaged Workbook (twbx) file allows you to view the original datasource. Unpacking is useful if your datasource is file-based (Excel/Access/CSV). To open this type of file, point at it then right-click and select the Unpackage option. Tableau will create a data folder that contains a copy of the file source.

FIGURE 7-13 *Crosstab with a sales column header added*

MAKE A PARAMETERIZED AXIS LABEL

Using parameters to alter the measure plotted in a view is an excellent way to make one chart serve many purposes. But, the default axis label isn't very informative as you see in Figure 7-14.

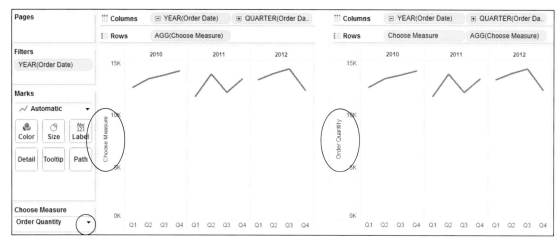

FIGURE 7-14 *Axis label default*

The time-series chart on the left of Figure 7-14 displays the default axis label for the parameter control Choose Measure. To enable a dynamic parameterized label for the axis, follow these steps:

1. Drag the parameter from the parameters shelf to the axis.

2. Drop the parameter on the axis.

3. Remove the default axis title by right-clicking on the axis.

4. Erase the default title in the titles area.

5. Right-click on the parameter heading and hide the field label.

6. Rotate the parameter label by right-clicking on it and selecting Rotate.

USING CONTINUOUS QUICK FILTERS FOR RANGES OF VALUES

When your worksheet or dashboard contains a continuous Quick Filter, many people don't realize you can restrict the range of values and then drag them from within the range to scroll. Figure 7-15 shows a bar chart that displays sales by customer and a Quick Filter using profit.

Restrict the range by dragging the bar handles in or by typing specific values in the filter values. You can see that the range has been restricted from 0 to 5,000. To scroll, point at the gray area in the filter bar and, while pressing your left mouse button, drag the range to the left or right to move through the entire set in $5,000 profit range increments.

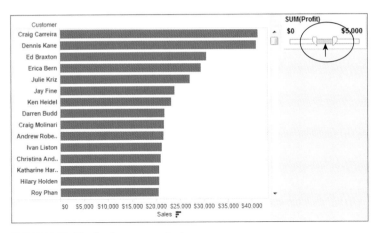

FIGURE 7-15   *Filtering for a range of values*

CREATE YOUR OWN CUSTOM DATE HIERARCHY

Tableau's automatic data hierarchies save a lot of time, but what if you don't want to display all of the hierarchy that Tableau provides? By creating custom dates you can combine them into hierarchies that meet your specific needs. Figure 7-16 shows a bar chart comparing sales values for specific dates.

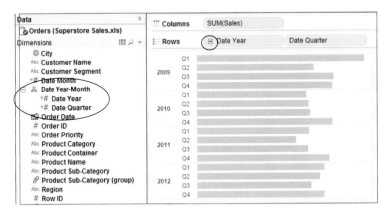

FIGURE 7-16   *Custom date hierarchy*

The custom hierarchy includes discrete year and quarter values and nothing more. Notice that the Date Year pill can be expanded by clicking the plus sign, but the grouping of the custom "Date Year" and "Date Quarter" overrides the normal date hierarchy structure within Tableau.

To create custom date hierarchies follow these steps:

1. Point at a date field in the dimensions shelf and right-click.

2. Select the Create Custom Date option.

3. Edit the date as you require.

4. Drag one date field on top of another to create the custom hierarchy.

5. Use the custom hierarchy in your view.

Figure 7-17 shows the custom date dialog box being accessed from the menu.

Complete the date by giving it a specific name. Use the Detail drop-down selector to pick the exact date granularity you desire. The radio buttons below that define whether the date is a discrete date (date part) or a continuous date (date value).

After the custom dates are defined, drag one on top of another in the dimensions window to create your custom date hierarchy. You can right-click and edit the name of the hierarchy as desired. This technique is particularly useful in dashboards when you might need to limit the expansion of the hierarchy so that the chart fits into the available space nicely.

FIGURE 7-17 *Creating a custom date*

ASSEMBLE YOUR OWN CUSTOM FIELDS

This is a favorite easy formula hack for creating key records on the fly if your datasource doesn't really include a truly unique key record. To create a new field that is the combination of two or more fields, use the Formula Editor. Figure 7-18 shows a concatenation formula.

Using the + sign between each field creates a concatenated (joined together) field that will be available in the dimensions shelf. This is also useful when you want to assemble addresses from discrete fields to create mailing lists. In Figure 7-18 the formula also inserts a literal string including a comma and a space between the Customer Name and City fields. If you experience performance degradation using this technique, try combining sets. Refer to the set section in Chapter 3 for more details.

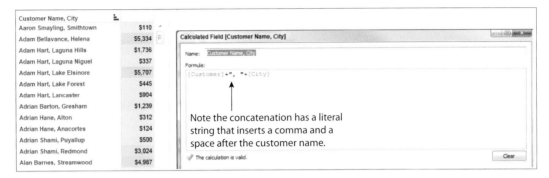

FIGURE 7-18 *Concatenating fields*

LET TABLEAU BUILD YOUR ACTIONS

Color or shape legends can be used to create highlight actions. Activate a color action by selecting the highlighting tool in the legend as you see in Figure 7-19 and then click on any color.

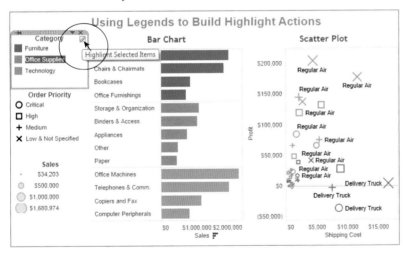

FIGURE 7-19 *Creating a highlight action from a color legend*

Similarly, the shape legend in Figure 7-19 can be used to create another highlight action. The resulting action in the dashboard will use the combination of color and shape when selecting marks from a scatter plot as you see in Figure 7-20.

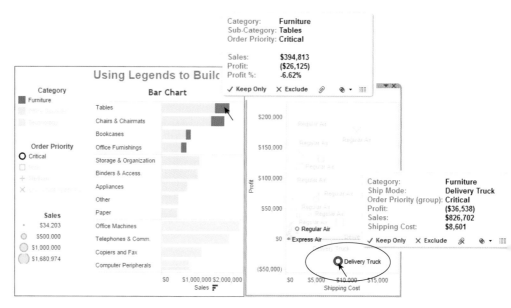

FIGURE 7-20 *Highlighting using actions generated by the color and shape legends*

Selecting a blue circle in the scatter plot triggers the highlight action—changing appearance of the scatter plot and bar chart. The combination of Order Priority (shape) and Product Category (color) are highlighted. Tooltips for both items have been displayed together in Figure 7-20 to expose the details for you to review. Tableau normally displays only one Tooltip at a time.

You can view the actions definitions by going to the Dashboard menu/Actions, then selecting edit. Figure 7-21 displays the menu details.

FORMATTING TABLE CALCULATION RESULTS

Table Calculations use your visualization to create new values. If the calculation defined results in a null value, Tableau provides a variety of formatting options that allow you to control exactly how the null results are presented in the resulting chart. Figure 7-22 shows an initial table calculation result and the five options provided to format the results.

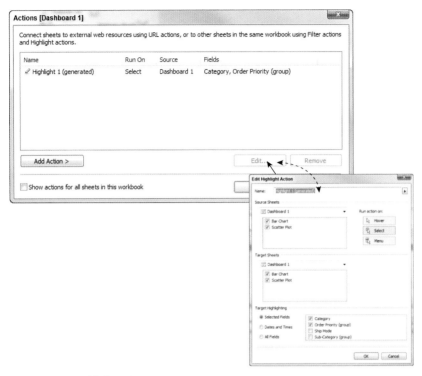

FIGURE 7-21 *Highlight action menu*

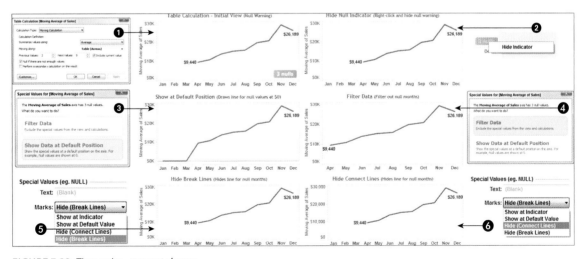

FIGURE 7-22 *Time series—percent change*

The dialog box displayed in Figure 7-22 area (1) shows the quick table calculation definition for a 3-month moving average. Note that the indicator in the dialog box (null if there are not enough values) is checked. Selecting this tells Tableau not to plot marks if there is insufficient data to correctly calculate the result. This means that no mark will be plotted if any month included in the time series does not have data for the three preceding months.

The result in the upper left section of the dashboard shows that a time series chart has been plotted with a small gray pill in the lower right corner indicating that three null values are included in the resulting plot. Notice that there are no marks for the January through March time period. This is because the data set did not include data for the preceding October through December time period.

One way to deal with the null warning is displayed in Figure 7-22 area (1). Right-clicking on the 3 nulls pill exposes the control seen in Figure 7-22 area (2), which exposes the Hide Indicator option. Selecting this option merely removes the null warning pill from view without defining how additional null values should be treated. If your source data is being updated regularly, this selection hides the null indicator without providing any additional formatting rules for Tableau to use if new null values appear in the data.

If the (3 nulls) pill is selected using the left mouse button, the dialog box seen in Figure 7-22 areas (3 and 4) is displayed. Showing the data at the default position causes Tableau to draw the line for the months with null values at zero. If the Filter Data option (4) is selected, Tableau will filter the null value months from view. Notice the axis for Figure 7-22 area (4) starts in April. This option might be misleading if the source data includes gaps in the middle of the time series. For this reason, Tableau provides two additional options to format null values.

The bottom charts in the dashboard of Figure 7-22 (areas 5 and 6) look similar to the chart in area (2) only because the null values in this example occur in the first three months of the time series. If the null values had occurred in the middle of the time series, these options provide slightly different treatments of the data breaks in the plot. To access the Special Values (e.g., Null) formatting dialog box, right click on the field pill that you are using to express the table calculation and select Format. This exposes the formatting menu for the pane as seen in Figure 7-22 areas 5 and 6.

Table calculations offer many options for deriving new information from your source data. Tableau's formatting options for null value provide for nuanced treatment of missing values so that information consumers are not mislead by gaps in your source data.

The key to understanding Quick Table Calculations and Table Calculation Functions is to grasp that the visualization you've created provides the source data for the result. If your visualization has missing values, then your result will include missing values.

WHEN TO USE FLOATING OBJECTS IN DASHBOARDS

Tableau supports the use of floating objects and this can be a great way to add information to your dashboards efficiently. This facility should be used with care.

Think about how the underlying visualization can change and ensure that the floating object doesn't obscure the data contained in the view. Figure 7-23 is an example of a potentially sub-optimal use of floating objects.

The floating year filter and color legend in Figure 7-23 are space-efficient, but could potentially obscure the data. Floating objects in this chart are not a good choice unless you can be certain that the products in the top third of the view won't extend into the floating controls. Figure 7-24 shows a better use case for floating objects.

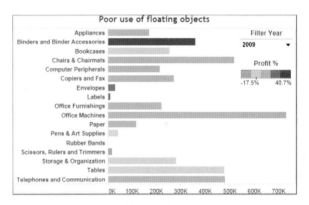

FIGURE 7-23   *A bad use of floating objects*

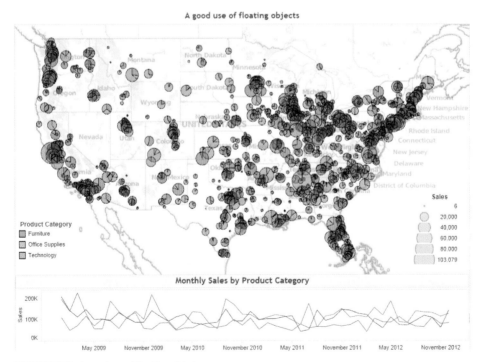

FIGURE 7-24   *A good use of floating objects*

Presuming that sales occur only in the lower forty-eight states, the floating objects in Figure 7-24 take advantage of the white spaces contained in the map to display color and size legends as well as a time series chart. A filter action could be added to the map and the time series to filter the view for selections made by the user—creating a more compact view than would otherwise be possible with the use of non-floating controls and Quick Filters.

CUSTOMIZING SHAPES, COLORS, FONTS, AND IMAGES

Tableau comes with a wide variety of pre-defined shapes, colors, and fonts, but you can style these objects to meet your specific needs.

CUSTOMIZING SHAPES

There is nothing wrong with using the default shapes as you see in Figure 7-25.

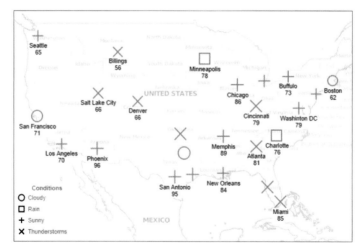

FIGURE 7-25 *Map with standard shapes*

Customizing the shape used to plot weather conditions does provide more immediate understanding. Figure 7-26 shows the same map, but with weather images to depict weather conditions.

The use of customized images in Figure 7-26 conveys weather conditions more intuitively. This example was created using one of the available standard shapes provided in Tableau's shape pallet. Editing shapes is done by accessing the Shape menu from the Shape legend you see in Figure 7-27.

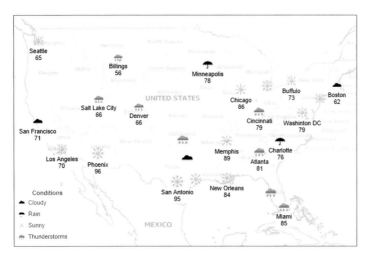

FIGURE 7-26 *Map with weather images*

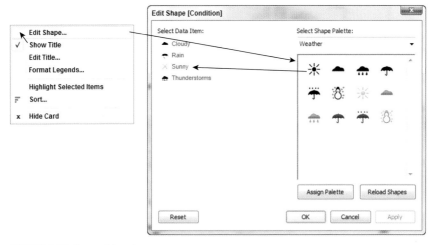

FIGURE 7-27 *Customizing shapes*

If Tableau's standard shape legend or pallets don't fit your requirements, import custom shape files (png, jpeg, bmp, gif) and make them available to use in your views by following these steps:

1. Create a folder to hold the image files under My Tableau Repository.

2. Give the folder a one or two word name (Tableau uses This Name).

3. Create a view that uses shapes.

4. Edit the standard shape by selecting the imported custom shape.

The best results are achieved using images that are sized at (32 × 32) pixels.

CUSTOMIZING COLORS

Creating customized colors for individual marks can be done easily using the color button in the marks tab. Make a custom color by clicking the color button and selecting the More Colors option. This exposes the window seen in Figure 7-28.

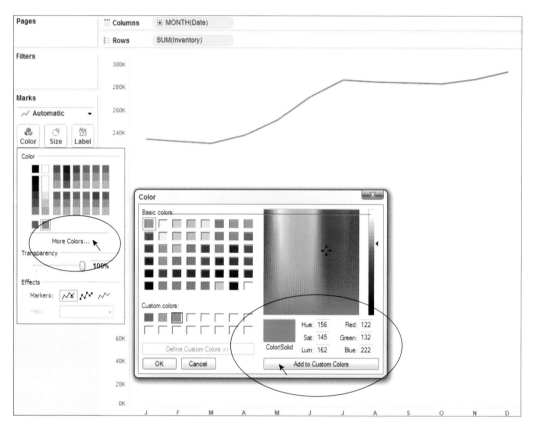

FIGURE 7-28 *Customize an individual color.*

You can scroll through color options using the color pane in the view or type in specific values. When the color is defined, click on the Add To Custom Colors option to make the color available for use.

It's also possible to create completely customized color pallets. Tableau took great care to create color pallets that effectively communicate. They considered factors like color blindness—providing gray scale and a specific color-blind-friendly pallet. If you have a specific need that the available color pallets don't fulfill, try mixing colors from different standard pallets. If you do have a very specific need (perhaps matching a logo color scheme), creating a completely customized pallet is possible, but you have to modify Tableau's preferences file located in: `\My Documents\My Tableau Repository\Preferences.tps`.

Search Tableau's website for a knowledge-based article called Creating Custom Color Palettes for specific details. You'll need to use a text editor (like Windows Notepad) to add the custom pallet by adding XML script that defines the palette name (as you want it to appear), then define the color values.

CUSTOMIZING FONTS

Tableau provides a wide range of fonts. You can customize the font style, size, color, boldness, and underlining for every element of text contained in headings, axis labels, mark labels, and Tooltips. In most cases the standard font selections work fine. Changing the font style of dynamic title elements is a very common use and helps people notice that values in dashboards change when selections are made. Figure 7-29 shows a dashboard with dynamic date headings.

FIGURE 7-29 *Customized title headings*

In this dashboard, the Year Filter in the left section of the title filters both charts contained in the dashboard for year. You can see that 2012 is selected and the title for each chart reflects that year's selections. In addition, the time series chart is filtered via an action from the product crosstab. Styling headings with dynamic elements is done by double-clicking on the title, inserting the variable, and then changing the font, color, or boldness of that element as seen in Figure 7-30.

Coloring the dynamic title elements black and the static title contents gray provides visual confirmation to the information consumer that the view is filtered for the desired selections.

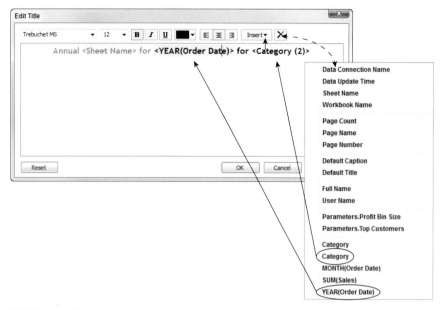

FIGURE 7-30 *Customizing a dynamic title element*

CUSTOMIZING IMAGES IN DASHBOARDS

The most typical use for an image in a dashboard is to add a company logo. By using the image object, logos can be placed and sized to fit in the title space. There are a couple of tricks you should be aware of that will help you fit images precisely. The InterWorks logo is a standard JPEG file. After placing the image object into the dashboard at the desired location, select the Pick Image option by pointing to the upper-right corner of the object to expose the menu you see in Figure 7-31.

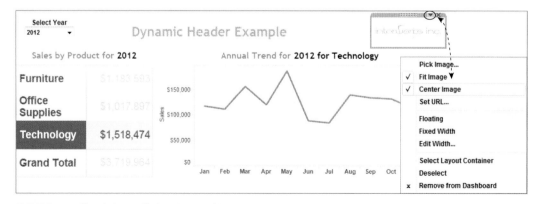

FIGURE 7-31 *Place in image file in an image object.*

After selecting the image, click on the Fit Image and Center Image options. These force the image file to resize automatically if you alter the image object size.

ADVANCED CHART TYPES

Tableau provides a complete range of chart styles. You really don't even have to understand why a particular chart is better. If you rely on the Show Me button, Tableau will provide an appropriate chart based on the combination of measures and dimensions you've selected.

There are some useful variations to the default chart types that require a little more knowledge to create. Knowing what default settings to modify makes all the difference. In this section you'll review six of the most commonly used non-standard chart types.

BAR-IN-BAR CHART

The bar-in-bar chart you see in Figure 7-32 provides another way to compare values.

In this example, color and size denote actual and budgeted sales. The height of each bar expresses the values of each measure for a particular region. The key to building this chart is to understand how to use color and size while altering Tableau's default bar-stacking behavior. To build this example using the coffee chain sample data set, follow these steps:

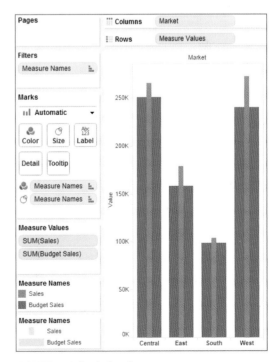

1. Multi-select Market, Budget Sales, Sales.

2. Using Show Me, select the Side-by-Side Bar Chart.

3. Move the Measure Names field pill from the column shelf to the size button in the Marks Card.

4. If you prefer budgeted sales to be the wider bar, drag the SUM (Budget Sales) below the SUM (Sales) pill in the Measure Values card. Alternatively, reorder the Measure Names color legend to accomplish the same thing.

5. Go to the main menu analysis/stack mark and select Off.

The bar-in-bar chart has more limited use than a bullet graph that we will cover at the end of the chapter, but this chart type also packs a dense amount of information into a small space. It is particularly useful when

FIGURE 7-32 *Bar-in-bar chart*

you want to compare a small number of measures across a larger number of dimensions.

BOX PLOTS

Box plots offer a way to show very granular distribution of a measure across multiple members of a dimensions set. Student test scores, website click-stream data, or per unit pricing are different analyses that might benefit from box plots. The box plot example in Figure 7-33 uses a sampling of website clickstream data for the past year. This data set was obtained using the Google Analytics connector provided with Tableau Software. In this analysis you see how to create a box plot of the "Time on Page" measure. This data is not part of the Tableau sample data sets. If you want to download a copy of the raw data file and solution, see Appendix C: "InterWorks Book Website" or the Wiley companion website for the download site URL.

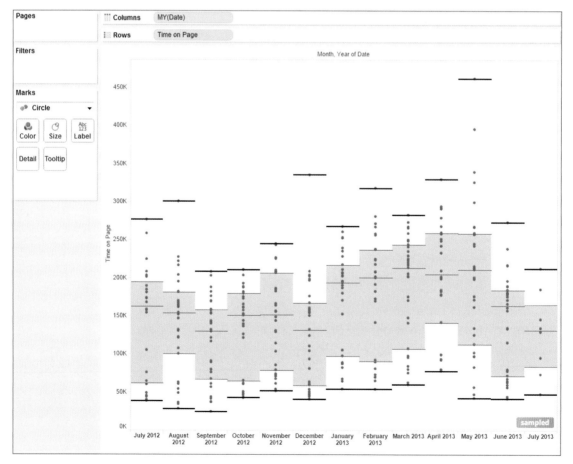

FIGURE 7-33 *Box plot of web page activity*

Each mark denotes average time that was spent on the website for a sampling of visitors. The thick black lines define the maximum and minimum time on site using a band-type reference distribution line. The thin red lines were plotted using a quartile reference distribution. For that type of distribution the middle red line represents the median value of the time on site for the month.

Generating the granular detail for the box plot requires that the source data be fully disaggregated so that every value is expressed by a mark in the chart. Expose all of the rows in the data set using the Analysis menu, then remove the check mark from the Aggregate Measures option. This will cause every row in the data set to be plotted in the view.

The specific steps used to create the box plot in Figure 7-33 are:

1. Place the date on the column shelf and select the month and year aggregation.

2. Place the Time on Page measure on the row shelf.

3. Disaggregate the measures using Analysis/Disaggregate Measures.

4. The mark size was then reduced using the slider control accessed by clicking on the size button on the marks card.

5. Define the Minimum/Maximum reference band by right-clicking on the left axis and selecting the Add Reference Line option. This exposes the dialog box you see in Figure 7-34.

6. Define the Quartile reference distribution that provides the box shading along with the median value reference line as well as the upper and lower quartile lines. View that dialog box in Figure 7-35.

Pay careful attention to the scope (cell) and the label settings (none). Test your definition by using the apply button first to visually confirm that the settings are correctly defined. When you're satisfied with the setting, lock them in by clicking the OK button.

FIGURE 7-34 *Define the Minimum/Maximum reference band.*

FIGURE 7-35 *Define the Quartile reference distribution.*

To complete the Quartile reference distribution note the formatting that uses a gray fill, red line, and the Symmetric color shading. Symmetric coloring provides consistent coloring of the quartile bands.

If you are building the box plot from the example data set, your chart should now look like Figure 7-33. Box plots combine fully-disaggregated data with the intelligent use of Tableau's reference line capabilities to provide insight into the trend in activity across dimensions. In the example, the time dimension was used to compare web activity over a twelve month period. The extremely high Time on Site in May 2013 might warrant additional digging into a more granular extract of the website activity in that month.

PARETO CHARTS

Known as the 80-20 Rule, the Pareto Principle was developed by Vilfredo Pareto in 1906 to describe the unequal distribution of wealth in his country.

In general, the (80-20) principle states that 20 percent of the inputs account for 80 percent of the outputs. For example, 80 percent of profits come from 20% of the products. Figure 7-36 shows a Pareto chart that displays profit by product. The following example was built using the Superstore Sales sample data set. You will learn how to create a Pareto chart that plots the cumulative profit generated by each distinct product that Superstore sells.

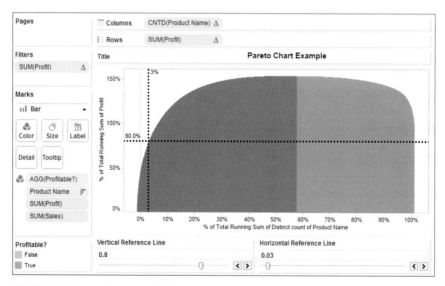

FIGURE 7-36 *Pareto chart—profit by item*

The vertical axis plots the cumulative profits expressed as a percentage of the total profits generated by the business. The horizontal axis plots the contribution of each individual product (item). Color encoding is being used to display positive and negative profit items as discreet groups. Parameterized reference lines are included, which allow the information consumer to move the lines on both the horizontal and vertical axes. In this way the user can determine how closely the sample conforms to the Pareto Principle. In the case of Figure 7-36 you can see that the sample data set has 80 percent of product profits being generated from a mere 3 percent of products. This is a much greater concentration than would normally be expected.

The trick to building this chart type is to understand how table calculations can be used to express the axis values as percentages of the total values. The following steps required to build this chart are:

FIGURE 7-37 *Vertical axis two-stage table calculation*

1. Drag the Product Name dimension to the Columns shelf.

2. Drag the Profit measure to the Rows shelf.

3. Sort the product name by descending profit (highest profit to lowest profit item).

4. Change the view from Normal to Entire View using the control on the menu icon bar. Then make the SUM(Profit) field on the Row Shelf into a Table Calculation by right-clicking on the field fill and creating a Running total table calculation.

5. Create a 2-stage table calculation by right-clicking on the field pill created in step 4 and editing Quick Table calculation as you see in Figure 7-37.

6. Perform a data extract on the Superstore Sales connection by right-clicking on the connection in the Data Shelf, and selecting Extract Data/Extract.

7. Drag the Product Name field from the dimensions shelf to the Marks card.

8. Edit the Product Name field just placed in step 7 by right-clicking on the field pill and selecting Measure/Count Distinct.

9. Add a 2-stage Table calculation to the field editing in step 8 by right-clicking on the pill and Add Table Calculation.

10. Edit the Table Calculation you create in step 9 to look like Figure 7-38.

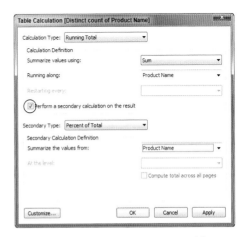

FIGURE 7-38 *Horizontal axis two-stage table calculation*

11. Drag the new Table Calculation created in step 10 to the column shelf and place it to the right of the Product Name pill. Then drag the Product Name field Pill from the Columns shelf to the marks card. Your chart will momentarily look broken. Don't worry it isn't.

12. Change the mark type in view on the Marks card from Automatic to Bar.

13. Create a calculated value called (Profitable?) to determine if profits are greater than zero using this formula: `SUM(Profit)>0`.

14. Place the (Profitable?) calculated value on the color button located on the marks card.

15. Add parameterized reference lines on each axis that allow the information consumer to change the location of the reference line from zero to 100 percent in .01 increments. Refer to Figure 7-39 to view the setting used to create the vertical reference line. The horizontal reference requires a second definition that should be initiated from the horizontal axis.

16. Edit the color scheme to match the gray/orange colors that indicate profitablity.

Once the parameterized reference lines are completed, the only remaining work is repositioning the screen elements to your task. The parameter controls in Figure 7-36 are positioned below the Pareto Chart to better utilize the worksheet by reducing the amount of unused white space.

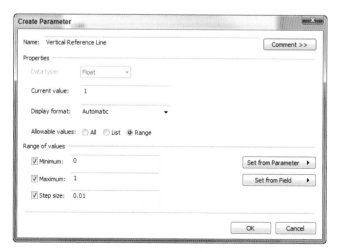

FIGURE 7-39 *Parameterized reference lines*

Don't be discouraged if it takes a few tries for you to get this chart type comfortably mastered. There are several ways you could build the chart. You may find another way to create the same effect.

The last two visualizations that you learn about in this chart are closely related to the next chapter on Dashboards. Sparklines and Bullet Graphs work well in dashboards because together they convey a lot of information even when space is restricted.

SPARKLINES

Edward Tufte conceived sparklines in his wonderful book, *Beautiful Evidence*. Graphics Press, 2006. He referred to them as "intense, simple, word-sized graphics." Sparklines can provide very effective time series charts in dashboards. When pixel height and width are constrained, you'll find that sparklines can convey a good deal of information in much less space than Tableau's default time series charts. Build sparklines using the following steps:

1. Create a standard time series chart.

2. Edit the axis and make each axis range independent.

3. Remove the axis headings.

4. Drag the right edge of the chart to the left.

5. Drag the chart bottom up.

6. Reduce the mark size from the Marks card.

7. If necessary, emphasize change using a table calculation.

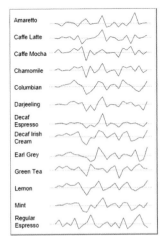

Figure 7-40 shows a sparkline made using the coffee chain sample database.

In this example it was necessary to use a Percent Change table calculation to emphasize the change in sales month over month. Why? The data was boring and contained very minimal dollar changes, resulting in the Dead Man EKG effect, or flat-lines on every row of the time series when the view was compressed. A nice feature of employing a table calculation for percent change is that a very light gray dotted line appears in each chart denoting the zero change level. In addition, some of the normal formatting elements have been removed from the view–axis titles, row and column headings, and the lines separating each product cell have been de-emphasized with a very light gray color.

You will build a Sparkline in combination with a Bullet Graph as part of an exercise in the next chapter on dashboard technique.

FIGURE 7-40 *Sales sparkline*

BULLET GRAPHS

Bullet graphs were developed by Stephen Few as another means for efficiently comparing metrics in a limited space. Basically, bullet graphs are bar charts (comparing one-to-many relationships) with the addition of comparative reference lines and reference distributions. Bullet graphs, in combination with sparklines, are an excellent combination in dashboards because they are space efficient and insightful. Look closely at the bullet graph in Figure 7-41.

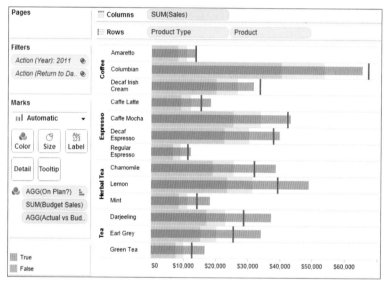

FIGURE 7-41 *Bullet Graph*

The bars in the bullet graph have been color-encoded to reflect the result of a Boolean (true/false) calculation that evaluates Actual versus Planned Sales. Products that are encoded in blue are below plan. The cell-level reference lines in red reflect the budgeted sales value. The gray encoding of the reference distribution behind the bars reflects levels of performance versus the budget as well (60 percent, 80 percent of budget). Also notice that the color of the actual sales bars has been faded to 6 percent using the Color button on the color shelf. So, this bullet graph was built using Show Me but includes several appearance tweaks to enhance understanding. The steps required to build the example in Figure 7-41 included:

1. Open the coffee chain sample database.
2. Multi-select Sales, Budget Sales, Product Type, and Product.
3. Click the Show Me button.

4. Check that the bars use Actual Sales.

5. Check that the reference line uses Budget Sales.

6. Items 4 and 5 will be wrong. Right-click on the bottom axis and choose the Swap Reference Line Fields.

7. Create a Boolean calculation `sum([Sales]) < sum([Budget Sales])`.

8. Drop the Boolean calculation result on the Color button.

9. Style the reference line to taste.

10. Style the reference distribution color scheme to taste.

The bars in bullet graphs should reflect the Actual Value. The reference line should reflect the Comparative Value (budget, prior year, etc.). Tableau doesn't try to determine the actual versus target value when the graph is created automatically using the Show Me button. You may have to use the Swap Reference Line Fields option that is accessed by right-clicking within the white space of the bottom axis. This swaps the pill placed in the Column shelf and the Marks card. It should make sense by now that the pill being expressed in the Column (or Row shelf) is plotted using the bar. The pill contained in the Marks card is used to create the reference line.

The combination of sparklines and bullet graphs in dashboards provides a very space efficient way to display one to many relationships, performance to plan, and performance versus prior years (if you add reference lines for that). The sparkline provides a very dense information-packed display of performance over time. Figure 7-42 shows them aligned in a dashboard.

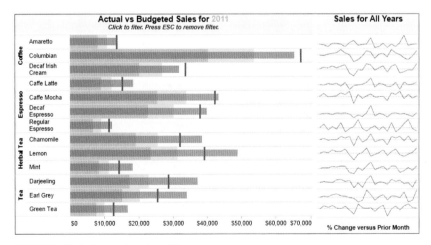

FIGURE 7-42 *Bullet graph and sparkline*

In the next chapter you will learn about best practices for dashboard design—using a Bullet Graph and Sparkline along with three other visualizations to create a compact, information-rich dashboard design.

CHAPTER 8

Bringing It All Together with Dashboards

Storytelling is the creative demonstration of truth. A story is the living proof of an idea, the conversion of idea to action.

ROBERT MCKEE[1]

An essential element of Tableau's value is delivered through dashboards. Allowing the audience to interact with a dashboard and change the details being displayed provides a means to shift context—leading to new and potentially important discoveries. Assembling dashboards in Tableau is fun for the designer, and good dashboard design can delight information consumers.

HOW DASHBOARD FACILITATES ANALYSIS AND UNDERSTANDING

When reviewing reports or creating new analytical reviews of data—you are looking for a story—something of value that you can share with others to enable change for the better. Dashboards fortify this storytelling by providing complementary views of the data and turning the data into actionable information that is supported by facts.

Well-designed dashboards are also visually interesting and draw the user in to play with the information, providing details-on-demand that enable the information consumer to understand what, who, when, where, how, and perhaps even why something has changed.

HOW TABLEAU IMPROVES THE DASHBOARD BUILDING PROCESS

Only three things really matter when it comes to business information—speed, accuracy, and the ability to make a new inquiry. Tableau delivers on all three. Tableau's ability to directly connect to a variety of datasources and render the data using the appropriate visualizations provides three distinct advantages over traditional data analysis tools:

- Reduced dashboard development time
- Reduced technical resource involvement
- Better visual analytics

Tableau reduces the need for technical staff in the dashboard development process by providing a user-friendly environment that doesn't require knowledge of database schema, SQL-scripting, or programming. Creating dashboards with Tableau is primarily a drag and drop operation. When individual chart panes are placed into the dashboard workspace, filtering and highlighting between panes is also accomplished with point and click efficiency.

Publishing your dashboard for consumption on personal computers, tablets, or the Internet requires no technical programming skills either. After learning a few basic principles, you will be creating compelling visual analytics in dashboards more quickly than was ever possible with older tools. Something magical happens the first time people use Tableau and gain a new insight. They begin to understand the potential unlocked when the tool disappears and the information becomes the center of attention.

In this chapter you'll learn field-tested techniques that will help you to build dashboards that effectively communicate to your audience by covering:

- Recommended best practices for building dashboards with Tableau
- The mechanics of the dashboard shelves and design objects
- Using actions to filter, highlight, and embed web pages
- Publishing dashboards via the desktop and Tableau Server
- Performance turning dashboards for fast load and query times

You will learn these techniques by building a dashboard that adheres to best practices using sample data included with your Tableau Desktop software. But, before building this example lets discuss the wrong and right ways to build a dashboard using Tableau.

THE WRONG WAY TO BUILD A DASHBOARD

Traditional providers of reporting tools have been companies that have a core competency in data collection and storage. These entities attract people that are very knowledgeable in the technical aspects of database building, data quality, and data storage, but not data presentation.

Traditional buyers of business information systems tend to be people from finance and accounting. The information technology group is normally involved because they possess the technical knowledge of database design, data collection, and data governance. Plus, IT is usually responsible for installing and maintaining the system.

Neither group possesses knowledge of the best practices related to data visualization. Their knowledge of charting typically comes from the commonly available spreadsheet programs, which often provide a lot of unnecessary and inappropriate chart styles. Historically older business information (BI) tools that information technology staffs are familiar with for report building have been more adept at data creation and storage—not information visualization.

Good report builders from both of these groups develop time-saving techniques that work well for creating dashboards in old-style tools. Unfortunately those techniques are more concerned with the technical challenges of building the report not the aesthetic qualities of the user experience.

Why would an experienced designer use overly complex graphics? One reason this happens is because dashboards created with legacy tools are more difficult to build—requiring more time and effort to produce. Often with legacy tools it makes sense to place as much information as possible into a single view to save time. This practice can lead to visualizations that are complex and difficult for end users to understand. Also, internal customers ask for what is familiar (grids of numbers) so that is what they receive. Unfortunately, these techniques are exactly the wrong way to build dashboards in Tableau.

Relying on grids or overly complex individual charts generally accomplishes two undesirable outcomes in Tableau. First, the dashboard doesn't communicate effectively. Second, it doesn't load as quickly as it should.

For example, a sales report displaying 12 months of history for twenty products, $12 \times 20 = 240$ data points, does not help the information consumer see the trends and outliers as easily as a time-series chart of the same information. Also, the quality of the data won't matter if your dashboard takes five minutes to load. Dashboard viewing is an activity that resembles browsing a website. Web browsing isn't very useful if you have a slow connection. Viewing a dashboard isn't either if it takes a long time to load or if the interactivity is slow.

The dashboard shown in Figure 8-1 displays some common pitfalls—overly dense and complicated charts and inappropriate chart types. Note the pie chart for comparing sales by product sub-category. The stacked bar chart uses a different (conflicting) color legend to display sales by region. The pie chart has too many slices, and performing precise comparisons of each product sub-category is difficult. The cross-tab at the bottom requires that the user scroll to see all the data.

The dashboard fails to convey important information quickly. Presenting the data this way can also lead to performance problems if there are a large number of rows being displayed in the product cross-tab.

Fixing these problems is normally not difficult. Tableau is designed to supply the appropriate graphics by default. Understanding why a dashboard loads slowly and how to ensure good speed requires only a basic understanding of how Tableau renders the information. We will dive into those details at the end of this chapter.

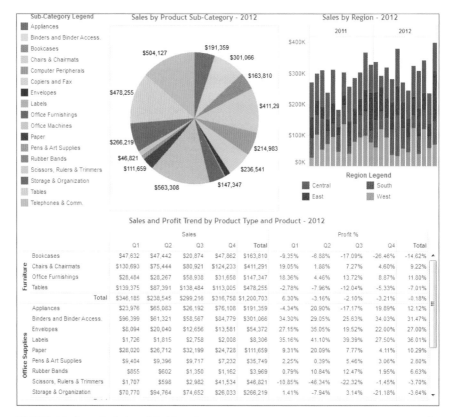

FIGURE 8-1 *A poorly-designed dashboard*

THE RIGHT WAY TO BUILD A DASHBOARD

How can you improve the previous dashboard and ensure that it loads quickly? Can the cross-tab be eliminated in order to reveal what is important in this data? A more effective dashboard conveys the information with less noise and provides details on demand.

The dashboard shown in Figure 8-2 uses a bar chart to provide a more precise comparison of sales by product sub-category (color-encoded bars). The time series combination line and bar chart at the bottom provides sales by month (bars—color encoded gray and black for a 5 percent profit threshold) and year-to-date sales by product category (color-encoded lines matching the bar colors in the bar chart above). The small cross-tab in the upper right corner of the dashboard provides summary information by region. The use of gray-scale to depict a profit ratio threshold in the time series combination line and bar chart provides additional insight into overall profitability. Darker gray is used to highlight product categories and months in which the profit ratio is under 5 percent.

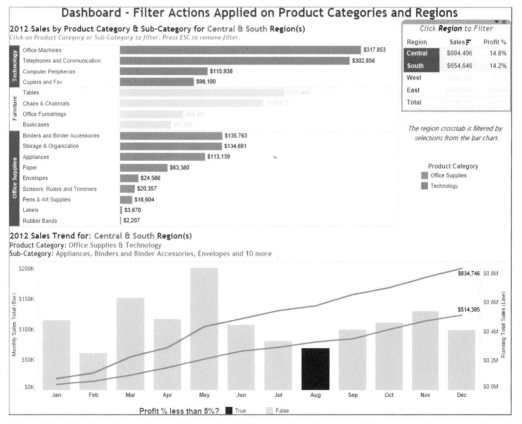

FIGURE 8-2 *A dashboard using simpler views*

The headings contain dynamic elements denoting the regions, product categories, and sub-categories that have been selected using filter actions embedded in the bar chart and region crosstab. The dashboard has been filtered for the central and south regions as well at the technology and office supply product categories. These selections are highlighted in the bar chart and region cross-tab.

This dashboard communicates more effectively by removing clutter and unnecessary details. The audience for this dashboard might include senior managers and regional sales staff. This design would serve both groups.

BEST PRACTICES FOR DASHBOARD BUILDING

After you have analyzed some data and determined what information you need to share, adhering to these principles will help you create better dashboard designs:

- Size the dashboard to fit the in the worst-case available space.
- Employ 4-pane dashboard designs.
- Use Actions to filter instead of Quick Filters.
- Build cascading dashboard designs to improve load speed.
- Limit the use of color to one primary color scheme.
- Use small instructions near the work to make navigation obvious.
- Filter information presented in crosstabs to provide relevant details-on-demand.
- Remove all non-data ink.
- Avoid One Size Fits All dashboards.

Work to achieve initial dashboard load times of less than ten seconds. These principles come from personal lessons learned building dashboards in a wide variety of use cases. They work well for 90 percent of the use cases across industry, government, and education.

You may find specific use cases for which violating one or more of these best practices performs well and communicates the information effectively. By all means then, do what works best for your specific case.

SIZE THE DASHBOARD TO FIT THE WORST-CASE AVAILABLE SPACE

Dashboard building would be easy if everyone had the best computer with high-resolution graphics. Unfortunately this normally isn't the case. So, you must design your dashboard to fit comfortably in the available space by determining the pixel height and width of the worst-case dashboard consumption environment. Tableau provides defaults for the typical sizes you will need or allows you to define a custom size. Doing a lot of design work without knowing the consumption environment is a recipe that results in unhappy information consumers and extra work for the designer.

Will the dashboard be consumed on laptops via Tableau Reader? If so, do you know the range of screen resolutions that are being used? Are tablet computers used? Is the dashboard going to be consumed via Tableau Server or will you have to embed the dashboard in a website? You need to understand the specific height and width of your dashboard space. For laptop consumption this can be as little as (800 × 600) pixels. For desktop computers or better resolution laptop monitors, (1000 × 800) pixels normally works well. Web embedded dashboards can be smaller but a typical worst-case minimum size might be as little as (420 × 420) pixels. Tableau has predefined sizes to help you layout the dimensions of your dashboard. Tableau also makes it easy to define custom size ranges if the default values don't meet your needs.

EMPLOY 4-PANE DASHBOARD DESIGNS

Four individual visualizations will fit well on most laptop and desktop computer screens, as shown in Figure 8-3. This style of presentation naturally highlights the upper-left pane because people in western societies have been taught to read from the upper left to the lower right of a page. Figure 8-3 shows a 4-panel design intended for laptop or desktop consumption.

A four visualizations design style will generally be read from the upper-left to the lower-right in a Z pattern unless you do something to grab attention elsewhere. Note that this design actually includes five panes—but the fifth pane, (the small Select Year cross-tab) acts as a filter for the rest of the dashboard. Ordinarily a Quick Filter would be used to permit the audience to select the year in view. Instead, the example in Figure 8-3 uses a small crosstab to trigger a filter action. The advantage using a crosstab instead of a Quick Filter is that additional information is provided (total sales for each year) in the same amount of space a multi-select Quick Filter would have required. The design employs a fifth data pane (an apparent contradiction to the best practice) but in a way that is consistent with the recommendation. Another reason to use a crosstab for this purpose leads to the next best practice recommendation.

Different rules apply when designing dashboards for tablet computers. Designing for tablet computers will be covered in detail at the end of this chapter.

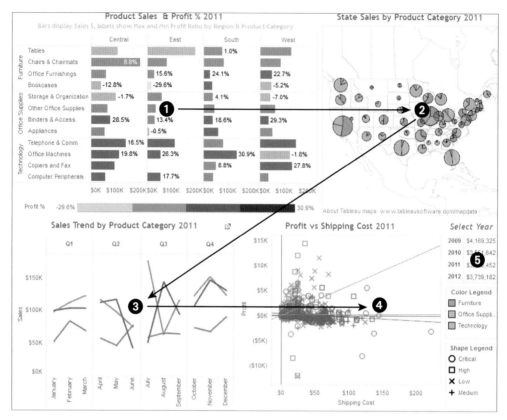

FIGURE 8-3 *A 4-panel design*

USE ACTIONS TO FILTER INSTEAD OF QUICK FILTERS

Using actions in place of Quick Filters provides a number of benefits. First, the dashboard will load more quickly. In order to visualize Quick Filters, Tableau must scan the source table from your database. If the table you are scanning is large, it can take some time for Tableau to render the filter. Tableau has improved Quick Filter load performance over the last several releases, but you may opt to use filter actions for another reason—aesthetics. In the same space that is required to display a multi-select filter you can provide a small visualization with a filter action that enables filtering, but in a way that also enhances content included in the dashboard.

Employing multiple Quick Filters in a dashboard is also potentially confusing to the audience. My personal worst-case scenario involved a client dashboard with two data panes and thirteen Quick Filters. The source database was very large (billions of records). It required six minutes and thirty seconds to load—all but eight seconds of that time was required to visualize the Quick Filters. Not only was it difficult to find the right filters, it was slow loading. By altering the design to a series of 4-panel dashboards and replacing the Quick Filters with filter actions, load time for each dashboard was reduced to less than eight seconds. This leads to the next best practice recommendation.

BUILD CASCADING DASHBOARD DESIGNS TO IMPROVE LOAD SPEEDS

Achieving fast load times can be challenging if the source data is very large. In the case mentioned in the preceding section, the load speed of the dashboard was terrible because many of the thirteen Quick Filters were scanning massive tables. The executive that requested the dashboard needed to be able to have data summarized globally, but also wanted to be able to drill into much more detailed subsets of the data. Unfortunately the initial design was slow-loading and didn't provide much insight. By creating a series of four-pane dashboards the load speed was improved dramatically and the understandability of the information presented was greatly enhanced.

The redesigned primary dashboard provided a good overview of operations by showing a bar chart (comparing different products), and a map (to show data geographically), a scatter plot (to provide outlier analysis), and a small crosstab with very high-level metrics. Filter actions were added to these visualizations that allowed the executive to see more detailed information in other dashboards that were pre-filtered by the selections made on the main dashboard. This cascading dashboard style provided all the information requested, but in a way that improved load speed and understandability.

The final design replaced the original dashboard (containing two data-objects and thirteen Quick Filters) with four cascading, four-panel dashboards. The top-level dashboard provided a summary view, but included filter actions in each of the visualizations that allowed the executive to see data for different regions, products, and sales teams. None of the new dashboards required more than eight seconds to load.

If you employ this recommendation and you are experiencing slow performance, Tableau's Performance Recorder provides visibility of the technical details you will need to troubleshoot the issues that may be degrading performance. The Desktop Performance Recorder is covered at the end of Chapter 8.

LIMIT THE USE OF COLOR TO ONE PRIMARY COLOR SCHEME

Too much color on a dashboard is confusing. Try to limit the use of color to expressing one dimension or one measure. You can effectively add a secondary use of color in the same dashboard if that secondary use of color employs a more muted color scheme. The dashboard in Figure 8-2 used two colors more effectively than the dashboard in Figure 8-1 because the secondary use of color expressed a limited set of values (true/false) and the color was expressed using a muted shade of gray. According to data visualization expert and author Stephen Few, up to ten percent of males and one percent of females have some form of color blindness.[2] The most prevalent form of color blindness limits the ability to distinguish red and green. Take this into consideration if your dashboard will be consumed by a large population. To avoid potential problems apply gray scale or blue-orange color pallets. These are visible to most color-blind people. Tableau also provides a color-blind pallet with ten colors. You may also consider building color-blind specific dashboards if you have a very large population of information consumers.

USE SMALL INSTRUCTIONS NEAR THE WORK TO MAKE NAVIGATION OBVIOUS

Quick Filters are obvious. Actions are not. Since actions are triggered by select-ing elements of your visualizations they will not be obvious to your audience unless you provide instructions within the dashboard. Placing instructions in the title bar of the worksheet that triggers the action is a good way to remind people of the availability of the action.

Use a consistent font style and color for these instructions in your dashboards so that your audience learns that style denotes an instruction. The instructions used in the Figure 8-2 dashboard are highlighted through the use of a brown italics font.

Another alternative is to place the instructions in Tooltips that appear when hovering over marks, as shown in Figure 8-4. This method offers the advantage of having the instructions appear in more complete text without crowding the dashboard space.

Note that the format of the instruction matches the color, font, and style of the instructions in the headers of the dashboard.

Give your audience even more explanatory information by adding a separate Read Me dashboard that includes additional details regarding the datasources used, formulas used, and navigation tips. You can even include links to websites that provide even more information, as shown in Figure 8-5.

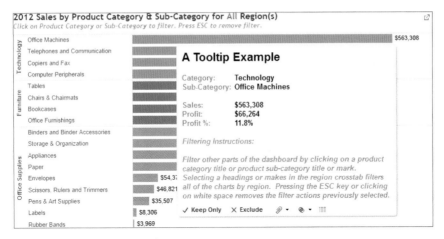

FIGURE 8-4 *Instruction in a Tooltip*

Finally, provide your contact information so that people can easily ask any other questions that may not be anticipated in your design.

FILTER INFORMATION PRESENTED IN CROSSTABS TO PROVIDE RELEVANT DETAILS-ON-DEMAND

Crosstabs are useful visualizations for looking-up specific values when you know exactly what you're looking for. Crosstabs are not the best visual style for quickly discovering trends and outliers. Figure 8-6 shows the poor use of a crosstab view. Even though the crosstab in view has been filtered for a specific dimension, vertical scrolling is still necessary in order to see all of the state values.

There is also a lot of white space generated by the column headers for Market and State in Figure 8-6. This dashboard could be improved by creating a filter action from the bar chart that could restrict the market displayed in the bar chart to a single market, but even with a filter action for market, the crosstab would still require scrolling to see all the values.

Read Me

Data Sources:

The data for this dashboard is provided by the company billing system and includes data from:

1. The sales transaction journal.
2. The customer master records.
3. The product master recordss.

Formulas:

Profit ratios are calculated using the following formula:
Profit $ / Net Sales $ = Profit Ratio

All numbers have be validated by the controller of the company and approved for distribution in this dashboard.

If you have any questions or comments please contact Joe Designer at:

Phone: 123-456-7890
Email: joe.designer@madeup.com

FIGURE 8-5 *A Read Me dashboard*

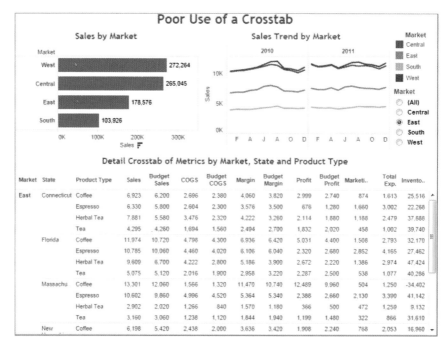

FIGURE 8-6 *A poor use of a crosstab*

In Figure 8-7 the crosstab is much more compact. The Market and State dimensions are being displayed in the title dynamically and the orientation of the crosstab has been changed to place the measures (11 fields) in rows and the Product Type (4 fields) in columns. This reduces white space and eliminates the need for scrolling.

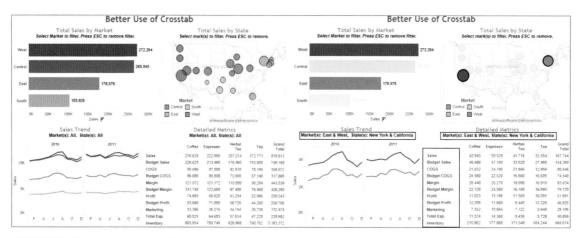

FIGURE 8-7 *A better use of a crosstab*

The unfiltered version of the dashboard on the left of Figure 8-7 clearly shows all the information without any scrolling. The filtered version on the right of Figure 8-7 shows more granular data in both the time series and the crosstab. This is accomplished using filter actions triggered from the bar chart and map—providing details on demand for the markets and states of interest. The use of dynamic titles in the time series and crosstab visualization (highlighted in Figure 8-7) communicates the information more effectively in less space.

REMOVE ALL NON-DATA-INK

This best practice is rule inspired by Edward Tufte, author of *The Visual Display of Quantitative Information*.[3] Remove any text, lines, or shading that doesn't provide actionable information. Remove redundant facts. If a company logo isn't required for promotion purposes—remove it. Ruthlessly eliminate anything that doesn't help your audience understand the story contained in the data.

AVOID ONE-SIZE-FITS-ALL DASHBOARDS

Trying to save time by making one dashboard serve many purposes will not result in the best performing dashboard or save design time. It is so easy to build dashboards and apply data restrictions within data extracts that I recommend making your dashboards fit the particular purpose of each audience. Generally, executives need to see high-level data across multiple geographies, product lines, and markets. Regional staff need more granular data but for restricted geographies, products, and customers.

While it is possible to make one dashboard that works for both groups, it normally doesn't produce the best possible format or the best performing dashboard for either. Strive to provide the best possible experience for each audience even if that requires a little extra effort.

WORK TO ACHIEVE DASHBOARD LOAD TIMES OF LESS THAN TEN SECONDS

Achieving fast load times is dependent on the size and complexity of your data as well as the type of datasource you are using. Slow loading dashboards can also be caused by poor dashboard design. There are several ways that the dashboard design itself can contribute to slow load speeds. Including high granular visualizations (that plot a large number of marks) can consume resources and cause slow load times. Using too many Quick Filters or trying to filter a very large dimension set can slow the load time because Tableau must scan the data to build the filters.

Tableau includes built-in tools for both Tableau Desktop and Tableau Server that help you identify performance issues. At the end of this chapter you'll learn about the desktop version of Tableau's Performance Recorder. The Server version will be covered in Chapter 9.

BUILDING YOUR FIRST ADVANCED DASHBOARD

Creating dashboards with Tableau is an iterative process. There isn't a "one best method." Starting with a basic concept, discoveries made along the way lead to design refinements. Feedback from your target audience provides the foundation for additional enhancements. With traditional BI tools, this is a time-consuming process. Tableau's drop and drag ease of use facilitates rapid evolution of designs and encourages discovery.

INTRODUCING THE DASHBOARD WORKSHEET

After creating multiple, complementary worksheets, you can combine them into an integrated view if the data is using the dashboard worksheet. Figure 8-8 shows an empty dashboard workspace.

The top-left half of the dashboard shelf displays all of the worksheets contained in the workbook. The bottom half of the same space provides access to other object controls for adding text, images, blank space, or live web pages into the dashboard workspace. The worksheets and other design objects are placed into the dashboard by dragging the selected object into the "Drop sheets here" area. The bottom left dashboard area contains controls for specifying the size of the dashboard and a checkbox for adding a dashboard title.

You are going to step through the creation of a dashboard using the Access database file that ships with Tableau called Coffee Chain. You will create the dashboard by employing the best practices recommended earlier in the chapter.

The example dashboard is suitable for a weekly or monthly recurring report. The specifications have been defined and are demanding. The example utilizes a variety of visualizations, dashboard objects, and actions. It will include a main dashboard and a secondary dashboard that will be linked together via filter actions.

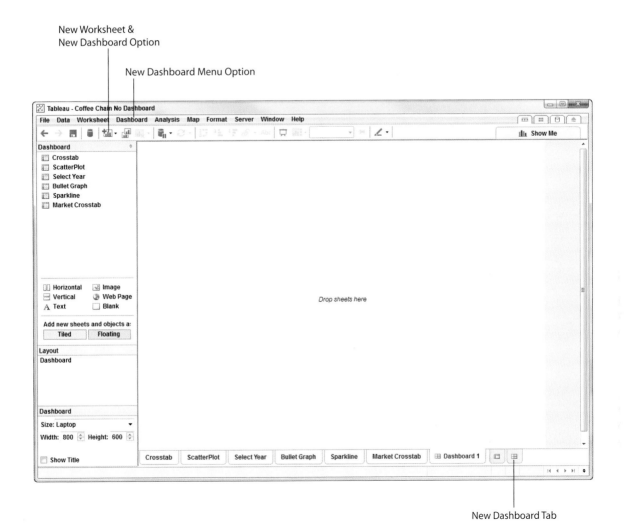

FIGURE 8-8 *Tableau's dashboard worksheet*

Read through the rest of the chapter first to get an overview of the process. Then, step through each section and build the dashboard yourself. When completed, your dashboard should look like Figure 8-9.

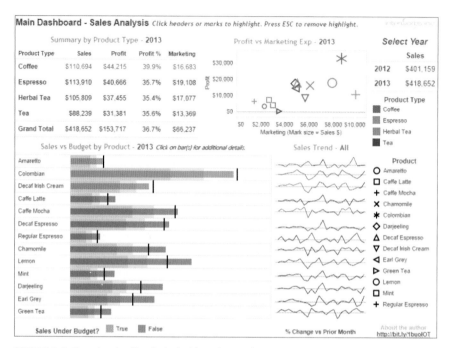

FIGURE 8-9 *Completed coffee chain dashboard example*

The dashboard follows the 4-pane layout recommended earlier in the best practices section of this chapter, but is actually a 5-panel design with the small Select Year cross-tab acting as a filter via a filter action. The main dashboard in Figure 8-9 includes a variety of worksheet panes, an image object with a logo, text objects, dynamic title elements, and a text object containing an active web link. The example employs a cascading design that links the main dashboard to a secondary dashboard via a filter action. The secondary dashboard contains more granular data in a crosstab and an embedded webpage that is filtered by hovering your mouse over the crosstab. This example is designed to use many of Tableau's advanced dashboard features included in Tableau Desktop Version 8. The major steps required to complete this example are:

1. Download the Chapter 8 Dashboard Exercise workbook from the book's companion website. Refer to Appendix C: "InterWorks Book Website" for additional details.

2. Define the dashboard size and position the dashboard objects in the dashboard workspace.

3. Enhance title elements, refine axis headers, and place image and text objects into the primary dashboard.

4. Create a secondary dashboard with a detailed crosstab, web page object, and navigation pane.

5. Add filter, highlight, and URL actions to the dashboards.

6. Finish the dashboard by enhancing the Tooltips and testing all filtering and navigation. Add a Read Me dashboard to explain how the dashboard is intended to be used, datasources, and any calculations created that may not be obvious to the audience.

DEFINING THE DASHBOARD SIZE

One of the first things you should consider when assembling worksheets in a dashboard is the available space that your audience has to view the dashboard. Will it be viewed on an old overhead projector with limited resolution and brightness? Or, will the audience consume the dashboard on a personal computer or a tablet computer? For this exercise assume that the majority of people will be viewing the dashboard on laptop computers. A small number of people will view it on desktop computers. The easiest way to start a dashboard is to click the new dashboard tab. Figure 8-8 shown earlier in the chapter highlights the new dashboard tab at the bottom of the workspace.

POSITION THE WORKSHEET OBJECTS IN THE DASHBOARD WORKSPACE

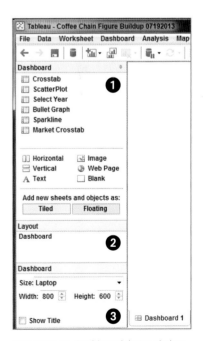

Placing worksheets into the dashboard workspace can be done by double-clicking on the worksheet objects at the top of the dashboard shelf. Tableau will automatically place them into the view. Alternatively, drag the worksheet object into the view and place it in the exact position you desire. Tableau provides a light gray shading as you drag objects into the workspace indicating the space that it will occupy when you release your mouse button.

Unless custom titles were added in the worksheets, the titles that are displayed in the dashboard for each worksheet reflect the worksheet tab names. A variety of dashboard objects can be accessed and placed into the dashboard workspace using the dashboard and layout objects displayed in Figure 8-10.

Dashboard area 1 includes worksheet objects, objects for controlling the orientation of groups of objects Horizontal and Vertical, objects for adding text, images, live web pages, or blank space. By default, Tableau uses Tiled to place objects in their own panes. Selecting the Floating option makes objects float over other objects already

FIGURE 8-10 *Dashboard design shelves*

in the workspace. As you add worksheet objects to the dashboard a small blue circle with a check mark will appear next to its icon.

Layout area 2 includes objects that have been added to the dashboard as well as layout options. Dashboard area 3 at the bottom allows you to define the sizing of the entire dashboard and the individual objects included in the workspace. Before any worksheets are added into the workspace, define the dashboard size to accommodate the worst-case scenario in which the dashboard will be viewed—(800 × 600) pixels. The option Laptop in the menu provides this exact size.

To view more options click on the size shelf as shown in Figure 8-11 for additional ways size can be controlled.

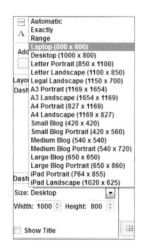

FIGURE 8-11 *Dashboard layout size definition*

■ Automatic—Expands the dashboard to fill the available screen space

■ Exactly—Allows you to lock the dashboard width and height

■ Range—Enables the designer to define minimum and maximum limits

The Exactly mode allows you to set the worst-case parameters for space. After completing your design you may want to change the size mode to Range and define specific limits that the dashboard can expand to fill.

Automatic mode expands or contracts the dashboard to fill the available screen resolution of each computer viewing the dashboard. If any of your audience has a high resolution graphics card, the dashboard might look out of place. The Range option allows you to define specific maximum limits so that dashboards designed for compact spaces don't look too sparse on large monitors. If someone is using a very low resolution monitor to view the dashboard, minimum limits can be set for the dashboard pixel height and width. Once the dashboard size has been defined you are now ready to add individual worksheet objects to the dashboard. Figure 8-10 displayed earlier shows six different worksheet objects that are available to add to the dashboard. There are two ways to add objects into the dashboard. Double-clicking on a worksheet object causes Tableau to place that object into the workspace automatically. To control the placement of an individual object more precisely, drag the object into the view. As long as your left mouse button is depressed Tableau will preview the area that the object will occupy by shading it in gray.

Double-clicking on each worksheet object in the order in which they appear in the dashboard (excluding the Market Crosstab which will be used in a separate dashboard) will result in the worksheets being displayed in the dashboard as you see in Figure 8-12.

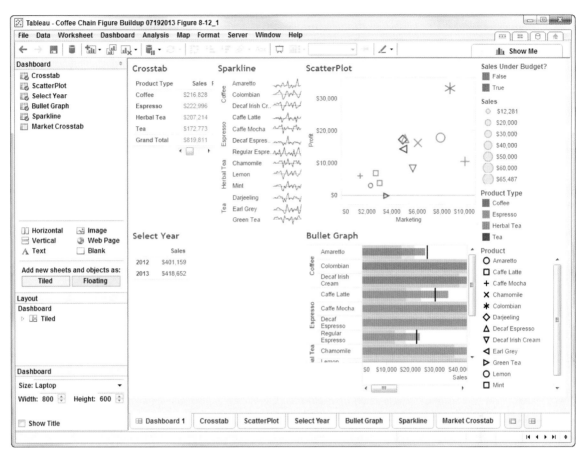

FIGURE 8-12 *Initial layout of the coffee chain dashboard*

Each worksheet has been added into the dashboard but the placement of the individual views can be improved. Reposition the Sparkline object by clicking inside the Sparkline object pane to activate it; then using the handle at the top and center of the object, drag it into the lower-right area of the workspace. Then, reposition the Select Year crosstab into the upper-right area above the color legend. When these steps are completed the dashboard pane should look like Figure 8-13.

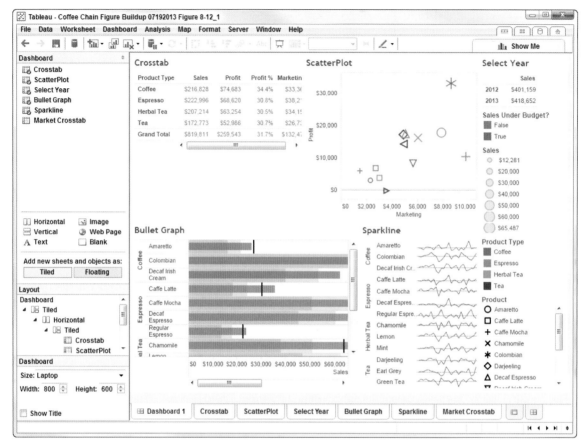

FIGURE 8-13 *Repositioned Worksheet Objects*

Add a title to your dashboard by selecting the Show Title option in the bottom left of your dashboard shelves. The default title will be the name of the dashboard worksheet that was created by Tableau. Edit the title text by double-clicking on the default name and type in **Main Dashboard - Sales Analysis**. Edit the title font to Arial, 12-point and select a light gray color. Make sure that the title is left-justified. After adding the title it should appear as you see in Figure 8-14.

Main Dashboard - Sales Analysis

Crosstab					ScatterPlot		Select Year	
Product Type	Sales	Profit	Profit %	Marketin				Sales
Coffee	$216,828	$74,683	34.4%	$33,3(	$30,000	✳	2012	$401,159
Espresso	$222,996	$68,620	30.8%	$38,2(			2013	$418,652

FIGURE 8-14 *Dashboard with title object added*

USING LAYOUT CONTAINERS TO POSITION OBJECTS

Layout containers allow you to group objects horizontally or vertically within the dashboard workspace.

Use a Horizontal Layout Container for the Dashboard Title

In Figure 8-15 the "InterWorks" logo is aligned horizontally to the right of the dashboard title.

Main Dashboard - Sales Analysis								
Crosstab					**ScatterPlot**		**Select Year**	
Product Type	Sales	Profit	Profit %	Marketin				Sales
Coffee	$216,828	$74,683	34.4%	$33,3(	$30,000	✳	2012	$401,159
Espresso	$222,996	$68,620	30.8%	$38,2			2013	$418,652

FIGURE 8-15 *Title and logo in a horizontal layout container*

The title and logo alignment in Figure 8-15 was achieved using these steps:

1. Drag a horizontal layout container to the top of the dashboard.
2. Drag the title object into the horizontal container.
3. Adjust the height of the horizontal layout container.
4. Place an Image object into the right side of the layout container.
5. Position the title and image within the layout container.

Add a horizontal layout container to the dashboard by dragging the Horizontal object from the dashboard shelf to the area above the title bar as you see in Figure 8-16.

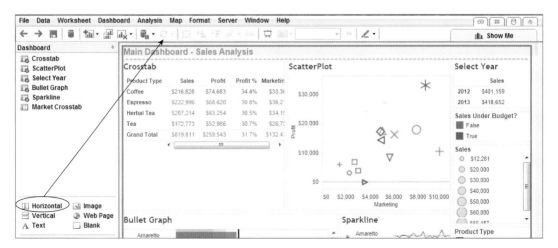

FIGURE 8-16 *Adding a horizontal layout container*

Before you let go of the object be sure that the gray area highlights the full width of the dashboard at the top. This will ensure that the title object occupies the entire width at the top of the dashboard. After releasing the mouse button, don't worry if the vertical space occupied by the layout container is very large—you can reposition it by dragging up from the bottom edge of the layout container. Then drag the title object into the horizontal layout container.

Now that the title is placed inside the horizontal layout container you can drag an image object into the layout container in the dashboard as you see in Figure 8-17.

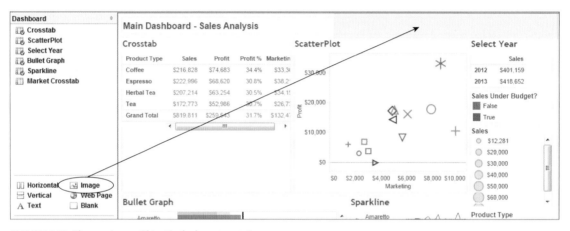

FIGURE 8-17 *Place an Image Object in the layout container*

Now it's time to assign a specific image to the image object. Use any image file you prefer for the logo. The example uses the "InterWorks" logo.

Reposition the title and image objects within the layout container by clicking in the title object space. Then, point the mouse at the right edge of the title object until your pointer changes to a horizontal pointer. Drag the edge to the right to align the logo with the left edge of the vertical space occupied by the Year Filter cross-tab object. Your logo should now be positioned directly over the right side vertical space over the legends.

Make the title bar narrower by pointing at its bottom edge and dragging up. The logo probably isn't centered within the image object. To fit and center the logo in the Image Object, click in the object to access the drop-down arrow and expose the object's menu as you see in Figure 8-18.

FIGURE 8-18 *Fit and center the logo*

Select Fit Image and Center Image. Your logo should now be resized to fit in the space.

To complete the title area, add the URL associated with the logo to the image pane. Set the website address by clicking on the image pane to activate the menu, pick the Set UR option and type in the website address. Now when the logo is clicked and web access is available, a browser session will open and the website will be displayed.

Now that the dashboard title is complete, turn your attention to the area on the right side of the dashboard containing the Year Filter crosstab along with the color, shape, and size legends.

Positioning the Select Year Crosstab and Legends

Look at the completed dashboard again in Figure 8-9 and notice that the color legend for Sales Under Budget? has been repositioned below the bullet graph, the Sales size legend is gone, and a text box containing a website link has been added to the bottom. At this point your legend area should look like Figure 8-19.

By default, Tableau places a vertical layout container in dashboards that have legends or Quick Filters. This means your dashboard already has a layout container in that space. You can view it by clicking on any pane within that space and select the menu using the drop-down arrow in the title bar—then click on Select Layout Container. Notice that all of the elements on the right side of the dashboard are in that space except the image pane containing the logo that you added to the horizontal layout container next to the title.

Insert a text object just below the Sales by Year cross-tab and type in **Scatter Plot** on one line, then **Legends** below that. Format the text box with a light gray using the object menu to access the formatting via the drop-down arrow in the title bar. Center the text from there as well.

Then place another text object below the Product Type color legend with the text **Click Below for the Author Information**, and below that add any website address you desire. I used a shortened version of my personal website (`http://bit.ly/1buoIOT`). This is another way active website links can be placed into a dashboard.

Delete the Sales size legend by accessing the legend menu via the small (x) appearing in the top right side of the object. Next reposition the Sales Under Budget? size legend by placing it below the Bullet Graph in the lower left area of the workspace. Resize the fit of the Select Year crosstab in the upper right of the dashboard so that it fills the entire view. Use the crosstab objects menu drop-down arrow and select the menu options Fit/Entire View.

Finally, reduce the amount of horizontal space used by the legend area by dragging the left edge of the vertical layout container to the right. Be careful not to obscure any of the legend text. You are done with the layout container

FIGURE 8-19
Right vertical layout container

styling for now. If necessary, you can come back and make additional refine-ments later. Your dashboard should now look like Figure 8-20.

The dashboard is starting to take shape but the worksheet objects don't utilize the available space well. The text used in the color legend below the Bullet Graph is partially obscured. In addition, the Bullet Graph and Sparkline objects are displaying identical row headers—creating redundant ink that can be removed if you ensure that the rows are sorted the same way. In the next section you'll learn how to deal with these issues so that the dashboard utilizes the available space more effectively.

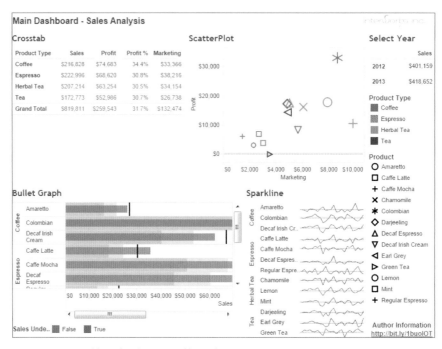

FIGURE 8-20 *Dashboard with improved legends*

POSITIONING AND FITTING THE DASHBOARD OBJECTS

The general layout of this dashboard is good. The upper left quadrant contains a Crosstab overview of performance. The Scatter Plot shows how promotional spending relates to profits and sales (although it isn't clear that the size of the marks in the scatter plot provide relative sales amounts). The Bullet Graph and Sparkline provide complementary views of actual sales performance versus budget. Color is used in two different ways. In the Scatter Plot color is used to distinguish Product Type. All of the other charts use a muted 2-tone color scheme to highlight under-budgeted sales.

To make this dashboard communicate the information more effectively requires the following steps:

- Ensure that each worksheet object fits its entire view.

- Create more descriptive titles for each pane.

- Make the Bullet Graph and Sparkline Sort in the same order.

- Hide the redundant row headers in the Sparkline chart.

- Reposition the worksheet objects to better utilize space.

Ensure That Each Worksheet Object Fits Its Entire View

Start by changing the fit within the Bullet Graph pane. The most straight-forward method to access the fit menu is one we've used a few times already—clicking on the title block of the pane and exposing the pane menu. Alternatively, you can expose the same controls from the layout shelf by selecting the Bullet Graph and right-clicking. Figure 8-21 shows that you can access the same menu using either method.

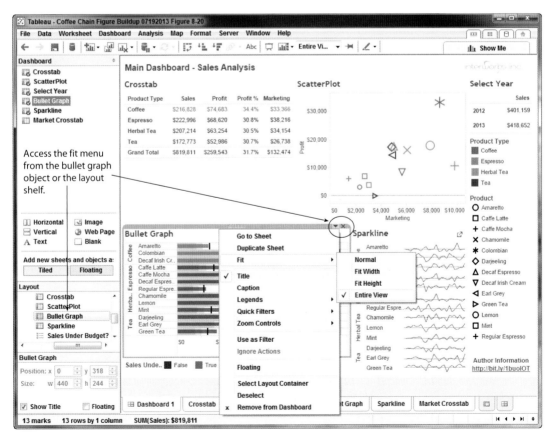

FIGURE 8-21 *Fitting the Bullet Graph Object*

Change the bullet graph fit from Normal to Entire View. You should see the graph fill the pane completely.

Notice when you click the bullet graph pane in the layout shelf, the context of the position and size shelf changes to display the values for the bullet graph pane. You now see the pixel positions and size of that particular pane. At the bottom of the shelf you will see that the Show Title option is selected and the Floating pane option is not. If the floating pane option were selected, this pane could be placed on top of other panes in the dashboard—floating over the area. This choice wouldn't be appropriate for the bullet graph. Later in the exercise we'll utilize a floating pane. Repeat the same process for all of the data objects so that all of them fill the available space.

Create More Descriptive Titles for Each Data Pane

Adding more descriptive data object titles will make it easier for the audience to interpret the dashboard. Edit the titles by double-clicking on each data object's title bar and replacing the `<sheetname>` text with the following title text:

- Bullet Graph—Sales vs. Budget by Product
- Sparkline—Sales Trend
- Cross-tab—Summary by Product Type
- Scatter Plot—Sales vs. Marketing Expense
- Select Year—Change the font to Arial, italics, 12 point, brown

Figure 8-22 shows the dashboard after completing the title editing.

The size, color, and style of the title font used for the Select Year crosstab in the upper right of the dashboard reminds the audience about the filtering provided within that object. Providing instructions this way accomplishes the intended purpose in minimal space. Later in this chapter an action will be added to the crosstab allowing the user to filter other charts in the dashboard by year. Next you'll see creative ways to use sorting, text objects, and mark labels to improve the legibility of the charts in the bottom half of the dashboard.

Improving the Bullet Graph and Sparkline Charts

In Figure 8-22 you can see that the bullet graph and sparkline have the same row headings. The duplicate headers are an inefficient use of space. The charts are meant to be used together to see performance versus budget and trends over time, but they are not perfectly aligned. The title of the color legend below the Bullet Graph is partially obscured and needs to be edited so that it is legible. Apply these improvements with the following steps:

1. Make the row sort order in both charts identical.

2. Hide the row labels in the Sparkline.

3. Turn on mark labels and hide the header in the Bullet Graph.

4. Improve the color legend below the Bullet Graph.

5. Precisely align the Sparkline and Bullet Graph rows.

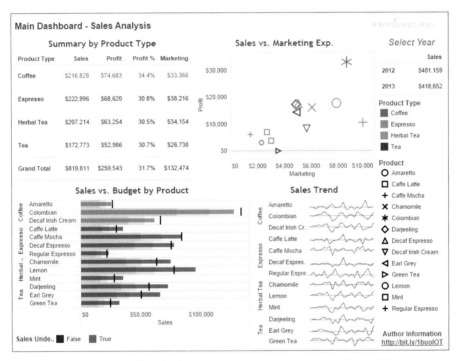

FIGURE 8-22 *Improved Dashboard titles*

Make the Row Sort Order in Both Charts Identical

Hover your mouse over the bullet graph title pane. This will expose the Go To Sheet navigation control. Click on the small box with the arrow (see Figure 8-23) to jump to the Bullet Graph worksheet.

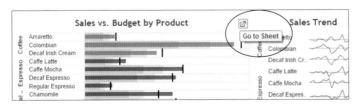

FIGURE 8-23 *Jump to the bullet graph worksheet.*

Edit the sort order of the product type and product field pills on the row shelf so that the rows in both charts sort identically. Access the sort menu for each field by right-clicking on the field pill on the row shelf, then select the Sort menu/Manual sort option as displayed in Figure 8-24.

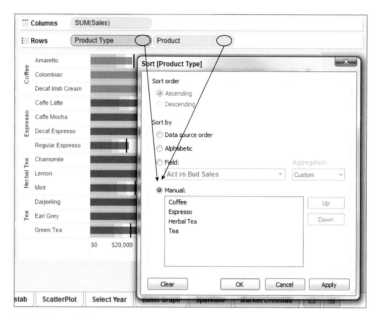

FIGURE 8-24 *Editing row sorting*

Repeat the same steps in the sparkline worksheet. When this step is completed Tableau provides a visual cue in the Product Type and Product field pills confirming that a sort has been applied to each field in both worksheets. The cue is a small bar chart that appears in the right side of each field pill.

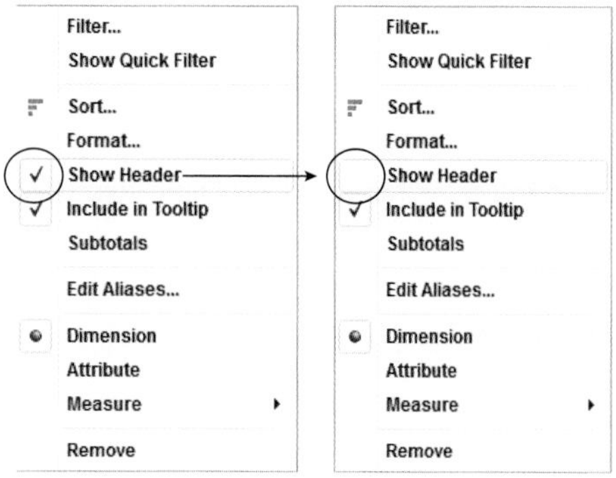

Now that the bullet graph and sparkline are sorted the same way, you can hide the product type and product row labels in the sparkline worksheet—saving space and eliminating redundant data ink. Right-clicking the Product Type and Product pills on the row shelf exposes the menu you see in Figure 8-25.

Hide the sparkline row headings by selecting any row header, right-clicking, and uncheck the Show Header option. Do this for both Product type and Product.

FIGURE 8-25 *Hiding the sparkline row headings*

Turn on Mark Labels and Hide the Axis Header in the Bullet Graph

The Bullet Graph can be edited to provide more vertical space by hiding the axis header at the bottom of the chart. These axis labels provide valuable context. If the dashboard were going to be printed and consumed on paper, it would not be a good idea to remove the axis header.

When dashboards are consumed interactively on a computer, mark labels can be used to replace axis headers by presenting important details on demand—when a mark or heading is selected. Mark labels can always be displayed, but in this case space would be better utilized if the labels displayed only when the user wants to see them. To make the mark labels appear on demand, go to the bullet graph worksheet and click the label button on the marks card to expose the menu seen in Figure 8-26.

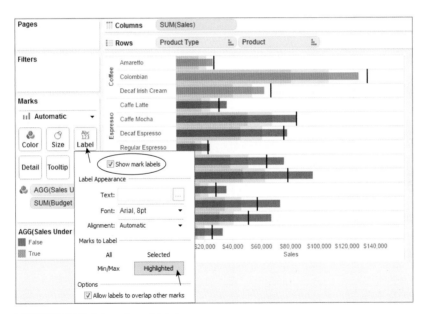

FIGURE 8-26 *Bullet graph mark label menu*

The axis header at the bottom of the Bullet Graph can be hidden by pointing at the axis header area, right-clicking, and unchecking the Show Header option. The view on the left side of Figure 8-27 shows the menu selection, and the resulting appearance of the Bullet Graph is shown on the right.

Removing the axis header in the Bullet Graph is a compromise that the mark labels enable by providing sales details via point and click selection of the mark or row header. Due to the limited space requirements for this dashboard, this is an acceptable compromise.

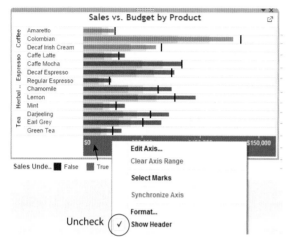

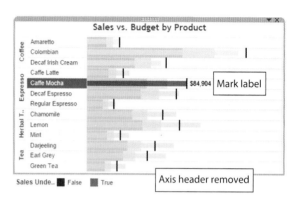

FIGURE 8-27 *Hiding the Bullet Graph Axis title*

Improve the Color Legend below the Bullet Graph

There is one more item near the Bullet Graph that needs to be addressed. In the view on the right side of Figure 8-27 you can see that the color legend title is partially obscured. This can be addressed by erasing the legend title, then adding a text object to the left of the legend. This technique allows for more precision in the alignment and positioning of the text to describe the legend colors. It also provides a means for centering the legend below the Bullet Graph.

Erase the legend title by accessing the legend menu via the drop-down arrow that appears when the legend is clicked-on, then uncheck the Show Title option. Now add a text box to the left of the legend by dragging a Text object to the left of the legend as you see in Figure 8-28.

The legend can be precisely positioned beneath the Bullet Graph by dragging the right edge of the new text object to the right or left. These changes have reduced the amount of space required for the Bullet Graph and the Sparkline.

Precisely Align the Scatterplot and Bullet Graph Rows

The Sales Trend Sparkline is not actually plotting the monthly sales value. It is showing the percent change versus prior month to accentuate the pattern of monthly changes. Refer to Chapter 7 for a full explanation of the reasons why this way of presenting the data may be helpful. This detail is an important fact that should be communicated to the audience.

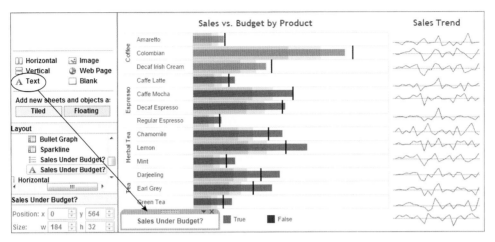

FIGURE 8-28 *Replace the legend title with a text object.*

You can see in Figure 8-28, the legend below the Bullet Graph is also causing a misalignment of the charts. While a Blank object could be placed below the Sales Trend Sparkline to address this problem, placing a Text object there addresses the alignment need, but also allows for the addition of text to describe exactly what is being plotted in the Sales Trend chart. Align the two charts by dragging the bottom edge of the chart objects to position them so that the rows in both graphs are perfectly aligned. Figure 8-29 shows the appearance of the full dashboard with these style enhancements completed.

The bottom half of the dashboard looks very good now. The color legend title is centered and the legend title is clear and legible. And, the rows in the Bullet Graph and Sparkline are aligned so users can see product sales compared to plan and the related sales trend.

Although this wasn't discussed in the preceding text, the blue/gray color scheme used to denote actual sales versus budget sales in the Crosstab and Bullet Graph, has also now been applied to the Sparkline. Blue trend line sections in the Sparkline now also denote sales that are under budget. This was achieved by placing the calculated value that was used in the two other charts Sales Under Budget? on the Marks Card for Color in the Sparkline worksheet.

To see more details regarding how the value was calculated, refer to the glossary entry for Boolean Value. If you have downloaded the workbook used for this example from the companion website, point at the field in the measures shelf, and select the Edit option to view the calculation.

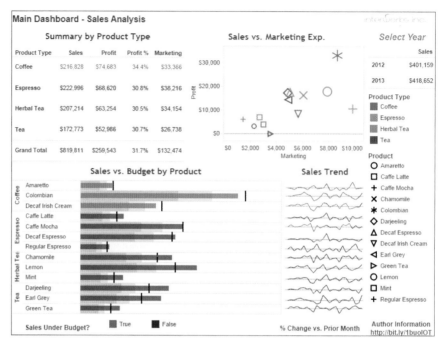

FIGURE 8-29 *The updated dashboard*

To finish refining the dashboard appearance there are a couple of items that need to be addressed—adjusting the vertical space used by the top and bottom halves of the dashboard and an edit to an axis header in the Sales vs. Marketing Scatterplot. These are addressed next.

Improving the Crosstab and Scatter Plot

Look at Figure 8-29 presented earlier. You can see that the Summary by Product Type chart contains too much empty space, but the lower half of the dashboard would benefit by having more pixel height—particularly the Sales Trend Sparkline. Compressing the vertical space used for the top half of the dashboard will address that issue and provide more room for the Bullet Graph and Sparkline at the bottom. Also, adjusting the amount of horizontal space provided to the row headers and the numbers may be necessary to ensure that larger numbers can be displayed in the object.

Note the addition of the text object containing "% Change vs. Prior Month" adds descriptive text but also helps to align the Bullet Graph and Sparkline charts.

Because the size legend for the Sales vs. Marketing Expense Scatterplot was removed earlier to conserve space, it would be useful to find a way to let information consumers know that the size of the marks in the Scatterplot denotes the relative sales value of each mark. These issues will be addressed with the following steps:

1. Adjust the horizontal space used by the row headings in the cross tab chart and reposition the horizontal space allocated to each chart.

2. Compress the vertical space occupied by the Crosstab and Scatterplot.

3. Edit the Scatterplot axis label to provide information related to the size legend that was removed earlier.

Figure 8-30 summarizes these steps visually.

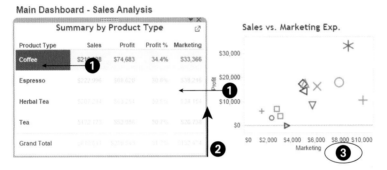

FIGURE 8-30 *List items to address.*

Reposition the amount of horizontal space occupied by the crosstab row header by clicking on the row and dragging to the edge of the header column to the left or right so that the heading fits comfortably on one row. Then drag the edge of the crosstab pane to the right or left and to allow enough room for the numbers in the crosstab to be expressed.

To reduce the amount of vertical space occupied by the top half of the dashboard, drag up from the bottom of the crosstab and scatterplot objects. Repositioning of dashboard objects like this is common, and you can make these kinds of adjustments at any time.

The axis title at the bottom of the scatter plot can be edited by pointing at the axis title, right-clicking, then selecting the Edit Axis menu option. This will expose the menu you see in Figure 8-31.

Add the text **Mark Size - Sales $** to the Title dialog box in the Edit Axis menu as you see in Figure 8-31. Clicking the OK button locks in the change. After completing these steps the dashboard will look like Figure 8-32.

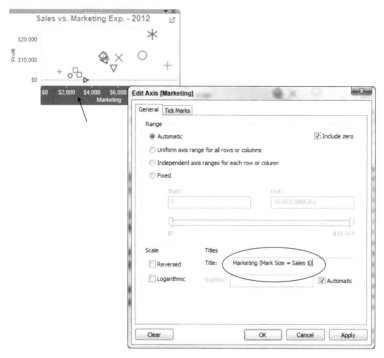

FIGURE 8-31   *Editing the Scatterplot Axis title*

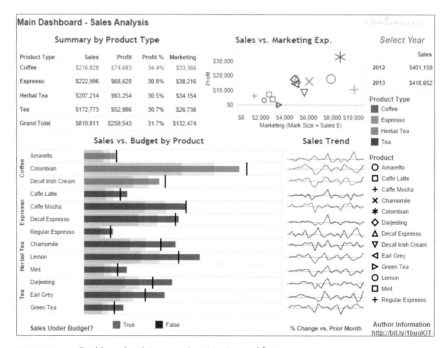

FIGURE 8-32   *Dashboard with improved positioning and fitting*

The dashboard looks finished now. The white space in the charts at the top has been reduced and the Bullet Graph and Sparkline have more room to breathe. The majority of the appearance editing in the main dashboard is complete.

In the next section you will learn how to use the data in the main dashboard to create actions for filtering and highlight related information in the main dashboard objects.

USING ACTIONS TO CREATE ADVANCED DASHBOARD NAVIGATION

Tableau's Quick Filters provide an easy method for filtering dashboards and worksheets. Refer to Tableau's manual for details on Quick Filters. This dashboard example purposefully avoids using Quick Filters because Tableau actions provide even more flexibility and in many instances provide better initial load speed than Quick Filters—consistent with the best practices recommended earlier in the chapter.

Actions facilitate discovery by altering the context of the dashboard based on selections made by the audience. In this section you will create actions that utilize all of the available ways Tableau can invoke actions. You'll build actions that:

- Filter and highlight the main dashboard.

- Facilitate navigation to the supporting dashboard.

- Filter a detailed crosstab in a new supporting dashboard.

- Call and filter an embedded website in the supporting dashboard.

- Return the audience to the main dashboard from the supporting dashboard.

Using the Select Year Crosstab to Filter the Main Dashboard

The Select Year crosstab in Figure 8-32 is titled using a different font style and color to make it stand out and provide a brief instruction identifying that the crosstab serves as a filter. Building filter actions in Tableau can be done in as few as three clicks. Create a filter action using the Select Year crosstab using these steps:

1. Click in the Select Year crosstab to activate the object.

2. Select the drop-down arrow to expose the menu.

3. Pick the Use as Filter menu option to create the filter action.

4. Edit the filter action so that the Sales Trend Sparkline isn't filtered.

Figure 8-33 shows the menus related to steps two and three from the list above.

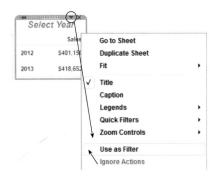

FIGURE 8-33 *Making a filter action*

After finishing step three you should be able to click on one of the years in the crosstab, and every chart in the dashboard will be filtered to show only the selected year. Clicking the Sales header in the crosstab will cause the dashboard to be filtered for both years.

Creating filter actions this way is very easy but it would be better if the Sales Trend Sparkline always showed both years. Tableau generated a filter action from the Use as Filter option. To make it so that the filter action does not apply to the Sales Trend Sparkline graph requires editing the generated filter action.

To edit the filter action generated by Tableau, access the Dashboard menu option, then select the Actions menu to expose the Actions dialog box. You can see the unedited filter action below on the left side of Figure 8-34.

The Edit Filter Action that Tableau generated applies to all of the Target Sheets in the main dashboard (Dashboard 1). The Edit Filter Action dialog box on the right side of Figure 8-34 shows the changes applied in that screenshot.

- Recommended—Give the action a more descriptive name.

- Required—Uncheck the Sparkline in the Target Sheets area.

- Optional—Select the Leave the Filter clearing option.

Naming the filter action very specifically makes it easier to identify the exact purpose of the action. This is useful in two ways. First, if you need to come back months later to edit the action, a specific name makes it much easier to find it. Second, if the Run Action On uses the Menu option, the name field will appear in Tooltips or when users point at headings—to trigger the action. Being descriptive there is important for users. You will see this type of action later in this chapter.

Unchecking the Sparkline in the Target Sheets area means that the Sparkline will no longer be filtered by year. Because the Sparkline requires very little space to clearly display two years of data, it makes sense to leave that chart unfiltered.

Finally, the Leave the Filter option causes the filter action to remain in place when the action is removed. For example, if the year 2013 is selected (and then the filter action is removed by pressing the escape key (ESC) or by clicking on white space within a chart) the chart objects affected by the filter action will continue to display only the year 2013—until another selection is made in the Select Year crosstab.

Created by "Use as Filter"   Edited from Dashboard.Actions menu

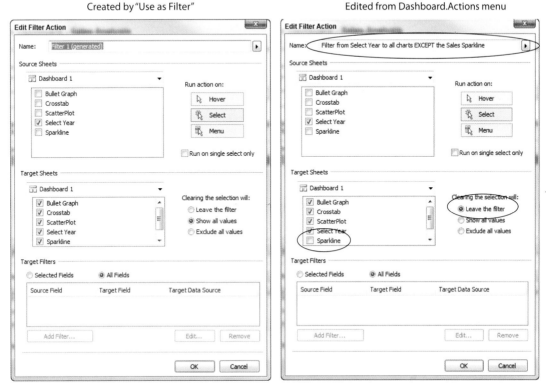

FIGURE 8-34 *Editing the filter action*

Adding Dynamic Title Content

The dashboard now includes a filter action that gives users the ability to filter for the year 2012, 2013, or both years. Dynamic titles are a good way to provide visual confirmation that the objects in the dashboard have been filtered correctly. Figure 8-35 shows the full dashboard filtered for the year 2013 with dynamic titles that include the year.

You can see that the Crosstab, Scatterplot, and Bullet Graph are filtered for the year 2013 while the Sparkline continues to display both years. Matching the font of the dynamic title elements to the Select Year Crosstab title color provides a visual link for the audience. Adding changeable title elements is done by inserting fields from your data into the title. Edit the title by double-clicking on the title; then select the insert menu option to position the field into the title as you see in Figure 8-36.

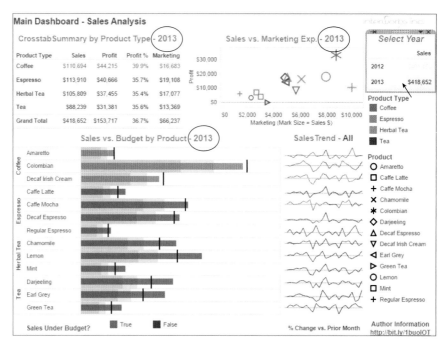

FIGURE 8-35 *Dashboard with dynamic titles*

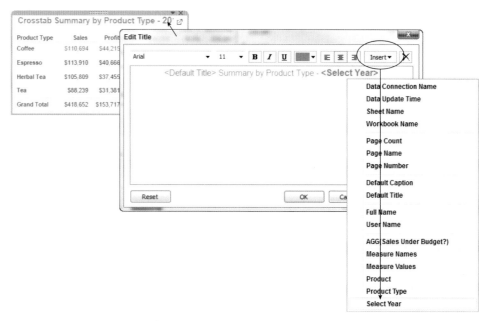

FIGURE 8-36 *Adding a dynamic field to chart titles*

Alternatively, you can directly type the field name in as long as you include the wrappers (<Select Year>) before and after the field name. Note that the (<Select Year>) added in the title is not the name of the crosstab. It is a similarly-named custom date field that was added to the source data. Refer to the "Creating Customized Date Fields" section of Chapter 3 for more.

The custom date is being used in the dashboard to override Tableau's default behavior, which gives users the ability to display Tableau's default date hierarchy (year, quarter, month, etc.). Due to the space limitations imposed for this dashboard, it is desirable to limit the display of dates in the Select Year Crosstab to show only year.

In the next section you'll learn how to use the color and size legends to create highlight actions.

Auto-Generating Highlight Actions from Legends

Highlighting helps users see related information in dashboards more easily. Users can generate highlighting from legends by activating the highlighting tool that appears when you point at a legend as shown in Figure 8-37.

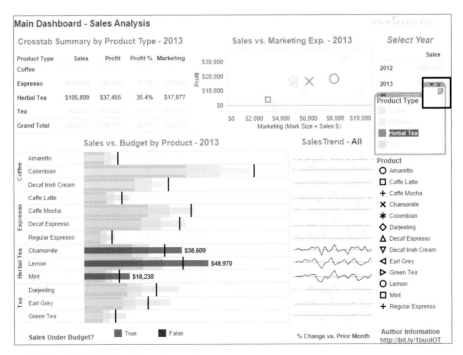

FIGURE 8-37 *Highlighting from a legend*

Highlighting this way is effective for looking at one dimension at a time. In Figure 8-37 the Product Type Herbal Tea is being highlighted in the dashboard. The same single dimension highlighting can be in the Product legend.

When these selections are made, Tableau creates a highlight action automatically. This is a power feature. By activating highlighting from both the Product Type and Product legends, Tableau generates a highlight action that is the combination of both the color and shape legends. To see the action that Tableau creates, access the Dashboard menu and Actions submenu just like you did for the filter action. Figure 8-38 shows the Actions dialog box and the Edit Highlight Action dialog box that is accessed via the edit button.

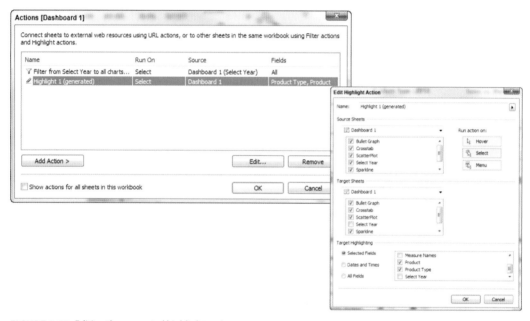

FIGURE 8-38 Editing the generated highlight action

When Tableau creates these highlight actions it will automatically apply them to every worksheet object in the dashboard. In this case, uncheck the Select Year Crosstab in the Target Sheets area so that the highlight action isn't applied to that object. Notice that the Target Highlighting area at the bottom includes the combination of both Product Type (color) and Product (shape) in the action.

This action will persist if the workbook is saved and will be available for anyone consuming the dashboard. Highlighting will now occur if marks or headings are selected within the dashboard as you see in Figure 8-39.

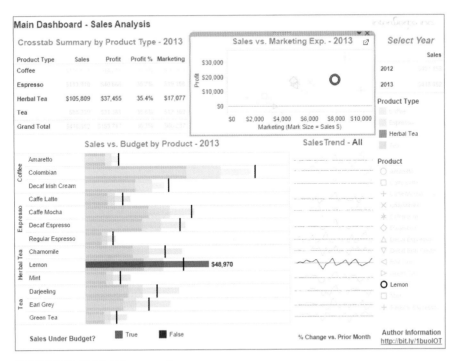

FIGURE 8-39 *Highlight from a mark*

The highlight in Figure 8-39 was triggered by selecting the green circle in the Scatterplot. The highlight action uses the combination of color and shape to highlight Product Type and/or Product in all of the other charts with the exception of the Select Year Crosstab that was removed from the action.

Because Tableau has built simple controls for triggering actions it is possible to build them even if you don't understand exactly how they work. If you know how to edit Actions, you can advance your knowledge through experimentation. If you want to understand more about the available options for Actions—details about the Action Dialog box are covered next.

Understanding the Action Dialog Box

Actions can apply to one or several Dashboards or Worksheets. This capability enables the creation of elegant cascading dashboard designs by using Filter Actions to link the contents of one dashboard to another related dashboard.

The steps to define Filter Actions and Highlight Actions are similar, but there are differences in how the data needs to be expressed for highlighting to work properly. For example, highlighting requires exact field names that are visually differentiated in each view, whereas filters don't have this requirement. Figure 8-40 shows the Filter and Highlight Action dialog boxes.

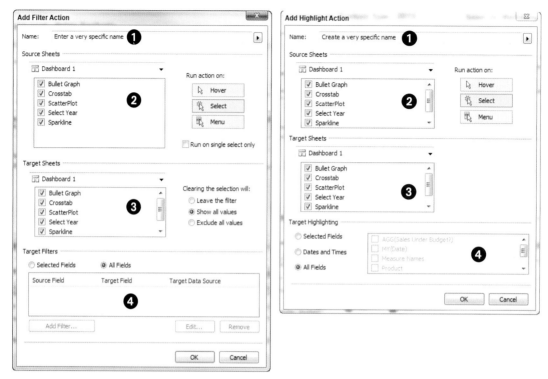

FIGURE 8-40 *Filter and highlight action menus*

The Filter/Highlight action screen is comprised of four main areas:

- Name—Define the name of the action as it appears in the dialog box and Tootips or Header menus if the action is run using a menu.

- Source Sheets—Controls where and how actions are invoked

- Target Sheets—Defines where actions are applied and their behavior when cleared (only for filter actions)

- Target Filters/Highlighting—Limits what fields are used to apply the actions

Name—Tableau automatically assigns action names sequentially by type. While this naming convention keeps things organized during the design process, it isn't helpful if you need to revise your design later. Giving actions very specific names will save time if later editing is necessary. When the "Run Action On" type is menu, the name also appears in related Tooltips and Header menus for executing the action.

Source Sheets—Contains a drop-down menu that allows you to select any of the worksheets included in your workbook at the source of the action. Dashboard is the source sheet in this example. The block directly below specifies where the action will be invoked from in the dashboard. The checked panes indicate panes that will invoke the action. Unchecked panes do not invoke the action. Run action on specifies how the action is invoked.

- Select—Action will run using a point and click.

- Menu—Runs via point and click in a Tooltip or by right-clicking the dimension heading in the pane

- Hover—Action runs as your mouse pointer hovers over a mark.

The examples you have seen so far have used the Select method to run on. Later in the chapter you will create actions that run on the Menu and Hover methods.

Target Sheets—This defines what places the action will be applied in, including the (dashboard or worksheet) and the individual worksheet objects that are changed by the action. This defines the places that actions will be applied. The radio buttons on the right side of this area define Tableau's behavior when the action is de-selected by the user.

For example, in Figure 8-35 presented earlier, a filter action for the year 2013 has been applied. In that example, pressing the escape (ESC) key, or clicking on blank space in a worksheet object, will de-select the filter action. However, because the "Clearing the selection will" is defined using the Leave the Filter option, the dashboard will remain filtered for the year 2013.

The Clearing the Selection Will area defines what happens when the action is cleared. Please note this particular control applies only to filter actions and does not exist for highlight actions. The different behaviors that can be selected to occur when a filter action is cleared are:

- Leave the filter—The filter action keeps only the last selected filter action.

- Show All Values—Returns the worksheet or dashboard to an unfiltered state within the context of the dashboard or worksheet

- Exclude All Value—Excludes the data from the view so the worksheets that are using the filtered data will not display any information when the filter action is removed

Target Filters—Tableau's normal behavior Highlight Actions is to use any possible common field existing between the source and the target sheets to apply the action. For Filter Actions, it is the fields that make up the mark selected in the source sheet that drive what fields are included in the filter.

The Target Filters area gives you the ability to specifically restrict the fields that Tableau uses to apply the action if you choose the Selected Fields option. For example, in the highlighting example presented earlier in the chapter, the Highlight Action was restricted to the Product Type and Product fields.

Filter and highlight action allow you to use the visualizations and legends in your views to create interactive dashboards that respond to selections users make—even if the source and target locations reside in different worksheets. These types of actions are confined to a single workbook.

Tableau provides a third kind of action that allows you to pass the data from your workbook to an external website. The website can be materials in a separate browser session or embedded into a dashboard. These are referred to as URL Actions. Figure 8-41 shows the URL Action dialog box.

FIGURE 8-41 *URL Action dialog box*

The Name and Source Sheets sections for defining URL Actions are similar to Filter and Highlight Actions. However, a webpage URL link field is used to define the target for the action. The small arrow on the right side of the URL field allows you to replace or append fields from your data to the web address.

The URL Options at the bottom of the dialog box allow you to deal with characters that may not be understood by the target URL via the URL Encode Data Values. The Allow Multiple Values option gives you a way to pass multiple list values (such as a list of products) as parameters to the URL. When passing multiple values you will also need to define how to separate each record (Item Delimiter), and the Delimiter Escape if the selected delimiter character is used anywhere in your data values.

In the next section you'll build another dashboard that will complement the Main Sales Dashboard just completed. This example will help you understand how to use your data interactively with data on an external website. You'll also learn how to create a menu action to navigate from the Main Sales Dashboard to the supporting dashboard, and another action will be used to provide navigation back to the Main Sales Dashboard.

EMBEDDING A LIVE WEBSITE IN A DASHBOARD

When completed, the next dashboard will include two primary objects—a crosstab with regional market metrics and an embedded website object. It should look similar to Figure 8-42.

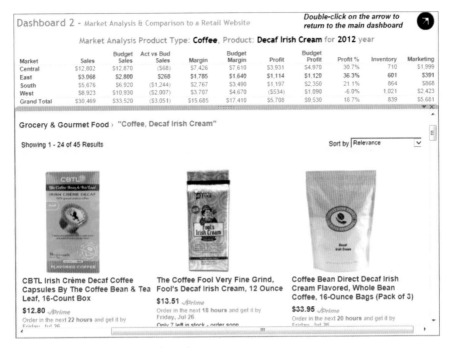

FIGURE 8-42 *Dashboard with a live web page*

This dashboard has the same size constraints as the parent Main Sales Dashboard. Navigation to and from the dashboard will be provided by Filter Actions. And the URL Action to search the embedded website will be triggered by hovering over the Market Analysis Crosstab.

Assemble Dashboard 2

Open the dashboard worksheet and set the size to exactly 800×600 pixels—a size consistent with the main dashboard. Then select the Show Title option to display a title object and type in the dashboard title that you see in Figure 8-42 (**Dashboard 2 - Market Analysis and Comparison to a Retail Website**).

Drag the Market Analysis worksheet into Dashboard 2. Edit the pane Fit setting to Fit Entire View so that the crosstab fills the full amount of space available. Next add a web page object to Dashboard 2 by dragging it into the bottom half of the dashboard pane and click the OK button on the Edit URL pop-up that appears without adding any website address. When you add the URL action—that data will be supplied by the action. Your dashboard should have two panes now. The web pane will be blank. It should look similar to Figure 8-43.

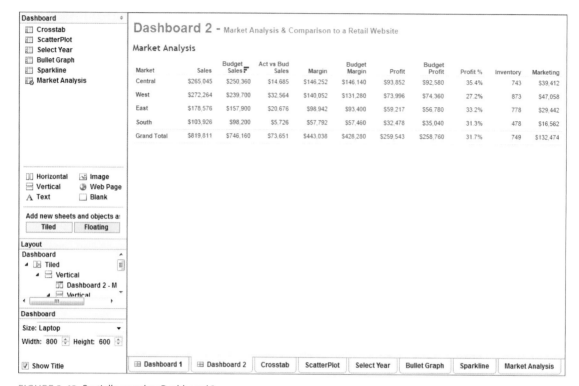

FIGURE 8-43 *Partially complete Dashboard 2*

The bones of the supporting dashboard are in place. Now you can perform actions to navigate between the dashboards and to activate the web page via a URL Action for the web page object. This requires three separate actions:

1. Create a filter action using the Bullet Graph in the Main Sales Dashboard to filter the Market Analysis Crosstab in Dashboard 2.

2. Make a URL action in Dashboard 2 to filter the web page object in Dashboard 2.

3. Add a filter action to return the user from Dashboard 2 to the Main Sales Dashboard.

Creating the Filter Action to Navigate from the Main Dashboard to Dashboard 2

You will now create a filter action that will be triggered from the Bullet Graph in the Main Sales Dashboard to the Market Analysis Crosstab in the supporting dashboard. The purpose of the action is to allow the audience to analyze sales of a selected product type and product—by market.

Understanding what information is passed in the filter action is important. When you create actions always check to ensure that the result is correct. If you don't, you could potentially present incorrect information. The Market Analysis Crosstab in Dashboard 2 doesn't currently include the Product Type, Product, or Select Year fields. This will present a problem that requires troubleshooting. Don't be concerned. It isn't unusual when assembling a new dashboard to revise the design as you build to accommodate filtering and highlighting needs. Duplicate the filter action you see in Figure 8-44.

Once you have completed the filter action, test it by trying to run the filter. Figure 8-45 shows the Tooltip that will appear when you point at a mark in the Bullet Graph.

The Tooltip is displaying the filter action created in the last step as blue text at the bottom of the Tooltip. Clicking on the blue text should take you to Dashboard 2. You can also execute the action by pointing at the row header and right-clicking to expose the action.

FIGURE 8-44 *Defining the navigation filter action*

Using either method to trigger the action, the Market Analysis Crosstab should be filtered for Coffee, Colombian, and the year of 2012. The result should look exactly like Figure 8-46.

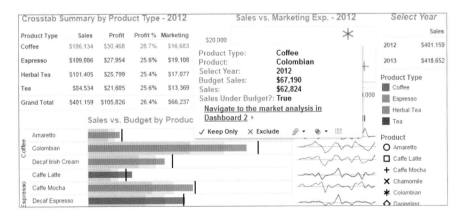

FIGURE 8-45 *Tooltip with a menu filter action*

Dashboard 2 - Market Analysis & Comparison to a Retail Website

Market	Sales	Budget Sales	Act vs Bud Sales	Margin	Budget Margin	Profit	Budget Profit	Profit %	Inventory	Marketing
East	$23,205	$21,390	$1,815	$15,762	$14,730	$11,129	$11,450	48.0%	636	$2,497
West	$14,862	$18,410	($3,548)	$8,803	$11,090	$4,593	$7,520	30.9%	762	$2,053
Central	$14,153	$14,260	($107)	$8,124	$8,300	$3,479	$4,490	24.6%	698	$2,686
South	$10,604	$13,130	($2,526)	$5,937	$7,450	$3,576	$5,440	33.7%	743	$1,437
Grand Total	$62,824	$67,190	($4,366)	$38,626	$41,570	$22,777	$28,900	36.3%	708	$8,673

FIGURE 8-46 *The filtered result in Dashboard 2*

The sales total in the target crosstab in Dashboard 2 should be $62,824 for the specific selection made above. Try using the filter action on a few different markets in the Bullet Graph just to be sure that it is working properly.

The first time your audience uses a menu action like this, the contents of the Market Analysis Crosstab in Dashboard 2 will not be obvious. The Bullet Graph displays Product Type and Product information. The Market Analysis Crosstab doesn't display any information about Product Type, Product, or Year in the headings. In this situation adding a title that inserts dynamic field entries is very helpful. Figure 8-47 shows the Market Analysis Crosstab with a title that includes those fields.

Dashboard 2 - Market Analysis & Comparison to a Retail Website

Market Analysis for Product Type: **Coffee**, Product: **Colombian**, for **2012** year

Market	Sales	Budget Sales	Act vs Bud Sales	Margin	Budget Margin	Profit	Budget Profit	Profit %	Inventory	Marketing
East	$23,205	$21,390	$1,815	$15,762	$14,730	$11,129	$11,450	48.0%	636	$2,497
West	$14,862	$18,410	($3,548)	$8,803	$11,090	$4,593	$7,520	30.9%	762	$2,053
Central	$14,153	$14,260	($107)	$8,124	$8,300	$3,479	$4,490	24.6%	698	$2,686
South	$10,604	$13,130	($2,526)	$5,937	$7,450	$3,576	$5,440	33.7%	743	$1,437
Grand Total	$62,824	$67,190	($4,366)	$38,626	$41,570	$22,777	$28,900	36.3%	708	$8,673

FIGURE 8-47 *Market crosstab with dynamic title*

You might have a problem initially getting your dynamic title elements inserted into the title because you don't have the Product Type, Product, or Select Year fields on your marks card. If those fields aren't included in the Market Analysis worksheet, you will not be able to achieve the result you see in Figure 8-47. This is a typical trouble-shooting situation. Go to the Market Analysis worksheet and add the fields to the marks card as shown in Figure 8-48.

Now that the Product Type, Product, and Select Year fields are available they can be inserted into the title. Use font colors in the title to highlight the dynamic fields and use a lighter gray font color for the static parts. This emphasizes the items that the filter action is currently displaying.

FIGURE 8-48 *Fields added to the marks card*

Making the URL Action

Earlier, you placed a blank Web Page Object in Dashboard 2. Now you are ready to build the URL action that will trigger a search on a retail website and display the result in the Web Page Object.

To demonstrate another way you can trigger the action, you will use the Run Action On Hover method to execute the action. This means when users hover anywhere over the Market Analysis Crosstab, the URL search will be executed. In an actual use case it might be better to trigger the action using Select or Menu.

Open your browser and search Amazon's website for "coffee, amaretto." When the search is completed copy the URL string from your browser. You will paste this code into the URL field to define the URL action in Figure 8-49.

FIGURE 8-49 *URL action menu*

To enable Tableau to automatically change the search sent to Amazon, you will replace the search keywords contained in the URL string you copied from the website with fields supplied by Tableau. Figure 8-50 shows the modified script with the field names inserted into the string.

Test the URL action by going back to the Bullet Graph in the Sales Analysis Dashboard and execute the menu action with a different product. When you hover your mouse pointer over the Market Analysis Crosstab that should trigger another search of the website, and the products displayed should reflect the new search criteria.

FIGURE 8-50 *Inserting URL variables*

Using embedded Web Page Objects with URL Actions provides a method for combining your data with information from the web without having to be a programming expert. URL actions can be used in many different ways. Hopefully you can see the potential for enhancing your dashboards with information from the Internet.

Creating a Home Button

To allow people using this workbook to easily navigate back to the main dashboard you are going to create one more action. There should be another worksheet in your workbook called Nav Button. You can see the crosstab in that worksheet in Figure 8-51.

The small navigation button crosstab displayed in the upper right of the dashboard (see Figure 8-52) uses a calculation to create the text "Double-click on the arrow to return to the main dashboard. The field is named Return Nav. The calculation is the text wrapped in single or double quotes. Placing the Return Nav field on the row shelf, then changing the mark type to shape allows you to select any shape available in Tableau's shape pallet. Use the size button on the marks card to increase or decrease the size of the shape in the crosstab.

This crosstab will be placed in Dashboard 2 and used to hold a filter action to return the user to the main dashboard. Figure 8-52 shows Dashboard 2 with the Return Nav worksheet placed next to the title at the top of the dashboard.

FIGURE 8-51 *Nav button worksheet*

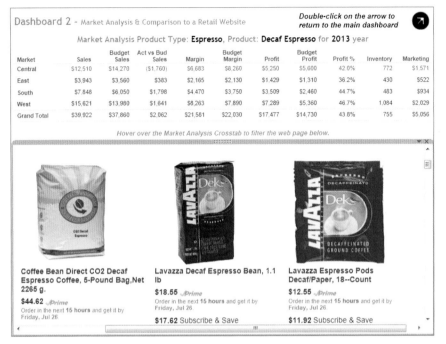

Dashboard 2 - Market Analysis & Comparison to a Retail Website

Double-click on the arrow to return to the main dashboard

Market Analysis Product Type: **Espresso**, Product: **Decaf Espresso** for **2013** year

Market	Sales	Budget Sales	Act vs Bud Sales	Margin	Budget Margin	Profit	Budget Profit	Profit %	Inventory	Marketing
Central	$12,510	$14,270	($1,760)	$6,683	$8,260	$5,250	$5,600	42.0%	772	$1,571
East	$3,943	$3,560	$383	$2,165	$2,130	$1,429	$1,310	36.2%	430	$522
South	$7,848	$6,050	$1,798	$4,470	$3,750	$3,509	$2,460	44.7%	483	$934
West	$15,621	$13,980	$1,641	$8,263	$7,890	$7,289	$5,360	46.7%	1,084	$2,029
Grand Total	$39,922	$37,860	$2,062	$21,581	$22,030	$17,477	$14,730	43.8%	755	$5,056

Hover over the Market Analysis Crosstab to filter the web page below.

Coffee Bean Direct CO2 Decaf Espresso Coffee, 5-Pound Bag,Net 2265 g.

$44.62 *Prime*
Order in the next **15 hours** and get it by Friday, Jul 26.

Lavazza Decaf Espresso Bean, 1.1 lb

$18.55 *Prime*
Order in the next **15 hours** and get it by Friday, Jul 26.

$17.62 Subscribe & Save

Lavazza Espresso Pods Decaf/Paper, 18--Count

$12.55 *Prime*
Order in the next **15 hours** and get it by Friday, Jul 26.

$11.92 Subscribe & Save

FIGURE 8-52 *The Home Button*

If you have trouble getting the placement right, remember that you can use a horizontal layout container object to group the dashboard title and the Return Nav button next to each other there. Also notice that some additional text has been added to the title. In addition, below the Market Analysis Crosstab a text object has been added with a navigation instruction explaining to users how to trigger the URL Action to the embedded website.

All that remains is to define the filter action to enable the Return Nav crosstab to navigate back to the main dashboard. Figure 8-53 shows the action dialog box to enable that feature.

This filter action completes all of the action examples for this workbook. Congratulations. It is now time to take a final tour of both dashboards to determine what additional information would enhance the information presented. Now that all of the navigation, filtering, titles, and other features have been completed, Tooltips can be customized to fill in

FIGURE 8-53 *Action to return users to the main dashboard*

any open questions. It might also be helpful to add a Read Me dashboard that contains text describing how the dashboard was designed to be used, while including contact information to users should unanticipated questions arise.

For all these reasons it is usually best to make Tooltip editing the last step in your dashboard design process.

ADDING DETAILS ON DEMAND WITH TOOLTIPS

The dashboard design is nearly complete. Getting outside feedback at this stage is helpful. Your audience may want to look at data in ways you didn't consider, which can lead to revisions to the layout, content, and filtering. Assuming that all of the design criteria have been fulfilled, finalizing the design normally requires adding textural content to provide relevant details on demand that enhance the content.

Tooltips are the pop-outs that appear when you hover over marks in worksheets and dashboards. They are an efficient way to convey textual information because they only appear on demand. Tooltips contain the fields used in your views by default, and any other field that is used as a filter or used on the marks card. They can also include manually added notes.

Dashboard and worksheet titles can also include explanatory information, but because of space limitations, the data added to them must be brief. In the remainder of this section you'll see how Tooltips and Titles can be used to enhance the example dashboards.

Using the Tooltip Editor

The Tooltip Editor is accessed from the Worksheet/Tooltip menu option. In dashboards, you can access the Title Editor by double-clicking in the title for Worksheet Object. Both editors provide light-duty word processing and other controls that allow you to insert fields into Tooltips and Titles. Figure 8-54 includes images of the Tooltip Editor and Title Editor for Bullet Graph in the Main Dashboard.

You can see that the editors are very similar but that the Tooltip Editor on the left contains a few additional controls that are not in the Title Editor. First, there is an indenting tool in the Tooltip Editor at the top that allows you to align individual rows exactly. The Tooltip editor also includes a check box called Include Command Buttons. If it is checked, additional controls appear at the bottom of the Tooltip as you see in Figure 8-55.

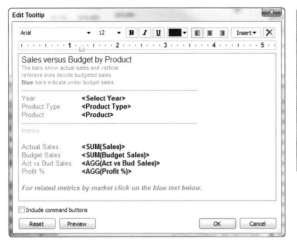

FIGURE 8-54   *Tooltip and Title Editors*

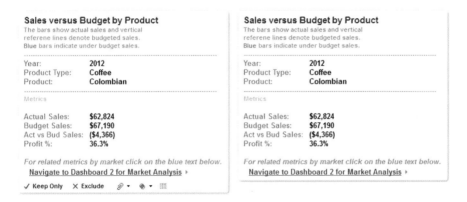

FIGURE 8-55   *Tooltips with and without command buttons*

Command buttons have been included in the Tooltip on the left and excluded from the one on the right. If your information consumers are viewing the dashboards using Tableau Reader, most of these controls, with the exception of the Keep Only and Exclude controls, will not be visible.

Notice that the Tooltip in Figure 8-55 has a variety of font sizes, colors, and styles being used. An underline is being used to divide the Tooltip into sections. At the bottom of the Tooltip there is instructional text followed by a Menu Action.

While you can be expansive in Tooltips, Titles have space restrictions. They serve the obvious purpose of identifying the content of the object they are associated with, but can also provide brief reminders. Figure 8-56 shows the completed Main Dashboard. Focus on the title areas.

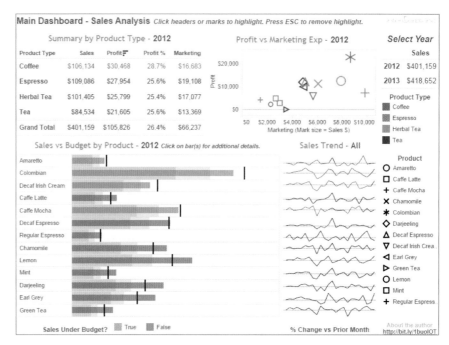

FIGURE 8-56 *Finished Main Sales Dashboard*

The titles include a few enhancements to provide small instructions. The dashboard's main title includes a small instruction to provide information on highlighting. Text was added to the Sales versus Budget Bar Chart providing a hint regarding available details. Three of the five Worksheet Objects include a dynamic field element that displays the year that has been selected from the Filter Action added to the Select Year Crosstab. These small instructions require very little space but improve the dashboard's understandability.

Enhancing Tooltips in the Main Dashboard

One of the big advantages to consuming interactive dashboards is the ability to utilize Tooltips to provide more detailed information without taking up valuable space in the dashboard layout. The Tooltips have been customized for every Worksheet Object in this dashboard. See Figure 8-57.

FIGURE 8-57 *Main Sales Dashboard Tooltips*

Each of the Tooltips is positioned in Figure 8-57 in the same area they appear in the dashboard. If you refer to Figure 8-56 you can see that each Tooltip is adding additional context in the view. The font color and style of instructions is consistently applied in the dashboard and the Tooltips. The Scatterplot, Bullet Graph, and Sparkline Tooltips support the more graphical views with field details. And the Bullet Graph includes the Menu Action along with a small instruction immediately above the action text. These are small things, but they greatly enhance the depth of information provided by the dashboard. This is why it is generally best to do your Tooltip editing at the very end of the design process.

Adding a Read Me Dashboard

Most people don't include Read Me worksheets in workbooks. If you are serving a large user base, the additional hour of time required to document your work in a Read Me dashboard could save you time in the long run. A well-documented workbook that provides an explanation of particularly complex calculated values, the datasources used, experts consulted, or other ancillary details will reduce your phone and e-mail traffic. If you have to manage a very large number of dashboards, a well-documented workbook can jog your memory if you need to revisit an old design or be an aid for training new staff.

The Coffee Chain data set used for creating the two sample dashboards in this chapter demonstrates that the size of your data isn't as important as the quality of information you can extract from it. The market analysis information contained in Dashboard 2 demonstrates how easy it is to use external information from websites with your data and make it interact with your proprietary data.

Next you learn about sharing your workbooks with others that may not have Tableau Desktop or Tableau Server licenses using Tableau's free Tableau Reader.

SHARING YOUR DASHBOARD WITH TABLEAU READER

The most secure way to distribute Tableau workbooks is via Tableau Server. But, when you want to share a workbook with someone that doesn't have access to Tableau Server, Tableau Reader provides a free alternative.

Distributing content with Tableau Reader requires that you save the Tableau workbook file as a packaged workbook. Tableau Packaged Workbooks (.twbx) require local file sources such as:

- Excel
- Access
- Text files (.csv, .txt, etc.)
- Tableau Data Extract files (.tde)

If the datasource for the workbook you want to share with Tableau Reader comes from a server-based database (SQL Server, Teradata, Oracle, etc.), you must extract the source data first—saving extracted data as a Tableau Data Extract—then save the workbook as a Tableau Packaged Workbook.

SECURITY CONSIDERATIONS FOR PUBLISHING VIA TABLEAU READER

Tableau Reader is intended to make your workbooks available to anyone—even those that do not have a Tableau licensed product. There are security considerations that you should be aware of when you distribute workbooks this way. Do not rely on filters to shield sensitive data that is included in the datasources used in the workbook. Tableau packaged workbooks are like zip files. They can be unpackaged which will expose the datasource file.

If your datasource includes sensitive information, you can exclude that data when the extract file is created. Figure 8-58 shows the Extract Data dialog box that is accessed by pointing at the datasource (in the data window) and right-clicking.

One way to exclude information when creating the extract is to exclude data by filtering. You can also use aggregation to reduce the granularity of the data included in the extract. For example, selecting Aggregate data for visible dimensions aggregates the extract file so that it will include only data to support the visualizations in your workbook. In addition, any fields that you hide in the data window will not be included in the data extract.

Excluding sensitive information from the data extract file allows you to control the risk of data loss caused by unauthorized distribution of proprietary data.

FIGURE 8-58 *The Extract Data dialog box*

SHARING DASHBOARDS WITH TABLEAU ONLINE OR TABLEAU SERVER

Tableau offers a cloud-based option called Tableau Online. This service provides a low cost alternative to sharing workbooks with licensed users of the service. Tableau Server is a self-managed solution that can be maintained inside or outside of your organization's firewall. Workbooks are published to Tableau Online or Tableau Server. People consuming the workbooks are granted access to them by a designated administrator that controls security.

The process for publishing workbooks to Tableau Server on Tableau Online is similar. Once the workbook has been published, authenticated users are able to access it using a web browser. See Chapters 10 and 11 for more details on Tableau Server and Tableau Online.

Over the past few years tablet computers have been growing in popularity. Tableau has made producing workbooks for table consumption a seamless experience for the designer.

In the next section you'll learn about designing workbooks for tablet computers including security considerations, and the difference in typical patterns of consumption between personal computer and tablet computer users.

DESIGNING FOR MOBILE CONSUMPTION

Just as the personal computer replaced the mainframe, and the laptop replaced the personal computer, even more mobile devices will eventually replace the laptop. This trend toward smaller and more powerful devices means more dashboards and visualizations will be consumed on mobile devices.

Leading technology research firms Gartner and International Data Corporation have reported on an explosion of growth in mobile devices—cell phones, and more recently tablet devices. In November 2012 Gartner reported:

Gartner says 821 million smart devices will be purchased worldwide in 2012; sales to rise to 1.2 billion in 2013.[4]

Gartner's forecast also said that tablet purchases by businesses would more than triple from 13 million units in 2012 to over 53 million units in 2016. Clearly business use of tablets is expanding rapidly.

This trend is echoed in the business information (BI) world with increasing numbers of people using mobile devices (tablets and smart phones) to consume data. Mobile deployment has become a key component of most successful Tableau implementations. The next section describes the physics of mobile data consumption, security considerations, usage patterns, and the design best practices for building dashboards for mobile consumption.

THE PHYSICS OF MOBILE CONSUMPTION

Mobile consumption of Tableau Dashboards is a function of the Tableau Server, Tableau Online, and Tableau Public environments. Since Tableau doesn't store data on your mobile device, a few prerequisites must be in place to enable mobile consumption:

- Installing Tableau's native iPad or Android application is not required (but desirable)
- Provide a server name and Internet address for the connection to Tableau Server.
- Username
- Password

Since mobile consumption is a default capability of Tableau Server, no additional configuration is required to enable mobile access. It should be noted that mobile device usage patterns can differ from non-mobile consumption.

Mobile users typically use more sessions of shorter duration than desktop users. The interesting result of this usage pattern typically means increased session counts at the server level as users exploit the "just-in-time" nature of mobile access to data.

SECURITY CONSIDERATIONS FOR MOBILE CONSUMPTION

Unlike the Tableau Reader or Tableau Desktop tools, Tableau's native apps for iOS and Android are completely Server based. This means neither mobile tool downloads a data file or workbook file onto the Tablet's physical storage. All data and reports are accessed entirely through the web connection to Tableau Server.

If a user were to lose a tablet, the only Tableau-related information residing there would be information about workbooks (publisher, date modified, and name) rather than the sensitive data contained within the workbooks being accessed. Of course, any machine with access to secure information should be password protected.

Since mobile devices normally exist outside of the corporate network, options for network accessibility should be considered before deploying Tableau for mobile consumption if they haven't already been separately addressed.

Whether the Tableau Server has been positioned inside or outside of the DMZ (a secure area in a private network providing access to authorized users from the public Internet) dictates what special procedures are necessary to enable mobile access. If the Tableau Server is not positioned within the enterprise DMZ, solutions to provide mobile access typically include virtual private networks (VPN), log-on, or corporate specific browsers (e.g., `http://www1.good.com/`).

Once access to the Tableau Server machine is established, users can view dashboards and reports with the same authentication protocols normally used for desktop browsing. In this regard, specific mobile permissions are not configurable at the Tableau Server level without duplicating accounts or servers. If a completely separate set of mobile reports is desired, this is a process typically mediated through a separate server or as a function of proxy-based relays.

TYPICAL MOBILE USAGE PATTERNS

Users accessing Tableau Dashboards and reports from a mobile device typically have quite a different set of goals/intent for their experience versus those accessing data on the desktop. While this rule is not hard and fast, mobile users normally have a narrower scope and more defined use criteria.

Just-In-Time Use

The Pew Internet Trust recently found that 86 percent of smart phone owners used their phone in the past month to make real-time queries to help them meet friends, solve problems, or settle arguments.[5]

The Pew report provided additional details regarding the activities mobile users engage in when using their portable devices. Do any of these items sound like needs your Tableau users might have?

- Solving unexpected problems that they or someone else encountered
- Deciding whether to visit a business
- Finding information to settle an argument regarding facts
- Looking up a score
- Getting up-to-the-minute information

All of these activities are supported by Tableau's mobile environment. If users are able to satisfy these Just-In-Time needs, they can seamlessly integrate that information into their daily activities.

Mobile Design Implications

Just-In-Time Use has significant implications for dashboard and report design. Clearly, the mobile market is not at all homogeneous. You should not assume all of your mobile users will have the same intent. But, you can make some reliable assumptions about mobile information consumers and their desire for Just-In-Time information.

Mobile users want the most up-to-date information possible for asking questions and solving problems. Mobile users are more likely to be looking for a specific answer to a specific question, rather than embarking on a multi-hour session of complex analysis. This tendency should inform your dashboard designs for mobile consumption.

These requirements imply that mobile dashboards need to be more focused on specific areas and answering the kinds of questions that arise most frequently.

Design Best Practices for Mobile Consumption

Mobile device screens are obviously smaller than personal computer monitors, and your input method will be less precise than a mouse pointer. These differences were carefully considered when Tableau enabled their products for mobile usage. You also need to think about how your dashboard designs need to be adapted for this kind of consumption. Mobile environment considerations include:

- No mouse and no multi-select through click and drag

- Lack of a control button and no multi-select through Ctrl+click

- Hover is not available as an action trigger.

- The finger for pointing and clicking

- Zoom by a pinch/expand gesture.

These differences have significant implications for mobile design and feature heavily in the following recommendations. The emergence of mainstream touchscreen-based operating systems, including iOS, Android, Windows 8, Smart Tables, and Smart Screens, means many of the design criteria specific to mobile will soon be applicable to a far larger user segment.

Design Implications Related to Screen Resolution

Consumer display resolution should always be a primary consideration for dashboard design, regardless of the consumption environment. Since there are fewer possible resolutions available for mobile devices, it is easier to create "table friendly" designs. Fixed dashboard sizing—desirable for mobile designs—also provides performance advantages at the Tableau Server caching level. As with all dashboard designs, it is best to err on the side of caution and size your view for the lowest resolution anticipated. This assures that information consumers won't be forced to scroll to see all of the content. Tableau has predefined dashboard resolutions for mobile devices. You can also specifically define any resolution required should your needs not fit industry standard sizes.

Best Practices for Mobile Design

Designing for mobile devices is similar to designing for personal computers. Many of the best practices in designing for the PC apply. There are some additional allowances that have to be made due to the smaller screen size.

- Design for a specific orientation.

- Consider the limits of finger navigation.

- Reduce the number of worksheet objects displayed.

Design for a Specific Orientation

The best dashboard designs for mobile devices should be optimized for a specific design. Most of the tablet dashboards that I've seen are designed for landscape mode viewing; however, what is most important is that you commit to an orientation and build the dashboard for viewing that way. Tableau's dashboard worksheet includes two predefined orientations for tablets—one for landscape mode (1020 × 625 pixels) and another for portrait mode (764 × 855 pixels). You can tweak those values to fit any resolution needed by using the Exactly mode. This selection allows you to define specific pixel height and width if the mobile devices you're designing for don't conform to the default values.

Consider the Limits of Finger Navigation

The primary interaction medium will be users' fingers, which do not have the precision of a mouse. If a dashboard design feature is actuated through a filter or highlight action, ensure that the selection options are large enough for users to easily select without accidentally hitting a neighboring point. Nothing makes for a grumpier tablet user than one waiting for a filter that they didn't intend to select.

To avoid this trap, design dashboards with one of two alternative navigations. Choose heat maps, bar charts, highlight tables, or bullet charts to trigger actions. These provide discrete layout boundaries and preclude overlapping or closely-spaced marks. Conversely, scatter plots have continuous axes that typically produce clusters of overlapping marks. This would not be a good choice for a filter action if precision is required. Figure 8-59 illustrates the point.

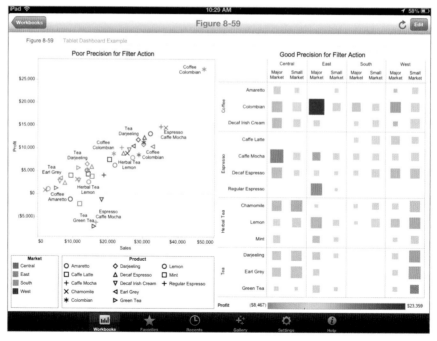

FIGURE 8-59 *Chart style and finger navigation*

The scatter plot on the left of Figure 8-59 includes many closely-spaced or overlapping marks. This makes it a poor tablet-based action trigger because it is nearly impossible for the user to select a particular mark unless it is one of the outliers that are not included in the cluster.

The heat map on the right side of Figure 8-59 has marks that are regularly spaced. No mark is too small to provide a good Click target. The heat map not only communicates data effectively, but also provides for easy action triggering. To ensure that the smallest values were large enough, the mark size was edited—increasing the minimum mark size to avoid all possibility of individual marks being too small to click.

Tableau has also tuned Quick Filters by changing their behavior, making them automatically expand into versions that are more easily selected using your finger on mobile devices. This doesn't require any special effort when you design the dashboard. Tableau detects the consumption environment and changes the design of the Quick Filter automatically.

These design differences provide a mobile-optimized interaction, though it does slow the experience slightly vis-a-vis consumption on a PC. For example, three selections are required to initiate a mobile Quick Filter—one click to activate the Quick Filter dialog, another to pick a value, and a third to return to the dashboard.

Reduce the Number of Worksheets Being Displayed

Due to the reduced screen size of mobile devices it is best to use no more than three worksheet objects in a dashboard. One of those may need to be a very small crosstab limited to a single measure. Designs with too many worksheet objects are generally difficult to see.

A Tablet Dashboard Example

The following example was created with the Superstore sample data. The dashboard has two primary data visualizations, two Quick Filters, one parameter control, and a filter action triggered by selections made in the heat map. You'll also see how using a small crosstab with a shape can be used to hold more detailed instructions within a Tooltip. Figure 8-60 shows a sales dashboard that is designed to be consumed using a tablet in landscape mode.

The dashboard in Figure 8-60 uses best practice techniques. The dashboard contains two data visualizations. The top heat map displays sales and profits using size and color. Region and project categories are displayed in rows providing discrete separation that will allow the user to filter using a filter action executed by selecting marks. The lower portion of the dashboard contains a histogram that displays sales or shipping cost information. A parameter control (select histogram measure) allows the user to change the measure being displayed in the histogram. The histogram also uses color to depict profit values. A Quick Filter allows the user to select the year being viewed in both charts. The histogram also contains a parameter control that allows the user to change the sales bin size range for each bar, and the small label at the top of each bar shows the record count for the sales bin.

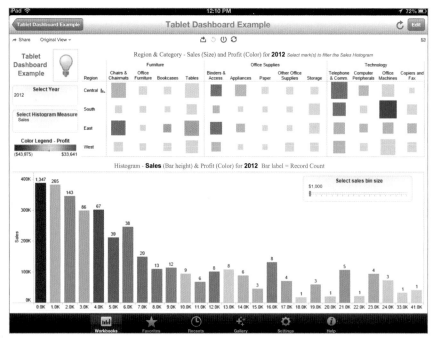

FIGURE 8-60 *Tablet dashboard in landscape mode*

Figure 8-61 shows how the Quick Filter for year pops out when the user selects the Select Year filter—making it easier to select the appropriate year. After the selection is made, the filter will collapse to its former size.

The histogram bin-size is changed using a slider-type parameter control that pops out as well, as you see in Figure 8-62.

A filter action placed in the heat map allows the user to filter the histogram to display the related values in the histogram below. As you can see in Figure 8-63, selecting a mark also causes a Tooltip to display related details.

In Figure 8-64, a small crosstab using a light bulb shape contains navigation instructions.

FIGURE 8-61 *Expanded year Quick Filter*

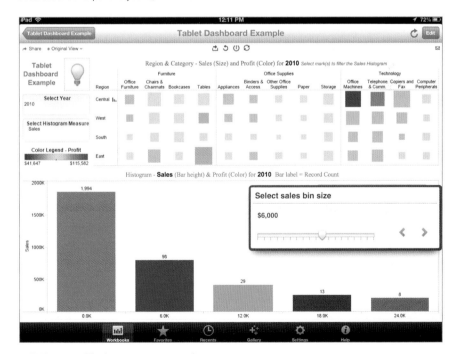

FIGURE 8-62 *Bin size parameter control*

FIGURE 8-63 *Filter action and Tooltip*

FIGURE 8-64 *Small instructions near the work*

When the user points at the light bulb image, a Tooltip is displayed that contains detailed instructions.

For someone needing timely information regarding sales by product line, this dashboard provides an easy to navigate, Just-In-Time environment for that purpose. The dashboard provides details in the worksheet object titles that change based on the filter and parameter selections made. The portions of the titles in bold confirm those selections. See Figure 8-65.

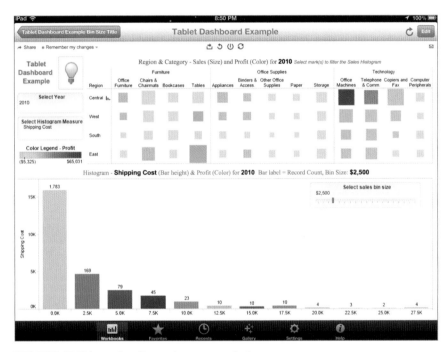

FIGURE 8-65 *Titles confirm filter and parameter selections.*

This mobile dashboard is designed to load quickly and answer a specific set of questions. It loads quickly, filters quickly, and is easy to read because it is designed to answer a specific set of questions related to sales and shipping costs.

USING THE TABLEAU PERFORMANCE RECORDER TO IMPROVE LOAD SPEED

Distributing content that loads fast and responds quickly to query requests is one of the most critical aspects of dashboard design. A slow-loading dashboard will not provide a good user experience.

Tableau provides a built-in tool called the Performance Recorder that provides detailed information about your workbook's performance characteristics. This tool analyzes Tableau's log files and builds a Tableau Workbook that analyzes the key performance attributes of your workbook.

To use the Performance Records start Tableau. Go to the Help menu and select the option Start Performance Recording, then open the workbook that you want to analyze. When you have the workbook open, refresh all of the worksheets, and use features so that queries are generated and rendering of visualizations occurs. When you are finished, return to the help menu and stop the Performance Recorder. Tableau will generate a dashboard that looks like Figure 8-66.

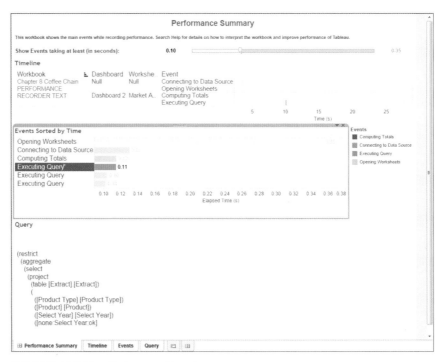

FIGURE 8-66 *Tableau Performance Recorder*

The dashboard generated by the Performance Recorder gives you information on the data connection, queries, and rendering speeds. If you have a workbook that loads slowly, the Performance Recorder gives you the ability to find speed leakages and test corrections by comparing updated performance recordings against your original record.

Now that you've seen how to create dashboards that perform and communicate well to your audience, in the next three chapters you will learn about installing, configuring, and managing Tableau's Server-based information sharing products.

NOTES

1. McKee, Robert. *Story: Substance, Structure, Style and the Principles of Screenwriting.* New York: Regan, 1997. Print. Page 113.

2. Few, Stephen. *Show Me the Numbers: Designing Tables and Graphs to Enlighten.* Burlingame, Calif: Analytics, 2012. Print. Page 79.

3. Tufte, Edward. *The Visual Display of Quantitative Information.* Cheshire, CT: Graphic, 1983. Print. Page 93.

4. "Gartner Says 821 Million Smart Devices Will Be Purchased Worldwide in 2012; Sales to Rise to 1.2 Billion in 2013," Gartner, Inc., accessed July 27, 2013, `http://www.gartner.com/newsroom/id/2227215`.

5. "Pew Internet: Mobile, Highlights of the Pew Internet Project's research related to mobile technology," by Joanna Brenner, last modified June 6, 2013, accessed July 27, 2013, `http://pewinternet.org/Commentary/2012/February/Pew-Internet-Mobile.aspx`.

PART II

TABLEAU SERVER

In this part

CHAPTER 9

Installing Tableau Server

The more you have in your cup, the more likely people are to want a drink.

SETH GODIN[1]

In the first eight chapters you learned how to use Tableau to connect to data, analyze data, visualize data, and build dashboards. Chapters 9, 10, and 11 are about installing, managing, and maintaining Tableau's information sharing products. Tableau provides three different tools for sharing information—Tableau Public, Tableau Online, and Tableau Server.

Tableau Public is a free cloud-hosted service aimed at bloggers, students, or data visualization enthusiasts that want to share their work publically. It is not designed for enterprise environments that require data security. In fact, anything published on Tableau Public is freely available for anyone to download. This tool is generally not used in enterprise environments that need to control access to the information.

Tableau Server is for customers that need to control where and how the data is stored and managed. It can be installed on hardware behind your firewall or on cloud services that you contract with directly. You can license it by named-user, or based on the server hardware that is installed.

Tableau Online (released in 2013) is another cloud-based information sharing environment (managed by Tableau Software) that provides data security without the need for installing any software or managing hardware. Your data is stored in a secure environment managed by Tableau Software. To start using Tableau Online just requires signing-up for the service and assigning access to your users based on your security needs.

Because Tableau Online is a service that doesn't require that you provision hardware and install any software, the majority of this chapter will be about your choices for installing and configuring Tableau Server. In the sections of the chapter related to setting-up security, differences between Tableau Server and Tableau Online will be discussed.

THE REASONS TO DEPLOY TABLEAU SERVER

Server's architecture provides the flexibility to scale from a single box to large multi-server deployments. User-friendly tools are provided for setup and maintenance of access rights, scheduling, and notification. Once setup is complete, continuing administration is normally minimal. Downloading and installing Tableau Server normally can be done in less than two hours.

A new feature in Tableau Server Version 8 provides users with the additional flexibility of editing or creating new reports and analysis. This functionality isn't a replacement for Tableau Desktop, but does allow staff that doesn't have a Tableau Desktop license to build and modify reports.

There are three primary reasons to deploy Tableau Server:

- Data governance (security)
- Efficiency (time savings)
- Flexibility (consumption and editing options)

DATA GOVERNANCE

Securing proprietary or confidential data is not only a business need, but also a legal requirement. Information managed by health care providers, insurance companies, and government entities is controlled by law. Businesses have a legal obligation to ensure that private employee and customer data is kept confidential and secure. Questions regarding policy implementation, data stewardship, and adaptability have to be balanced against this need for security.

Technology staff must be concerned about the accuracy and consistency of the data being consumed by staff without being overly controlling. Tableau Server balances these different needs very well by supporting data governance best practices. It allows information technology staff to maintain control over datasources (providing a single version of the truth) while simultaneously providing information consumers with the ability to adapt reports to their own purposes—without the need for additional technical staff or needing to resort to creating new (unauthorized) datasources.

EFFICIENCY

Sharing reports is very easy via Tableau's free desktop report consumption tool—Tableau Reader. However, this approach doesn't scale well and provides only limited means for securing the underlying data. Updating desktop reports is easy, but can be time-consuming if you have dozens of weekly reports to deliver. Tableau Server provides a secure environment for report consumption and can automatically update reports and inform users of new report availability via Server's subscription service. Administrators can monitor report consumption, server utilization, and performance.

Tableau Online provides similar benefits at a lower price point but requires publishing your Tableau reports outside of your firewall.

Many times the datasource doesn't include all of the information desired. Domain experts inside your entity may create initial workbooks that address aggregation needs, dimension grouping, and other particulars that would be desirable to share with everyone using Tableau. Server facilitates this sharing by allowing users to publish that metadata via datasource files through the server—saving everyone time and ensuring report consistency. If those datasource files are modified, then changes are automatically propagated to everyone using that datasource.

Personnel consuming reports don't need to install any software to view reports because everything is viewed via a web browser. Internet Explorer, Firefox, Chrome, and Safari are all supported.

FLEXIBILITY

While Tableau connects directly to a wide variety of sources, if you desire to run reports from data extracts, extract updates can be scheduled to run automatically at any time interval desired. Do not underestimate the level of demand that Tableau generates. In short order, your deployment may go from a few users to hundreds, and then thousands. The number of reports will increase as well. Server provides the users with an easy-to-navigate consumption environment that allows them to ask questions and get answers. It provides administrators with the means for managing and updating reporting needs without the need for daily manual intervention.

Reports published via Server can include direct connections to datasources or data extracts that are automatically updated by Server. Administrators can assign rights for publishing, consuming, and even modifying reports. Reports can be embedded into existing company websites, and Tableau can pass through the security layer without requiring the user to enter redundant login information. Information consumers can securely view and edit reports via the web on their desktop, laptop, and on iOS or Android tablet devices.

Tableau Server is a robust environment that provides technology managers with the tools to secure and maintain the environment while also providing information consumers with fast access to the information they need.

LICENSING OPTIONS FOR TABLEAU SERVER AND TABLEAU ONLINE

Tableau Server can be licensed two different ways:

- Per-named-user basis
- Server core license

Core licensing provides unlimited access to any number of users. Pricing is based on the number of processor cores contained on the physical box or multiple boxes on which you deploy the software. Per-named-user licensing starts with a minimum of ten users. Core licensing requires an eight-core minimum. Although many factors can affect performance in a server deployment (hardware, network traffic, dashboard design), an eight-core configuration can support up to 225 concurrent users.

Tableau Online is a named-user license that requires a one-year commitment. You can start with a single license and add more as your needs grow.

DETERMINING YOUR HARDWARE AND SOFTWARE NEEDS

Tableau Server is a scalable system that is capable of meeting the demands of the most intense enterprise environments. Proper planning is an important first step before you settle on the appropriate hardware configuration and licensing options. At a minimum, you should consider the following details when planning your deployment:

- User count
- User concurrency rate
- Workbook complexity
- User Locations
- Database Locations
- Database size
- Extract Usage—number and size

The user count and user concurrency rate provide an expectation of the volume of requests that Server will be handling. This is normally fairly easy to estimate. User count represents the number of licensed users on Tableau Server that are able to make requests to the server. User concurrency rates represent the percentage of the licensed users that will be making requests at any single moment. For example, a deployment anticipating 1,000 licensed users with an expected concurrency rate of 10 percent implies that approximately 100 users would be active in the system at any moment.

Workbook complexity is more difficult to anticipate. For this reason, before you plan your Server environment it may be advisable to identify a core group of report designers, train them, and have them build some initial reports that can serve as a basis for planning. This typically doesn't require more than a month to accomplish and doesn't need to involve many staff. Not all requests made to Tableau Server are equivalent. Server will spend more resources to render dashboards with complex designs and large volumes of data than dashboards with simple designs and low record counts. Poorly designed dashboards are the most common cause of poor performance in Tableau Server.

If you have users across many locations or database services deployed across multiple geographies, you may need to have a correspondingly larger number of Tableau Servers to support local demands if a central service isn't able to provide the desired responsiveness.

The amount of data you have, as well as the type of database sources you are using, must also be considered. Massive data or heavy demand along with a database that wasn't designed for the analytical loads can create the need for shifting some of the analytical burden to Tableau Server from the database by utilizing more Tableau Data Extract files.

DETERMINING WHAT KIND OF SERVER LICENSE TO PURCHASE

If you don't require that your data and reporting be within your company network—behind your firewall, Tableau Online provides a very convenient option. Tableau Software manages the hardware and is responsible for maintaining network performance. It is a very good option if you are comfortable with Software-as-a-Service (SaaS) models. The administrator of a Tableau Online deployment is only directly responsible for controlling the access by setting permissions for publishing and viewing the data.

If your organization is unable to reside your data in the cloud outside of your firewall, Tableau Server's named-user licensing or Core-Server licensing allow you to directly control every aspect of Tableau Server's setup and configuration—inside or outside of your company's firewall. For most large enterprise customers, Tableau Server offers the most flexibility.

Tableau Server named-user licensing is exactly what it sounds like—one license purchased per user—meaning that a license must be purchased for each individual user of the system. If there are ten distinct employees that need access to Tableau Server, then all ten of them must have a named-user license.

A question that many people ask is whether or not Tableau can be deployed on any kind of multiplexing device so that individual users can share the per-named-user license. The answer is no. Licenses are transferable but this is not a practical way to split a single named-user license among an active user base. Named-user licenses are also referred to as Interactor licenses.

Core licensing allows customers to license Tableau Server by the server processor core—avoiding the need to purchase licenses for specific named-users. Core licensing provides greater flexibility, allowing for as many users as a server can support from a resource perspective. These licenses are typically sold in multi-core quantities in eight-core multiples. Pricing for core licensing reflects the fact that a single core can support many users. It also provides the option of enabling a special guest account to enable unrestricted access to reports assigned by the administrator.

The number of users you anticipate accessing the system normally determines which licensing model you choose. Smaller entities with low user counts typically find that named-user licensing provides a better value. Tableau Online will also appeal to this segment if externally-hosted security is permitted. Large organizations with user counts exceeding 250 normally find core licensing more cost effective.

In some cases mixed licensing models might be desirable since hardware limitations imposed by the core licensing model can be alleviated though the selective use of named-user licensing and/or Tableau Online.

TABLEAU SERVER'S ARCHITECTURE

Tableau Server is comprised of several processes operating together. These may run concurrently, but typically all processes won't be running all of the time. These include:

- Application Server (`wgserver.exe`)
- VizQL Server (`vizqlserver.exe`)
- Data Engine (`tdeserver.exe, tdeserver64.exe`)
- Backgrounder (`backgrounder.exe`)
- Data Server (`dataserver.exe`)
- Repository (`postgres.exe`)

The application server handles requests to the web application such as searching, browsing, logging in, generating static images and managing subscriptions. The VizQL server handles the task of loading and rendering requested views. The data engine receives queries made to Tableau Data Extracts present on the server. These queries come from the VizQL processes. To service these queries, the Data Engine loads the Tableau Data Extracts into memory and returns the requested record set. The backgrounder runs maintenance tasks and data extract refreshes. The data server handles requests to Tableau Datasources. These requests can come from the Tableau Server or from Tableau Desktop users. The repository is the Postgres database Tableau Server uses to store settings, metadata, usage statistics and workbooks.

With the notable exception of the data engine, all of these processes are 32-bit processes. The data engine has a 64-bit executable code, which will be used by default if a 64-bit architecture is detected. All processes except the backgrounder are multi-threaded.

SIZING THE SERVER HARDWARE

Tableau Server runs well within a variety of hardware configurations. It can be deployed for small organizations on a relatively inexpensive single system. It can also be deployed for large organizations with thousands of users on clusters containing many powerful machines. You get what you pay for in terms of performance from hardware expenditures. The current minimum recommended hardware configuration for Tableau Server is a single machine with 32-gigabytes of memory and 8-CPU cores. Specific recommendations regarding the size and configuration of your deployment are affected by many factors including the complexity and size of the dashboards, the datasources, the timing and frequency of usage, the network, and the hardware configuration running the software. For these reasons specific benchmarks are not provided. Consult with Tableau Software's technical staff or a qualified Tableau Software Partner to obtain specific recommendations.

As your deployment grows you can increase capacity by scaling-up to a more powerful single server, or by splitting the increased demand across multiple physical servers.

A Scale-Up Scenario

To scale Tableau Server up on a single system, choose a platform that can provide more physical CPU cores and more system memory. At this time, major hardware manufacturers are shipping servers that support up to 32 physical CPU cores and far more memory than Tableau Server will require. The above ratio of CPU cores to system memory (1-CPU to 4-GB memory) is a good general guideline to follow—plan for more memory when use of very large Tableau Data Extracts is expected. The data engine will hold data extracts in memory if possible. This improves query performance.

Disk performance is a secondary consideration when planning for Tableau Server in most cases. The major exception being situations in which there is heavy use of the data engine with extracts that will not fit into memory. In this case the data engine is forced to go to disk frequently—making faster I/O potentially worthwhile. Otherwise, even with heavy use of the data engine, Tableau Server does not benefit a great deal from more exotic I/O setups, such as arrays of Solid State Drives (SSD).

An example of a scale-up configuration for Tableau Server is a single machine with 24-CPU cores and 96-GB of memory. Based on the current Tableau Server scalability tests, it's expected that this server could handle somewhere between 108 and 378 concurrent requests depending on workbook complexity.

A Scale-Out Scenario

To scale Tableau Server out, multiple servers will need to be provisioned and the server processes will be split across them. In this case, the servers are not required to be configured identically. It is a common pattern to tailor each machine in a cluster to the processes running on it. Deploying Tableau Server on multiple servers will be discussed in greater detail later in this chapter in the section on High Availability Environments.

An example of a scale-out configuration for Tableau Server is a cluster consisting of three machines each configured with 8-CPU cores and 32-GB of memory. This configuration will provide slightly lower performance than the sample scale-up configuration due to the server communication overhead introduced by the cluster. A fourth machine can be used to run the Gateway server. If this is done, any machine running Gateway services exclusively is not counted against the Tableau Server Core license.

Regardless if you plan to scale-up or scale-out, if you decide to purchase under the core-license model you need to determine the number of cores that you'll be required to purchase. Do this by counting the number of physical cores across all of the machines that will be running Tableau Server processes excluding servers that are running Gateway services only.

ENVIRONMENTAL FACTORS THAT CAN AFFECT PERFORMANCE

There are many environmental factors that can affect performance of Tableau Server. Normally the most significant factors relate to network performance, the browser, and resource contention.

Network Performance

Users will be connecting to Tableau Server either through an internal network or via the public Internet. Any poor performing network links in between users and the Tableau Server can cause erratic behavior of dashboards, and slow loading Internal networks are not normally a problem. Spotty Internet connections are a common cause of long dashboard load times. If you do experience slow connection speeds, the best solution is to increase the available bandwidth of the connection.

Browser

The user experience of Tableau Server is heavily dependent on JavaScript. As such, some browsers can cause Tableau Server to feel unresponsive or sluggish because of their sub-par JavaScript performance. Internet Explorer 7 is a major offender in this case. Chrome, Firefox, Safari and modern versions of Internet Explorer all have superior JavaScript performance. If it frequently takes a few clicks to get a Quick Filter drop-down selection to apply, you might be running into a browser performance issue.

Resource Contention

Tableau Server will not perform well in environments with other resource hungry applications and services running on the same machine. Resource contention can cause slowness in each component process of Tableau Server. To get the most out of your Tableau Server license expenditure, ensure that Tableau Server is the only application running on the machine(s).

CONFIGURING TABLEAU SERVER FOR THE FIRST TIME

When installing Tableau Server there are many configuration options to evaluate. Most of these options can be adjusted after the installation, but some of these options cannot be changed without reinstalling the software. It is therefore important to place careful consideration behind the configuration options below.

GENERAL: SERVER RUN AS USER

Server Run As User refers to the Windows username that the Tableau Server service (tabsvc) will run under. By default, this is configured as the Network Service account. This can be changed to either a local machine account or a domain account. If choosing a domain account, specify the domain with the username. One reason to use a domain account is to provide access to datasources that require Windows NT authentication without prompting users for credentials. In this case the account specified here logs into the datasource.

GENERAL: USER AUTHENTICATION AND ACTIVE DIRECTORY

Tableau Server can be configured to authenticate users in one of two ways:

- A Local Authentication
- An Active Directory Authentication (ADA)

It is very important that you choose the authentication method carefully because this cannot be changed once the server is installed. In the Local Authentication option users are added to the server by configuring a username and a password. In the Active Directory authentication option, users who are added to the Tableau Server must already exist within Active Directory. Active Directory manages the user's password. Selecting Active Directory authentication allows clients to reuse their existing security structure.

Be sure to enter the domain name and nickname when choosing to authenticate with Active Directory. This domain name must be a fully qualified domain name. Using the (ADA) method allows an additional option—Enable Automatic Log-on. This option enables users to automatically log in to Tableau Server with the currently logged in Windows account credentials via the Microsoft Security Support Provider Interface (SSPI). Additionally, Automatic Log-on should not be enabled if the guest account is enabled or trusted ticket authentication is used.

General: Port Number

By default, Tableau Server accepts requests on port 80. If this needs to be changed for networking reasons, reset the port number using this option.

General: Open Port in Windows Firewall

This opens the above port number in the Windows Firewall to ensure that requests can be received on the specified port. This setting normally shouldn't need to be edited unless you have changed from the default port 80.

Data Connections Caching

The caching options within Tableau Server dictate how often cached data will be reused and how frequently data will be queried from the datasource. These are the options:

- Refresh Less Often.
- Data in the cache is reused for as long as possible.

- Balanced (data is removed from the cache after a specified number of minutes)

- Refresh More Often.

- Data in the cache is refreshed on each page reload by a query to the datasource.

Caching option selections can significantly affect performance. Reading from the cache is much quicker than querying the datasource directly. In most cases leaving this option set to Refresh Less Often will provide the best performance. The main reason to change to Balanced or Refresh More Often, is to prevent old data from being reported when you have a rapidly changing datasource.

Data Connections: Initial SQL

When connecting to a database, an initial SQL statement can be sent to set up an environment. For security reasons some administrators may want to disable the Initial SQL setting. Selecting the "Ignore initial SQL Statements for all datasources" setting will cause the workbooks created using the initial SQL statement to open, but the initial SQL command will not be sent.

Server: Number of Processes per Server

The server tab of the configuration dialog box allows the user to configure the machines in the Tableau Server cluster and the number of each type of process per server. These are the default configurations for an 8-core instance:

- VizQL—Two processes

- Application—Two processes

- Background—One process

- Extract engine—One process

Use the Edit dialog box to adjust the numbers of processes if needed. You should plan on at least one CPU core and one gigabyte of memory per process at a minimum. These settings are made in the configuration dialog box after installation. Cluster configurations will be covered in the High Availability section later in this chapter.

E-mail Alerts for Administrators

To have an e-mail notification sent to a specified administrator when the server detects problems, enable Send E-mail Alerts. Add the e-mail address of the person to be notified.

Subscriptions

Use the Enable E-mail Subscriptions option to allow users to subscribe to workbooks on Tableau Server so that they receive e-mail notification when the workbook is updated. This subscription will send the most recent version of a workbook to users at scheduled intervals.

If either e-mail notification is enabled (for problem alerts to the administrator or for subscriptions) the relevant SMTP Server information must be provided.

Secure Sockets Layer (SSL)

Select the Use SSL for Server Communication setting to enable Tableau Server to use SSL to secure communications. If this setting is enabled, the required certificate files must be provided. Tableau Server currently uses SSL only over Port 443. For more information about the requirements of the SSL certificate files, check the Configuring SSL reference in the Tableau Server Administrator's Guide.

To adjust these settings after installation, select the Configure Tableau Server shortcut under the Tableau Server folder in All Programs.

SETTING-UP SECURITY RIGHTS

Tableau Server has a robust system for managing security. To fully grasp it, you must understand the hierarchy of objects that contain reports and data within Tableau's environment.

Workbook

The Workbook object represents the Tableau workbook file published from Tableau Desktop. It contains dashboards and worksheets, which in terms of Tableau Server are all known as Views. Permissions can be applied to specific Views within a Workbook or at the whole Workbook level. Workbooks and Views can belong to projects and must be published to a site.

User

The User object represents a named-user who has access to the Tableau Server. Users must be granted a licensing level of Interactor or Viewer to log in to the server. It's possible to leave a user account on the server in an effectively disabled state by setting its licensing level to unlicensed. This can be useful for audit purposes. Users can be granted access to Views, Workbooks, Projects, and Sites. They can also be placed into groups. Also note that unlicensed Tableau Server users (that have been given publishing rights) can publish workbooks to Server even when they cannot view the published results on the server.

Project

The Project is an object used to organize and manage access to Workbooks. Workbooks are placed into Projects within a Site. This can be used as an organization tool by placing Workbooks with similar content into a single project. It can be used as an access restriction tool by granting access to a Project to a user or group and then publishing Workbooks into that Project.

Group

The Group is an object used to organize users in Sites on the Tableau Server. Users can be placed into Groups and these Groups can in turn be given permissions to objects on the server. Groups can be created locally on the Tableau Server or, if Active Directory authentication is in use, they can be imported from an Active Directory Group. Groups make managing user permissions within Tableau Server much easier.

Site

The Site is the top level of the security hierarchy. Sites are essentially completely separate Tableau Server instances from the user perspective. Users cannot log in to, or view, any information about Sites to which they do not have access. The base Tableau Server site is known as the Default Site. Users that belong to more than one site must choose which site they want to see when they log in. Additional Tableau Server sites are accessed using a name extension string appended on the URL using this format: `(/t/[name])`.

Permissions

Where sites define separate work environments in Tableau Server, permissions define what users or groups are permitted to do within a site. Tableau Server comes with several standard permission roles that can be assigned to Users or Groups.

The Interactor role represents the common user who can access and use Objects but not edit them. The Publisher role allows users to publish reports from Tableau Desktop to the server. The Editor role allows the user to make changes to Workbooks. Users can also be granted several more specialized roles. Additionally there are two administrative permissions that can be granted at the Site and Instance level—System Administrator and Site Administrator. These last two permission types allow high-level control of the particular Instance.

When the standard roles aren't enough, it is possible to add very specific permissions to Groups or Users. More detail around specific permissions that are available can be found in the Tableau Server Administrator's Guide.

Using Groups and Projects to manage access is much easier than assigning user permissions to workbooks individually. Depending on the sensitivity of data contained in workbooks on the server, some organizations choose to make heavier use of individual Sites rather than Projects. It is important to understand that moving content between projects is very easy, but moving content between sites requires republishing the workbook. A common example of this is having separate Sites configured for departments such as human resources. Another common usage of Sites is using the default instance as production and creating an alternate test site for development and testing on Server.

ENABLING ROW-LEVEL SECURITY VIA FILTERS

Row-Level security is the ability to restrict access to specific data elements within a datasource to specified users. It is enabled by employing user filters. Using the Superstore sample data you will see an example that restricts access to records using the region dimension. Figure 9–1 shows a map visualization of Superstore that uses color to define regions.

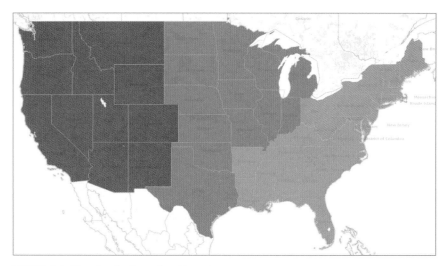

FIGURE 9–1 *Map visualization colored by region*

Start by creating a user filter in Tableau Desktop by selecting Server ➢ Create User Filter ➢ Region from the main menu. Users created for this example include the East Region, West Region, and the All Region groups. East and West can see only their regions. The All Region user will be able to view everything in the data set. Clicking the OK button defines the filter. You can see the members selected for the All Region option in Figure 9–2.

Once the user filter is created it will appear on the Set Shelf at the bottom left of the desktop. Dragging the set to the Filter Shelf applies the filter. You can simulate the results of the filter for other users by using the toggle at the bottom right of the Tableau Desktop interface by selecting other users. This will change the view to simulate how it will appear for each user you select so that you can verify that the filter produces the desired result. Figure 9–3 shows the region filter set placed on the Filter Shelf. Notice that the All Region user is being simulated using the drop-down filter at the bottom right.

When a user filter is placed on a worksheet, the Publish Workbook to Tableau Server dialog box changes to include a new Generate Thumbnails As User option. You can see it in the lower right

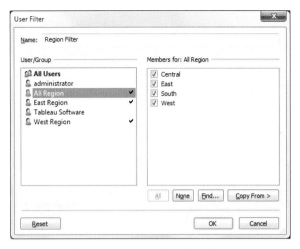

FIGURE 9–2 *Tableau Desktop user filter dialog box*

of Figure 9–4. This option allows you to select what thumbnail will display for each user in Tableau Server—ensuring that sensitive data isn't seen by unauthorized users. The View Permissions dialog box can contain many users with different view filters.

FIGURE 9–3 *Filter shelf with region filter added*

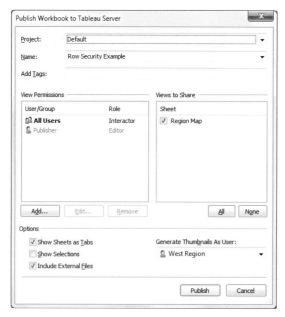

FIGURE 9-4 *Thumbnail filtering*

FIGURE 9-5 *Thumbnail generated for a West Region user*

In Figure 9-5 you see how the thumbnail in Tableau Server appears to a West Region user.

Logging into Tableau Server as an East Region user results in the thumbnail view being restricted for access to the eastern states in that territory. When the user selects the View, the actual map view will look like Figure 9-6, and include only the states that comprise that region.

An All Region user logging in will see every state as you see in Figure 9-7.

User filters are an effective and simple method of implementing Row-level security within Tableau Server. However, if the users are allowed to download the workbook from Tableau Server—and open it in Tableau Desktop—they can remove the filter and expose the unfiltered report. Keep this in mind to prevent unrestricted data access. Also remember that users with publisher access can republish reports after removing the filter and provide unrestricted access to the report. Ensure that individuals with publishing rights on Server are trained to prevent unauthorized distribution of sensitive data. Using datasource user filters can also be helpful for limiting the quantity and scope of data exposed.

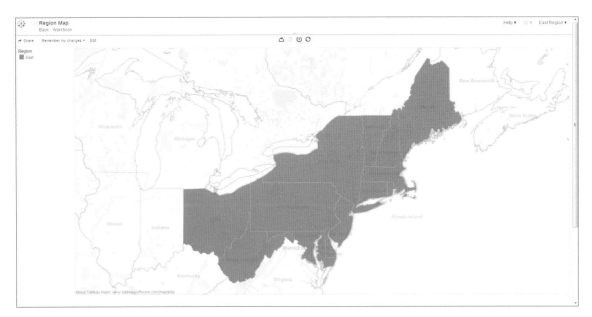

FIGURE 9-6 *Map visualization restricted by the user filter*

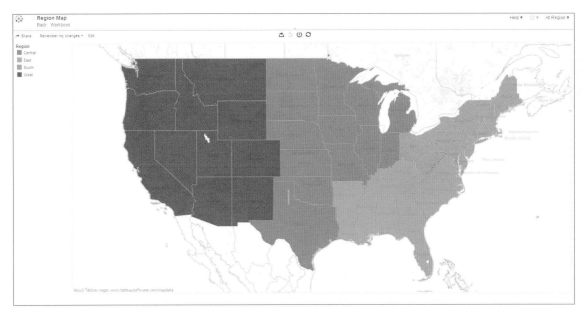

FIGURE 9-7 *Map filter for an All Region user*

There are other more complex methods of implementing Row-Level security. Be mindful that unless the data is secured at the datasource level, it isn't possible to prevent unrestricted access if the users are allowed to download the workbook, and they have access to Tableau Desktop. Implementing Row-Level filtering requires diligent user permission management to ensure no unexpected data access occurs.

WHEN AND HOW TO DEPLOY SERVER ON MULTIPLE PHYSICAL MACHINES

Earlier in this chapter you read about considerations for sizing hardware for Tableau Server—specifically the concepts of scaling-up and scaling-out. Scaling-up refers to using more powerful single server hardware. Scaling-out refers to bringing in more machines to help carry the workload. Clustering, distributed environments, and scaling-out all refer to the same concept: running Tableau Server on more than one machine, to spread the workload.

The decision to scale-out Tableau Server in a cluster is normally made when a single server cannot support the expected workload, and when adding additional machines represents a lower expected cost than scaling-up to a substantially more powerful single machine. Tableau's multiple processes can be assigned to different machines in the cluster to achieve efficient division of the workload.

For instance, an environment that makes use of very large data extracts could devote an entire machine in the cluster for running data extract engine processes. This machine could include a larger amount of system memory and fast I/O to support the need to quickly load and query many data extracts. In addition, another machine with very fast CPU cores could be dedicated to VizQL processes if high numbers of concurrent view requests are anticipated. Clustering Tableau Server can also provide high availability capabilities by creating redundant core processes on multiple machines. High availability configurations will be in the next section of this chapter.

In Tableau Server clustered environments, the first machine Tableau Server is installed on is known as the Primary Tableau Server, or, the Gateway. All other machines are known as Workers. The Gateway handles all of the requests to the Tableau Server and communicates with the workers to satisfy those requests. To set up a distributed cluster environment follow these steps:

1. Install Tableau Server on the primary machine. (Note the IP address of this machine.)

2. Stop the Tableau Server service on the primary machine.

3. Install the Tableau Server worker software on all of the Worker machines.

4. Return to the primary (Gateway) server and open the configuration utility.

5. Select the Servers tab and click the Add button.

6. Type the IP address of one of the Worker machines in the dialog box.

7. Specify the number of, and each type of, processes to deploy on the Worker.

8. Click OK.

9. Repeat the same steps for each Worker machine.

Once all of the Workers are added to the cluster, save the changes within the configuration utility and restart the Tableau Server service on the primary machine. For more information about clustered Tableau Server deployments see the "Distributed Environments" section of Tableau Software's Tableau Server Administrators Guide.

DEPLOYING TABLEAU SERVER IN HIGH AVAILABILITY ENVIRONMENTS

As Tableau Server usage increases, the need to ensure its continuous availability also rises. Strategies to guarantee constant availability are broadly referred to as high availability. These strategies necessitate that core components of Tableau Server be redundant to minimize the chance of unplanned downtime. Realizing this goal requires deployment in a distributed environment and running redundant critical processes on separate servers.

Achieving significant redundancy can be realized using a three-server cluster, but to achieve a fully redundant configuration, at least four servers are necessary.

THE THREE NODE CLUSTER

In this configuration, one node hosts the Gateway, which routes requests to the other two Worker servers. The two Worker servers both run all of the server processes. Even though all of Tableau Server's processes should be made redundant, the three processes that must be made redundant are the Gateway, the data engine process, and the repository process. Prior to Tableau Server Version 8, both Workers have instances of the repository and data engine processes, but only one of the two Workers was actively accepting requests. Now both data engine processes actively accept requests, even though one is considered primary. In prior releases, the secondary Worker has standby copies of the processes and is automatically promoted to active status if the main Worker fails. This promotion is called fail-over.

The loss of a Worker machine can occur without making the cluster inaccessible. However, since there is only a single Gateway machine, should that server go offline the cluster will be inaccessible to users. To have complete fault tolerance, a four-node cluster is required.

THE FOUR NODE CLUSTER

In a four-node cluster, a second Gateway machine is added to make that critical node redundant. However, this standby Gateway server must be promoted to active status manually. There is currently no automatic fail-over for Gateway machines.

The high availability setup process is similar to the basic cluster configuration detailed in the When and How to Deploy Server on Multiple Physical Machines section of this chapter.

The steps to set up a high availability configuration are:

1. Install Tableau Server on the primary machine (note the IP address of this machine).
2. Stop the Tableau Server service on the primary machine.
3. Run the Tableau Server Worker installer on the other machines included in the cluster (the primary server IP is needed for this step).
4. Open the configuration utility.
5. Select the Servers tab and click the Add button.
6. In the Add Tableau Server dialog box type the IP address of the first of the Workers.
7. Specify the number of each type of process.
8. Ensure that both the extract storage and repository storage are included on this host's settings. Click OK.
9. Start the Tableau Server service on the primary machine.
10. View the server status and observe that the instances of the extract engine and repository on the new worker appear to be down. This will be resolved once the primary server has transmitted all data for these processes to the new worker machine.

11. After the worker extract engine and repository processes switch from Service Down to Service Standing By, stop the Tableau Server service on the primary machine again.

12. Open the configuration utility on the primary server.

13. Clear the extract storage in the configuration utility on this host and the repository storage on This Host check boxes for the primary server. Remove all other processes to configure this machine as a Gateway only. Click OK.

14. Click the Add button on the servers tab.

15. In the Add Tableau Server dialog box, type the IP address of the second Worker and specify the number of each type of process. Be sure to check both the Extract Storage and Repository Storage on this host's settings. Click OK.

16. As an optional step, you can configure e-mail alerts about the cluster status from the E-mail Alerts tab in the configuration utility.

17. Close the configuration utility and restart the Tableau Server service.

18. Once the service comes back up check the status of the cluster from the Tableau Server maintenance page. You should see the IP address of the primary server listed with only the Gateway service. You should also see the two Worker server IP addresses listed with the remaining Tableau Server processes. One Worker will have an active data engine and repository and the other Worker will have standby copies of these processes.

The three-node configuration presented earlier may be augmented with a redundant Gateway server to increase reliability. For information about making the Gateway redundant and the manual fail-over process see the "Configuring a Highly Available Gateway" section of the Tableau Server Administrator's guide.

LEVERAGE EXISTING SECURITY WITH TRUSTED AUTHENTICATION

Tableau Server is frequently deployed in landscapes that contain legacy systems that already contain security protocols to prevent unauthorized access. These systems may include internal portals, content management systems, or existing reporting interfaces. Is it possible to embed an interactive Tableau visualization into a site that already contains a legacy security protocol? The answer is yes. This is commonly referred to as Single Sign-on. The Tableau Server system for enabling this is called Trusted Authentication.

When using Trusted Authentication, it is assumed that the web server containing the embedded views will handle the user authentication. The person attempting to access the embedded view must be a valid user on both the web page and Tableau Server. The web page server passes the username of the person that has logged in to the Tableau Server. So, the usernames must match or be programmatically transformed to match.

Tableau Server must also be configured to acknowledge the web page server as a trusted server. This is configured using the Tableau Server Administration Tabadmin tool. The web page server must also be able to perform a POST request and transform the response into a URL. This means that static web pages that are not supported by a scripting language will not be able to support these requirements.

If the web page server uses Security Support Provider Interface (SSPI), configuring Trusted Authentication is unnecessary as long the users are valid members in Active Directory. In that case, Tableau Server authenticates the user via Active Directory as long as the users are also licensed to access Tableau Server. The flowchart in Figure 9–8 illustrates how security data travels between each component.

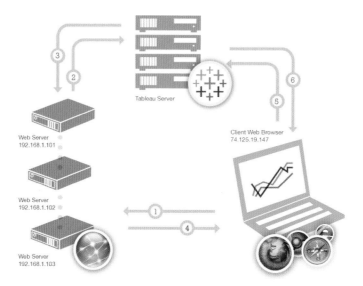

FIGURE 9–8 *Trusted Authentication*

If all of the above requirements are met, then Trusted Authentication works in the following way:

1. **A user visits the web page**—When a user visits the web page with the embedded Tableau Server view, a GET request is sent to your web server from the HTML for that page.

2. **Web server POSTS to Tableau Server**—The web server sends a POST request to Tableau Server. That POST request must have a username parameter. The username value must be the username for a licensed Tableau Server user. If the server is running multiple sites and the view is on a site other than the Default site, the POST request must include a target site parameter.

3. **Tableau Server creates a ticket**—Tableau Server checks the IP address of the web server that sends the POST request. If it is set up as a trusted host, then Tableau Server creates a ticket in the format of a unique nine-digit string. Tableau Server responds to the POST request with that ticket. If there is an error and the ticket cannot be created Tableau Server responds with a value of -1.

4. **Web server passes the URL to the browser**—The web server constructs a temporary URL for the view using either the view's URL or its object tag (if the view is embedded) and inserts it into the HTML for the page. The ticket will include a temporary address (for example: `http://tabserver/trusted/<ticket>/views/requestedviewname`). The web server passes the HTML for the page back to the client's web browser.

5. **Browser requests a view from Tableau Server**—The client's web browser sends a request to Tableau Server using a GET request that includes the URL with the ticket.

6. **Tableau Server redeems the ticket**—Tableau Server sees that the web browser requested a URL with a ticket in it and redeems the ticket. Tickets must be redeemed within three minutes after they are issued. Once the ticket is redeemed, Tableau Server logs the user in, removes the ticket from the URL, and sends back the final URL for the embedded view.

The Tableau Server installation manual provides examples of the code required for the web server to handle the POST to Tableau Server, converting the ticket into a URL and embedding the view in many languages. These examples are included as a part of the Tableau Server installation. Navigate to the following directly to view them:

```
C:\Program Files (x86)\Tableau\Tableau Server\8.0\extras\
embedding
```

For tips on using Trusted Ticket Authentication with views that you wish to embed in other websites, see the section on "Use Trusted Ticket Authentication as an Alternative Single Sign-On Method" in Chapter 10.

DEPLOYING TABLEAU SERVER IN MULTI-NATIONAL ENTITIES

Tableau Desktop and Server support a wide range of locales and languages. This makes is easy to deploy in organizations with diverse nationalities. Language settings refer to the translation of text in the user interface elements within Tableau. Locale refers to the format of numbers and dates. Tableau Server supports English, German, French, Portuguese, Japanese, Chinese, and Korean. It also has support for more than three hundred locales.

Default language and locale options can be configured at the server level by users with system administrator permission. This option is located on the Maintenance page of the Tableau Server web interface. The default language is initially determined by the language settings of the server on which the software is installed. Figure 9–9 shows the dialog box.

FIGURE 9–9 *The language and locale dialog box*

Users can also configure their individual language and locale settings from the User Account page. However, users must do this from their view of the User Account page. Administrators cannot set language and locale options for a specific user. When a user changes these settings, this overrides the default language and locale settings designated by the administrator.

If the user does not have a language and locale specified on their user account page, those settings can also be taken from the user's web browser—if the browser is using a language that Tableau supports. Also, keep in mind that the author of a workbook in Tableau Desktop can specify language and locale settings there as well. Settings specified in the workbook take precedence over all other language and locale settings.

The order of precedence—from highest to lowest priority—is designated as follows:

1. The Tableau workbook
2. The user preferences page
3. The locale specified by a user's browser
4. The Tableau Server maintenance page
5. The computer on which Tableau Server is installed

Keep in mind that language options do not translate any report text—only Tableau user interface elements.

USING PERFORMANCE RECORDER TO IMPROVE PERFORMANCE

Earlier, at the end of Chapter 8 you learned how to use Tableau's Performance Recorder to improve workbook performance in Tableau Desktop. There is also a separate Performance Recorder that allows you to record and view information about Tableau Server performance at the workbook level.

Prior to Tableau Version 8, this data had to be collected and analyzed manually from log files or via a third party application that was created by InterWorks. The Performance Recorder basically creates a Tableau workbook of your Tableau workbook's performance. Information about the following events is captured and displayed visually:

- Query execution
- Geocoding
- Connections to datasources
- Layout computations
- Extract generation
- Data blending
- Server rendering

Performance Recorder is disabled on Tableau Server by default. To begin using it you must enable it on a per site basis. To activate Performance Recorder on the server, navigate to the Administration-Sites page and check the site you wish to enable. Click Edit. In the Edit Site dialog, check the Allow Performance Recording check box and click OK. Figure 9–10 shows the edit dialog box properly checked.

To use the Performance Recorder on a view you must append the following code

```
?:record_performance=yes
```

o the view URL. If everything is working correctly, you should see a Show Performance Recording command in the view status bar. Clicking this link will open a view that is generated from the recorded performance data.

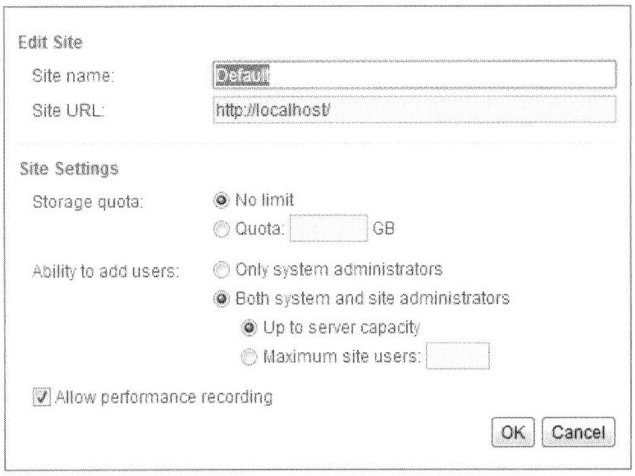

FIGURE 9–10 *Enabling Performance Recording*

This view does not automatically update. To see the most current data, close and open the view again. The Performance Recording will continue capturing data about interactions with the view until the user navigates away or removes the string from the URL. Figure 9–11 displays an example of the information available in the Performance Recording summary display.

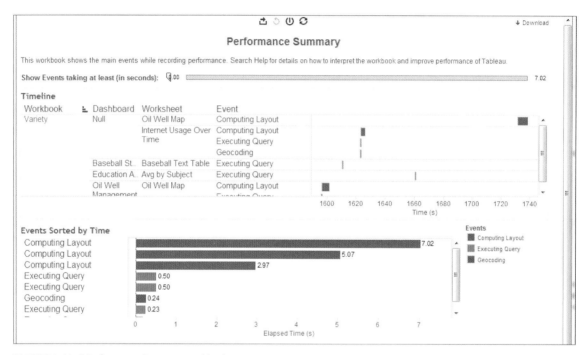

FIGURE 9–11 *A Performance Summary workbook*

The example recording was taken while interacting with one of the sample Tableau Server workbooks supplied with your server license. The dashboard that the Performance Recorder generates contains three views:

- Timeline—A Gantt chart displaying event start time and duration

- Events Sorted by Time—A bar chart showing event duration by type

- Query Text—Optionally appears when clicking-on an Executing Query event in the bar chart

TIMELINE GANTT CHART

The Timeline Gantt Chart displays by workbook, dashboard, or worksheet when each event occurred. Event start time is indicated by the bar's horizontal position, and the duration of each event is indicated by the individual bar length.

THE EVENTS SORTED BY TIME

This section of the workbook shows the duration of recorded events in descending order. This is useful for observing the execution time of each event that occurred during the Performance Recording. This will help you identify any lengthy events that may be the cause of performance problems.

QUERY TEXT

Optionally, the workbook also displays the query text for any specific event that you want to examine in detail. You access the detail by clicking on any of the green Executing Query events in the bar chart. This is a handy feature that allows you to review any query text that may be of interest without having to leave the Tableau Performance Summary Dashboard.

PERFORMANCE-TUNING TACTICS

The Performance Summary report generated by the Performance Recorder informs you about the specific events that may be contributing to slow performance. Once you understand the events most affecting performance try the following tactics to address the performance problem.

Query Execution

Query Execution represents the time that it takes for the datasource to execute a query and retrieve the data requested by the worksheet. If the datasource is a database, it is very helpful to see the queries issued by Tableau in order to identify inefficiencies. Common issues include poor indexing strategies, fragmented indexes, database contention, insufficient database resources, and inefficient SQL queries. If the datasource is the Tableau data engine, there are fewer troubleshooting options.

Geocoding

Geocoding represents the time Tableau needs to locate geographical dimensions. If this event type is consuming too much time, consider geocoding your records in the source data set and passing a pre-calculated latitude and longitude to Tableau rather than having Tableau generate the geocodes when rendering the map view.

Connecting to the Datasource

Connecting to the Datasource conveys the time required for Tableau to connect to the datasource. This event is typically not a large percentage of total worksheet time. In rare cases there can be a network or datasource issues that extend connection times. To rule out these issues examine the network topology between the Tableau Server and the datasource server.

Layout Computations

This is the time needed for Tableau Server to compute the visual layout of the worksheet in the Layout Computation event. This can be influenced by server resource contention as well as worksheet complexity. The more marks that are visualized within the workbook, the more time that workbook will require to load and refresh. It may be necessary to restrict the number of marks simultaneously displayed through techniques such as actions, filters, and aggregation. Large crosstabs can be particularly costly, and are not a good visual analytic technique. If all these tactics fail to result in noticeable improvement, it may be necessary to provide additional resources to the server.

Generating Extract

The amount of time that the data engine spends generating an extract is called the Generating Extract event. The size of the datasource (the numbers of rows and columns) along with the time Tableau spends compressing and sorting the data are the major factors affecting the time required to generate extract files.

If your extract file is taking too long to refresh in your environment, it may be possible to speed up the process by removing unnecessary columns from the extract. This will reduce the time required for generating, sorting, and compressing the remaining columns. Should the problem persist, you may want to ensure that all fields have the appropriate data type assigned to them in the underlying database. Improperly defined field types in the source database can affect the performance during the extract creation, as well as any subsequent queries needed to be performed against the extract file.

If extract generation speeds are still not good enough, try running more data engine processes or placing them on their own Worker instance.

Blending Data

The amount of time that Tableau Server spends performing data blends is the Blending Data event. This event can take a long time when working with large amounts of data from the blended datasources. Filtering before the blend at the datasource level can be effective. If possible, consider moving data into a single datasource so that joins can be used instead of blending.

Server Rendering

The amount of time that Tableau Server spends rendering the computed layouts into a format to send to the client browser is the Server Rendering event. The time it takes to complete this event can be impacted by the load on the VizQL processes as well as the complexity of the layouts. Refer to the Computing layouts' event for guidance.

Whether specifically mentioned or not, most of these events can be quickened by restricting the amount of data visualized through filtering or aggregation. This can also be achieved by using faster hardware or adding more resources on Tableau Server. As far as workbook performances go, if it doesn't perform well in Tableau Desktop, it won't perform well in Tableau Server either. For this reason you should use the Performance Recorder on the desktop to troubleshoot performance issues there before publishing an under-performing workbook to the server.

MANAGING TABLEAU SERVER IN THE CLOUD

Increasingly, organizations are choosing to move away from hosting on-premise servers by migrating to cloud-based solutions. Flexibility and decreased initial costs are two reasons for pushing software into the cloud.

WHAT DOES IT MEAN TO BE IN THE CLOUD?

Before discussing cloud-based Tableau Server hosting options, it might be helpful to define what we mean by cloud-based. The term, "In the Cloud" has become a catch-all term in recent years for any service that isn't hosted by an on-premise server. That definition doesn't quite capture the scaling implications of the cloud though. Cloud solutions are typically hosted and rapidly scalable systems. As mentioned at the beginning of this chapter, Tableau Software has two server versions that operate only in the cloud.

TABLEAU'S CLOUD-BASED VERSIONS OF SERVER

Tableau Public is a Tableau Server implementation hosted by Tableau Software that is free to use but comes with some caveats. Chief among these is that all workbooks and data hosted on Tableau Public are just that, public. This is probably a deal breaker for most organizations. However, if your organization wants to make data available to the public anyway, this is a great (free) solution. Other caveats with Tableau Public are:

- Datasources are limited to 1,000,000 rows per datasource.
- Only file-based datasources can be used.
- Data is limited to 50 megabytes per account.

Data extracts are the most common datasource used on Tableau Public.

For groups wanting to present reports to the public, but also needing to maintain control of their underlying data, Tableau has an offering called Tableau Public Premium. A fee-based service, Tableau Public Premium allows users to restrict access to the underlying data in a workbook and also prevent downloads of that workbook. Additionally, it removes the maximum row limit imposed by Tableau Public. As these two offerings can't restrict access to reports in any way, they are clearly not for organizations with sensitive data.

Tableau Online provides an added measure of control and security beyond Tableau Public. It is a cloud-based version of Tableau Server that is licensed on a per-named-user basis with no minimum requirement on the number of licenses. The software is installed and maintained by Tableau Software in a secure hosting facility. It is very easy to use Tableau Online. Once you have signed-up, you can start publishing workbooks for other licensed Tableau Online users to view.

There are a few differences between Tableau Online and Tableau Server including:

- Workbooks published to Tableau online must use Tableau Data Extract that must be refreshed regularly. Live connections to Amazon Redshift are supported as well.
- No guest access. Everyone using Tableau Online must be licensed to use the service.
- No custom branding in the Tableau Online environment
- Tableau Software creates and maintains your site.
- No minimum user requirement

At the beginning of this chapter, Tableau's three different server products: Tableau Server, Tableau Pubic, and Tableau Online were introduced. Currently, the majority of Tableau Server customers want to host Tableau Server on-premise, behind their company firewall. But, an increasing number of organizations are choosing to host Tableau Server in the cloud.

PUTTING TABLEAU SERVER IN THE CLOUD

Although Tableau Server is most frequently hosted within company networks, it too can be hosted in the cloud by utilizing Amazon EC2 instances and most other services that provide cloud-based Windows Server platforms. Amazon EC2 is not currently a platform supported by Tableau Software, but it does work. There are a few items to consider if you want to deploy Tableau Server using a cloud service provider. You are still fully responsible for the installation and maintenance of Tableau Server deployed this way—unless you also want to farm-out this work on a contract basis to consultants.

Tableau Server needs to be accessible to your users, so make sure ports are opened in any firewalls and that the server will accept traffic from your users' network addresses. Active Directory integration can be tricky with these platforms so consider local authentication if you encounter issues.

When deploying Tableau Server in multi-node configurations, ensure that the IP addresses of the nodes are static so that node communication won't be impaired through system restarts. Also ensure that firewall rules are in place to allow nodes to communicate with each other. The most common issues with running Tableau Server in a cloud environment are networking related. Once the Tableau Server is installed and accessible, administering it is very similar to administering a locally-installed host.

MONITORING ACTIVITY ON TABLEAU SERVER

As your server deployment grows you can monitor usage activity to ensure the best experience for your users. Tableau server includes an administrative maintenance menu that displays most of the information you'll need in order to monitor the status of the processes running on each server. There are also a series of Tableau workbooks accessed via the analysis section that you can see in Figure 9–12.

FIGURE 9–12 *Tableau Server maintenance menu*

THE STATUS SECTION

The status section displays the current status of processes that are available on each machine deployed. The example in Figure 9–12 is for a single server. If you have a multi-cluster setup you will see each machine's IP address shown on its own row.

THE ANALYSIS SECTION

The Analysis section provides links to embedded Tableau workbooks that provide metrics on these areas of interest:

- Server Activity—Displays thirty days of views with information on workbook counts, users, and sites
- User Activity—Shows user activity by server with detailed user activity available as well
- Performance History—Provides information on particularly taxing workloads impacting performance
- Background Tasks—Gives you views of the tasks, primarily those triggered by user actions
- Space Usage—Shows you how much space is being used by user, project, workbook, and by datasource
- Customized Views—Displays the user-modified views changed using the Remember My Changes feature

THE ACTIVITIES SECTION

There may be some problem in your server setup that causes Tableau Server's search index to become corrupted. If this happens, users may not get the correct results when searching for workbooks or datasources. Run the Rebuild Search Index if searches are not bringing back the expected results.

If you enabled the Saved Passwords option for people accessing Server, this allows users to save passwords for datasources in multiple browsers and visits. If you need to force everyone to enter passwords again, the Cleared Saved Data Connection Password For All Users option will require everyone to enter a password the next time they visit. This can also be done more selectively for individual users via the user preferences menu.

THE SETTINGS SECTION

The options included in this section allow you to control how the behavior of credentials embedded in workbooks assign workbooks with embedded credentials to schedules, and provide a way for users to save datasource passwords for multiple browsers and visits. You can also change Tableau Server's default start page, default menu language, and locale for displaying numbers. Another feature is the ability to return any altered settings to the default values. See Tableau Server's on-line manual for more details.

Tableau has recognized the need to provide enterprise class management tools for monitoring activity, security, and performance. Tableau Version 8 provides significantly more tools than prior releases. In Chapter 10 you'll see how easy it is for users to publish and consume reports in Tableau Server.

NOTES

1. Godin, Seth: *Linchpin: Are You Indispensable?* Penguin Group (USA), 2010. Print. Page 154.

Using Tableau Server to Facilitate Fact-Based Team Collaboration

All good-to-great companies began the process of finding a path to greatness by confronting the brutal facts.

James Collins[1]

Tableau Server facilitates information sharing and team collaboration by making interactive dashboards and views accessible to authorized individuals via any of the popular web-browsing software tools available today. Reports can be directly consumed via iOS (Apple) or Android tablets. Beginning with Tableau Server Version 8, authorized staff can also edit existing reports or create completely new analysis using Tableau Server.

Authorized Tableau Server users can also share metadata including joins, groupings, sets, name aliases, and other customized data by publishing Tableau Datasource files to Server. You will learn how to take advantage of these features and more in this chapter.

PUBLISHING DASHBOARDS IN TABLEAU SERVER

After Tableau Server is installed, those creating reports and analysis must be provided with publishing rights. Staff that will be consuming reports must be granted access rights. Once you've created a workbook containing at least one worksheet, you can publish that information to Tableau Server. Workbooks containing many different worksheets and dashboards can be published in full, or by selecting any combination of worksheets and dashboards. The Tableau Desktop menus used for publishing to Tableau Server are shown in Figure 10–1.

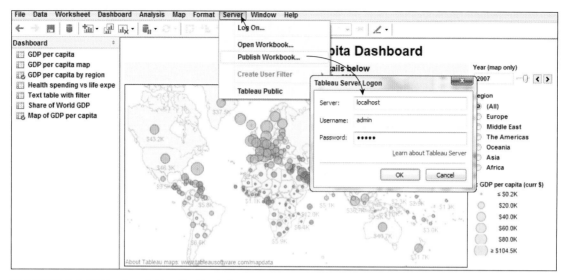

FIGURE 10–1 *Publishing from Tableau Desktop to Server*

Publishing a workbook requires three steps:

1. Open the workbook you wish to publish.

2. Select the Server menu and click on Publish Workbook.

3. Enter the server URL, your username, your password, then click OK.

The Publish Workbook to Tableau Server dialog box will appear as you see in Figure 10–2.

Using this menu you define when, how, and what details will be published to the server. If your workbook's datasource is a Tableau Data Extract (tde) file, you can also schedule regular data updates using the Scheduling & Authentication button at the bottom of Figure 10-2.

Tableau organizes and secures published workbooks using a variety of methods:

- Project—Folders for grouping workbooks

- Name—Naming workbooks

- Tags—Allowing for user-defined tagging of workbooks

- Permissions—Controlling what users are permitted to do

- View—Hiding or sharing specific views

Creatively combining these entities facilitates secure access at the appropriate level for individuals, teams, work groups, and projects. The specific purpose of each is explained in more detail below.

PROJECT

Projects are folders for organizing your reports and controlling access to those reports. Server comes with one Default project folder. Those with administrative rights can create additional projects. Figure 10–2 shows an additional project called Demo Dashboards, which was added to hold the reports being published.

NAME

You can accept the name assigned to the workbook when it was created in Tableau Desktop or choose to define a new name that will appear in Tableau Server when the workbook is published. You define new workbook names using the Name field seen in Figure 10-2.

FIGURE 10–2 *Publishing dialog box*

TAGS

Tagging published workbooks is optional but provides another way to search for reports. They can be helpful if you publish a large number of reports. Enter each tag separated by a comma or space. If the tag you are entering contains a space, surround the tag by quotation marks (e.g., "Production Benchmarks").

VIEW PERMISSIONS

Those authorized to do so can optionally add, edit, or remove permissions for all users, groups, or individual users through the View Permissions tool. When editing permissions another dialog box opens, which you can see in Figure 10–3. This box allows you to edit permission types for different roles (viewer, interactor, editor, or custom).

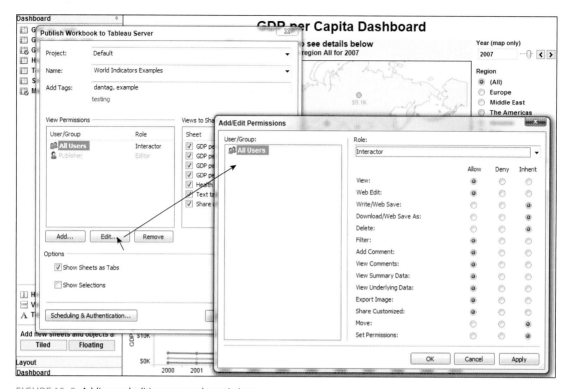

FIGURE 10–3 *Adding and editing users and permissions*

VIEWS TO SHARE

The Views to Share option allows you to select specific sheets you wish to share. Any sheets that are not selected are hidden on Tableau Server, but these are still available within the workbook if it is downloaded from Tableau Server.

OPTIONS

Appearing at the bottom of the publishing dialog box are more optional selections that control the appearance of what is published.

Checking the Shows Sheets as Tabs option will generate tabs when the report is published to Tableau Server—facilitating navigation between worksheets and dashboards in the published workbook. The Show Selections option allows selections you've made on a worksheet or dashboard to persist when the workbook is published to Server and will be displayed to users consuming the workbook.

If the datasource that you are using for the report being published comes from an external database or file, you will also see a check box for the inclusion of external files; checking that option generates a copy of the source file on Tableau Server. Custom image files used in any view will also be saved. If you have a live database or an extract file being utilized by the workbook, you should also see a button in the lower left for Scheduling and Authentication. Selecting that button allows you to set the refresh schedule for data extract sources or to change how a live database connection is authenticated on Tableau Server. Details regarding scheduling updates and authentication are covered in depth later in this chapter in the sections on "Sharing Connections, Data Models, and Data Extracts" and "Using Subscriptions to Deliver Reports via E-mail."

Select the Publish button seen at the bottom of Figure 10-2 to initiate the upload to Tableau Server. Upon completion a pop-up will appear displaying the newly-published workbook.

If your Tableau Server instance is configured for multiple sites, you will also see a Select Site dialog box to define on which server site the workbook will be published. Tableau's default is a single site. Multiple sites are partitions of the same physical server.

ORGANIZING REPORTS FOR CONSUMPTION

Publishing reports to the web is the first step in effectively sharing information on Tableau Server. As your user base grows and reports proliferate, finding reports you're interested in requires organization. User security, group security, and site security were discussed in Chapter 9. Tableau Server provides two additional ways to organize reports, projects, and tags. Projects are virtual folders in which you publish workbooks and datasources. Tableau also provides built-in support for adding security to each project—allowing you to more easily manage security across multiple workbooks and datasources. Users can also tag particular workbooks or datasource files with keywords. This provides you with a user-defined search term that is helpful for locating files when there are a lot of published workbooks. Defining a sensible framework for projects and tag recommendations might be helpful to your user base and provide some consistency across your enterprise. These could be defined in advance, but you may allow users to define additional tags that meet their specific needs as well.

For example, you may define projects by business unit or function—leveraging tags and adding context to each search. In a university setting three different departments might be consuming reports:

- Admissions
- Financial Aid
- Career Services

The Admissions office might be concerned with tracking the number of students applying each year and whether they were accepted and enrolled. Financial Aid would like to track the amount of aid offered and accepted. Career Services might be interested in monitoring the progress of students that have graduated and are seeking employment. Setting up projects for each office could be advantageous because it will facilitate security while organizing the reports logically for the staff of each department.

Adding tags to each workbook could provide additional context regarding the details. Examples in a University might include:

- Admissions—Undergraduate, admissions, "accepted vs. denied," enrolled, declined, graduate
- Financial Aid—Aid, grants, loans, scholarships, transfer scholarships, undergraduate, graduate
- Career Services—Offers, accepted offers, max salaries, median salaries, undergraduate, graduate

And please look closely at the admission tag example "accepted vs. denied." When tags include spaces, they must be wrapped in quotations. Notice the same tags being used in different projects and workbooks. This allows a user to search for similar analysis performed across different departments.

For example, if the dean of a college wanted to quickly find all the reports available analyzing undergraduate students, the dean could search using the Undergraduate tag and quickly access reports related to admissions, financial aid, and career services.

ADDING TAGS TO WORKBOOKS

Users can add tags to any workbook they have the right to access. Figure 10–4 shows a Global tag being added to one workbook contained within a project.

On the left side of the window in Figure 10–4 you can see the view has been filtered for the Dan Playground project. Selecting a workbook and clicking on the tag menu option exposes existing tags that can be applied to the selected workbook. If none of the existing tags work, clicking the Add option opens a dialog box for entering a new tag. In Figure 10–4 you can see a Global tag being added.

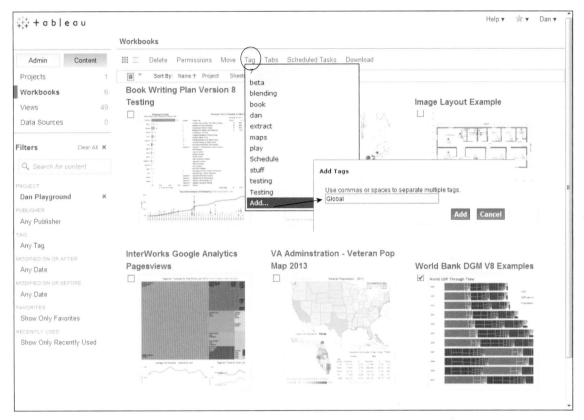

FIGURE 10-4 *Adding a tag to a workbook*

Tags can also be added directly when publishing a workbook. This additional option is located in the menu that is presented when you publish a workbook.

CREATING A FAVORITE

Favorites are workbook views or dashboards that you use often and want to save for quick access. Favorites are accessible via a drop-down menu in the upper right corner of the browser window or from the menu on the left side of the screen. Figure 10–5 displays a favorite menu showing a list of favorites. Favorites are indicated using a small star—visible in the upper right area of Figure 10-4 and Figure 10-5.

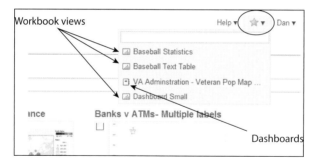

FIGURE 10-5 *The favorites menu*

Figure 10-5 shows three worksheets and one dashboard have been defined as favorites. Any workbook or worksheet can be made into a favorite from the thumbnail or list views. Figure 10-6 shows a list view of the reports.

		Name	↑	# Sheets	Size	Publisher	Modified	Project	Tabs
☐	☆	Book Writing Plan Version 8 Testing		17	460.8 KB	Dan	Jan 22, 2013 10:41 AM	Dan Playground	🗀
☐	☆	Figures for Chapter 5		5	5.5 MB	Dan	Feb 15, 2013 6:45 AM	Dan Playground	🗀
☐	☆	Image Layout Example		3	145.5 KB	Dan	Feb 14, 2013 1:56 PM	Dan Playground	🗀
☐	☆	InterWorks Google Analytics Pageviews		3	746.9 KB	Dan	Jan 22, 2013 10:38 AM	Dan Playground	🗀
☐	★	VA Adminstration - Veteran Pop Map 2013		9	4.4 MB	Dan	Jan 28, 2013 11:01 PM	Dan Playground	🗀
☐		World Bank DGM V8 Examples		12	833.7 KB	Dan	Feb 26, 2013 2:03 PM	Dan Playground	🗀

Workbooks

Delete   Permissions   Move   Tag   Tabs   Scheduled Tasks   Download

Help ▼   ☆ ▼   Dan ▼

Click to toggle favorite

Rows per page: 25   Pages: 1 / 1   Prev   Next

FIGURE 10-6 *List view with a favorite*

To make any workbook a favorite select the star associated with the item. This will toggle the star—coloring it yellow—and will add the item to the favorites menu in the upper right as seen in Figure 10-5. You can also add a favorite from the thumbnail view. The most convenient way to access favorites is via the star drop-down menu that you see in the upper right of Figure 10-6. You can also filter for favorites by using the menu on the left. The filter menu also allows you to select specific projects, publishers, tags, or recently used items.

By combining user and group security with projects, favorites, and tags you can control access to sensitive information and allow users to set up their own means for facilitating easy access to the information that is most important to meet their particular needs.

OPTIONS FOR SECURING REPORTS

Managing the security of data and reports is an important consideration. With the exception of a core-licensed server (with guest accounts enabled) all users must log in to Tableau Server before they have access to view any information. Applying permissions at the project level, you can efficiently manage access to a large number of workbooks and datasources while still providing the flexibility to alter security for a single group or user at any time. Securing reports is done using a combination of application layer and data layer controls.

- The Application Layer—Tableau Server credentials
- The Data Layer—database security

THE APPLICATION LAYER

Tableau Server provides application layer security through user credentials. Users can be managed in one of three ways:

- Local authentication
- Microsoft Active Directory
- Trusted Ticket Authentication

In Chapter 9 you learned about details related to managing security for users. Once a user has been authenticated to access the Tableau Server environment, you specify which projects, workbooks, and datasources that user is permitted to see. This is called object-level security. Tableau supports the assignment of object-level permissions for any user group or user by utilizing any of the following objects:

- Project
- Workbook
- Datasource

Using a top-down approach, permissions can be assigned at the project level—which may be inherited by any workbook or datasource published to that project. Permissions assigned to a user group will automatically propagate to all users within the group unless a user has explicit permissions overriding the group settings. The publisher has ultimate control over whether to accept the default permissions or define customized permissions. Tableau server comes with three standard permission levels already defined. These are called Roles and include viewer, interactor, and editor. Figure 10–7 shows the interactor role permissions.

FIGURE 10–7 *Interactor permission role menu*

The permissions menu is accessed when your workbook is published by clicking the Add button below the View Permissions area seen in Figure 10–7. Other roles can be viewed by selecting the Role menu drop-down arrow. Custom roles can be defined by selecting a user or group, and then choosing the custom role option from the Role menu. This allows you to set customized permissions when assigning your custom role to a specific user or group. Tableau's manual provides step-by-step instructions for defining permissions. Access the appropriate section of the manual from the help menu in Tableau and search for Setting Permissions.

DEFINING CUSTOM ROLES

Customizing roles is done by defining the permissions for the role. Understanding the permissions that you allow is important. Depending on the selections made, you may grant the ability for people to republish reports, change filters, redesign the workbook views, build new views, export data, download the workbook, share custom views, or even set new permissions. For a detailed description of each capability use Tableau's help menu and search for Permissions.

Care should be taken when granting permission to prevent the unauthorized dissemination of data. The list below categorizes permissions by risk level. High risk items provide the ability for the user to override permissions or disseminate data. Medium risk items convey the ability to alter or export views. Low risk permissions pertain to viewing and commenting capabilities.

High Risk Permissions

- Write/Web Save
- Download/Web Save As
- Move
- Set Permissions
- Connect

Medium Risk Permissions

- Web Edit
- View Summary Data
- View Underlying Data
- Export Image

Low Risk Permissions

- View
- Delete
- Filter
- Add Comment
- View Comments

These risk assessments are meant to be guidelines only. If your data is highly sensitive, care should be taken to mask confidential information at the datasource level to assure that confidential information is not inappropriately exposed.

A PERMISSION-SETTING EXAMPLE

Permissions can be defined so that it is possible to reuse a single workbook for groups with different access rights. For example, you may choose to group users by office. This was described in the university example mentioned earlier in this chapter (admissions, financial aid, and career services). Permissions for related projects could be set so that each office only gains access to the workbooks specifically related to their individual (office) groups.

At the same time, the university president's office could access the workbook, but with different permission settings that permit access to all of the projects and all of the related data details.

As a result, financial aid users won't see the admissions or career services reports. Instead, they will only see and have access to their financial aid reports. Yet, the university president's group will be able to view reports related to all three groups. Using this model, administrators can efficiently manage security for large and diverse entities.

The Data Layer

When employing a live database connection in Tableau Desktop you must provide credentials to authenticate the database server. This data-level security is persisted on Tableau Server as well. When publishing a workbook or datasource you must choose what type of authentication you'll associate with your live connection.

It's important to understand the difference between application layer and data layer security. When a user logs into Tableau Server, the user is authenticated at the application layer but not the data layer. When accessing any report that utilizes a live connection, the user must also be authenticated by that datasource. How the user is authenticated is predicated upon what settings you select when publishing the workbook or datasource. Your choices boil down to four options:

- Prompting the user to enter credentials
- Using embedded credentials
- Using a Server Run As Account
- Using SQL Server Impersonation (available for SQL Server only)

Embedded Credentials

Tableau also offers administrators the option to permit users to save their datasource credentials across multiple visits and browsers. This is enabled through the Embedded Credentials settings option in the administrative maintenance screen in Tableau Server. Figure 10–8 shows the menu with the appropriate selection checked. You also have the option to embed the connection username and password for the database form within Tableau Desktop.

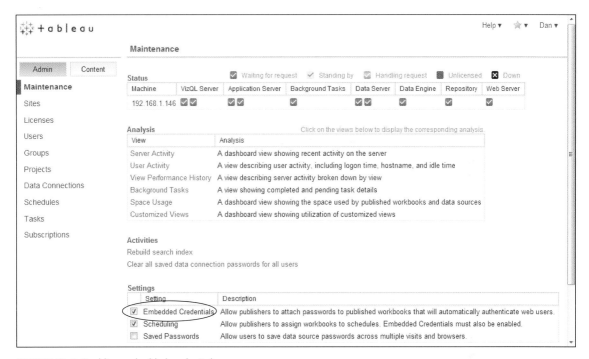

FIGURE 10–8 *Enabling embedded credentials*

By using this option, all users that utilize the connection will have the same level of access as the publisher of the workbook. This is a convenient feature for users that saves them from having to log in a second time. However, enabling embedded credentials removes the ability to manage data-level access on a per-user basis.

Server Run As Account using Windows Active Directory

Tableau Server runs in Windows Server environments. Therefore, Tableau Server installations utilize an active directory service account to run. A beneficial consequence of this fact is that Windows Active Directory (AD) can be used to eliminate redundant logins for Tableau Server users.

When a report is viewed on Tableau Server using a data connection employing this method, the Server Run As Account will be used to authenticate against the database. Your database administrator will need to ensure that the Server Run As Account has the proper access to connect to and query the tables and views used in your connection. Use Tableau Server's online manual and search for Run As User to view the setup details for this feature.

SQL Server Impersonation

As an option that is only available when connecting to a SQL Server database, impersonation is another way of eliminating the need for users to log in twice while still preserving the ability to manage data level access on a per user basis. This also allows the SQL Server database administrator to control security policy from the database and propagate those policies to Tableau Server.

To use SQL Server Impersonation each Tableau Server user will need individual accounts on SQL Server with credentials matching those on Tableau Server. For instance, if you have chosen to use Active Directory to manage your Tableau Server users, you must grant the same Active Directory accounts access to SQL Server. The user will either need to be the Server Run As Account or have their credentials embedded in the workbook during the publishing step by selecting the Impersonate Via Embedded Password option in the authentication menu.

When a user views a workbook that has implemented SQL Server Impersonation, they are authenticated using the Server Run As Account or via embedded SQL Server credentials. This account then impersonates the user connecting and accesses the database with their defined permissions. Search Tableau Server's online manual for SQL Server Impersonation for more details regarding setup and configuration.

Tableau Server provides a variety of ways to manage security. In the next section you'll find out how Tableau Server provides more flexibility and efficiency through the Data Server.

IMPROVE EFFICIENCY WITH THE DATA SERVER

The Tableau Data Server provides a way to manage datasources that have been published to Tableau Server. These published sources can include direct connections to a database, or Tableau Data Extract files. Authorized staff can set permissions associated with the connections and also set refresh schedules for data extract files. The metadata associated with these published sources becomes available to any workbook that uses the datasource. Metadata includes:

- Custom calculated fields
- Ad hoc groupings
- Ad hoc hierarchies

- Field name aliases
- Custom fonts and colors

The Data Server is efficient because it provides a flexible way to spread heavy workloads by enabling Tableau Server to absorb some of the demand normally handled by the primary database server.

While using data extract files is not a requirement, data extract files frequently perform better than the host database. The Data Server also saves time— enabling the work of a single individual to be shared by many. Datasources published to the Server can be accessed by authorized Tableau Desktop users to create new analysis.

Next you'll learn how to publish a datasource to Tableau Server and then use the Data Server to centrally host and share files, schedule automatic updates, and leverage incremental extract refreshing for near real-time data.

Publishing a Datasource

Publishing a datasource file to the data server is done from Tableau Desktop by opening the workbook containing the datasource you wish to make available for others to use. From the workbook, access the menu for publishing the datasource by right-clicking in the data window containing the datasource in the upper left section of the worksheet as seen in Figure 10–9.

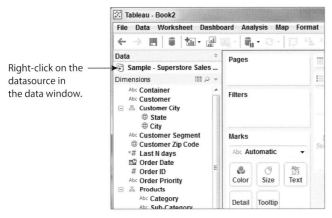

FIGURE 10–9 *Publishing to the data server*

After right-clicking and selecting publish to server, a server login dialog box appears. You will be required to enter the server URL, your username, and password to access the server. If you have a multiple site deployment you'll also need to enter the site you want to publish to as well. Once the server login is completed a dialog box will appear as you see in Figure 10–10.

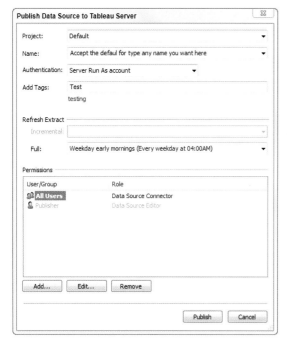

FIGURE 10–10 *Dialog box for publishing a datasource*

Define the parameters for publishing the datasource by selecting the project, the datasource name, the authentication method, tags, how and when you want the Server to refresh the extract, and finally what permissions you wish to assign to the extract. Most of these topics have already been covered in Chapter 9 or in earlier sections of this chapter. In the next two sections you will learn more about the options for updating datasource files and how to use incremental updates.

Manual vs. Automatic Updates

One potential benefit of using an extract—a portable copy of your original data set—can also be a drawback. The extract may not reflect the latest changes occurring in the datasource until the extract is refreshed. Tableau provides two different methods for updating extract files—manual and automatic updates.

Manual Updates Using Tableau Desktop

Manually updating data extracts can be done via the data menu or by right-clicking on the data menu. Follow these steps to refresh the datasource file:

1. Start Tableau Desktop if it is not already running.

2. Open the workbook containing the extract you wish to refresh.

3. Select the data menu and refresh all extracts (or add data from a file to append new data).

4. A dialog box will appear displaying the extracts that are available to update.

5. Click on the refresh button to update the extract files.

If your workbook contains multiple extract files, they will all be updated using this method. You can also update individual extract files in the workbook by pointing at the datasource in the data window, right-clicking, and then selecting extract, then refresh.

This manual process is one way you can append data from a separate source file or database—assuming the separate source contains the same fields as the original datasource. To do so, follow the same steps as above but in the last step choose Add Data From File instead of Refresh. In Chapter 11 you'll see how Tableau Server's command line tools can be used to automate manual processes.

Automatic Updates Using Tableau Server

If you have many different datasources and workbooks using datasource files published to Server, manually updating large numbers of files would be impractical. Tableau Server comes with a pre-defined update schedule and allows you to create your own custom update schedules.

To schedule updates you'll need to first publish your extract to Tableau Server directly using Data Server or indirectly by publishing the workbook that uses an extract as its datasource. During the publishing process you have the option to select a refresh schedule to have Tableau Server automatically update the extract.

Tableau Server includes predefined schedules or your server administrator can define custom schedules set to recur at a monthly, weekly, daily, or hourly time interval. Schedules can also be defined to allow jobs to run concurrently or sequentially, with an option to change the priority of the schedule relative to others that may occur at the same time. Figure 10–10 presented earlier, shows the schedule option in the Refresh Extract section. The drop-down box next to Full contains the available options. You can see in the example that the extract will be refreshed during weekdays at 4:00AM.

Defining a Custom Refresh Schedule

For those users granted administrative rights, creating custom refresh schedules is done from the Tableau Server admin menu. You can see these schedules in Figure 10–11.

Accessing the admin/schedules menu provides a list of what is available and summary information regarding the available schedules—their type, scope, the number of times run, how they run, as well as the next scheduled run time. To define a new custom schedule, you must select the New menu option you can see above the check boxes in Figure 10-11. Selecting that exposes the custom schedule dialog box you see below in Figure 10-12.

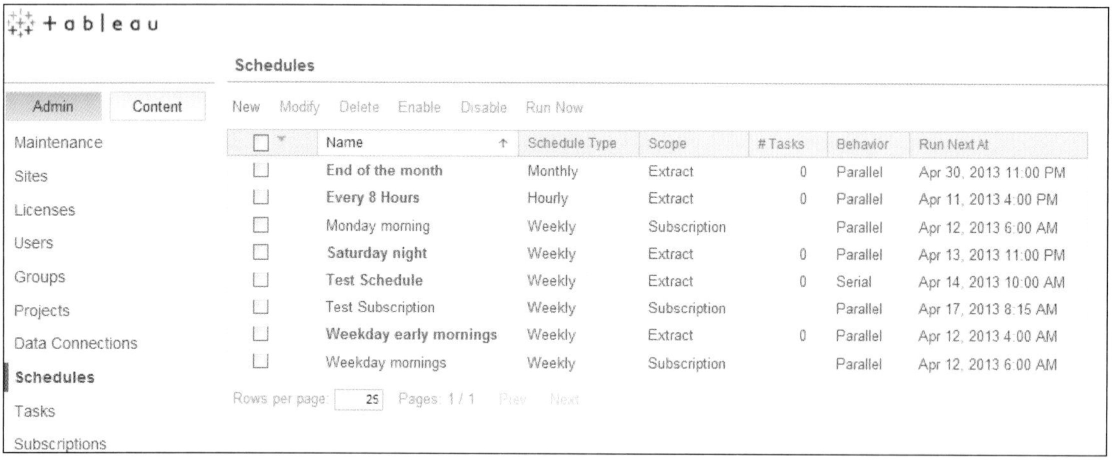

FIGURE 10-11   *Admins schedules menu*

FIGURE 10-12   *Creating a custom schedule*

Give the schedule a clearly descriptive name and fill in the highlighted blanks. Then, click the Create Schedule button. This makes the schedule available for use. As you can see, there is plenty of flexibility for controlling when data extracts are refreshed.

INCREMENTAL UPDATES

What if you have a particularly large or very active datasource? Very large source files can take time to update. You can reduce the time required for extracting data by employing incremental updates. Typically when refreshing extracts, the current rows are truncated and completely replaced by a new copy of the data set. In contrast, incremental refreshes allow you to specify a date, date-time, or an integer value field contained in your data, to specifically identify new records in a datasource.

When an incremental refresh is used, Tableau will check for the maximum value of the field in your extract and compare that value to each row in the original datasource—importing only the rows with a later or higher value. This approach will reduce the time required to update your extract. The larger the source file, the more significant will be your potential time savings.

You define this option in Tableau Desktop when you build the extract definition by selecting the incremental refresh option, then selecting the field that you want to use to identify the new data. The field options you see in Figure 10–13 include the order date or ship date fields.

If you choose to use incremental refreshes, you are not excluding the option for a full refresh. On the contrary, you are only allowing for the additional choice of an incremental refresh when either performing a manual or automatic update. It is advisable to run full refreshes of the data on a regular basis because the incremental refresh may not capture all of the changes in the source data set.

CONSUMING INFORMATION IN TABLEAU SERVER

As your Tableau deployment matures you may have hundreds of reports and datasources being published, updated, and consumed. Facilitating access

FIGURE 10–13 *Enabling incremental updates*

to information and encouraging collaboration is of primary importance, and that is the principle value business information systems provide. Tableau Server provides tools for finding information, commenting on reports, sharing discoveries, or customizing views; Tableau Server even allows information consumers to create completely new visualizations from within Tableau Server.

FINDING INFORMATION

Tableau's security structure provides an initial level of categorization, but Tableau Server also allows information consumers to customize access further though tagging, marking favorites, and even altering existing workbooks without the need for a Desktop license.

Tagging

You learned about tagging from the publishing perspective earlier in this chapter. However, users having only interactor access can also tag projects, workbooks, views, and datasources. While interactor users can add and remove their own tags, administrators and publishers have the visibility of all tags applied to workbooks. Tags are applied from the content menus for projects, workbooks, views, or datasources. To apply the tag, select the Tag menu option at the top, and either select an existing tag or enter a new tag. Figure 10–14 shows a tag being applied from within the content thumbnail view for workbooks.

The thumbnail workbook views checked in Figure 10–14 will have the Version8 tag applied to them. This tag will provide a means for filtering based on that tag. If no existing tag is appropriate, use the Add option at the bottom of the tag menu and create a new tag. Note, the new tag won't appear in the tag's menu until the view is refreshed in your browser.

Removing Tags

If you want to delete a tag associated with a project, workbook, view, or datasource, navigate to the server view containing the item from which you wish to delete the tag. Scroll to the bottom of the page below the comments area. You will see the tags associated with the item there as displayed in Figure 10–15.

The version tag will be deleted in Figure 10–15 by clicking on the X in the tag area. Note that administrators and publishers may remove any tag, but interactor users can only remove tags they have created.

FIGURE 10–14 *Tagging workbooks*

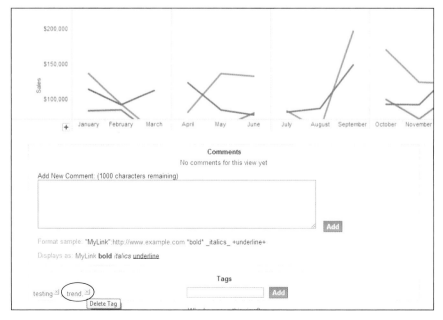

FIGURE 10–15 *Deleting a tag*

Favorites

Next to every workbook or view listing in Tableau Server is a star icon that allows your users to create a personal favorites list. If the icon is colored yellow, that item is a favorite. Greyed items are not. Clicking on the star will add it to the favorites list. Clicking a second time toggles it off the list. The Favorites list is a bookmarking mechanism that provides fast access to your most frequently used items. Refer to Figure 10–5, presented earlier in the "Creating a Favorite" section of this chapter to review the details regarding how favorites are added.

SHARING COMMENTS AND VIEWS

Comments can be applied in any server view if the user has the proper permission and assuming the comment save option has not been disabled through an embedded view. Comments are found at the bottom of the view in Server, giving users the opportunity to share ideas and ask questions.

Views can be shared with anyone via the Share Link found at the top of the page. If the view is embedded, you will find the Share Link at the bottom of the page. Figure 10–16 shows the dialog box that appears when the share menu option is selected.

FIGURE 10–16 *The share view dialog box*

The Share Links option allows you to send a link in an e-mail or to embed the view within a website. Both of the options allow you to optionally set the pixel height and width of the view, and to define whether or not the toolbar or tabs are displayed.

CUSTOMIZED VIEWS

Users can make mark selections, apply filters or highlights, and then save those settings in a customized view. Figure 10–17 shows a visualization in which the color legend for the Americas has been saved as a custom view called Americas Highlighted View.

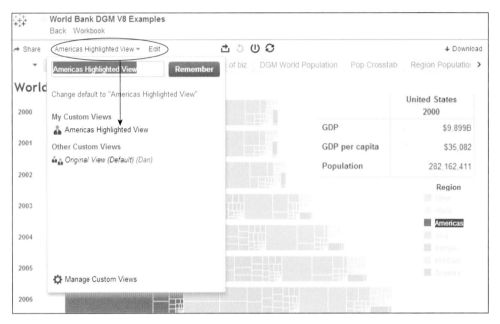

FIGURE 10–17 *Saving a custom view*

Saving any customized view requires three steps:

1. Click on the Remember my changes link.

2. Provide a name for the customized view.

3. Click the Remember button to save the view.

Your customized view is saved, and you are redirected to a unique URL that is generated for the view. The Remember My Changes link is also changed to the name of your customized view. If you click the link, you'll see a list of all the customized views you have saved along with a link to the original view published. To rename or delete any of your customized views, click the Manage Custom Views link at the bottom of the listing.

Other users accessing the view on their own will still be presented with the original view as originally published, unless they use the unique URL for your customized view. Customized views provide a good way for users to save frequently used filter combinations without the need to rely on the publisher.

A significant new feature that arrived with the release of Tableau Version 8 is web authoring. This goes beyond saving customized views by allowing users that lack a Tableau Desktop license to alter and create totally new visualizations within Tableau Server.

AUTHORING AND EDITING REPORTS VIA SERVER

Tableau Server's in-browser editing functionality provides a simplified version of the Desktop experience. It allows users to edit existing workbooks, create new visualizations, and save that work back to Server. This feature now provides for an under-supported component of the Enterprise community—the middle tier of users who do not require the complexity and power of the Desktop tool, but want the ability to probe the data in ways that were not anticipated by the report publisher. Web-Tablet authoring provides the ability to self-serve information from any device capable of accessing the Tableau Server and creating a web-session, without installing any software.

WHAT IS REQUIRED TO AUTHOR REPORTS ON THE WEB?

In Chapter 8 you learned about web and mobile access to Tableau Server reports. You observed that a personal computer's web-based interaction is very similar to the tablet-based interaction. This is also true when considering the Web-Tablet authoring functionality. This functionality, like all web-based interfaces to Tableau, is exclusively a function of the Tableau Server environment and is not possible utilizing only the Desktop or Reader products. To author on the web you need:

- A live web connection
- A Tableau Server Interactor license
- A standard web browser with a live web connection
- A pre-existing workbook must be published to Tableau Server.
- Appropriate permissions to be able to Web Edit

If you want to author via a tablet, you must download Tableau's iPad application from Apple, or the Android application from Google Play if you plan to use an Android tablet. While these elements are essential, they are not sufficient. The server permission for Web Edit must be allowed as you see in Figure 10–18.

As with all permissions on Tableau Server, web editing can be configured at multiple levels—user, group, workbook, project, or Site. Tableau Server users can also access saved datasources via the content tab and create a new workbook using that datasource. One Desktop license is required to publish the original report template to the server but any number of Tableau Server Interactor licensees can edit the report or create new reports from published datasources. This is the first iteration of Server-based authoring. Tableau does not impose additional licensing fees to access the Web-Tablet authoring tool.

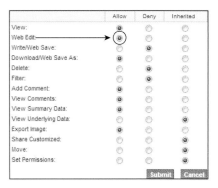

FIGURE 10–18 *Permitting web editing*

SERVER DESIGN AND USAGE CONSIDERATIONS RELATED TO WEB AND TABLET AUTHORING

Tableau's Web-Tablet authoring system is largely a client-side functionality provided through an HTML5 layer. This means that the Web-Tablet authoring system will have limited impact on the majority of Tableau Server processes.

The Tableau Server administrator should be aware that users editing views via this method will generate activity on the Server's VizQL process. And, if the workbook being edited is based on a data server extract-driven datasource, those processes will also experience increased loads. This impact is identical to the effective impact of adding additional Tableau Desktop interactions—presuming a server-mediated data connection.

Should Web-Tablet authoring result in a high number of workbook saves or creates via the server Save As dialog, Tableau Server will experience additional demand placed on its repository and storage systems in a manner similar to the load that would be expected via Tableau Desktop utilization.

These additional loads are a good thing. They mean that your user-base is engaged and actively using the system.

DIFFERENCES BETWEEN DESKTOP AND WEB OR TABLET AUTHORING

The experienced Tableau Desktop user will immediately notice that the web-tablet editing interface closely mirrors the familiar desktop environment. Editing through the web or tablet is very similar to the Desktop tool, though it is simplified and limited in a few ways. This section will detail the functional differences between the two authoring experiences. While limitations in the Web-Tablet authoring environment are highlighted, you should not interpret this section as a negative critique. Web authoring is a significant innovation that will provide benefits to the majority of your user base.

The goal is to highlight the differences so that you are aware of what can be done via the web versus what must be done using the Desktop application. The Web-Tablet authoring environment is designed to provide a simplified version of the Desktop experience. It is not intended to replace the Desktop application. Tableau Version 8 is also the first iteration of this functionality, and it will probably evolve and improve in future releases.

Drop Areas for Rows and Columns but No Show Me! Drop Area

Many of the standard Desktop Options and layouts are available within the Web-Tablet authoring interface. The left-hand side re-creates the data window, including any datasource(s), measures, and dimensions. The Column and Row shelves, along with the pages, filters, and marks cards also exist in their standard positions. Users can create visualizations in the same drag/drop manner that is fundamental to Tableau's Desktop authoring experience. One difference is that all fields must be dragged to the shelves and that the in-view drop areas for rows and columns do not exist, nor does the default Show Me! drop-area function in the view's center. See the web-authoring interface in Figure 10–19.

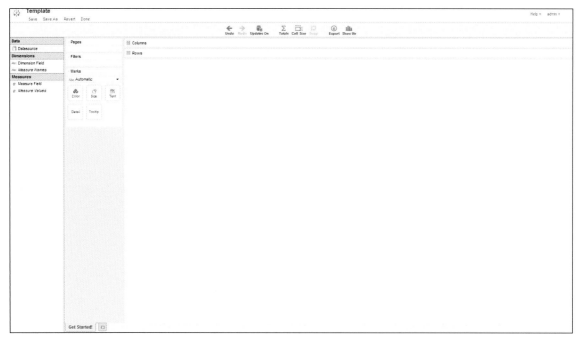

FIGURE 10–19 *The Web-Tablet authoring view*

Notice that some of the tools found in the desktop product icons or main menu appear in the web environment at the top of the authoring space.

No Dashboard Support

There is no dashboard display in the server authoring environment. In fact, Dashboard's editing is not interpreted in the Web-Tablet editing experience. Any workbook that contains Dashboards will display those views broken into their component parts (even if hidden) versus being displayed as the combined entity you see in the desktop application.

Datasource Manipulation Is Not Supported

All datasources needed for analysis must be included at the time of publishing from Tableau Desktop. The web authoring system does not allow for any manipulation of the metadata layer. You can't add new datasources, remove unused datasources, create calculated fields or parameters, change default field properties, or edit relationships between datasources. In general, the web authoring environment doesn't support metadata management. These capabilities exist exclusively in the desktop tool.

No Right-Mouse Button Click Functionality

While Tablet users won't be surprised at the lack of a secondary click option, this may surprise PC-based web authors. Any functionality accessed through right-clicking in Tableau's Desktop tool is not supported in the Web-Tablet authoring system. Some of these functions facilitated by right-button clicks in the Desktop are enabled through simple menu-based controls in the web-table environment. Dimension-specific controls are shows in Figure 10–20.

The dimension specific controls in Figure 10–20 were exposed by selecting the small drop-down arrow in the market dimension pill. Similar measure-specific controls are shown in Figure 10–21.

Quick table calculations are referenced using the drop-down arrow in the sales pill on the column shelf.

Quick Filters Only: No Complex Filtering

Desktop users accustomed to creating "complex" filters like "Top 10," or utilizing specific conditions, will notice that these filters will persist in the web authoring session. However, web editors can't add new versions of these complex filters. Web editors are able to add Quick Filters to views, and the full suite of Quick Filter types are available.

FIGURE 10-20 *Dimension-specific controls*

FIGURE 10-21 *Measure-specific controls*

Cell Sizing Is Exclusively Menu-Based

Cell sizing is controlled exclusively through the cell size menus; users can't drag elements of the visualization to resize those items—nor can they drag to resize the sheet as a whole. And, web editors cannot drag to control the "Fit" of the view within the design space. Figure 10–22 displays the web tools Fit and Sizing controls.

FIGURE 10–22 *Web fit and cell-sizing controls*

Even though Desktop dragging to resize elements isn't available in the web environment, the cell-size menu provides this facility.

Sheets Cannot Be Renamed

While creating new worksheets is supported, web-authors cannot enter customized names for the worksheets. New sheets created are numbered sequentially.

Sorting Is Only Available through Quick Sorts

Unlike Tableau Desktop, authors cannot set sorts based on specific fields, default sorts, or pre-sort information in a robust manner. Sorting is exclusively allowed through the in-visualization Quick Sorts that are omnipresent on headers in all Tableau visualizations.

Limited Control of Color, Size, Text, and Tooltips

Tableau Desktop allows nearly infinite control of color palettes, size ranges, shapes, and Tooltip content. The Web-Tablet environment provides none of these fine-grain controls.

Multi-Select/Ctrl-Key Functions Are Not Available

Tableau's Show Me! facility is available and works very well. However, Desktop users fond of using the Ctrl+Select technique to multi-select fields and then apply Show Me! to create visualizations, will notice that this isn't possible through the Web-Tablet system. All of Tableau's standard visualizations are available in the web authoring system as you see in Figure 10–23.

FIGURE 10–23 *Web authoring with Show Me!*

As fields are placed on shelves in Figure 10–23, relevant chart types will be highlighted just as they are in the Desktop. Even though this doesn't quite match the desktop authoring experience, the web-authoring environment provides robust visualization capabilities.

SAVING AND EXPORTING VIA THE WEB-TABLET ENVIRONMENT

The Web-Tablet environment provides a number of options for sharing work and insights.

Export

Similar to the Desktop tool, Web-Tablet authors have a full suite of export functions in addition to the standard server-based export functions. Figure 10–24 displays the available web options.

FIGURE 10–24 *Web-Tablet export functions*

Exporting images, data, crosstabs, and pdf documents are all supported.

Save and Save As

Recall in Figure 10–3 the web/edit permission must be allowed to enter the web edit system. Similarly, the ability to overwrite the existing workbook is also permission based. Should a user have sufficient permission to save their work from the Web-Tablet editing system, they will be given the option to save the workbook, which will overwrite the original Desktop version. Note that Tableau Server does not save a copy of the original document by default, so saving in the Web-Tablet system is equivalent to a republishing through the Desktop tool. The Save As dialog does provide the user with the ability to republish the altered workbook under a new name, or into another project.

RECOMMENDATIONS FOR IMPLEMENTING WEB-TABLET AUTHORING

Web-Tablet based design has not been designed to entirely replace the Desktop tool. Enterprises should view Web-Tablet authoring as a supplementary tool that enables a previously under-served cohort group to access Tableau's ad-hoc analysis and reporting capabilities.

Paired with relevant datasource access and training, the Web-Tablet authoring tool facilitates self-service business analysis in a controlled environment—providing users with the ability to ask questions that were not anticipated within the original design of the report. Key points to remember when designing reports that will be open to Web-Tablet authoring are:

- Give component worksheets logical name(s) that will not be obscured by the standard Desktop practice of hiding sheets that have been added to Dashboards.

- Design template workbooks and template datasources that can be readily approached by non-technical users that may not have data analysis expertise or experience with the Tableau Desktop tool.

- Provide transparent information about datasources—including refresh rates, sources, assumptions, and contact information for the original publisher.

- Do not presume users will understand how to use the Web-Tablet authoring environment, provide training, and help motivated individuals use the system effectively.

- Create a specific Sandbox project/area where new users can save work and gain confidence.

SHARING CONNECTIONS, DATA MODELS, AND DATA EXTRACTS

Tableau's data server can lower the data access barrier while still providing data governance controls. Database administrators can define data connections once, publish them to the data server, and manage access by applying Tableau's object level. Consequently, data analysts using Tableau require no knowledge of the underlying tables, joins, or related criteria driving the connections.

OFFERING A COMMON DATA LIBRARY

It's common for organizations to manage and use a variety of datasources. Transactional data may live in one database while historical data is maintained in another completely different database. Business users may maintain their own spreadsheets of forecasts and budgets. While Tableau can easily connect to each of these disparate datasources, Data Server offers the capability to host these connections in a central place. This reduces the potential for data misuse because Tableau users can simply connect to Tableau Server and the data they need access to, regardless of source system. Data Server simply acts as a proxy to databases while also serving as a host for items such as Excel and Access files, or even data extracts.

SHARING DATA MODELS

Earlier in the Chapter in the section related to the Tableau Data Server you learned how datasources can be published and used by many different users. The related metadata that comes with the shared datasources allows data administrators to manage inconsistencies through:

- Consistent field name aliasing
- Consistent field grouping
- Consistent application of field hierarchies

This permits the organization to tap into the best subject matter experts to create and validate calculations and publish the resulting data models for your entire organization to benefit from. These capabilities can reduce variations in how business rules are interpreted and applied, while giving analysts the ability to do their own ad-hoc analysis by adding their own customizations on a per-workbook basis.

INHERITANCE OF UPDATES

Once a datasource has been published to Data Server, workbooks using the connection automatically inherit any future updates to the datasource. This greatly simplifies the process of datasource maintenance, while reducing the risk of outdated business rules persisting in production when an underlying change has been made.

EMBEDDING TABLEAU REPORTS SECURELY ON THE WEB

If your organization is accustomed to consuming information via a specific web portal, Tableau provides a variety of ways to embed your reports as interactive dashboards or static images—all the while persisting the same licensing and security framework available to you on Server.

WHEN TO EMBED A DASHBOARD

When does it make sense to embed a dashboard rather than simply having your users access it directly from Tableau Server? If your user base is already familiar with a particular web portal, it makes sense to use that website as a repository for interactive Tableau visualizations and Dashboards. In addition, there may be advantages to leveraging the existing security options that the web portal may already have defined.

Going to Your Users

It can be frustrating for some people when they are given yet another website and login to access for information that they need to effectively perform their job and make critical decisions. Many people don't enjoy the accelerating change fostered by advances in technology. At work, people are constantly presented with new software and initiatives designed to make them more efficient, but that (at least during the transition) make them less efficient.

By embedding Tableau into an existing web portal that is familiar to users, you can provide them with the benefits that Tableau has to offer while keeping them in a familiar environment that they are already used to accessing for their reporting needs.

When Your Reports Are a Piece of a Larger SaaS Offering

Anytime you are offering a service to your clients you'll want to control the overall branding of the product you create. When including Dashboards the process is no different. Rather than providing what appears to be a third party solution by redirecting your users from your product to Tableau Server, you can embed the Tableau reports directly into your product instead. The result can often be a seamless integration where your users are unaware of—and need not know—the underlying technology driving the reports you provide them with. Instead, the details blend into the background while you offer a single cohesive product to your users.

Providing a More Robust Environment

We've already discussed situations where your users are already concentrated in another environment, and how it can be advantageous to embed Tableau reports in that environment. Now, let's explore the opposite situation. What happens when, over the years, multiple reporting environments have been created as the result of various initiatives spread over multiple departments? One part of the company may rely on Business Object reports created a decade earlier. Other teams depend on SSRS reports to make their day-to-day decisions. Now, you look to open a new world of analytical discovery by implementing Tableau.

So, do you go about re-creating the existing Business Objects and SSRS reports in Tableau and redirect all users to Tableau Server? Does this always make sense when specific reports work perfectly well and already directly impact a critical business need? Why not create a single environment that combines these disparate systems into a single environment that you can further enhance through documentation and an interactive user community?

What is worse than bad business intelligence? Good business intelligence that nobody can find. By creating a single seamless environment for your users, they no longer have to track down and find the reports that may be out there. You mitigate the risk of users reinventing the wheel by re-creating existing reports. Most important of all, you remain agile because you can blend in future technologies while servicing your users in the same location you do now.

HOW TO EMBED A DASHBOARD

Embedding Dashboards usually boils down to one of these methods:

- Using Tableau's JavaScript code
- Using the Dashboard's URL in an iFrame or Image tag
- Writing your own code using Tableau's JavaScript API

No matter which method you choose to use, you can control your embedded view through the use of Passed Parameters. We'll explore all three methods below while also diving into the details of all the parameters you can use.

Note that all the embedded solutions in this section require the user to log in via the embedded view as they normally would when accessing Tableau Server directly. For information relating to providing a single sign-on experience for your users, see Tips and Tricks for Embedding Dashboards.

Using Tableau's JavaScript Code

The easiest way to embed a Dashboard in another web page is to use the JavaScript code provided by Tableau in its Share button. With the options for setting the width and height of your Dashboard and the ability to turn on/off the toolbar and tabs, this provides a mechanism for quickly embedding your Dashboards into another web page. Below is a quick example of the resulting code:

```
<script type="text/javascript" src="https://yourtableauserver.com/javascripts/
api/viz_v1.js"></script><div class="tableauPlaceholder" style=
"width:979px; height:662px;"><object class
="tableauViz" width="979" height="662"
style="display:none;"><param name="host_url"
value="https%3A%2F%2Fyourtableauserver.com%2F" /><param name=
"site_root" value="&#47;t&#47;YourSite"
/><param name="name"
value="YourWorkbook&#47;YourView" /><param name="tabs"
value="yes" /><param name="toolbar" value="yes" /></object></div>
```

Notice the use of <param> tags to pass specific values to Tableau Server. Through the use of these tags, it is possible to pass additional parameters such as an initial filter. For example, the following entry will initially filter the embedded view by restricting the Region dimension to West only:

```
<param name="filter" value="Region=West"/>
```

The name and site root parameters are the only ones required when embedding a view.

Using an iFrame or Image Tag

Another option is to use the URL for a dashboard or a view in an iFrame or image tag. Additional parameters can still be passed but must be included at the end of the URL. The embed parameter is required, but all others are optional. An example of an embedded view using an iFrame is displayed below this paragraph. The Dashboard is once again filtered to the West Region only, while also restricting to the date June 1st, 2012.

```
<iframe src="https://yourtableauserver.com /t/views/MyWorkbook/MyDashboard?:
embed=yes&Region=West&Date=2012-06-01" width="800" height="600"></iframe>
```

Note the required embed parameter is set first. A value of Yes hides Tableau's default navigation options and comments section below the view, while also moving the toolbar and share options below the view.

Writing Your Own JavaScript API

You can also write your own code by leveraging Tableau's JavaScript API. This is often the preferred choice by web developers looking to embed Tableau views into their existing web applications as it offers a deeper level of control.

Tableau provides developers with the ability to interact with embedded views in real time. By listening for events generated by Tableau views, developers can capture actions performed by a user and respond to them in rich, interactive ways. For instance, developers can respond to a user selecting marks on an embedded view and trigger a response in their web application. Developers can also interactively set filters and select marks within an embedded view in real time—no longer limited to simply setting initial values prior to a view loading. The best part is that each of these API functions are enacted as they would be if the user had performed the action in the view itself, meaning no page refreshes occur. The result is a completely seamless experience between your application and the embedded Tableau reports. Check this book's InterWorks book website or the Wiley companion website for an example of how you might use the JavaScript API to create interaction between a Tableau Dashboard and a website.

Further Control Using Passed Parameters

Whether you choose to use an iFrame or JavaScript, you can pass additional parameters to the view. Search Tableau's website to find a complete list of supported parameters.

TIPS AND TRICKS FOR EMBEDDING DASHBOARDS

Tableau has streamlined the embedding process to a great extent. You may get some additional benefit from the following tips and tricks.

Filter Formats for Dimensions, Measures, and Dates/Times

When passing dimension filter parameters, simply list each value in a comma-separated list. To filter on multiple dimensions, separate each with an ampersand. The general form is:

```
Field=Value1,Value2,Value3&Field2=Value1,Value2
```

You can filter on measures in the same manner by passing explicit values. However, Tableau Server does not support filtering by a range of values or using greater than or less than logic.

To filter on a Date or Date/Time field, use the following form:

```
DateField=yyyy-mm-dd hh:mm:ss
```

When filtering a Date/Time field, the time component is considered optional.

Know Your Character Limits

Theoretically there is no limit to the number of parameter values you may pass to an embedded view. However, you may ultimately run into a URL length restriction imposed by the end user's browser.

While HTTP protocol does not impose a cap on URL length and many modern browsers can handle URLs with up to 80,000 characters, Internet Explorer 8 and 9 have a maximum character limit of only 2,083 characters.

As a result, you should strive to keep your URLs under this limit to ensure compatibility. Keep in mind that the complete URL—not just the parameters and corresponding values—are included in this length.

Use Trusted Ticket Authentication as an Alternative Single Sign-On Method

When an embedded view is accessed, the same authentication mode enabled on Tableau Server is used to verify the user's identity. For instance, if your server is configured to use local authentication, your users will be required to log in via a form provided by the embedded view. This can be cumbersome if the user has already authenticated in the web application. To work around this, Tableau provides a couple of options for single sign-on authentication—a process where your user is authenticated by your web application and is not required to further authenticate themselves by any embedded Tableau views.

If your server is configured to use Active Directory and SSPI, you can enable SSPI on your web server as a single sign-on solution given the user is in your Active Directory and is a licensed Tableau Server user. In all other situations, you will need to use Trusted Ticket Authentication as an alternative single sign-on method.

When using Trusted Ticket Authentication, the web server assumes all responsibility for authenticating users. Before embedding the view, the web server passes two POST parameters to Tableau Server:

- Username (must match a licensed Tableau server user)
- Client_ip

The web server will receive a response in the form of a unique_id, which is used in the embedded view's URL, as shown in this form:

```
https://yourtableauserver.com/
trusted/unique_id/t/views/MyWorkbook/MyDashboard?:embed=yes
```

If you are using JavaScript, the ticket parameter can be used:

```
<param name="ticket" value="unique_id"/>
```

Once a unique_id has been issued, it must be redeemed within 15 seconds from a machine matching the client _ip specified or it is considered no longer valid. When Tableau Server receives the request, the user is logged in as they would be if using forms authentication, and the trusted ticket URL is resolved to that of a standard request.

Before a web server can make a Trusted Ticket Authentication request, it must first be "White Listed" on Tableau Server. This can be accomplished using the following `tabadmin` command, where `xxx.xxx.xxx.xxx` represents IP addresses for any trusted web servers:

```
tabadmin set wgserver.trusted_hosts "xxx.xxx.xxx.xxx, xxx.xxx.xxx.xxx"
```

USING SUBSCRIPTIONS TO DELIVER REPORTS VIA E-MAIL

Busy managers sometimes like to have their reports delivered. Tableau supports this though subscriptions. By subscribing to a workbook or a view, users can have an image of the report delivered directly to their e-mail. The user will be notified via e-mail when the report is updated. These schedules are defined by a server administrator, allowing administrators to ensure that any additional server load is balanced appropriately. Subscription e-mails also contain links to their live and interactive counterparts located on Server.

To subscribe to a report, a user follows these steps:

1. Log in to Tableau Server.

2. Open the view or dashboard to which you wish to subscribe, or subscribe to an entire workbook by opening a single view or dashboard belonging to that workbook.

3. Click the Subscribe icon in the top right corner of the dashboard. This is represented by the small e-mail icon on the left side of the download link.

4. This causes the subscribe dialog box to appear.

Select or enter the following values:

1. To—Verify the e-mail address associated with your account.

2. Subject—Enter the desired subject for the subscription e-mail.

3. Schedule—Select the schedule you'd like your snapshots sent on. These schedules are created and maintained by Tableau Server administrators.

4. Content—Choose whether to subscribe to the current sheet only or all sheets in the Workbook.

5. Click on subscribe to finish.

ADMINISTRATORS SUBSCRIPTION MANAGEMENT

Allowing subscriptions on Tableau Server requires a few additional steps to be performed by an administrator. You can change these in the Tableau Server configurations to Enable Subscriptions using the following steps:

1. Log in to the Tableau Server machine, stop the server, and open the Tableau Configuration utility.

2. Click the E-mail Alerts/Subscriptions tab.

3. Check Enable E-mail Subscriptions.

4. In the SMTP Server section, ensure that an SMTP Server and Port is specified. Enter a Username and Password if required by your SMTP Server.

5. Enter a Send E-mail From an Address. This e-mail will send out all subscription e-mails.

6. Enter your Tableau Server URL.

7. Click OK to finish.

8. Start the server.

CREATING SUBSCRIPTION SCHEDULES

Administrators have to enable the subscription notification system in Tableau Server in order for the feature to be available to users. To create subscription notification schedules, the administrator should follow these steps:

1. Log in to Tableau Server using a System Admin account.

2. From the Admin tab click Schedules ➢ New.

3. The Create New Schedule page appears.

Define the desired schedule ensuring Schedule Scope is set to Subscriptions and click on the Create Schedule button to finish the definition.

Your users will now have the option to subscribe to workbooks and views using the schedule(s) you've defined. Like all scheduled tasks you have the option to initiate them manually by using the Run Now option on the Schedules page.

In the last two chapters you've learned how to install Tableau Server and were introduced to the features available to Tableau Server users.

The next chapter is geared toward administrators charged with the responsibility of keeping information up to date and maintaining the environment. You will learn how Tableau's command line tools (`tabadmin` and `tabcmd`) can help you automate repetitive administrative tasks.

NOTES

1. Collins, James C. *Good to Great: Why Some Companies Make the Leap—and Others Don't*. New York, NY: HarperBusiness, 2001. Print. Page 88.

CHAPTER 11

Automating Server with Tableau's Command Line Tools

As your Tableau Server deployment expands, the number of users and amount of data you have to manage will grow. Tableau provides two command line tools that will help you automate routine tasks. Most of the functions the command line tools provide are available directly within Tableau Server's user interface.

Using Windows Notepad (or your favorite text editor) you can automate `tabcmd` to run via a batch file. Then by using Windows Task Scheduler you can trigger the batch file to run at a specific time or based on a specific triggering event. Of course many popular scripting or programming tools can call Tableau's command line functions to automate tasks. How you use these tools is only limited by your desire and creativity.

If you are a system administrator and accustomed to writing script and using the Windows Command Processor and Windows Task Scheduler, you will not have difficulty incorporating `tabcmd` or `tabadmin` into your existing toolset. Many people don't use the command line utilities because their full functionality is not clearly understood, or they have not seen specific use case examples. Tableau Software provides some good introductory videos on their website. You can find those by searching for On Demand Training and looking in the server section for the tabcmd and tabadmin videos.

WHAT DO TABCMD AND TABADMIN DO?

Tableau's two command line tools are `tabcmd` and `tabadmin`. Tabcmd provides functions for performing workflow tasks like publishing workbooks, adding users, or exporting workbooks as image or data files. Tabadmin is designed for server administration—configuring server options, activating users, resetting passwords, and other tasks associated with managing the deployment and usage of Server within the enterprise.

A person with publishing rights might want to use `tabcmd` to automate repetitive tasks associated with updating and publishing datasources. A server administrator can leverage `tabadmin` to set up a new site, grant or revoke user rights, back up data, alter default session time-out settings (get input from Tableau Support or a qualified Tableau Partner before changing these settings), or reset user passwords. Think of tabcmd as a tool for helping those who publish and share. Tabadmin is an automation tool for staff with administration responsibilities—helping them control access, tweak settings, or observe system status.

INSTALLING THE COMMAND LINE TOOLS

When Tableau Server is installed `tabcmd` and `tabadmin` are automatically installed in Tableau Server's bin folder. Depending on the operating system being used (Windows 32-bit or 64-bit) the program will be installed in one of these locations:

- **32-bit**—`C:\Program Files\Tableau\Tableau Server\8.0\bin`
- **64-bit**—`C:\Program Files (x86)\Tableau\Tableau Server\8.0\bin`

If you are using an older version of Tableau Server the portion of the address that says 8.0 would be replaced with the specific version number that you are using. If you are running a distributed environment—with multiple worker machines—and you want to utilize `tabcmd` on one or more of the worker boxes, you must install `tabcmd` on those other machines. Tableau provides an installer program for doing that. Those programs are:

- **32-bit**—`C:\Program Files\Tableau\Tableau Server\8.0\extras\Tabcmdinstaller.exe`
- **64-bit**—`C:\Program Files\Tableau\Tableau Server\8.0\extras\Tabcmdinstaller.exe`

Copy the `Tabcmdinstaller.exe` program to the computer that you want to install it on and double-click on the file to run the program. The program provides prompts as it installs. Tableau Software recommends installing the `tabcmd` program on the root drive (`C:\tabcmd`).

Since the setup program doesn't automatically add the bin folder containing `tabcmd` or `tabadmin` to the Windows PATH system variable, you have to manually navigate to the bin folder subdirectory to use the programs. This can be avoided if you modify your computer's PATH system variable to include the path to the bin folder. Doing this allows you to run the executable commands without needing to manually enter the directory location of the bin folder. To start using `tabcmd`, open the Windows Command Prompt. Figure 11–1 shows you how to do that in a Windows 7 environment.

If you are using a different version of Windows, find the accessories folder by searching your computer's hard disk. Once you've entered the accessories folder, click on Command Prompt to open the command prompt window. In order for you to have access to the tabcmd program files you must first navigate to one of the bin folders listed in the first section. If you are using a 64-bit version of Windows, type in the following command and press enter:

```
cd "C:\Program Files(x86)\Tableau\Tableau Server\8.0\bin"
```

This will change the active directory to the bin folder that holds the tabcmd program. Assuming that your Tableau Server address is `http://mytableauserver.com`, and that your Tableau Server uses port 80, start a tabcmd session by typing the following into the command prompt window:

```
tabcmd login -s http://mytableauserver.com -u USER -p PASSWORD
```

The end of the string immediately following the ".com" is case sensitive.

After entering the `tabcmd login` command, and the `-s` site URL, substitute the URL location of your Tableau Server installation. Then enter your username and password after the `-u` and `-p` global option variables.

The instance of Tableau server used in this example is a local installation on a laptop. The username is `Admin` and the password is `Admin`. The command line entry to log into this server can be seen in Figure 11–2.

FIGURE 11–1 *Opening Windows Command Prompt*

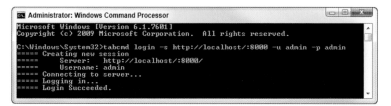

FIGURE 11–2 *Tabcmd login example*

Notice that the portion of the script that includes the server address also includes an additional element (`:8000`). This defines the TCP/IP port for the local server instance and is required because the port assigned to the local server isn't the default value that Tableau Server normally uses. You can find more details regarding the default port settings in the Tableau Server online manual by searching for TCP/IP Ports. After completing this step you can now issue other commands to Tableau Server.

SETTING THE WINDOWS PATH

If you want to avoid having to manually change your current directory to the Tableau Server bin folder every time you want to run an executable file, add the bin folder to your Windows PATH system variable. Edit PATH by going to the Windows Control Panel, click on System, then Advanced System Settings, and selecting the Environmental Variables button to expose the dialog box you see in Figure 11–3.

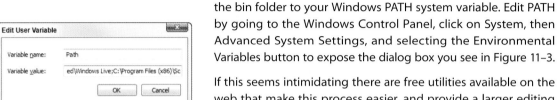

FIGURE 11–3 *Editing the PATH system variable through the Windows Control Panel*

If this seems intimidating there are free utilities available on the web that make this process easier, and provide a larger editing window. Figure 11–4 shows a free utility called Eveditor in which the PATH has been edited to include the bin folder.

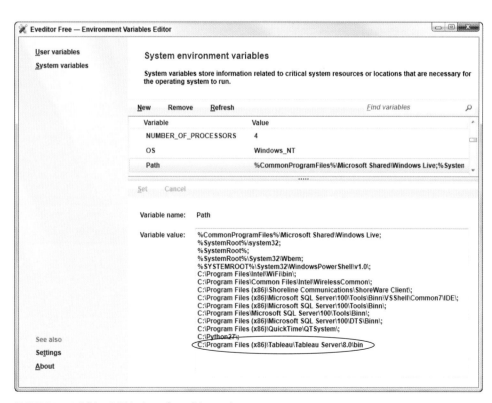

FIGURE 11–4 *Editing PATH using a free editing tool*

Adding the path for the Tableau Server bin folder eliminates needing to manually type in the path every time you want to start tabcmd or tabadmin in a batch file. Later you'll see how to dynamically set PATH commands inside executable batch files—enabling dynamic setting of the file path so that tabcmd can always find the script it needs to execute.

Keep in mind that any third-party tools (like Eveditor) are not supported by Tableau Software. You may be successful with Eveditor or other tools that you enjoy using, or you may experience problems. This is outside of Tableau Software's control.

WHAT KINDS OF TASKS CAN BE DONE WITH TABCMD?

The tabcmd utility provides the ability to automate routine tasks concerning workflow management activities related to:

- Users, groups, projects, and sites
- Data management, publishing, updating
- Session management
- Security, site listings
- Server version information

The level of access and control is dependent on the type of administration rights assigned to the person using tabcmd. System Administrators can manage data connections, groups, projects and workbooks. They can add users to groups and projects. But, they are not able to alter user licensing levels. Systems administrators have full rights—including the assignment of licensing levels for users and managing the server itself. System Administrators can assign some administrative roles to Site Administrators. That role determines how much control will be given to a Site Administrator. Site Administrators can manage groups, projects, workbooks, and data connections. If the System Administrator permits it, they can also add or remove site users.

The tabcmd utility currently provides 24 functions with an additional 12 global option settings.

You can access a complete function reference in the Tableau Server's online manual in the `tabcmd` Commands section. Located at: `http://onlinehelp` `.tableausoftware.com/current/server/en-us/tabcmd.htm`.

Tabcmd also has a built-in help function for listing the available commands by entering Tabcmd Help Commands. Figure 11–5 shows the help command display.

FIGURE 11–5 *The tabcmd help function display*

Entering Tabcmd Help and then a specific command name causes more complete options for that single command to be displayed.

LEARNING TO LEVERAGE TABCMD

In the following examples you'll see progressively more advanced ways to use tabcmd including:

■   Manually creating and running a tabcmd script

■ Creating a Windows batch (.bat) file to run a saved script

■ Using Windows Task Scheduler to automatically run a saved script

MANUALLY ENTERING AND RUNNING A SCRIPT IN TABCMD

The most basic way of using tabcmd is to manually enter commands that can also be accessed from the Tableau Server manual. This is also a good way to test tabcmd before you attempt to create script that automatically runs tabcmd.

A common task required of a content administrator is to create groups on Server and assign users to those groups. Figure 11–6 displays the script used to create a new group called Executives.

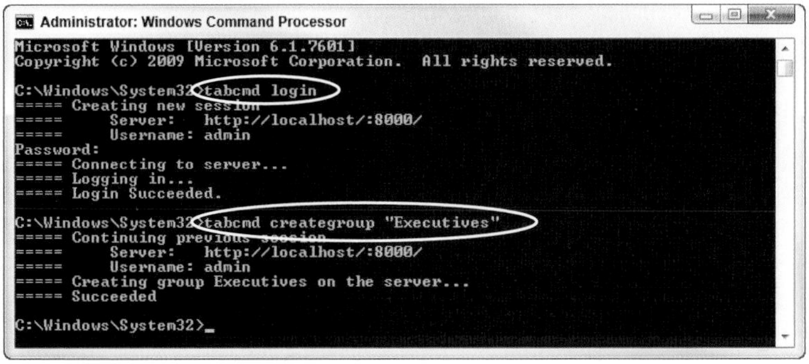

FIGURE 11–6 *Adding a new group to Server*

The first command in Figure 11–6, `tabcmd login`, initiates a new session and prompts the user to enter a password. It is also possible to append the password to the end of the login command by adding -p or -password followed by your actual password. The script Tabcmd Creategroup `"Executives"` triggers the addition of the new group to Server. At the bottom of the script you can see that tabcmd provides a status while processing and then confirms that the operation succeeded.

The next step is to assign users to the group. By creating a list of valid usernames (`egroupadd.csv`) and saving it in the Tableau Server bin folder, tabcmd can assign the specified users to the executive group. Figure 11–7 shows a list of Server users on the left (Allen, Bill, Cal, Dave, Eric). On the right you see the executed script.

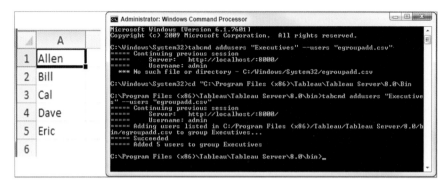

FIGURE 11–7 *Adding users to the new group*

This is the script used to add the users:

```
tabcmd addusers "Executives" —users "egroupadd.csv".
```

These activities can be done directly in the Tableau Server GUI environment, but tabcmd may be a more efficient way to make group assignments if they change frequently or you have a large number of users to assign.

RUNNING TABCMD SCRIPTS VIA BATCH FILES

If you find yourself using the same script repeatedly, you can use a text editor to create and save the script for reuse later. Windows includes a text editor program called Notepad that can be used to enter and save `tabcmd` script. Notepad is normally located in the Windows accessories folder. Another Windows application—Task Scheduler—can be used to launch the script saved using Notepad. There are many other programming tools you can use for this purpose, but these are part of the Windows toolset.

The Steps Required to Create Batch Processing Scripts

Regardless of whether you prefer to use Windows Notepad or some other text editing software, the basic steps to create a batch process are the same:

1. Create the `tabcmd` script in Notepad or another text editor.

2. Save the script as a (.bat) executable file.

3. Double-click the batch file to execute the script.

In this scenario the script is still run manually but you no longer have to type all of the instructions every time you want to make changes, export data, or update files. These may be activities you repeat periodically—often enough to warrant saving a script—but not so often that you need to fully automate processing.

In the next example you'll see how to create a script in a text editor, save the script as a batch file, and then run the script using a CSV source file that provides the usernames and permissions needed to update Tableau Server.

Assume you have five new users to add and will be provisioning Interactor licenses for all of them. Figure 11–8 shows the CSV file with the names of the users.

Creating a robust script that will work flexibly is the goal. To do that requires a little knowledge of Windows commands and tabcmd. Figure 11–9 shows one way to accomplish adding the users.

	A	B
1	Username	Password
2	Brenden	b1
3	Phil	p1
4	Joe	j1
5	Paul	p1
6	Darren	d5

FIGURE 11–8 *CSV file containing new user list*

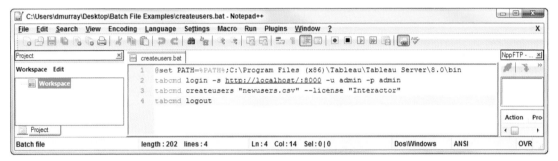

FIGURE 11–9 *Creating and saving script in a .bat file*

For the batch file to run properly, place it in the same directory as the CSV file that contains the users that need to be added to server. The first line of the code in Figure 11–9—`@set PATH=%PATH%`—defines the path for the file to search if any elements are not located there. These Windows commands allow you to define the path for the batch session only. This is a better practice than blending data files in with Windows system files (not a good practice). It also has the virtue of persisting only while the batch file is being executed—rendering the earlier example of permanently editing the PATH system variable unnecessary.

The rest of the script in Figure 11-9 includes tabcmd commands that are located in the bin folder specified by the set path command. In fact, you can define many different paths using this method for files that you want to keep separated.

The bulleted list below may be easier for to read than Figure 11-9. Alter the specific code where applicable to match your system's setup and the name of the CSV file that you created to load new users.

- Line 2—Log in to Tableau Server.
- Line 3—Create the users from the `newusers.csv` file.
- Line 4—Log out of Tableau Server.

When the program starts you'll see each command run and when it is finished the command window will close automatically. Figure 11–10 shows a screenshot of the Windows Command Processor window—running the script.

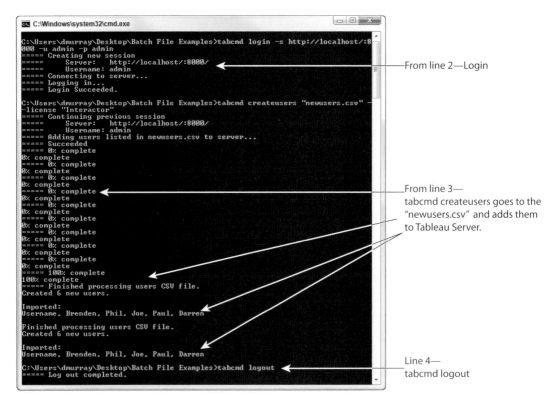

FIGURE 11–10 *The executed script*

As the program finishes, the screen automatically clears. If you want to keep it in view, add a fifth line to the script using the Pause command. With just a few lines of code you can update many records this way. If you aren't using Active Directory to secure Tableau Server, this method provides a quick way to mass load hundreds of users from a file.

Using Windows Scheduler to Fully Automate Scripts

By adding the batch file from the previous example to Windows Task Scheduler, the file can be updated based on a trigger event or a specific time schedule. For example, if you have an actively expanding user base it might be necessary to create new users in the system every day. The system administrator could add new users to the `Createuser.csv` and schedule updates every day at a specific time. Figure 11-11 shows the Task Scheduler application. A new task was created to ADD USERS to Tableau Server (daily). The following steps were used to define the schedule:

1. General tab—Name and describe the task and set security options.

2. Triggers tab—Define what causes action (daily at 7:00AM).

3. Actions tab—Select the batch file to run (point to the `Createuser.bat` file).

4. Conditions tab—Set desired limitations for the run to occur.

5. Settings tab—Specify additional settings affecting the task behavior.

This will cause the file to be updated on a regular basis without the need for the batch file to be manually selected. Figure 11-11 shows the task scheduled for automatic updates of new user additions.

FIGURE 11-11 *Windows task scheduler*

Even if you're on vacation, updates can continue if you delegate the task of adding the usernames and license level to the `Newusers.csv`.

COMMON USE CASES FOR TABCMD

There are many different ways to utilize tabcmd to automate repetitive or intensive production issues. If you find yourself doing repetitive tasks consistently, you should consider using tabcmd to automate the process to Save time, improve accuracy, and enhance the way you can share and update files.

The examples presented next are intended as a sampling of the ways you could use tabcmd. You will undoubtedly think of many more ways to automate processes that repeatedly require your attention.

RETRIEVING FORECAST DATA FROM WORKBOOKS

Tableau's forecasting ability can be used to create initial projections based on historical patterns. The tabcmd Export function can be used to publish forecasted data points from a workbook view. Exporting data in CSV format can then be used to update a source database or a spreadsheet. This first-pass view of the forecast can then be tweaked and returned to a database and stored.

Even more commonly, historical data can be published as well. Even though it may be easier to analyze data using Tableau, some users my lack license access. You may wish to share exported PDF, PNG, or CSV files with vendors that don't have access to Tableau. Alternatively, you might publish packaged workbooks specifically for partners and allow them to access specific groups on your server.

MANAGE DATA GOVERNANCE VIA TABCMD

You may want to create a quality control directory that you publish raw files to for review, then after auditing and approval use the Publish command to move the preliminary file into a production group or project. This is an interesting alternative to heavy-handed quality control. Instead of focusing on the end report, IT can focus on ensuring the quality of the data extract file and provide information to consumers with a vetted preliminary view that can be modified to suit specific needs.

USING TABADMIN FOR ADMINISTRATIVE TASK AUTOMATION

The Tabadmin Toolset is intended for use by the designated server administrators responsible for configuring and maintaining Tableau Server's data and metadata. Tabadmin has its own set of commands that are exclusively used for these purposes. You can find a categorized list of these in Appendix A.

Normally, a very limited number of technical staff members are tasked with the responsibility of developing, maintaining, and monitoring system performance. The tasks performed using Tabadmin include:

- Tabadmin help
- Conducting system backups and restores
- Displaying information on system status
- Cleaning service log files
- Resetting the password for the Tableau Server account
- Enabling or disabling access to Tableau Server's Postgres database
- Creating zipped log files
- Stopping Tableau Server

STARTING TABLEAU SERVER

The tabadmin command tool may also be useful for additional tasks. The recommendations in the list below should only be attempted under the direction of Tableau Software Support or a qualified Tableau Server Partner.

- Altering default time-out provisions for queries
- Changing default time-out limits for idle users
- Creating a server log file
- Configuring Tableau Server processes
- Printing Tableau Server license information
- Printing information on active users
- Setting primary and secondary gateway hosts
- Executing system changes via the configure command

The Tabadmin command line utility is the primary tool maintaining the safety and performance of the server. Tableau software provides extensive documentation on their website.

Finally, Tableau provides online reference material that covers all of the details well. You can find this by navigating to the Admin view and selecting the help menu in the upper right of the screen, then Get Help and Support.

That will take you to the online help screen where you will find the online administrator guide. Specific sections related to Tabadmin activities include Tabadmin, Database Maintenance, and Troubleshooting.

The first eleven chapters of this text have been about introducing you to Tableau Desktop, Tableau's Server products (Server, Online, and Public), and Tableau Server's command line toolset. In the final chapter, short case studies will be presented that show how others have used Tableau to address their business needs.

PART III

CASE STUDIES

In this part

CHAPTER 12

Use Cases for Rapid-Fire Visual Analytics

Relating a few stories about how people are deploying and using Tableau will hopefully inspire you to think of ways you can use it to turn data into understandable information. The case studies presented include a variety of industries, healthcare, and education. Keep an eye on the book's InterWorks book website and the Wiley companion website for additional case studies and additional example material.

RAPID-FIRE ANALYSIS AT A PUBLIC UTILITY

Newnan Utilities is a local water utility in Newnan, Georgia. The company has experienced significant fluctuations in call volume within their call center that were proving to be challenging to resolve. Traditional call center software was too expensive. Director of Administration, Jeff Phillips, and Business Analyst, Paul Lisborg, were charged with solving the problem. They achieved this goal by using Tableau Software to visualize the data that was already being captured by their telephone system database. Figure 12–1 shows an example call analysis dashboard.

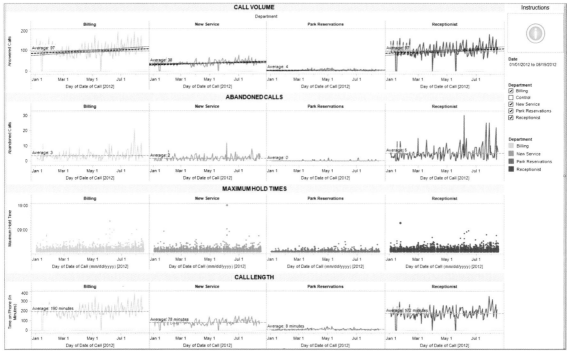

SOURCE: CASE STUDY AND FIGURE PROVIDED BY PAUL LISBORG, NEWNAN UTILITIES.

FIGURE 12–1 *Call analysis dashboard*

This dashboard has a number of desirable attributes. When users point at the instruction icon in the upper right side of the dashboard, they receive detailed navigation instructions regarding navigation and filtering. The dashboard provides time series analysis of call volume for selected departments and information on abandoned calls, maximum hold times, and average call duration.

Newnan Utilities was able to deploy the dashboard in less than an hour. They were able to make immediate and significant improvements in staff utilization during peak periods, and managers were more quickly alerted to staffing needs. Best of all, a single dashboard design is able to be deployed easily across multiple platforms—including smart phones and tablet computers.

The company has also realized significant benefit by using Tableau for residential rate analysis and for monitoring and managing potential storm water infiltration into a wastewater system. All of these solutions were envisioned, developed, and deployed in days.

AGGREGATING DISPARATE DATASOURCES AT A LARGE UNIVERSITY

Ted Curran is the Executive Director of Finance of the Tepper School of Business at Carnegie Mellon University. Ted was charged with overhauling the business school's data evaluation information—a system affecting over two hundred and fifty faculty and staff. The project would potentially uncover necessary modifications to the school's reporting and analytics. The university's ability to generate and collect data far outpaced its capacity to utilize the data to drive favorable outcomes. After considering a number of different solutions, Tepper selected Tableau Software.

GETTING STARTED WITH TABLEAU

Initially, Tepper wanted to use data to give the dean a high-level view across the school's operations, including admissions, financial aid, marketing, faculty, and course evaluations. The scope also had to consider undergraduate and master's programs along with career opportunities and other key decision metrics. The project was time-sensitive, and Tepper management felt that Tableau offered the best possibility for a rapid deployment. Ted's team engaged consulting help and developed a specific project plan to deliver an initial set of reports.

PROTOTYPE REPORT DEVELOPMENT

Prototyping reports required detailed sessions with ten different business units to identify goals and define the specific content needed to support those objectives. Data had to be corralled from multiple sources to create the first series of reports. Data architects were brought in to develop data models that would be used for the data warehouse design and to extract, transform, and load logic (ETL) that was developed to automate data collection and storage.

In less than ten days a presentation was made to the business school staff and deans that outlined the project scope and objectives. Most importantly, over twenty interactive dashboards were presented using actual Tepper data. The presentation focused on what was currently being tracked and reported, but added new information needed for decision-making. This presentation provided a convincing demonstration of rapid results. Key stakeholders—the dean and senior associate deans—were convinced of the efficacy of the plan during this meeting.

LEVERAGING TABLEAU FURTHER

Soon after the initial prototype designs were implemented, other departments and colleges around the campus became aware of the project and began to investigate how they might improve the quality and timeliness of their reporting using Tableau.

Teppers' systems team was able to leverage the ad-hoc data models produced in Tableau to create an extensive data warehouse. The warehouse and accompanying ETL processes aimed to centralize data access that had been isolated in separate systems. These made it easier for non-technical users to combine data sets, track changes, and provide a repository for more extensive visual analysis using Tableau.

TEPPER'S OUTCOME AND EXAMPLE DASHBOARDS

Ted reports that the payback on the project investment was about twelve months. The school uses Tableau to provide information on student outcomes and instructor evaluations. Figure 12–2 includes scatter plots comparing student grades, course evaluations, and instructor evaluations.

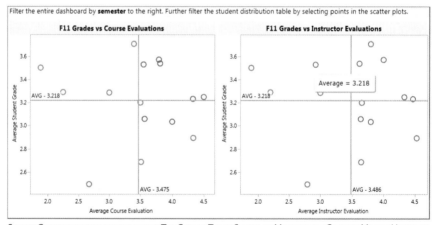

SOURCE: CASE STUDY AND FIGURE PROVIDED BY TED CURRAN, TEPPER SCHOOL OF MANAGEMENT, CARNEGIE MELLON UNIVERSITY.

FIGURE 12–2 *Scoring student and instructors*

Faculty research and editorial visibility is also immediately accessible via Tableau as you see in Figure 12–3.

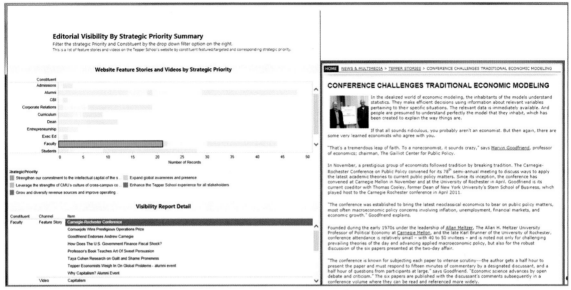

FIGURE 12-3 *Faculty editorial visibility*

This dashboard displays interactive content from the Internet as well, that can be viewed after making selections from the bar chart and crosstab panes.

Financial metrics are also reported visually in dashboards. Figure 12–4 shows an example of revenue and expense analysis for academic, administration, and research centers.

When specific areas are selected in the bar chart, transaction details are displayed as follows.

Tepper achieved their goal of centralizing key reports and providing critical information needed to improve decision-making. The ability to summarize key items in the budget process quickly helps managers make better decisions. Tableau has also enabled Tepper to maintain sound data governance and provide consumption on personal computers and tablet devices.

The college continues to work on opportunities to advance its academic mission while increasing revenue and capacity, decreasing costs, and increasing efficiency. Tableau has proven to be a key component in the school's toolset for bringing together a diverse mix of best of breed ERP, custom, and legacy systems —to better understand their data for decision-making.

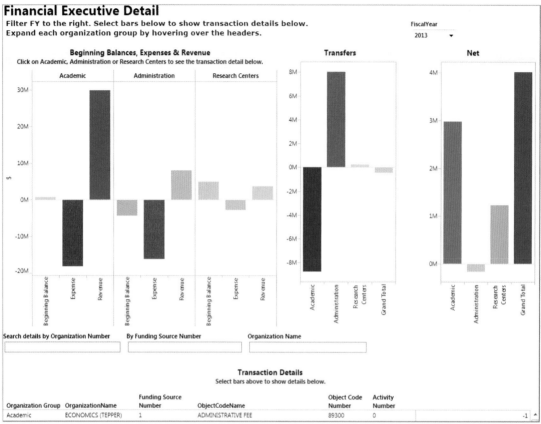

SOURCE: CASE STUDY AND FIGURE PROVIDED BY TED CURRAN, TEPPER SCHOOL OF MANAGEMENT, CARNEGIE MELLON UNIVERSITY.

FIGURE 12-4 *Financial performance*

ANALYSIS IN A MAJOR RAILWAY LOGISTICS TEAM

Norfolk Southern is one of six major railways operating tracks in North America. With over 22,000 miles of track, their operations are diverse and complex. This case study focuses on their Atlanta-based Modalgistics Supply Chain Solutions Group. Modalgistics provides consulting services with the aim of increasing asset utilization and reducing costs. These services include supply chain strategy, merger and acquisition support, advanced business analytics, and site location analysis. John Hoover is Modalgistics General

Manager of Supply Chain Services, and Andy Piper is a key member of his team providing analysis using Tableau. John and Andy were founding members of the Atlanta Tableau User Group (ATUG). They continue to be actively involved in ATUG.

MODALGISTICS DOES TRANSPORTATION RESEARCH

Transportation Research can be a very involved process. Specialized applications and models can take years to develop. These tools deliver value, but often at high cost. Data analysis, hardware, software, coding, labor, research and development, and many other related areas can add-up to expensive and time consuming analysis. The underlying value of the project can be solid, but not all projects get launched, and not all projects get completed. Providing meaningful analysis quickly can directly affect project viability.

HOW MODALGISTICS USES TABLEAU

Norfolk Southern utilizes Tableau to access raw data in a variety of datasources including Oracle, DB2, Teradata, SQL, and others. Much of the work includes commercially available industry data that is used to enhance client data. Prior to Tableau, the Modalgistics team did most of its analysis using Access, Excel, or flat files. That data was normally confined to a single computer. Typically, the information was presented in static form and presented using presentation software. Distribution of the results included maps, spreadsheets, slide decks and other files. Tableau's design allowed the Modalgistics team to produce useful client information more quickly and with greater flexibility. Tableau's distribution capabilities allow them to provide interactive, packaged workbooks. Clients are able to open the workbooks using a web browser on a personal computer or mobile device without needing to install any special software. Best of all—the client can interact with the data—it is no longer static!

These workbooks support a broad spectrum of users from transportation and marketing to external customers siting new plants or calculating carbon footprint impacts.

Transit and Dwell Analysis

Figure 12–5 displays transit and dwell analysis over time.

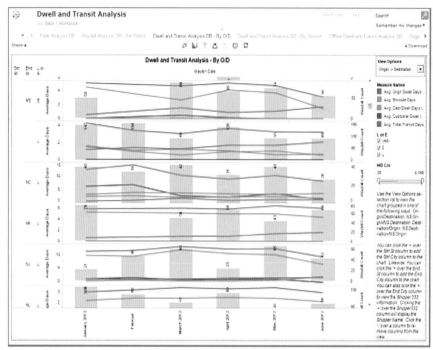

SOURCE: CASE STUDY AND FIGURE PROVIDED BY JOHN HOOVER AND ANDY PIPER, NORFOLK SOUTHERN MODALGISTICS TEAM.

FIGURE 12–5 *Transit and dwell analysis*

Transit and Dwell analysis helps clients improve asset utilization and provides interactive drill-down analysis of outlier events that require tactical attention to resolve.

Transit Path Analysis via GPS Movement Records

Geospatial analysis is facilitated within Tableau as well, using GPS coordinates and movement records. Figure 12–6 shows a typical geographic view used.

Carbon Footprint Site Comparison Analysis

Rail and truck distribution networks can provide aggregated network visualizations showing the carbon emission footprints within states or specific facilities—in the same dashboard. Figure 12–7 shows one example. Notice the icon in the upper right of the dashboard providing additional navigation instructions for information consumers.

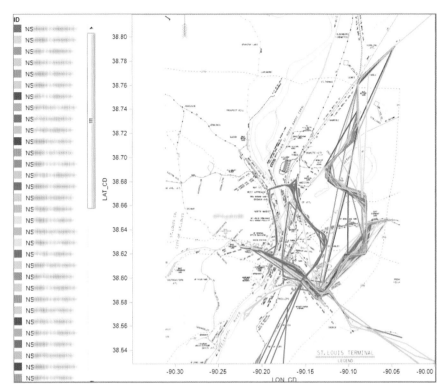

Source: Case study and figure provided by John Hoover and Andy Piper, Norfolk Southern Modalgistics Team.

FIGURE 12–6 *GPS movement records*

The design of the dashboard allows users to see the big picture, but also to drill into the granular details of a particular site.

THE OUTCOME FOR MODALGISTICS

Tableau has allowed the Modalgistics team to deliver insight faster, more flexibly, and at a lower cost than provided by the traditional tools used before Tableau. The output provided now is more visual, more understandable, and more interactive, and the analysis can be completed faster with fewer resources. Tableau is also used as a prototyping tool when other technologies are employed for client solutions.

This has generated interest in other parts of Norfolk Southern including their Roanoke and Norfolk, Virginia locations. Early results from desktop licenses justified the addition of a Tableau core server license for report delivery. This has resulted in higher quality analysis that is timelier.

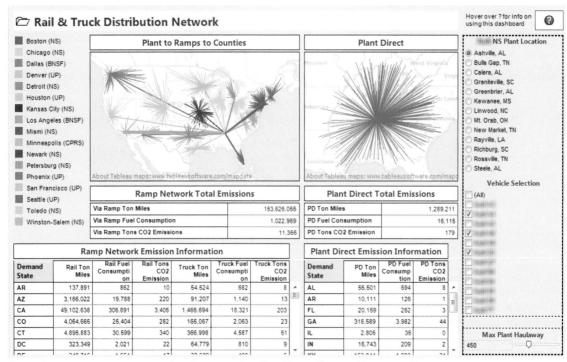

Source: Case study and figure provided by John Hoover and Andy Piper, Norfolk Southern Modalgistics Team.

FIGURE 12-7 *Carbon footprint analysis*

QUALITY METRICS IN A HOSPITAL

Jonathan Drummey is a Data Analyst in the Quality Management Department at Southern Maine Medical Center, a healthcare system with a 150 bed hospital and 17 physician practices located south of Portland, Maine. Jonathan was recognized as one of the first class of Tableau Zen Masters for his active contributions to the Tableau user community. Check out his blog, Drawing with Numbers, at http://drawingwithnumbers.artisart.org/.

OBAMACARE AND MEDICARE REIMBURSEMENTS

This story is about how Tableau is used to monitor metrics, save money, and identify previously hidden cost savings. During the early part of the last decade, a series of bills passed under the Bush administration that directed the Centers for Medicare and Medicaid Services (CMS) to begin paying hospitals for reporting on quality measures. You can view the results online at Hospital Compare: http://www.medicare.gov/HospitalCompare/.

The Affordable Care Act of 2010 (also known as Obamacare) extended those reforms and authorized Medicare to begin paying hospitals based on the delivery of quality care and patient experience in a program called Value Based Purchasing (VBP). This might not seem that radical, but it is the first time in the history of the Medicare program that hospitals are being paid for the quality of care, not just for the volume of care. Donald Berwick, former Director of CMS, said, "Instead of payment that asks, 'How much did you do?' the Affordable Care Act clearly moves us toward payment that asks, 'How well did you do?' and more importantly, 'How well did the patient do?'"

In fiscal year 2013 Medicare withheld one percent of all Diagnosis Related Group (DRG) payments—the standard payments for treatments at hospitals—for almost every hospital in the United States. Based on performance on a set of measures, each hospital could lose that revenue or gain up to one percent or more.

The Value Based Purchashing (VBP) program increases the amount at risk by one quarter percent each year, up to two percent for fiscal year 2017. One percent might seem trivial, but for a non-profit hospital with 60 percent or more of revenue dependent on Medicare (and less than one-half percent margin or less in a difficult year), failure to perform well can mean negative margins. So, when the VBP program became active, the hospital's CFO asked for monthly updates during the performance period.

HOW TABLEAU WAS USED TO ANALYZE VBP

VBP started out with two baskets of measures. One was a set of process of care measures (a subset of the Core Measures), such as whether patients diagnosed with heart failure had written discharge instructions, or whether patients diagnosed with pneumonia had an appropriate antibiotic selection made.

The second basket was made up of patient experience measures, such as how well patients communicated with their nurses and doctors. Performance for each measure is counted in two ways—compared to national benchmarks, and improvement compared to a baseline period from 2010. In addition, a consistency grade contributed to a minimum score goal to ensure that the hospitals were motivated to do well in all areas. All of these scores are then blended into a combined score.

Part of what made this interesting is that even though Southern Maine's management team had a good idea of how much revenue would be at risk (one percent of projected DRG payments), they did not know how much might be retrieved through VBA.

After the performance period was over, Medicare combined the scores from all over the country and pooled all of the withheld money, then ran that through an algorithm to generate a multiplier. In other words, Southern Maine Hospital's performance was being graded on a curve, with their ultimate revenue gain or loss dependent on the "Final Linear Exchange Function (FLEF)." This function became the input to a model that Southern Maine created to analyze the effect of the FLEF on the hospital's profitability.

The original profit model was built like many projection spreadsheets; any time Jonathan wanted a new range of numbers he had to make a copy of the Excel workbook. There was no view over time, and no per measure gain or loss, only the range of the one big number. Jonathan's mission in the Quality Management Department is to look for places where they can take action to improve patient safety and quality of care.

After dissecting the spreadsheet to understand the algorithms used by the American Hospital Association to derive the values, Jonathan generated a table of data in Excel, and pulled all of the results into Tableau. Later in the same day, he was able to create a dashboard in Tableau that allowed them to view change from the prior month, and quickly see what measures have the most potential loss and/or smallest gain. Figure 12–8 shows the resulting dashboard. For confidentiality reasons, the exact numbers have been hidden.

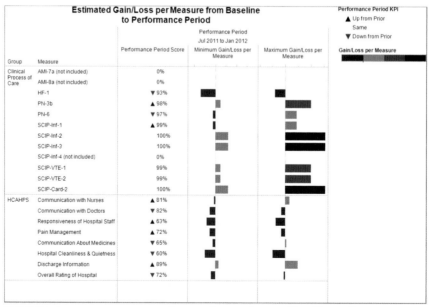

SOURCE: CASE STUDY AND FIGURE PROVIDED BY JONATHAN DRUMMEY, SOUTHERN MAINE MEDICAL CENTER.

FIGURE 12–8 *Estimated baseline gain/loss*

This dashboard helped Southern Main focus on the patient experience scores. Beyond just asking the staff to do a better job, executive leadership (VPs and above) regularly walked the floors and talked with staff. They realized some great improvements in a short period of time.

Tableau was also used to monitor per-measure performance over time. You can see an example dashboard in Figure 12–9. Some changes really jump out.

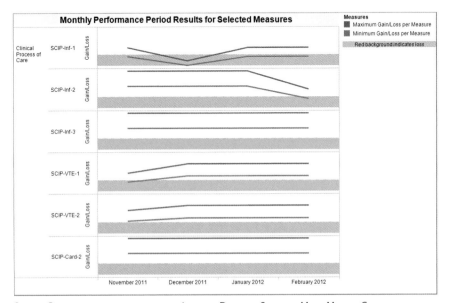

SOURCE: CASE STUDY AND FIGURE PROVIDED BY JONATHAN DRUMMEY, SOUTHERN MAINE MEDICAL CENTER.

FIGURE 12–9 *Performance over time*

See that big dip for February 2012 next to SCIP-Inf-2? That reflected a single failure to prescribe appropriate antibiotics prior to surgery. Going beyond the fact that a patient did not get the care they deserve and the complications that may have resulted, that single failure—which reduced their score from 100 to 99 percent—cost the hospital thousands of dollars in VBP revenue.

This dashboard instigated an inquiry, and they discovered that a temporary surgeon was responsible for the error. They also discovered over time that most of their surgical measure failures were due to temporary surgeons that were less familiar with hospital procedures. This pointed out two areas for improvement, one for training, the second that they could incentivize the temporary surgeons with either bonuses or penalties for "Core Measure" failures during their contract.

SOUTHERN MAINE'S OUTCOME

These dashboards enabled a process that provided Southern Maine with an opportunity to quantify quality improvement in dollar terms. They have two registered nurses who do concurrent abstraction of the Core Measures (that have complicated rules for inclusion and exclusion). They are sometimes able to identify gaps in care, work with staff to correct the issue, and prevent an exception in the measure.

A lunchtime conversation led to questions about what would happen to their VBP numbers if these nurses weren't catching these "near misses"? Within a few minutes, Jonathan was able to re-run the core measure numbers to identify what their performance scores would have been if all the near misses had been actual failures. These prospective results can then be shown clearly in Tableau.

In this way Jonathan was able to show that the savings generated by the concurrent abstractors *was more than their salary*. In the fall of 2012, Medicare published the final numbers for Value Based Purchasing, and Southern Maine came out in the black, receiving (1.024 percent). This placed the hospital in the top quartile nationally.

Jonathan provided this case study in early 2013. Southern Maine continues to monitor progress using Tableau in this way because they were able to create meaningful and actionable analysis that directly translated to improved financial results, and more importantly, better patient care.

PLANNING FOR A SUCCESSFUL TABLEAU DEPLOYMENT AT ACT

The ACT organization is a non-profit based in Iowa City, Iowa that provides a variety of testing and assessment services. You've probably heard of the ACT test—a college admission readiness test that was administered to over 1.6 million students in 2012. Tim Kuhns is the Principle for Innovation Research and Analytics Evangelist at ACT, and is responsible for finding new ways for the organization to analyze, understand, and communicate information within the organization. The ACT organization has been providing testing services for over fifty years. They have a lot of data.

VALUE DRIVERS FOR ACT

The introduction and expansion of Tableau within ACT was driven by four primary observations about Tableau made during their initial evaluation:

- Tableau provides a means for democratizing data.

- Tableau helps non-experts transform data into insights.

- Tableau creates visually appealing output.

- Tableau enabled management to clearly see value in the output.

In addition, Tableau's licensing model enabled ACT to start with a small investment, prove value, then expand as the user base was trained and value-proven, and demand naturally increased.

BUILDING USER BASE INTEREST AND SKILL

The ACT's Tableau deployment was aggressive but controlled. They also came up with innovative ways to spur interest and build competency. A visual analytics shoot-out competition was held early in the deployment to encourage desktop users to build skills. Prizes were awarded to the top entries and participation awards recognized all of the attendees. This built team competency and increased enthusiasm for the tool across the organization. If you're considering a large scale Tableau deployment, this staged rollout provides a good template to follow.

A PROPERLY STAGED EVALUATION AND ROLL OUT

Beginning with a demo of Tableau in September of 2011, ACT went through several stages of awareness and usage.

First two months—initial evaluation

- Initial Tableau demo

- Purchase five desktop licenses

- Concept and business case development

- Bring your own data workshop

- Business case one accepted

Next four months—train and deploy

- Purchase of 75 desktop and one eight-core server licenses

- Hire consultant to conduct onsite training for 60 staff

- Develop internal application prototype

- Usage expands to 80 staff

- Business case two accepted

Next five months—increasing the number and variety of uses

- Developed first production application

- Training in visual analytics from Stephen Few

- Visual analytics shootout (internal competition with prizes)

- Usage expands to 120

- Second eight-core server license purchased

This deployment plan considered all of the key needs that applied regardless of the type of organization. The initial evaluation phase was thorough and fast. Once the decision was made to purchase a significant number of licenses, a consultant was hired to provide customized on-site training that used ACT data to build competency and enthusiasm. As the roll-out achieved critical mass and more users came in, training was supplemented by inviting a well-known data visualization expert to provide additional training, and a visual analytics contest encouraged early usage and awarded the best competitors with prices.

HOW ACT USES TABLEAU

ACT generates a lot of test data, and one of the most obvious use cases for Tableau was analyzing test score results. Figure 12–10 shows one example.

The scoring distribution dashboard provides data on score distribution via a histogram. Less obvious is the ability to change the distribution viewed from a composite score to individual test section results. The scatter plot provides comparisons of student count and score results with average results being displayed via a reference line. The bar charts on the right-side of the dashboard allow information consumers to view results for a variety of parameterized dimensions.

ACT continues to expand the variety of ways Tableau is utilized, including test material usage by geography and stage of completion, job profile analysis by industry for other ACT test products, security testing and investigation, response analysis, and production performance.

ENSURING SUSTAINABILITY

Tim and his team have adopted best practices to ensure the continued expansion of the ACT team's competency by establishing policies to ensure continuous communication, creating an internal help desk, implementing on demand question and answer sessions with an experienced consulting partner, and establishing an internal user group to share the team's best ideas and provide examples for less experienced users to follow.

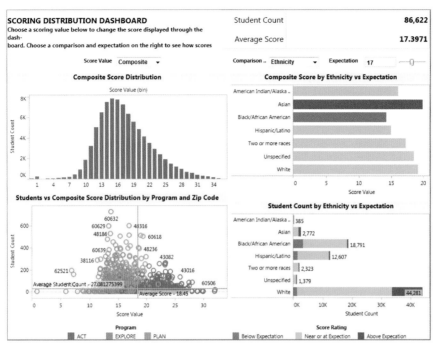

SOURCE: CASE STUDY AND FIGURE PROVIDED BY TIM KUHN, THE ACT ORGANIZATION.

FIGURE 12–10 *Scoring distribution dashboard*

EMPLOYING VISUAL ANALYTICS TO AID SUCCESSION PLANNING

A few years ago InterWorks was engaged to work with a human resource ana-lyst—Adrian Abarca—on a visual analytics project. At the time he was working for a global insurance provider with over 60,000 employees. Adrian's job was to provide human resource analytics. He had just discovered Tableau and wanted to use it to prepare presentation materials for a meeting, but didn't feel he knew it well enough to finish the work on-time without experienced help. InterWorks provided that help.

A FRAMEWORK FOR SPURRING EFFECTIVE CONVERSATION AND ACTION

Adrian's mission was to provide fact-driven research that supported workforce analysis to facilitate strategic workforce planning. The insight gleaned from this work helped human resources professionals at the company assist operating managers in making fact-based decisions. He also wanted to provide proactive information that would give managers insight that would aid strategic planning rather than just giving managers' historical views.

PROVIDING PROGRESSIVE INFORMATION FOR SUCCESSION PLANNING

Succession planning data is vital to an organization's talent development strategy. Normally, this information is not structured in a way that allows leaders to easily identify potential pitfalls in the leadership pipeline, but if the data is presented in a way that helps people identify future issues before they arise, plans can be laid to prepare for smooth transitions. The dashboard in Figure 12–11 was used to facilitate conversation between leadership and their human resource support partner.

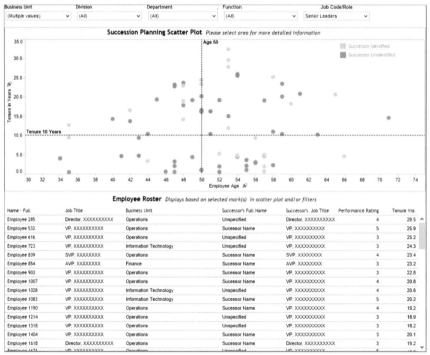

FIGURE 12–11: *Succession planning dashboard*

This dashboard assists in identifying successors' needs using two ambiguous dimensions: the employee's tenure with the organization and age. By using parameters, the users can change the view to fit specific organizational requirements. For example, if the expected retirement age for the company is 55 and tenure is 15 years, the reference lines can be changed to express those facts via the reference lines in the scatter plot.

Selecting one or more marks (individuals) in the scatter plot, allows users to filter the crosstab and display pertinent information related to those selections. The scatter plot is also broken into four quadrants that help the user identify where the urgent needs for successors exist. This data alone is not enough to fully understand the critical requirements. Adding competencies and critical skills to the dashboard enables deeper analysis and understanding of the specific skills and talents needed—providing a means for identifying talent gaps in prospective replacements for each position. For confidentiality, this information has been removed from Figure 12–11.

Human capital is every entity's most valuable asset. By expressing appropriate facts and dimensions visually, it becomes easier to see outliers that require attention. But, progressive dashboards like the one presented here offer more than typical historical headcount reports—they provide a means for progressive plans.

In mid-2013, Tableau Software started trading publically on the New York Stock Exchange. Considering that the company has been in existence for a mere 10 years, it is exciting to imagine what the next 10 years will bring.

Our ability to capture, use, and analyze data has improved considerably since the 1970s when database tools started to become commercially available. In the early 1980s the spreadsheet became the "killer application" on early personal computers because spreadsheets provided a quantum leap in our ability to model different scenarios. Tableau provides yet another breakthrough in the ability to understand large and diverse data sets by making data easier to see and understand.

The ultimate goal of storing data is to turn it into information that can be used to make better decisions. It is my hope that this book will help you reach your goals with Tableau faster.

PART IV

APPENDICES

In this part

- **APPENDIX A:** Understanding and Using Tableau Functions
- **APPENDIX B:** Tableau Data Shaper Excel Plug-In
- **APPENDIX C:** InterWorks Book Website
- **APPENDIX D:** Glossary

Understanding and Using Tableau Functions

Rarely does the datasource provide all of the information necessary to answer all of the questions asked. Using inputs from fields in the source data or from user-defined input entered though parameters—additional data can be added to your visualizations that enhances content. If you are accustomed to creating SQL statements in a database, the functions and syntax of Tableau's calculated values should look familiar. If you are a spreadsheet expert the syntax will be new but should not pose a significant challenge for you to learn.

Tableau's formula-editing window provides help and error-checks the syntax of the formulas you create. Even if you have no experience, with a little practice you'll find that you use some functions frequently. Tableau groups functions into nine major categories as shown in Table A-1.

TABLE A-1: Tableau function categories

FUNCTION CATEGORY	FUNCTION CATEGORY CAPABILITIES
Number	Perform arithmetic and trigonometric operations.
String	Manipulate strings.
Date	Calculate and parse date fields.
Type Conversion	Change values from one data type to another
Logical	Conditional operations based on your data
Aggregate	Mathematical and statistical summaries of your data.
RawSQL Pass Through	Pass SQL statements directly to the datasource that are executed at the datasource level. These are only available for certain database types.
User	Information on the identity, domain, and membership of the current user
Table Calculation	Functions that are executed within Tableau using the structure of the visualization you've created

SOURCE: TABLEAU SOFTWARE MANUAL

Tableau Software provides abbreviated help on every function within the formula editing window, the product manual, and the website. This appendix supplements those resources by providing:

- An alphabetically-sorted listing of every function by type
- An alphabetically-sorted list with brief function descriptions
- In-depth analysis of every function with syntax examples.

ORGANIZATION AND KEY FOR APPENDIX A

The in-depth analysis section of the Function Appendix is organized alphabetically by function name. Color encoding is used to identify fields, functions, and parameter entries.

- `Fields are orange`
- `Functions are blue`
- `Parameters are purple`

Care has been taken to exactly match the color hues as they appear in Tableau's formula editor.

Function syntax is broken down, and each entry contains one to three examples. Examples are listed as basic, intermediate, or advanced level. Please note that some function types—RAW SQL for example—are inherently more complicated than basic functions like those for aggregation or dates. The difficultly is gauged within the function category only.

WHAT IS RAW SQL AND WHY DO YOU NEED IT?

The RAW SQL functions are a special type of function in Tableau known as a pass-through function. These functions allow the user to send statements to the underlying database that are not evaluated by Tableau. This allows the user to call database functions that Tableau is unaware of. Tableau is aware of many built-in database functions and has mapped many of them to functions within Tableau, but, depending on your datasource, there are probably functions that Tableau doesn't yet support. In addition to built-in database functions, the RAW SQL function allows you to call any function that the underlying datasource supports—including user-defined functions. This makes the RAW SQL functions particularly powerful.

The RAW SQL functions are broken into two broad categories based on whether or not the expected result is a scalar or an aggregate. You'll observe functions with names of the form RAW SQL and RAW SQLAGG. When the expression is passed to the underlying database it produces a scalar-value choose command, the RAW SQL version of the function. Conversely, when the expression sent to the database produces an aggregate value, choose the appropriate RAW SQLAGG function. These functions are then both broken down even further by the type of the resulting scalar or aggregate. In addition to choosing whether or not to use the scalar or aggregate version of the function, you should also choose the function that matches the type returned by the expression. These types are as follows:

- BOOL—A Boolean value

- DATE—A date value. Note that date types in databases usually omit time.

- DATETIME—A date time value. Note that date time types usually include date and time.

- INT—An integer value. Numbers without a decimal component

- REAL—A numeric value. Numbers with a decimal component

- STR—A string value. Text data

For instance, when passing an expression to the database that will return an aggregated numeric sum with a decimal component you should choose the `RAWSQLAGG_REAL()` function. Choosing the incorrect scalar or aggregate function will cause an error within Tableau. There is some leniency in the function types you can choose. As long as Tableau can convert the value into the type the function returns will work.

Another thing to keep in mind when you are working with RAW SQL functions is that your underlying database will not understand the dimension and measure names within Tableau. To pass a dimension or measure into the RAW SQL expression you must use a substitution syntax provided by Tableau. This syntax is similar to substitution syntax seen in other languages. This is demonstrated in the example below:

```
RAWSQL_INT("1000 + %1", [Order ID])
```

In this example, the `RAWSQL_INT` function is being used to pass a simple expression to the database. The `%1` will be replaced by the value of Order ID in the expression. Notice that you should be using the scalar function and specifying the integer return type.

Using the RAW SQL functions will let you expand the capabilities of Tableau in many ways. If you can write a function to perform the operation you require at the database level then you can expose it to Tableau with these functions. Keep in mind whenever you come across examples of RAW SQL usage that the examples are dependent upon the functions present in the database. For the examples in the remainder of this section you will be using a copy of the Superstore Orders data set included with Tableau Desktop that has been loaded into a SQL Server 2012 instance. Some of the expressions used to demonstrate the pass-through queries may not work with your datasources.

ALPHABETICAL FUNCTION LIST—SUMMARY

Table A-2 shows every Tableau function available for the typical user. Depending on your datasource, additional functions may be available from a particular database. Consult your database manual for information commands not listed below. The remainder of Appendix A provides detailed explanations of each function. Code examples are provided for each function and are classified as basic, intermediate, and advanced.

TABLE A-2

#	FUNCTION NAME	TYPE FUNCTION	#	FUNCTION NAME	TYPE FUNCTION
1	ABS	Number	57	PREVIOUS_VALUE	Table Calculation
2	ACOS	Number	58	RADIANS	Number
3	ASCII	String	59	RAWSQL_BOOL	Pass Through
4	ASIN	Number	60	RAWSQL_DATE	Pass Through
5	ATAN	Number	61	RAWSQL_DATETIME	Pass Through
6	ATAN2	Number	62	RAWSQL_INT	Pass Through
7	ATTR	Aggregate	63	RAWSQL_REAL	Pass Through
8	AVG	Aggregate	64	RAWSQL_STR	Pass Through
9	CASE	Logical	65	RAWSQLAGG_BOOL	Pass Through
10	CHAR	String	66	RAWSQLAGG_DATE	Pass Through
11	CONTAINS	String	67	RAWSQLAGG_DATETIME	Pass Through
12	COS	Number	68	RAWSQLAGG_INT	Pass Through
13	COT	Number	69	RAWSQLAGG_REAL	Pass Through
14	COUNT	Aggregate	70	RAWSQLAGG_STR	Pass Through
15	COUNTD	Aggregate	71	REPLACE	String
16	DATE	Type Conversion	72	RIGHT	String
17	DATEADD	Date	73	ROUND	Number
18	DATEDIFF	Date	74	RTRIM	String
19	DATENAME	Date	75	RUNNING_AVG	Table Calculation
20	DATEPART	Date	76	RUNNING_COUNT	Table Calculation
21	DATETIME	Type Conversion	77	RUNNING_MAX	Table Calculation
22	DATETRUNC	Date	78	RUNNING_MIN	Table Calculation
23	DAY	Date	79	RUNNING_SUM	Table Calculation

#	FUNCTION NAME	TYPE FUNCTION		#	FUNCTION NAME	TYPE FUNCTION
24	DEGREES	Number		80	SIGN	Number
25	ENDSWITH	String		81	SIN	Number
26	EXP	Number		82	SIZE	Table Calculation
27	FIND	String		83	SPACE	String
28	FIRST	Table Calculation		84	SQRT	Number
29	FLOAT	Type Conversion		85	SQUARE	Number
30	FULLNAME	User		86	STARTSWITH	String
31	IF	Logical		87	STDEV	Aggregate
32	IFNULL	Logical		88	STDEVP	Aggregate
33	IIF	Logical		89	STR	Type Conversion
34	INDEX	Table Calculation		90	SUM	Aggregate
35	INT	Type Conversion		91	TAN	Number
36	ISDATE	Date, logical, String		92	TODAY	Date
37	ISFULLNAME	User		93	TOTAL	Table Calculation
38	ISMEMBEROF	User		94	TRIM	String
39	ISNULL	Logical		95	UPPER	String
40	ISUSERNAME	User		96	USERDOMAIN	User
41	LAST	Table Calculation		97	USERNAME	User
42	LEFT	String		98	VAR	Aggregate
43	LEN	String		99	VARP	Aggregate
44	LN	Number		100	WINDOW_AVG	Table Calculation
45	LOG	Number		101	WINDOW_COUNT	Table Calculation
46	LOOKUP	Table Calculation		102	WINDOW_MAX	Table Calculation
47	LOWER	String		103	WINDOW_MEDIAN	Table Calculation
48	LTRIM	String		104	WINDOW_MIN	Table Calculation
49	MAX	Aggregate, date, number, string		105	WINDOW_STDEV	Table Calculation
50	MEDIAN	Aggregate		106	WINDOW_STDEVP	Table Calculation
51	MID	String		107	WINDOW_SUM	Table Calculation
52	MIN	Aggregate, date, number, string		108	WINDOW_VAR	Table Calculation
53	MONTH	Date		109	WINDOW_VARP	Table Calculation
54	NOW	Date		110	YEAR	Date
55	PI	Number		111	ZN	Logical, number
56	POWER	Number				

SOURCE: TABLEAU MANUAL, ADAPTED

1. ABS

The ABS function returns the absolute value of the given number. The absolute value can also be seen as its distance from zero. This function is useful when you want to find out the difference between two values, regardless of whether that difference is positive or negative.

```
ABS (number)
```

> Number = any given number.

Basic:

```
ABS([Budget Variance])
```

> This function returns the sum of all absolute values for all the rows in the database for Budget Variance.

Intermediate:

```
ABS (SUM([Budget Sales])-SUM([Sales]))/SUM([Budget Sales])
```

> This example provides the absolute value of the variance between the sum of Budget Sales and the sum of Sales, and is expressed in a percentage from Budget Sales. The ABS function can be used to highlight exceptions when comparing to variance tolerance levels.

2. ACOS

The ACOS function returns the arccosine of the given number. This is the inverse of the COS function.

```
ACOS(number)
```

> Number = any given number between -1 and 1.

Basic:

```
ACOS(0.5)
```

> This function returns 1.0471975511966 radians.

Intermediate:

```
DEGREES(ACOS(0.5))
```

> This function calculates the arccosine of number 0.5 and converts the result to degrees. The return is 60 degrees.

3. ASCII

ASCII is a character-encoding scheme that allows English characters, numbers, and symbols to be encoded into a corresponding number in the ASCII character set. The ASCII function returns the ASCII code for the first character in a given string. A Standard ASCII character set comprises 128 characters. These 128 ASCII characters can then be divided further into 4 equal groupings of 32 characters. The ASCII groups contain the following:

- 0–31 Non printing characters/control characters

- 32–63 Numeric values, punctuation characters, and special characters

- 64–95 Uppercase Alphabet characters and special symbols

- 96–127 Lowercase Alphabet characters and special symbols

```
ASCII(String)
```

Basic:

```
ASCII("Aaron Barker")
```

This function example returns the ASCII character for the first character within the customer name string. This example returns 65, as the first letter of the string is an "A."

Intermediate:

```
IIF (ASCII([Customer])<=32,'Non Printable Characters','Printable Characters')
```

This function example provides a basic data validation mechanism for the ASCII Printable Characters.

Advanced:

```
ASCII(LTRIM( MID(([Customer],FIND([Customer]," ")))))
```

This function example uses three other Tableau functions within its logic. The Customer field contains the customer name with a space between the Forename and Surname. We can use the logic above to determine the initial of a customer's Surname in ASCII format.

4. ASIN

The ASIN function returns the arcsine of the given number. This is the inverse of the SIN function.

```
ASIN(number)
```

Number = any given number between -1 and 1.

Basic:

ASIN(1)

> This function returns the arcsine of value 1. The result is 1.5707963267949 radians.

Intermediate:

DEGREES(ASIN(1))

> This function calculates the arcsine of number 0.5, and converts the result to degrees. The return is 90 degrees.

5. ATAN

The ATAN function returns the arctangent of the given number. This is the inverse of the TAN function. The result is given in radians in the range between -π/2 and π/2.

ATAN(number)

> Number = any given number, where the number is given in radians.

Basic:

ATAN(1)

> This function returns 0.785398163397448 radians, which is equal to π/4.

Intermediate:

DEGREES(ATAN(1))

> This function calculates the arctangent of number 1 and converts the result to degrees. The return is 45 degrees.

6. ATAN2

The ATAN2 function returns the arctangent of two given numbers (x and y). The result is in radians in the range between -π and π, excluding -π.

ATAN2(y number,x number)

> The y number = any given number and the x number = any given number.

Basic:

ATAN2(1,1)

> This function calculates the arctangent where y and x values are 1. The return is 0.785398163397448 radians, which is equal to π/4. Note: If both x and y values are 0, then this will return a NULL value.

Intermediate:

DEGREES(ATAN2(-1,-1))

> This function calculates the arctangent of point 1,1 and converts the result to degrees. The return is -135 degrees.

7. ATTR

The ATTR function evaluates all of the members contained within the field it is applied toward and returns a single value (if all of the values are identical) or the symbol "*" if more than one value exists in the set. The "*" symbol is meant to denote a special kind of NULL—one containing many values, instead of the more typical use of NULL—no values.

When the ATTR function is applied to a dimension that is expressed in a hierarchal view of the data, it will treat that field as a label and will cause aggregate values that would otherwise be calculated (for example: table calculations or subtotals) not to be displayed. Figure A-1 shows this result:

Columns	⊞ YEAR(Order Date)				Columns	⊞ YEAR(Order Date)		
Rows	⊟ Category	⊞ Sub-Category			Rows	ATTR(Category)	⊞ Sub-Category	
Title	No ATTR Aggregation on the Category Field				Title	With ATTR Aggregation on the Category Field		
Category	Sub-Category	2011	2012	Grand Total	Category	Sub-Category	2011	2012
Furniture	Bookcases	$140,925	$163,810	$304,736	Furniture	Bookcases	$140,925	$163,810
	Chairs & Chairmats	$457,000	$394,181	$851,181		Chairs & Chairmats	$457,000	$394,181
	Office Furnishings	$164,923	$147,347	$312,270		Office Furnishings	$164,923	$147,347
	Tables	$506,812	$478,255	$985,067		Tables	$506,812	$478,255
	Total	$1,269,661	$1,183,593	$2,453,254				
Technology	Computer Peripherals	$190,364	$214,620	$404,984	Technology	Computer Peripherals	$190,364	$214,620
	Copiers and Fax	$280,821	$236,541	$517,362		Copiers and Fax	$280,821	$236,541
	Office Machines	$426,103	$563,308	$989,412		Office Machines	$426,103	$563,308
	Telephones & Comm.	$469,518	$504,005	$973,523		Telephones & Comm.	$469,518	$504,005
	Total	$1,366,807	$1,518,474	$2,885,281				
Grand Total		$2,636,468	$2,702,067	$5,338,534	Grand Total		$2,636,468	$2,702,067

FIGURE A-1: *ATTR function example*

A good explanation of ATTR can be found in a Tableau Forum entry by Joe Mako[1] in which Joe expresses the logic used by the ATTR function using this formula:

```
IF MIN([field])=(MAX([field]) THEN MIN([field]) ELSE "*" END
```

Restating Joe's logic—if the minimum value and the maximum value of the set of numbers returned from the database are the same, then use the minimum value, and if they are not the same—return the "*" symbol.

Basic

```
ATTR([dimension])
```

The ATTR function is normally invoked within a view in combination with a table calculation function when you need to remove partitions (panes) from the view in order to achieve the proper aggregation for result. For example, if the view contains two related dimensions that combine to form a hierarchy, making the higher-level dimension an attribute will remove that partition from the view. This permits more granular control over how table calculations behave.

Basic

```
ATTR ([field])
```

The result of this formula would be a single number, or the "*" symbol.

8. AVG

The AVG function returns the average value for an expression. It is calculated as the sum of all of the numbers for the expression divided by the count of the number of records in that expression. For example, if you have a set containing (24, 30, 15, 5, 18) the average of those five numbers will be: (24 +30+15+5+16)/5 =15.

Basic:

```
AVG([Discount])
```

The result is the average discount for whatever level of detail is exposed in the view.

Intermediate:

```
AVG(DATEDIFF('day',[Order Date],[Ship Date]))
```

> This will calculate the number of days between the order date and the ship date, and then provide the average for the level of detail displayed in the view.

Advanced:

```
AVG(IF(DATEDIFF('day',[Order Date],[Ship Date])<=[Time to Ship Goal])
THEN 1 ELSE 0 END)
```

> This calculation compares the number of days it takes to ship an item to a parameter (variable) [Time to Ship Goal]. If the time is less than or equal to the parameter, a 1 is returned. If it's greater than the parameter a 0 is returned. Then, the average of those values is calculated and could be used to derive the percentage of items that shipped within the time specified by the selected parameter value.

9. CASE

The CASE function is provided with an expression/data field, which can be defined as the CASE statement source. The data values located within this source field are compared against a sequence of values determined by the user within the CASE statement. If any of the values within the expression match the user-determined values, then a return expression is created. If no match is found, then a default return expression is used. These return expressions must be coded; otherwise, NULL values are returned. CASE functions are only applicable to string expressions.

```
CASE expression WHEN value1 THEN return1 WHEN value2 THEN return2 ......
ELSE default return
END
```

Basic

```
CASE [Month]
WHEN 1 THEN "January"
WHEN 2 THEN "February"
WHEN 3 THEN "March"
WHEN 4 THEN "April"
ELSE "Not required"
END
```

> This example will look at the month field—containing integers—and return the corresponding month strings defined.

Intermediate

```
STR (DAY([Order Date])) + " " + (CASE [Month]
WHEN 1  THEN "January"
WHEN 2  THEN "February"
WHEN 3  THEN "March"
WHEN 4  THEN "April"
WHEN 5  THEN "May"
WHEN 6  THEN "June"
WHEN 7  THEN "July"
WHEN 8  THEN "August"
WHEN 9  THEN "September"
WHEN 10 THEN "October"
WHEN 11 THEN "November"
WHEN 12 THEN "December"
ELSE "Data Error"
END) + " " + STR(YEAR([Order Date]))
```

> The function examples above highlight the flexible nature that the CASE statement allows. It allows for multiple descriptive return expressions to group the results returned.

10. CHAR

CHAR is a function that changes an ASCII code into its relevant String character. ASCII and CHAR functions perform the reverse of each other and both are fundamentally linked.

```
CHAR(Number)
```

Basic:

```
CHAR(65)
```

> This function example returns the corresponding String value for the integer value 65. 65 in the ASCII character table is A.

Intermediate:

```
CHAR(IIF (ASCII([Customer])>96 and ASCII([Customer])
< 122,ASCII([Customer])-32,
ASCII([Customer]))))
```

> This function example provides an effective way of ensuring the CHAR output is CASED correctly when dealing with letters from the alphabet. The uppercase letters of the alphabet are maintained within the 3rd grouping of 32 ASCII characters, with the lowercase letters being maintained within the 4th grouping. With this in mind, it is easy now for us to determine the case of the letter and apply some logic to ensure that the ASCII code is returned as a Capital letter.

Advanced:

```
CHAR(ASCII([Customer]))+"."+
CHAR(ASCII(LTRIM(MID([Customer],FIND([Customer]," ")))))
```

> The function example shown displays the customer initials that have been obtained from the Customer field, separated by a full stop. Example output would be D.W. The additional String functions are detailed within this section of the book.

11. CONTAINS

The CONTAINS function gives the user the ability to search for any sequence of characters (SUBSTRING) that may be present within a searchable string. The CONTAINS function returns a Boolean value of True or False.

```
CONTAINS(String, Substring)
```

Basic:

```
CONTAINS([City],"New")
```

> This function returns a True value for all the Customer Cities held within the data that has New within its name and in that sequence of characters. The case of the letters within the substring is irrelevant and does not affect the outcome. new, New, and nEw are all valid and will return the same result.

12. COS

The COS function returns the cosine of a given number specified in radians.

```
COS(number)
```

> Number = any given number, where the number is in radians.

Basic:

```
COS(PI()/8)
```

> This function calculates the cosine of π/8 radians. This function returns 0.923879532511287.

Intermediate:

```
COS(RADIANS(60))
```

> In this function the number is known in degrees. First the degrees are converted to radians before the cosine is calculated. The result is 0.5.

13. COT

Returns the cotangent of a given number specified in radians. The number is expressed in radians.

```
COT(number)
```

Number = any given number, where the number is given in radians.

Basic:

```
COT(PI( )/4)
```

This function calculates the cotangent of π/4 radians. This function returns 1.

Intermediate:

```
COT(RADIANS(45))
```

In this function the number is known in degrees, in this case 45. First the degrees are converted to radians before the cotangent is calculated. The result is also 1.

Advanced:

This is an application of combined trigonometry functions in Tableau. This is the syntax of calculating distance between two geographical locations, whereby 3959 is the value of the average radius of the earth.

```
3959 * ACOS(SIN(RADIANS([Lat])) *  SIN(RADIANS([Lat2]))
+ COS(RADIANS([Lat])) * COS(RADIANS([Lat2])) *
COS(RADIANS([Long2])-RADIANS([Long])).
```

Location1: Lat, Long. Location2: Lat2, Long2

```
3959*ACOS(SIN(RADIANS(50.7397))*SIN(RADIANS(36.1051))
+COS(RADIANS(50.7397))*COS(RADIANS(36.1051))
*COS(RADIANS(-97.1038)-RADIANS(-1.73336)))
```

The return of this function is 4553.

14. COUNT

This function returns the count of the items in a group. NULL values are not counted.

Basic:

COUNT([Ship Date])

> The formula returns the count of records that have a ship date value. Records missing a ship date entry will be NULL and the record will not be counted.

Intermediate:

COUNT([Ship Date]) / COUNT(1)

> This example divides the number of records that have a ship count by the count of all records. Using a constant value as the expression will mean it is never NULL, so COUNT(1) is equal to the count of records. Every Department has 100 percent of the items shipped, so that means there were no NULL values in Ship Date.

Advanced Example:

COUNT(IF([Discount]=0 THEN NULL ELSE 1))/COUNT(1)

> This formula will look at the discount field and if the value is 0 it will not be counted. The resulting count is then divided by the total number of rows to derive the percentage of items that have a discount.

15. COUNTD

Count distinct returns the number of distinct items in a group. NULL values are not counted. Each unique value is counted only once.

Basic:

COUNTD([Customer Name])

> This formula returns the count of unique customer names. Any record where customer name is NULL will not be counted. It will count each unique name only once regardless of the number of records including the name. Note: If your datasource is Excel, Access, or a text file, you must extract the data for this function to be available.

Intermediate:

COUNTD([City]+[State])

> This formula combines the city and state fields to create a new field in order to count the number of unique city-state combinations. Note that the + sign concatenates the city and state fields together.

Advanced:

```
COUNTD(IF([Country]=[Country Parameter])
THEN [Customer Name] ELSE NULL END)
```

The formula counts the unique customer instance for a selected country. The parameter (variable) permits the user to select the country to count customer names. Any other country is viewed as NULL so it will not be counted.

16. DATE

The DATE function converts a given input into a date. This is similar to the DATETIME function, but doesn't include time. This is especially useful when you have string dates in your datasource or are building your own dates using other datasources.

Basic:

```
DATE("March 15, 2013")
```

The preceding example converts the string to a date value of March 15, 2013.

Intermediate:

```
DATE([DateString])
```

The preceding formula returns a date if [DateString] is a valid date type; otherwise, it will return NULL.

Advanced:

```
DATE(STR([Year]) + '/'+ STR([Month]) + '/' + STR([Day]))
```

The previous formula returns a date constructed from various components in the datasource. This is especially useful when the datasource has date elements in it, but no true date dimension. This allows you to create that date dimension so you can use Tableau's auto-generated date hierarchy in views.

17. DATEADD

The DATEADD function adds a specified time period to a given date. This function is useful when you want to calculate new dates off of another date in your data set, to create reference lines in time series analysis, or to create dimensions to use for filtering.

```
DATEADD(DatePart, Increment, Date)
```

The DatePart specifies the type of time period that is being added. It is always specified in single quotes and lower case (for example: 'day'). Increment specifies the exact amount of time to add. Table A-3 below displays value data parts that can be used with date functions to specify granularity of the date and/or time contained in the result.

TABLE A-3: Valid date function date parts

DATEPART	VALID INCREMENT VALUES
'year'	Four digit year
'quarter'	1–4
'month'	1–12 or "January", "February", and so on
'dayofyear'	Day of the year; Jan 1 is 1, Feb 1 is 32, and so on
'day'	1–31
'weekday'	1–7 or "Sunday", "Monday", and so on
'week'	1–52
'hour"	0–23
'minute'	0–59
'second'	0–60

SOURCE: TABLEAU DESKTOP MANUAL

Date is the actual date used for the addition. This value can be a constant value, field, parameter, or another function that returns a date.

Basic:

DATEADD('day', 3, Date)

The preceding formula returns a date three days after the given Date. In this case, if Date was equal to June 3, 2012 the function would return June 6, 2012.

Intermediate:

DATEADD('day', -30, TODAY())

The preceding formula returns a date 30 days before today's date. If today is March 18, 2013 then this function will return February 16, 2013. This can be very useful in filtering for specific periods (like 30 rolling days) or highlighting a period on a timeline where data may be uncertain.

Advanced:

```
DATEADD('month', -12, WINDOW_MAX(MAX([Date])))
```

> The advanced example formula returns a date that is 12 months before the last date in the defined window (see the WINDOWMAX calculation for more details). It's common in many businesses for data to be days, weeks, or even months old. This method gives you a date 12 months from the end of the data set, no matter how big (or small) the gap is between the end of the data set and the current date.

18. DATEDIFF

The DATEDIFF function calculates the time between two given dates. This is useful for creating additional metrics or dimensions for your analysis. It returns an integer value of a specified unit of time.

```
DATEDIFF(DatePart, Date1, Date2)
```

DatePart specifies the type of time period that is being returned. It is always specified in single quotes and lower case (for example: 'day'). See the DATEADD entry for valid DatePart values. Date1 and Date2 are the actual dates used for subtraction. The values can be constants, fields, parameters, other functions that return dates, or combinations of any of these.

Basic:

```
DATEDIFF('day', #June 3, 2012#, #June 5, 2012#)
```

> The preceding formula uses the DATEDIFF function to calculate the difference In days between the two date literal values in the formula—which in this example results in the answer of 2 days. Keep in mind you can use date fields in your data set to specify flexible date values as well.

Intermediate:

```
DATEDIFF('day',[InvoiceDate], TODAY())
```

> The preceding formula is returning the number of days between the two dates. This is a common setup for aging reports. The example derives the current age of the invoice in days. If today is March 18, 2013 and we have an invoice with an [InvoiceDate] of January 10, 2013, the function would return 67 (days). This can be very useful, especially when combined with Bins.

Advanced:

```
CASE [Parameter].[Date Unit]
WHEN 'Day' THEN DATEDIFF('day',[OrderDate],[ShipDate])
WHEN 'Week' THEN DATEDIFF('week',[OrderDate],[ShipDate])
END
```

The preceding formula returns an integer, either the number of days or weeks between the two dates. In this example you're using a parameter, [Date Unit]. This parameter is a string type that allows the user to input the time period they want returned in the result (days or weeks). This allows the user to determine the best way to express the answer.

19. DATENAME

The DATENAME function returns part of date as text. This function is useful for creating custom labels that go beyond what Tableau formatting can provide.

```
DATENAME(DatePart, Date)
```

The DatePart operator defines exactly how you want the date to be expressed, such as week, month, or year. Date is the actual date you want to extract from.

Basic:

```
DATENAME('month', #June 3, 2012#)
```

The preceding formula returns June from the literal date of June 3, 2012.

Intermediate:

```
DATENAME('month',[StartDate]) + ' to ' + DATENAME('month',[EndDate])
```

The preceding formula returns a string describing the start and end dates for each row in the datasource. If [StartDate] is equal to January 1, 2013 and [EndDate] is equal to March 1, 2013 then the function will return January to March.

Advanced:

```
DATENAME('month', TOTAL(MIN([Date]))) + ' '
DATENAME('year', TOTAL(MIN([Date]))) + ' to ' +
DATENAME('month', TOTAL(MAX([Date]))) + ' '
DATENAME('year', TOTAL(MAX([Date])))
```

The preceding formula returns a string describing the first and last date that exists in the view. The key to this is using the TOTAL function with MIN and MAX (see those function entries for more details). This is useful when you'd like to have a header, annotation, or other label that describes the period of analysis. If TOTAL(MIN([Date])) is equal to January 1, 2013 and TOTAL(MAX([Date])) is equal to March 1, 2013, then the function will return January 2013 to March 2013.

20. DATEPART

The DATEPART function returns part of a date as an integer. This can be useful for certain calculations when you need to parse portions of a date.

```
DATEPART(DatePart, date)
```

DatePart defines the portion of the date you require, such as week, month, or year. Date is the actual date you want to extract from the original date.

Basic:

```
DATEPART('month', #June 3, 2012#)
```

> The preceding formula returns 6, which represents the 6th month, June.

Intermediate:

```
DATEPART('dayofyear',[Date])
```

> The preceding example returns a numeric representation of the day of the year (in other words, how many days into the year it is). For example, if the [Date] is June 3, 2012 it will return 155.

Advanced:

```
IF DATEPART('hour',[Datetime]) < 12 THEN 'Morning'
ELSEIF DATEPART('hour',[Datetime]) < 16 THEN 'Afternoon'
ELSEIF DATEPART('hour',[Datetime]) < 21 THEN 'Evening'
ELSE 'Night'
END
```

> The preceding formula is using the hour to categorize the time into different groupings. In this case, if [Datetime] is between Midnight and Noon it will categorize it as Morning. If [Datetime] is between Noon and 4pm it will say it's the Afternoon. If [Datetime] is between 4pm and 9pm it will be the Evening, while anything else will be Night. This function can be useful for categorizing time periods, such as shifts in manufacturing or day parts in advertising. Note that DATEPART returns a 24-hour time period (i.e., 1pm will return 13).

21. DATETIME

The DATETIME function converts a given input into a date and time. This is similar to the DATE function, but includes the time. This is especially useful when you have string dates in your datasource or are building your own dates off of other datasources.

Basic:

```
DATE("March 15, 2013 5:30 PM")
```

> This formula converts the string to a date time value of March 15, 2013 at 5:30 PM.

Intermediate:

```
DATETIME(STR([Date]) + ' ' + [Time]),
```

> The preceding example returns a date time. The [Date] field is simply a date with no time. The formula first converts [Date] to a string, and then adds the [Time] component from another dimension. This is accomplished through concatenation of the two separate fields. Once concatenated, the result is converted into date time.

Advanced

```
DATE(STR([Year]) + '/' + STR([Month]) + '/' + STR([Day]) + ' ' + STR([Time]))
```

> This example returns a Date time constructed with various components from the datasource. This is especially useful when the datasource has date elements in it, but no true date time dimension. This formula converts three different fields into a single date dimension to take advantage of Tableau's built-in date hierarchy.

22. DATETRUNC

This function returns a date—truncated to the nearest specified date part. Think of this as an aggregating method for converting time into the desired level of detail while maintaining the date format. The date returned will always be the first day in the time period.

```
DATETRUNC(DatePart, date)
```

The DatePart defines the date aggregation displayed (week, month, or year, etc.). Date is the actual date used to extract the desired DatePart.

Basic:

```
DATETRUNC('Month', #March 14, 2013#)
```

> The preceding formula returns the date March 1, 2013. Since you selected Month as your DatePart, it returns the first of the month—presuming that you defined the date granularity in the view as month/day/year.

Intermediate:

```
DATETRUNC('week', MIN([Date]))
```

> The preceding formula returns a date that is the start of the week of MIN ([Date]). In this case, the date represents the start of the first date for any mark in the view. This function could be useful when looking at dimensions for which the start date is important, like customer sales or internal projects.

Advanced:

```
CASE [Parameter].[Date Unit]
WHEN 'Day' THEN DATETRUNC('day', [Date])
WHEN 'Week' THEN DATETRUNC('week', [Date])
WHEN 'Month' THEN DATETRUNC('month', [Date])
END
```

> The preceding formula returns a flexible expression of the date through the use of a parameter. The parameter, [Date Unit] is a string type that allows the user to input the time period they want to aggregate the result. This is ideal when the same report needs to be viewed at different levels of detail, for instance a trend report in which users would like to see the monthly trend, but also drill down into other specific time periods—like week or day.

23. DAY

This function returns an integer representing the day of any given date. This is a shortened form of DATEPART ('day', Date).

```
DAY(Date)
```

Date is the date you want to extract from.

Basic:

```
DAY(#March 14, 2013#)
```

> The preceding formula returns 14.

Intermediate

```
DAY(DATEADD('day',[Date], 5 ))
```

> The preceding formula returns the day [Date] + five days. If [Date] is March 14, 2013 then this function will return 19.

Advanced:

```
CASE [Parameter].[Date Unit]
WHEN 'Day' THEN DAY([Date])
WHEN 'Month' THEN MONTH([Date])
WHEN 'Year' THEN Year([Date])
END
```

> The preceding example returns an integer. The parameter for the `[Date Unit]` controls the specific date level that will be returned in the answer set. If the user selects Day, the function will return the day of `[Date]`.

24. DEGREES

The DEGREES function converts a given number in radians to degrees.

```
DEGREES(number)
```

> `Number` = any given number.

Basic:

```
DEGREES(PI()*2)
```

> This function converts the radian value of 2π. The result is 360 degrees. The conversion from radians to degrees can also be calculated with the `PI` () function. (`PI` ()*2) * (180/`PI` ()) which gives the same return.

25. ENDSWITH

The `ENDSWITH` function does exactly the same role as the `STARTSWITH` function; however, its focus is on the end of a string.

```
ENDSWITH(String, Substring)
```

BASIC:

```
ENDSWITH([City],"Orleans")
```

> The function example returns a true value only if the END of the search field matches the substring. The `STARTSWITH` and `ENDSWITH` functions ignore any leading or trailing spaces that may be present in the string field.

26. EXP

The EXP function is the inverse of the LN function. EXP returns "e" raised to the power of the given number, where *e* has the value 2.71828182845905. In Tableau the return is truncated to 14 decimal places.

`EXP(number)`

Number = any given number.

Basic:

`EXP(2)`

The result of this function is 7.38905609893065, where *e* is multiplied by itself. Tableau will first calculate the function before the return is truncated to 14 decimal places.

27. FIND

The `FIND` function takes the premise behind the `CONTAINS` function; however, it does not return a Boolean Value. The `FIND` function returns an index position that indicates where the substring that is being searched for begins within the search string. If the substring is not found then the function will return a 0 value. The `FIND` function uses similar logic by way of trying to find a substring within a string field; however, an additional optional feature allows us to add a search start position. This start option is an index position where the `FIND` function begins its search.

`FIND(String,Substring,[start])`

Basic:

`FIND(([City],"Orleans")`

Caution must be taken should you create the above example within a Tableau workbook. Tableau will automatically create a Measure, as the resulting output is a numeric value. If we displayed this field within a summary worksheet, Tableau would produce an aggregated value of the index number returned "*" the number of instances with the data. This would be incorrect as we are specifically after the index number. It would be best practice to change the field type to a DIMENSION once this is created. The function example is looking for the index number for a city in our data that has Orleans within the [City] string. New Orleans is found and the `FIND` Function returns a value of 5, (character 5 is where our substring starts).

Intermediate:

```
FIND(([Customer] ," ' ",4))
```

The function can be used to search for any character within a String. The example above searches for customers who have an apostrophe within their name. We assume that our customer name field is stored in the following structure: 'Forename|space|Surname' and can make assumptions that no customer has a Forename containing an apostrophe, and that no forenames are less than 3 characters long. Enter the index position as 4, for the first character to begin the search.

Advanced

```
IIF(CONTAINS([Customer],"'"),
(RIGHT([Customer],LEN([Customer])—FIND([Customer],"'",4)+2)),NULL)
```

The function example shows how combined string functions can be useful within Tableau. The function first searches for any field with an apostrophe. If this returns a true value, the combination of RIGHT, LEFT, and FIND functions finds the apostrophe, determines its position, moves the indexing position back two places, and extracts all string characters from this new index position. In a nutshell, you are looking to extract surnames that have an apostrophe within them. If the CONTAINS function returns a False value then the field is given a NULL value.

28. FIRST()

The FIRST() table calculation function returns the number of rows back to the first row of the view/partition. This function does not require any arguments.

Basic:

```
FIRST()
```

This function returns the amount of rows back to the first row.

Intermediate:

```
WINDOW_AVG(SUM([SALES]),FIRST(),LAST())
```

This function returns the average of the sum of sales from the first row to the last row of the window (or frame). Note: If the values are incorrect or inconsistent, ensure that you are properly using the Compute By portion of the table calculation.

Advanced:

```
IF FIRST()=0 THEN WINDOW_AVG(SUM([SALES]),0,IIF(FIRST()=0,LAST(),0)) END
```

> This function assumes there are a large number of marks in the view or that the user is dealing with a big data set. Through the use of if/then logic, table scans, which cause noticeable performance degradation, can be bypassed. In the end, the calculation takes the average of the sum of sales for the specified window (or frame).

29. FLOAT

The Float function returns a floating point number, or in other words, a decimal number.

Basic:

```
FLOAT(5)
```

> The preceding example returns a floating decimal number of 5.000.

Intermediate:

```
INT([Teachers]) + FLOAT([Students])
```

> The prior formula returns a decimal that represents the total amount of Teachers and Students. Despite one of the dimensions being an integer, Tableau will return the type with the most precision.

Advanced:

```
FLOAT(MID(2,[DollarString]))
```

> In the preceding formula, the field [DollarString] contains a string that represents a dollar amount, $ 5.00. The MID function is used to dispose of the dollar sign and get only the number, then the FLOAT function is used to convert the string to a floating decimal point number that will be conducive for further calculations.

30. FULLNAME()

Assumptions used for the examples.

User 1

- Full Name: Malcolm Reynolds
- Active Directory Name: DOMAIN\m.reynolds

User 2

- Full Name: River Tam

- Active Directory Name: DOMAIN\r.tam

User 3

- Full Name: Jayne Cobb

- Active Directory Name: DOMAIN\j.cobb

`FULLNAME()` returns the full name of the user logged on to Tableau Server. For example, if Malcolm is the user currently logged in to Tableau Server, `FULLNAME()` will return Malcolm Reynolds. In design mode, the author has the ability to impersonate any registered user on the server. Expression = a valid discrete argument.

Basic:

```
FULLNAME()='River Tam'
```

> This will return a Boolean result dependent on whether or not River Tam is the user logged on to Tableau Server.

Intermediate:

```
FULLNAME()=[Sales Person]
```

> Returns a Boolean result (true/false) if the user logged-in matches the [Sales Person] dimension on a given row of data. This can be used to provide a global filter to enforce row-level security.

Advanced:

```
CASE FULLNAME()
WHEN [Sales Person] Then 'True'
WHEN [Junior Manager] Then 'True'
WHEN [Snr Manager] Then 'True'
ELSE 'False'
END
```

> This will compare `FULLNAME()` to several fields in the database returning a True whenever the logged-on user matches a name in either the Sales Person, Junior Manager, or Snr Manager field. This can be applied to a global filter to enforce row level security.

31. IF

The `IF` statement is a basic version of the `IIF` statement; however, it uses the same logical processing. It has less logic that can be used in simple calculations.

```
IF test THEN value END / IF test THEN value ELSE else END
```

Basic:

```
IF([Order Quantity] > 10 THEN "Bulk Buy" ELSE "Non Bulk" END
```

This example provides simple segmenting of the order quantities greater than ten units to be named Bulk Buys, while all lesser order quantities are classified as Non Bulk. Adding more `ELSEIF` clauses provides a means for adding more logical criteria.

```
IF test1 THEN value1 ELSEIF test2 THEN value2 ELSE else END
```

Intermediate:

```
 IF [Ship Mode] = "Regular Air"
THEN "Customs Required"
ELSEIF [Ship Mode] = "Express Air"
THEN "Express Customs"
ELSE "No Customs" END
```

This formula evaluates the `[Ship Mode]` field. If it contains "Regular Air" then the answer returned will be "Customs Required." If it contains "Express Air," the answer returned will be "Express Customs." Any other value in the field will return "No Customs."

32. IFNULL

The `IFNULL` statement is a simple reference function against a field. It contains two expressions. The first expression is a testing expression, and the second is the override expression. If the first expression is FALSE, then it returns the override expression as the result. If the first expression is TRUE then it retains that value.

```
IFNULL(expresson1,expression2)
```

This formula will evaluate expression1. If expression1 is FALSE, then expression2 is returned. If expression1 is TRUE, then it returns the expression1 value.

Basic:

```
IFNULL([Customer],"Unidentified")
```

This example determines if the Customer record has a `NULL` value. If the customer field *does* have a `NULL` value then it will return the string Unidentified; otherwise, the customer name will remain.

33. IIF

The `IIF` function uses similar logic to the CASE statement; however, its arguments and return values are not as flexible. The IIF statement contains a TEST argument, followed by a THEN statement, and an ELSE statement. The test argument is first calculated; if the result is a TRUE Boolean value then it returns the THEN statement as an answer. If the result of the argument is FALSE then it returns the ELSE statement as an answer. An additional UNKNOWN value can be added to the end of an IIF statement should the TEST argument not return either a TRUE or FALSE value.

```
IIF(test,then,else)
or
IIF(test, then, else,[unknown])
```

Basic:

```
IIF(1<2,True,False)
```

> The expression will return True.

Intermediate:

```
IIF([Time to Ship]>12,"Within SLA", "Outside SLA" )
```

> If the time to ship is greater than 12, then the function returns Within SLA. Otherwise, the function returns Outside SLA.

Advanced:

```
IIF([Order Date]< Today()-14 and [Ship Mode] = "N"
,"High Priority",IIF([Order Date]<Today()-4 and
 [Ship Mode] = "N","Medium Priority","Low Priority"))
```

> This more complex example checks first for order dates that are 14 days before today's date and with a ship mode of N, returning high priority in this case. More recent orders that are within four days of today's date are classified as Medium priority if ship mode is N. Otherwise, they are classed as low priority orders. Nested IIF statements can be used to embed intricate logic in comparisons.

34. INDEX()

The `INDEX` function returns the row number of the current row within the window (pane) or partition. This function does not require any arguments.

Basic:

INDEX()

This table calculation function is useful for creating ranking lists or as a row number function.

Intermediate:

WINDOW_MAX(INDEX())=INDEX()

This table calculation allows a user to filter for the TOP X fields within the view/partition. For example, if one needs the TOP 5 products within a category, this function will provide such a filter. Note: Ensure that you are properly using the Compute By portion of the table calculation.

Advanced:

IF INDEX()=1 THEN WINDOW_AVG(SUM([SALES]),0,IIF(INDEX()=1,LAST(),0)) END

This function assumes there are a large amount of marks on the view and/or that the source data set is large. The if/then logic bypasses table scans which can cause noticeable performance degradation. The calculation takes the average of the sum of sales for the specified window (or pane). LAST() returns the number of rows from the current row to the last row in the view/partition.

35. INT

The function INT converts a value to an Integer. If the value is a floating point number, it will round down to the nearest integer (this can be used as a FLOOR function).

Basic:

INT(3.7)

The preceding formula returns the integer 3.

Intermediate:

INT([Date])

The preceding formula returns the integer representation of a date. This can be useful in certain calculations, or to create a BIN on a date (Tableau will only allow you to create bins on measures).

Advanced:

```
FLOAT(MID(4,[QtyString]))
```

> In this example, [QtyString] is a string that contains a quantity that you want to use in additional calculations, QTY 5. The MID function is used to dispose of the text (QTY) and return the number only. The INT function then converts the string into an integer.

36. ISDATE

The function ISDATE checks to see if a text is a valid date. The resulting output is a Boolean value. If the date string is valid, it will return TRUE; otherwise, an invalid date string returns a FALSE value.

```
ISDATE(Text)
```

Text is the value you want to test.

Basic:

```
ISDATE("This is not a date")
```

> The preceding formula returns FALSE.

Intermediate:

```
ISDATE("01 January 2013")=TRUE
ISDATE("1st January 2012")=FALSE
ISDATE("1/9/2012")=TRUE
```

> The preceding formula returns TRUE values for strings that are appropriately formatted as dates. The FALSE result is due to the 1st not being recognized as a valid date format.

Advanced:

```
ISDATE(STR([Year]) + '/' + STR([Month]) + '/' + STR([Day]))
```

> The preceding formula returns TRUE if the date constructed is valid.

37. ISFULLNAME()

Assumptions used for the examples.

User 1

- Full Name: Malcolm Reynolds
- Active Directory Name: DOMAIN\m.reynolds

User 2

- Full Name: River Tam

- Active Directory Name: DOMAIN\r.tam

User 3

- Full Name: Jayne Cobb

- Active Directory Name: DOMAIN\j.cobb

ISFULLNAME() returns a Boolean (true/false) value when the string or dimension specified in the brackets matches the user's full name for the user logged on to Tableau Server. In design mode the author has the ability to impersonate any registered user on the server. Expression = Any valid discrete argument.

Basic:

```
ISFULLNAME('River Tam')
```

Returns a Boolean depending on whether or not River is the user logged on to Tableau Server. Unlike using FULLNAME() within an IF or CASE statement, using ISFULLNAME() requires that you input the string value manually. You cannot reference another dimension.

Intermediate:

```
IF ISFULLNAME('Malcolm Reynolds') THEN 'Management'
ELSEIF ISFULLNAME('River Tam') THEN 'Sales'
ELSEIF ISFULLNAME('Jayne Cobb') THEN 'Public Relations'
ELSE 'Unknown'
END
```

The ISFULLNAME() function is used to put the users into logical groups. It could be used to customize dynamic titles or color schemes.

38. ISMEMBEROF()

This user function returns a Boolean (true/false) based on the logged-in user's group membership defined on Tableau Server. Expression = Any valid string argument.

Basic:

```
ISMEMBEROF('Sales')
```

If the user is a member of the group (local or Active Directory) Sales, then the function returns a true value; otherwise, it returns false. This could be used to manage row level security.

Intermediate:

```
IF ISMEMBEROF('Management') THEN 'Access Permitted'
ELSEIF ISFULLNAME('Sales') THEN 'Access Permitted'
ELSE 'Access Denied'
END
```

> This example is being used to drive permissions for a sales dashboard while providing row-level access only to sales team members and senior management. Other staff could access the dashboard but would return no data.

39. ISNULL

The ISNULL statement is a simple Boolean function. It only requires one expression and only returns the Boolean value of TRUE or FALSE.

```
ISNULL(expression)
```

Basic:

```
ISNULL([Customer])
```

> The ISNULL example above will return a TRUE value if a customer name exists, or a FALSE value if the Customer field is NULL.

40. ISUSERNAME()

Assumptions used for the examples:

User 1

- Full Name: Malcolm Reynolds
- Active Directory Name: DOMAIN\m.reynolds

User 2

- Full Name: River Tam
- Active Directory Name: DOMAIN\r.tam

User 3

- Full Name: Jayne Cobb
- Active Directory Name: DOMAIN\j.cobb

`ISUSERNAME()` is a function for username. It is not compatible with dimension fields and is used only for manual text input. Expression: Any valid string argument.

Basic:

`ISUSERNAME('j.cobb')`

> Returns a Boolean (true/false) value of true if Jayne is logged on the server and false if someone else is logged in.

41. LAST()

This table calculation function does not require any arguments.

Basic:

`LAST()`

> This function returns the amount of rows from the current row to the last row in the view/partition.

Intermediate:

`WINDOW_COUNT(SUM([SALES]),FIRST(),LAST())`

> This function returns the count of the sum of sales from the first row to the last row of the window (or frame). Note: If the values are incorrect or inconsistent, ensure that you are properly using the Compute By portion of the table calculation.

Advanced:

`IF INDEX()=1 THEN WINDOW_COUNT(SUM([SALES]),0, IIF(INDEX()=1,LAST(),0)) END`

> This function assumes there are a large amount of marks on the view and/or that the user is dealing with Big Data. Through if/then logic, we can bypass the table scans, which cause noticeable performance degradation. In the end, the calculation takes the count of the sum of sales for the specified window (or frame). Bonus: Try making the window frames dynamic with a parameter.

42. LEFT

`LEFT` is a String function that returns the left-most characters from its designated string. This function can be used to create new dimensions directly or combined to create advanced calculated fields.

`LEFT(String,Number)`

Basic:

LEFT([Customer Zip Code],3)

> The function example is a simple way of identifying the sectional center facility used within the current U.S. Zip code system. LEFT can be used in more advanced queries when only the beginning sections of a string are required to be separated or queried.

43. LEN

LEN is a function that returns a number value for the total length of a string. Note LEN counts spaces between string characters to contribute to the LEN total value.

LEN(String)

Basic:

LEN("Bob Hope")

> The value returned for the above calculation is (8), (3) for Bob, (1) for the space, and (4) for Hope.

Advanced:

The Advanced FIND example that was provided previously uses the LEN statement to help complete the calculation.

RIGHT([Customer],LEN([Customer])-FIND([Customer],"'",4)+2)

> This formula calculates the length of the field [Customer], subtract the index value for the location of any apostrophes within [Customer], and take the RIGHT most number of characters. The number of characters is the result of the simple subtraction that is taking place.

44. LN

The LN function returns the natural logarithm of a number. This is the logarithm to the base e, where e, has the value 2.71828182845905. In Tableau the return is truncated to 14 decimal places. The natural logarithm of the expression is the power to which e would have to be raised to equal the expression.

LN(number)

> Number = any given number greater than zero. If the number is less than or equal to zero the LN function returns a NULL.

Basic:

LN(7.38905609893065)

> The result of this function is 2. In this case *e* would need to be raised to the power of 2 to equal the expression.

45. LOG

The LOG function returns the logarithm of a number for the given base. The logarithm of the expression is the power to which the base would have to be raised to equal the expression. If the base value is omitted, then base 10 is used.

LOG(number,[base])

> Number = any given number greater than zero. If the number is less than or equal to zero the LOG function returns a NULL, and [base] = any given number (not required).

Basic:

LOG(1000)

> The return of this function is 3, as base 10 needs to be raised to the power of 3 to return the expression. In other words the calculation 10*10*10 would return 1000.

LOG(8,2)

> This function also returns 3. In this case base 2 is used, and 2 should to be raised to the power of 3 to return the expression. In other words the calculation 2*2*2 would return 8.

46. LOOKUP

LOOKUP(expression,[offset])

> Expression = Any valid aggregate calculation (e.g., SUM([Sales])) [offset]=target row from first/last.

Basic:

LOOKUP(SUM([SALES]),2)

> This example returns SUM([SALES]) in each row for the sales from the forward-looking or future sales. Put simply, it grabs the value of sales from two rows up.

Intermediate:

```
LOOKUP(SUM([SALES]), FIRST()+1)
```

> This function returns SUM([SALES]) in the second row of the view/partition. Notice the other table calculation can be used as a helper in this function.

Advanced:

```
LOOKUP( MIN([Region]),0)
```

> This function enables the user to filter on a field without affecting any other calculations (e.g., percent of total). The reason a calculation (percent of total) is not 100 percent if you just have one attribute in your view is because Table Calculations are evaluated *before* a filter.

47. LOWER

This function allows the user to lowercase all characters within a string. The LOWER function will only change the Uppercased characters that exist in a string and thus ignore all lowercase characters that already exist.

```
LOWER(String)
```

Basic:

```
LOWER("BatMan")
```

> The function example will output the following all-lowercase string: batman.

48. LTRIM

The LTRIM function removes leading spaces that may be present within the data. This function can be used as a data cleansing function so that the data is consistent and set correctly.

```
LTRIM(String)
```

Basic:

```
LTRIM("Bob Hope" )
```

The output for this would simply be `"Bob Hope"`. You need to remove leading spaces as these can cause a number of issues if you try to apply any additional functions to the data. An example of this would be:

```
LEFT("Bob Hope", 4) which result is "    ".
```

49. MAX

The `MAX` function is normally reserved for numbers; however, this function can also be used on strings within Tableau. When `MAX` is applied to strings, the `MAX` value returns the string that is highest within the data's sort sequence for that particular string.

`MAX(a,b)`

Basic:

`MAX("Maureen","William")`

> On the assumption that the name field that you are considering above is sorted in ascending alphabetical order within the database, the function examples' output would be `"William"`. It considers the first name in alphabetical order to be the lowest and the last name to be the highest, and thus `"William"` is returned. If any of the strings used in the comparison logic have a value of `NULL`, then `NULL` will be the resulting output.

Intermediate

`MAX([Sales])`

> This example returns the maximum value across all the rows in the database.

`MAX([Sales],[Profit])`

> This example returns the maximum value between sales and profit for every row in the database.

The `MAX` function can also be used as a String Function or Date Function, whereby expression1 and expression2 are string or date data types respectively.

Advanced:

`MAX(ABS([Sales]-[Sales est]))`

> This formula returns the difference between the estimated sales and actual sales. In this example the largest differences (positive or negative) would be derived and displayed for any dimension expressed in the view.

50. MEDIAN

This function returns the median of a single expression. `MEDIAN` can be used with numeric fields only. NULL values are ignored. If your datasource is Excel, Access, or a text file—this function will not be available unless the datasource is extracted.

Basic:

MEDIAN([Discount])

> This formula will return the MEDIAN value of discount for whatever dimension, or level of detail in view.

Intermediate:

MEDIAN(DATEDIFF('day',[Order Date],[Ship Date]))

> This formula returns the MEDIAN difference between the order date and ship date, and expresses the result in days for any dimension displayed in the view.

51. MID

The MID function returns a partial string as its output. The MID function allows extraction of specific segments from within a string. This function requires an index position, from which the read begins. The function then extracts all parts of the string from the index position onwards, or an optional argument can be used to only extract a certain number of characters from the start index position.

MID(string,start,[Length])

Basic:

MID("Michael Gilpin",9)

> The function example output will be Gilpin. The MID function only begins extracting the string at index point 9. Michael contains 8 characters, the space is also classed as a character, and hence the extraction begins at the G and returns the remaining data from within that string.

Intermediate:

MID("Michael Gilpin",9,4)

> The function example is similar to the first example, but an additional argument has been applied. This adds another option to the function. This example begins extracting the string at index position 9; the letter G, the length function that has now been added then limits the extract to 4 characters starting at the index position. The result of this new calculation is Gilp.

52. MIN

The MIN function is very similar to the MAX function, whereby this function returns the minimum value when applied to a single field in an aggregate calculation. The `MIN` function can also be applied to return the minimum of two arguments. These arguments must be of the same type. When used with two arguments the function returns NULL if either argument is NULL.

```
MIN (expression1, expression2)
```

Expression1 = A valid number or aggregate calculation. Expression2 = A valid number or aggregate calculation (not required).

Basic:

```
MIN([Sales])
```

This function returns the minimum value across all rows in the database.

```
MIN([Sales],[Profit])
```

This function returns the minimum value between Sales and Profit for every row in the database. Note that this function can be used as a String or Date type function, where expression1 and expression2 are string or date data types.

Intermediate:

```
MIN([Shipping Cost],[Maximum Shipping Cost])
```

Another use case for `MIN` allows you to pass in two fields and return the minimum value between the two. In this example a parameter (variable) is used to permit the user to select the maximum allowable value for comparison.

Advanced:

```
DATEDIFF('day',MIN([Order Date]),MAX([Ship Date]))
```

This formula derives the difference between the minimum order date and the maximum ship date. This could be used in conjunction with an order identification dimension to calculate how long it takes for the entire order to be filled if there were multiple shipments.

53. MONTH

This function returns an integer representing the month of any given date. This is a shortened form of `DATEPART` (month, date).

```
MONTH(Date)
```

The `Date` is the date the function will use to extract the month.

Basic:

```
MONTH(#March 14, 2013#)
```

> The preceding formula returns 3.

Intermediate:

```
MONTH(DATEADD('day',[Date],5))
```

> The preceding formula returns the day that [Date] + 5 days lands on. If the [Date] is March 30, 2013 the function will return 4 (since [Date] + 5 days is April 4, 2012).

Advanced:

```
CASE [Parameter].[Date Unit]
WHEN 'Day' THEN DAY([Date])
WHEN 'Month' THEN MONTH([Date])
WHEN 'Year' THEN Year([Date])
END
```

> The preceding formula returns an integer. In this example, a parameter for the [Date Unit] is used to control the level of detail of the result:—day, month, or year.

54. NOW

The NOW function returns the current date and time.

Basic:

```
NOW( )
```

> Presuming today's date is March 12, 2013 at 3:04 PM the preceding formula will return the date March 12, 2013 03:04:00 PM.

Intermediate:

```
DATEADD('hour', -5, NOW())
```

> The preceding formula returns a date time that is 5 hours before the current date time. If today is March 18, 2013 at 3pm then this function will return March 18, 2013 at 10 am. This can be very useful in filtering for specific time periods.

55. PI

The function PI returns the mathematical constant pi, also expressed with the symbol π. The value is approximately equal to 3.14159265358979. In Tableau the return is truncated to 14 decimal places.

```
PI()
```

The PI function returns the constant value 3.14159265358979. Note: There is no expression for this function—simply add the open and close parentheses ().

Basic:

```
2*PI()*5
```

This function returns 31.4159265358979. This is the formula where PI is used to calculate the circumference of a circle with the formula 2π*radius, where in this example 5 is the value for the radius of the circle.

56. POWER

The POWER function raises the number to the specified power.

```
POWER(number,power)
```

Number = any given number. Power = any given number.

Basic:

```
POWER(4,3)
```

This function raises 4 to the power of 3. The result is 64. The ^ symbol can also be used in the calculation instead. The calculation 4^3 therefore returns the same result as POWER(4,3).

Intermediate:

```
[Profit]*POWER(1+0.12,6)
```

The POWER function can be used to apply exponential growth factors over time. This function reflects a growth factor of 12 percent (for which the number expression is 1.12) over 6 periods.

57. PREVIOUS_VALUE

This function is a table calculation function that returns the previous value in the partition.

```
PREVIOUS_VALUE(Expression)
```

Expression = Any valid aggregate calculation (e.g., SUM([Sales])) or constant (e.g., 1).

Basic:

```
PREVIOUS_VALUE(SUM([SALES]))
```

This table calculation function returns the SUM ([SALES]) if the current row is the first row in the view/partition.

Intermediate:

```
SUM([SALES])*PREVIOUS_VALUE(0)
```

This function returns (SUM([SALES])) as the product of constant zero. Note: If the values are incorrect or inconsistent, ensure that you are properly using the compute by portion of the table calculation.

Advanced:

```
SUM([SALES])*PREVIOUS_VALUE(1)
```

This function returns the running product of SUM([SALES]). Note: Experiment with different values/constants in the PREVIOUS_VALUE (expression) function.

58. RADIANS

The RADIANS function converts the given number from degrees to radians.

```
RADIANS(number)
```

Number = any given number.

Basic:

```
RADIANS(360)
```

This function converts the value of 360 degrees to the radians value. The result is 6.28318530717959, which is equal to 2π. In Tableau the return is truncated to 14 decimal places. The conversion from degrees to radians can also be calculated with the PI() function. 360 * (PI()/180), which yields the same return.

59. RAWSQL_BOOL()

The `RAWSQL_BOOL()` function is a pass-through function that allows the user to send an arbitrary expression to the underlying datasource. The expression must return a scalar value of a type that Tableau can convert into a Boolean. This expression will not be checked in any way by Tableau and may produce an error at the datasource level. The user must respect the syntax conventions of the datasource when constructing the expression. The generalized syntax for the function is below:

`RAWSQL_BOOL("expr",[arg1],...[argN])`

The `expr` in quotes is the expression to be passed through to the datasource. `N` number of arguments can be specified in a comma-separated list as shown. These arguments are referenced in the expression with a %1, %2, and % `N` syntax.

Basic:

`RAWSQL_BOOL("%1=%2",[Order Date],[Ship Date])`

> In this example we're checking whether or not the [Order Date] and [Ship Date] fields are equivalent. The function will return true if they are equivalent and false if they are not.

Intermediate:

`RAWSQL_BOOL("%1='Oklahoma' AND %2 > 100.00",[State],[Sales])`

> This formula checks whether or not the [State] field is equal to Oklahoma and if the [Sales] field is greater than 100.00. If both of these are true the function will return true. It will return false if either is false.

Advanced:

`RAWSQL_BOOL("PATINDEX('%Henry%',%1)>0 AND %2>100.00",[Customer Name],[Sales])`

> This formula performs the SQL Server PATINDEX() function on the [Customer Name] field to look for the presence of the substring Henry. If that string is contained in the [Customer Name] field and the [Sales] field is greater than 100.00 the function returns true. If either condition is false the function returns false.

60. RAWSQL_DATE()

The `RAWSQL_DATE()` function is a pass-through function that allows the user to send an arbitrary expression to the underlying datasource. The expression must return a scalar value of a type that Tableau can convert into a date. Tableau will ignore any time component if a date time is returned. This expression will not be checked in any way by Tableau and may produce an error at the datasource level. The user must respect the syntax conventions of the datasource when constructing the expression. The generalized syntax for the function is below:

```
RAWSQL_DATE("expr",[arg1], ...[argN])
```

The `expr` in quotes is the expression to be passed through to the datasource. `N` number of arguments can be specified in a comma-separated list as shown. These arguments are referenced in the expression with a %1, %2, and % `N` syntax.

Basic:

```
RAWSQL_DATE("%1 + 10", [Order Date])
```

> This example adds 10 days to the [Order Date] value.

Intermediate:

```
RAWSQL_DATE("COALESCE(%2, %1)", [Order Date], [Ship Date])
```

> This example uses the SQL Server COALESCE() function to choose the first value from [Order Date] and [Ship Date] that is not NULL.

Advanced:

```
RAWSQL_DATE("CASE WHEN %1 = 'Critical' THEN %2+2
WHEN %1 = 'High' THEN %2+3
WHEN %1 = 'Medium' THEN %2+4
ELSE %2+10 END", [Order Priority], [Order Date])
```

> This example uses a SQL Server CASE statement to add a different number of days to the [Order Date] field depending on which [Order Priority] value is found.

61. RAWSQL_DATETIME()

The `RAWSQL_DATETIME()` function is a pass-through function that allows the user to send an arbitrary expression to the underlying datasource. The expression must return a scalar value of a type that Tableau can convert into a date time. This expression will not be checked in any way by Tableau and may produce an error at the datasource level. The user must respect the syntax conventions of the datasource when constructing the expression. The generalized syntax for the function is below:

```
RAWSQL_DATETIME("expr", [arg1], ...[argN])
```

The `expr` in quotes is the expression to be passed through to the datasource. `N` number of arguments can be specified in a comma-separated list as shown. These arguments are referenced in the expression with a %1, %2, and % `N` syntax.

Basic:

```
RAWSQL_DATETIME("%1 + '06:30:00'", [Order Date])
```

> In this example, you're adding the time literal '06:30:00' (6 hours, 30 minutes, 0 seconds) to the [Order Date] value.

Intermediate:

```
RAWSQL_DATETIME("DATETIMEFROMPARTS(2013,2,24,9,40,35,0)")
```

> This example uses the SQL Server function DATETIMEFROMPARTS() to build a date time value from time parts. The resulting date time literal in SQL Server would be expressed as 2013–02–24 09:40:35:000.

Advanced:

```
RAWSQL_DATETIME("CASE WHEN %2 = 'East'THEN %1 + '01:00:00'
WHEN %2 = 'West' THEN %1—'02:00:00'
ELSE %1 END", [Order Date], [Region])
```

> The above example uses the SQL Server CASE statement to add or subtract a time literal depending on the value in the [Region] field. When the [Region] is East you will add 1 hour and when the [Region] is West you will subtract 2 hours. If the [Region] is any other value it will simply return [Order Date] without any change.

62. RAWSQL_INT()

The `RAWSQL_INT()` function is a pass-through function that allows the user to send an arbitrary expression to the underlying datasource. The expression must return a scalar value of a type that Tableau can convert into an integer. This expression will not be checked in any way by Tableau and may produce an error at the datasource level. The user must respect the syntax conventions of the datasource when constructing the expression. The generalized syntax for the function is below:

```
RAWSQL_INT("expr",[arg1],...[argN])
```

The `expr` in quotes is the expression to be passed through to the datasource. `N` number of arguments can be specified in a comma-separated list as shown. These arguments are referenced in the expression with a %1, %2, and % `N` syntax.

Basic:

```
RAWSQL_INT("1+2")
```

> This formula returns the addition of the integers 1 and 2. If the result is not 3, something has gone seriously awry.

Intermediate:

```
RAWSQL_INT("CEILING(%1)",[Unit Price])
```

> The above example uses the SQL Server function CEILING() which takes in numeric values and returns the smallest integer that is larger than the argument. You're passing [Unit Price] into the CEILING() function.

Advanced:

```
RAWSQL_INT("DATEDIFF(day,COALESCE(%2,%1),GETDATE())",[Order Date],[Ship Date])
```

> In this example you're using the SQL Server functions DATEDIFF(), COALESCE() and GETDATE() to return the difference in days between the current SQL Server date time and either the [Ship Date] or the [Order Date] depending on if either value is NULL.

63. RAWSQL_REAL()

The RAWSQL_REAL() function is a pass-through function that allows the user to send an arbitrary expression to the underlying datasource. The expression must return a scalar value of a type that Tableau can convert into a number. This expression will not be checked in any way by Tableau and may produce an error at the datasource level. The user must respect the syntax conventions of the datasource when constructing the expression. The generalized syntax for the function is below:

```
RAWSQL_REAL("expr",[arg1],...[argN])
```

The expr in quotes is the expression to be passed through to the datasource. N number of arguments can be specified in a comma separated list as shown. These arguments are referenced in the expression with a %1, %2, and % N syntax.

Basic:

```
RAWSQL_REAL("5.39 + 3.56")
```

> This example adds the two numeric values 5.39 and 3.56 together. The result is 8.95.

Intermediate:

```
RAWSQL_REAL("RAND()")
```

This example uses the SQL Server function RAND() to generate a pseudo random number. The generated value is a numeric type between 0 and 1.

Advanced:

```
RAWSQL_REAL("ROUND(CASE WHEN %1 = 'East' THEN %2 * 1.15
WHEN %1 = 'West' THEN %2 * 0.85
ELSE %2 END, 2)",[Region],[Sales])
```

This formula uses a SQL Server CASE statement to selectively multiply the [Sales] value by either 1.15 or 0.85 depending on what the [Region] value is. We then use the ROUND() function to round the result to 2 decimal places.

64. RAWSQL_STR()

The RAWSQL_STR() function is a pass-through function that allows the user to send an arbitrary expression to the underlying datasource. The expression must return a scalar value of a type that Tableau can convert into a string. This expression will not be checked in any way by Tableau and may produce an error at the datasource level. The user must respect the syntax conventions of the datasource when constructing the expression. The generalized syntax for the function is below:

```
RAWSQL_STR("expr",[arg1],...[argN])
```

The expr in quotes is the expression to be passed through to the datasource. N number of arguments can be specified in a comma-separated list as shown. These arguments are referenced in the expression with a %1, %2, and % N syntax.

Basic:

```
RAWSQL_STR("'Trivial Case'")
```

This basic example defines the string literal Trivial Case with the RAWSQL_STR function. This is truly the trivial case.

Intermediate:

```
RAWSQL_STR("%1 + '-' + CONVERT(varchar, %2)",[State],[Zip Code])
```

This example concatenates the value in the [State] field with the string literal '-' and the string representation of the value in the [Zip Code] field. The CONVERT(varchar, %2) is necessary in SQL Server to avoid a type error.

Advanced:

```
RAWSQL_STR("STUFF(%1,CHARINDEX(' ', %1), 0,' ''' + %2 + ''' ')",
[Customer Name],[State])
```

In this example we're using the SQL Server `CHARINDEX()` function to locate the first instance of a space in the value of the `[Customer Name]` field and then using the SQL Server `STUFF()` function to insert the value in the `[State]` field there. Observant readers might notice that the case where the blank space isn't found in the `[Customer Name]` hasn't been handled. If that happens, the `[State]` will just get tacked on to the front of the `[Customer Name]`.

65. RAWSQLAGG_BOOL()

The `RAWSQLAGG_BOOL()` function is a pass-through function that provides a means to send an arbitrary expression to the underlying datasource. The expression must return an aggregate value that Tableau can convert into a Boolean. This expression will not be checked in any way by Tableau and may produce an error at the datasource level. The user must respect the syntax conventions of the datasource when constructing the expression. The generalized syntax for the function is below:

```
RAWSQLAGG_BOOL("agg_expr", [arg1], ...[argN])
```

The `agg_expr` in quotes is the expression to be passed through to the datasource. `N` number of arguments can be specified in a comma-separated list as shown. These arguments are referenced in the expression with a %1, %2, and % `N` syntax.

Basic:

```
RAWSQLAGG_BOOL("SUM(%1) = SUM(%2)", [Sales], [Profit])
```

This example compares the sum of the `[Sales]` values with the sum of the `[Profit]` values and returns true if they are equal. It returns false if they are not.

Intermediate:

```
RAWSQLAGG_BOOL("SUM(CASE WHEN %1='Oklahoma' THEN %2 ELSE 0 END)
> 100.00", [State], [Sales])
```

This formula uses the sum of the `[Sales]` values when `[Region]` = `'Oklahoma'` and then checks whether or not it is greater than 100.00. The calculation returns true if the sum is greater than 100.00 and false if it is not.

Advanced:

RAWSQLAGG_BOOL("SUM(CASE WHEN PATINDEX('%Henry%', %1) > 0 THEN %2 ELSE 0 END)
> 100.00",[Customer Name],[Sales])

> This example performs the SQL Server PATINDEX() function on the [Customer Name]
> field to look for the presence of the substring Henry. It sums the [Sales] values where
> that string is contained in the [Customer Name] field. If that sum is greater than 100.00
> the function returns true. Otherwise, it returns false.

66. RAWSQLAGG_DATE()

The RAWSQLAGG_DATE() function is a pass-through function that allows the
user to send an arbitrary expression to the underlying datasource. The expression must return an aggregate value that Tableau can convert into a date. This
expression will not be checked in any way by Tableau and may produce an
error at the datasource level. The user must respect the syntax conventions
of the datasource when constructing the expression. The generalized syntax
for the function follows:

RAWSQLAGG_DATE("agg_expr",[arg1],...[argN])

The agg_expr in quotes is the expression to be passed through to the datasource. N number of arguments can be specified in a comma-separated list
as shown. These arguments are referenced in the expression with a %1, %2,
%N syntax.

Basic:

RAWSQLAGG_DATE("MIN(%1)",[Order Date])

> This example returns the minimum value of the [Order Date] field.

Intermediate:

RAWSQLAGG_DATE("MAX(COALESCE(%2, %1))",[Order Date],[Ship Date])

> This formula returns the maximum value of the SQL Server function COALESCE() on
> [Order Date] and [Ship Date]. The COALESCE() function returns the first non-NULL
> field from its argument list.

Advanced:

RAWSQLAGG_DATE("MAX(CASE WHEN %1 = 'Critical' THEN COALESCE(%3, %2) END)",
[Order Priority],[Order Date],[Ship Date])

> This formula returns the maximum value of the SQL Server function COALESCE() on
> [Order Date] and [Ship Date] when [Order Priority] is critical. The COALESCE()
> function returns the first non-NULL field from its argument list.

67. RAWSQLAGG_DATETIME()

The `RAWSQLAGG_DATETIME()` function is a pass-through function that allows the user to send an arbitrary expression to the underlying datasource. The expression must return an aggregate value that Tableau can convert into a date time. This expression will not be checked in any way by Tableau and may produce an error at the datasource level. The user must respect the syntax conventions of the datasource when constructing the expression. The generalized syntax for the function is below:

```
RAWSQLAGG_DATETIME("agg_expr",[arg1],...[argN])
```

The `agg_expr` in quotes is the expression to be passed through to the datasource. *N* number of arguments can be specified in a comma-separated list as shown. These arguments are referenced in the expression with a %1, %2, and %N syntax.

Basic:

```
RAWSQLAGG_DATETIME("MAX(%1)",[Ship Date])
```

This formula returns the maximum value, or most recent date within the [Ship Date] field.

Intermediate:

```
RAWSQLAGG_DATETIME("MAX(%2-%1)",[Order Date],[Ship Date])
```

This formula returns the maximum of the date time difference between [Ship Date] and [Order Date]. In SQL Server this difference will be returned as a date time that is offset from 1900–01–01.

Advanced:

```
RAWSQLAGG_DATETIME("MAX(CASE WHEN %2 = 'East' THEN %1 + '01:00:00'
WHEN %2 = 'West' THEN %1-'02:00:00'
ELSE %1 END)",[Order Date],[Region])
```

The preceding example uses the SQL Server CASE statement to add or subtract a time literal depending on the value in the [Region] field. When the [Region] is East one hour is added, or when the [Region] is West two hours are subtracted. If the [Region] is any other value we simply return [Order Date] without any change. The maximum value from the CASE statement across all records is returned. This all works perfectly if you process orders in the central time zone.

68. RAWSQLAGG_INT()

The `RAWSQLAGG_INT()` function is a pass-through function that allows the user to send an arbitrary expression to the underlying datasource. The expression must return an aggregate value that Tableau can convert into an integer. This expression will not be checked in any way by Tableau and may produce an error at the datasource level. The user must respect the syntax conventions of the datasource when constructing the expression. The generalized syntax for the function is below:

```
RAWSQLAGG_INT("agg_expr",[arg1],...[argN])
```

The `agg_expr` in quotes is the expression to be passed through to the datasource. *N* number of arguments can be specified in a comma-separated list as shown. These arguments are referenced in the expression with a %1, %2, %N syntax.

Basic:
```
RAWSQLAGG_INT("FLOOR(SUM(%1))",[Sales])
```

> The preceding example uses the SQL Server function `FLOOR()` to return the greatest integer value less than the sum of the `[Sales]` field.

Intermediate:
```
RAWSQLAGG_INT("CEILING(STDEV(%1))",[Unit Price])
```

> This example uses the SQL Server function `CEILING()` to return the smallest integer value greater than the standard deviation of the `[Unit Price]` field.

Advanced:
```
RAWSQLAGG_INT("AVG(DATEDIFF(day, COALESCE(%2, %1), GETDATE()))",
[Order Date],[Ship Date])
```

> The preceding example returns the average difference in whole days between the current date time on the SQL Server and the first non-NULL value in `[Ship Date]` and `[Order Date]` returned by the `COALESCE()` function.

69. RAWSQLAGG_REAL()

The `RAWSQLAGG_REAL()` function is a pass-through function that allows the user to send an arbitrary expression to the underlying datasource. The expression must return an aggregate value that Tableau can convert into a number. This expression will not be checked in any way by Tableau and may produce an error at the datasource level. The user must respect the syntax conventions of the datasource when constructing the expression. The generalized syntax for the function is below:

```
RAWSQLAGG_REAL("agg_expr",[arg1],...[argN])
```

The `agg_expr` in quotes is the expression to be passed through to the datasource. *N* number of arguments can be specified in a comma-separated list as shown. These arguments are referenced in the expression with a %1, %2, and %N syntax.

Basic:

```
RAWSQLAGG_REAL("SUM(%1)",[Profit])
```

> The preceding example returns the sum of the [Profit] values with the decimal component intact.

Intermediate:

```
RAWSQLAGG_REAL("VAR(%1-%2)",[Product Base Margin],[Discount])
```

> The preceding example uses the SQL Server function VAR() to return the statistics variance of the [Product Base Margin] value minus the [Discount] value.

Advanced:

```
RAWSQLAGG_REAL("ROUND(SUM(CASE WHEN %3='East' THEN %1*%2*0.85
WHEN %3='West' THEN %1*%2*1.15
ELSE %1*%2 END),4)",[Unit Price],[Order Quantity],[Region])
```

> In the advanced example the sum of a SQL Server CASE statement selectively multiplies the [Unit Price] value and the [Order Quantity] value by either 1.15 or 0.85 depending on what the [Region] value comes from. The formula then uses the ROUND() function to round the result to 4 decimal places.

70. RAWSQLAGG_STR()

The `RAWSQLAGG_STR()` function is a pass-through function that allows the user to send an arbitrary expression to the underlying datasource. The expression must return an aggregate value that Tableau can convert into a string. This expression will not be checked in any way by Tableau and may produce an error at the datasource level. The user must respect the syntax conventions of the datasource when constructing the expression. The generalized syntax for the function is below:

```
RAWSQLAGG_STR("agg_expr",[arg1],...[argN])
```

The `agg_expr` in quotes is the expression to be passed through to the data-source. `N` number of arguments can be specified in a comma-separated list as shown. These arguments are referenced in the expression with a %1, %2, and % `N` syntax.

Basic:

`RAWSQLAGG_STR("MIN(%1)",[Order Date])`

This example returns the minimum value of the `[Order Date]` field. It's worth noting that it returns it as a string value. The expression that the `RAWSQL` function is calling can return a different value than the function returns as long as it is convertible into the outer function return type.

Intermediate:

`RAWSQLAGG_STR("MAX(LEFT(%1, 3))",[City])`

In the preceding example the function uses the SQL Server function `LEFT()` to get the left-most three characters from the `[City]` field and then returns the maximum value of that string.

Advanced:

`RAWSQLAGG_STR("CASE WHEN (SUM(%1)/SUM(%2)) > 0`
`THEN 'Compliant' ELSE 'Noncompliant' END",[Profit],[Sales])`

The preceding example calculates a profit ratio by dividing the sum of `[Profit]` by the sum of `[Sales]` and then returns the string Compliant if this value is greater than 0. It returns `Noncompliant` if the calculated value is less than 0.

71. REPLACE

The `REPLACE` function is an advanced function that allows specified data replacement within a string field. This does *not* change the data at the source level by using this function, but instead merely creates a new field that now includes the replacement strings. The function searches a string field to find the necessary stated substring. Once the substring is found, the replacement string then replaces the substring data.

`REPLACE(String,Substring,Replacement)`

Basic:

`REPLACE("[Order Priority]","Not Specified","High")`

The function example searches the `Order Priority` field to find any orders that have not got a specified priority within the database. The `REPLACE` function then replaces the `Not Specified` orders to a new status of `High`.

Intermediate:

```
IIF([Order Date] < dateadd('month',-2,today()) ,
REPLACE([Order Priority],"Not Specified","High"),[Order Priority])
```

The function example is being used to determine the validity of each order priority assigned to every order id. The calculation only investigates orders that are older than 2 months. The REPLACE stage then assigns a new Order Priority to all orders older than 2 months and that have a Not Specified priority. The function replaces the Not Specified with a High Priority. The REPLACE function is highly dependent on the source data. The Replace function is not available against all datasources. Using a data extract does allow a more robust solution when planning on using the REPLACE function.

72. RIGHT

RIGHT is a String function that returns the right-most characters from its designated string. This function can be used to create new dimensions directly or combined to create advanced calculated fields. This has the same principles as the LEFT function.

```
RIGHT(String,Number)
```

Basic:

```
RIGHT([Customer Zip Code],3)
```

The function example is an additional way of using U.S. Zip Codes; however, using the RIGHT function helps identify the area of the City or metropolitan area.

73. ROUND

The ROUND function rounds numbers to the number of digits as specified with the decimals argument within the function. The decimals argument specifies how many decimal points of precision to include in the final result, although it is not required. If the decimals variable is not included, then the number is rounded to the nearest integer. Tableau uses the following rounding rules:

- If the value of the number to the right of the rounding digit is less than five, the rounding digit is left unchanged.

- If the value of the number to the right of the rounding digit is five or higher, the rounding digit is raised by one.

```
ROUND(number, [decimals])
```

Number = any given number. Decimals = any given number (not required).

Basic:

ROUND([Sales])

> This function returns all sales values in the database to the nearest integer. If this function is used to round the sales for one year, then it will first round the results for every row in the database before the aggregation is applied.

Intermediate:

ROUND(SUM([Profit])/SUM([Order Quantity]),2)

> This function will first calculate the sum of profit divided by sum of order quantity and then round the result to 2-digits. If the sum was not used, and non-aggregate arguments were used instead, then the function would round all underlying rows in the database first before any result is aggregated as defined by the dimension.

74. RTRIM

The RTRIM function removes trailing spaces that may be present within the data. This function, like the LTRIM function, can be used as a data cleansing function so that the data is consistent and set correctly.

RTRIM(String)

Basic:

RTRIM("Ruby Young")

> The output for this would simply be Ruby Young. Just like LTRIM, trailing spaces may cause an issue if using additional functions and trying to blend data from different sources.

75. RUNNING_AVG

This is a table calculation function that returns the running average of the provided expression from the first to the current row of the view/partition.

RUNNING_AVG(expression)

> Expression = Any valid aggregate calculation (e.g., SUM ([Sales])).

Basic:

RUNNING_AVG(SUM([SALES]))

> This table calculation function returns the running average of the sum of sales within the window (or frame). Note: When the [start] and [end] arguments are omitted, the entire frame (window/pane) is used. If the values are incorrect or inconsistent, ensure that you are properly using the Compute By portion of the table calculation.

Intermediate:

```
RUNNING_AVG(SUM([SALES]), FIRST(),LAST())
```

This formula returns the running average of the sum of sales from the first row to the last row of the window (or pane). Note: If the values are incorrect or inconsistent, ensure that you are properly using the Compute By portion of the table calculation.

Advanced:

```
IF INDEX()=1 THEN RUNNING_AVG( SUM([SALES]) ) ELSE NULL END
```

This function assumes there are a large amount of marks on the view and/or that the user is dealing with Big Data. Through if/then logic, you can bypass the table scans, which cause noticeable performance degradation. In the end, the calculation takes the running average of the sum of sales for the specified window (or frame) and does not repeat the values.

76. RUNNING_COUNT

This table calculation function returns the running count of the provided expression from the first to the current row of the view/partition.

```
RUNNING_COUNT(expression)
```

Expression = Any valid aggregate calculation (e.g., SUM([Sales])).

Basic:

```
RUNNING_COUNT(SUM([SALES]))
```

This formula returns the running count of the sum of sales within the window (or frame). Note: When the [start] and [end] arguments are omitted, the entire frame is used. If the values are incorrect or inconsistent, ensure that you are properly using the Compute By portion of the table calculation.

Intermediate:

```
RUNNING_COUNT(SUM([SALES]), FIRST(),LAST())
```

This formula returns the running count of the sum of sales from the first row to the last row of the window (or frame). Note: If the values are incorrect or inconsistent, ensure that you are properly using the Compute By portion of the table calculation.

Advanced:

```
IF INDEX()=1 THEN RUNNING_COUNT(SUM([SALES]),0, IIF(INDEX()=1,LAST(),0)) END
```

This formula assumes there are a large number of marks on the view or that the user is dealing with a large data set. Using IF/THEN logic, the formula can bypass the table scans, which can cause noticeable performance degradation. In the end, the calculation returns the running count of the sum of sales for the specified window (or frame). Bonus: Try making the window frames dynamic with a parameter.

77. RUNNING_MAX

This table calculation function returns the running maximum of the provided expression from the first to the current row of the view (partition).

```
RUNNING_MAX(expression)
```

Expression = Any valid aggregate calculation (e.g., SUM ([Sales])).

Basic:

```
RUNNING_MAX( SUM([SALES]) )
```

This formula returns the running maximum of the sum of sales within the window (or pane). Note: When the [start] and [end] arguments are omitted, the entire frame is used. If the values are incorrect or inconsistent, ensure that you are properly using the Compute By portion of the table calculation.

Intermediate:

```
RUNNING_MAX( SUM([SALES]) ), FIRST(),LAST()
```

This formula returns a running maximum of the sum of sales from the first row to the last row of the window (or frame). Note: If the values are incorrect or inconsistent, ensure that you are properly using the Compute By portion of the table calculation.

Advanced:

```
IF INDEX()=1 THEN RUNNING_MAX( SUM([SALES]) ) ELSE NULL END
```

This formula assumes there are a large amount of marks on the view or that the user is dealing with a large data set. Through IF/THEN logic, you can bypass the table scans, which cause noticeable performance degradation. The calculation returns the running maximum of the sum of sales for the specified window (or pane) and does not repeat the values.

78. RUNNING_MIN

This table calculation function returns the running minimum of the provided expression from the first to the current row of the view or partition.

`RUNNING_MIN(expression)`

Expression = any valid aggregate calculation (e.g., SUM ([Sales])).

Basic:

`RUNNING_MIN(SUM([SALES]))`

This formula returns the running minimum of the sum of sales within the window (or frame). Note: When the [start] and [end] arguments are omitted, the entire frame is used. If the values are incorrect or inconsistent, ensure that you are properly using the Compute By portion of the table calculation.

Intermediate:

`RUNNING_MIN(SUM([SALES]) ), FIRST(),LAST())`

This formula returns the running minimum of the sum of sales from the first row to the last row of the window (or frame). Note: If the values are incorrect or inconsistent, ensure that you are properly using the Compute By portion of the table calculation.

Advanced:

`IF INDEX()=1 THEN RUNNING_MIN (SUM([SALES]))ELSE NULL END`

This formula assumes there are a large amount of marks on the view or that the user is dealing with a large data set. The use of IF/THEN logic bypasses table scans which cause noticeable performance degradation. In the end, the calculation returns the running minimum of the sum of sales for the specified window (or frame) and does not repeat the values.

79. RUNNING_SUM

This table calculation returns the running sum of the provided expression from the first to the current row of the view/partition.

`RUNNING_SUM(expression)`

Expression = Any valid aggregate calculation (e.g., SUM ([Sales])).

Basic:

```
RUNNING_SUM(SUM([SALES]))
```

This formula returns the running sum of the sum of sales within the window (or frame). Note: When the `[start]` and `[end]` arguments are omitted, the entire pane is used. If the values are incorrect or inconsistent, ensure that you are properly using the Compute By portion of the table calculation.

Intermediate:

```
RUNNING_SUM( SUM([SALES]) ), FIRST(),LAST())
```

This formula returns the running sum of the sum of sales from the first row to the last row of the window (or pane). Note: If the values are incorrect or inconsistent, ensure that you are properly using the Compute By portion of the table calculation.

Advanced:

```
IF INDEX()=1 THEN RUNNING_SUM ( SUM([SALES]) ) ELSE NULL END
```

This formula assumes there are a large amount of marks on the view or that the user is dealing with a large data set. The use of if/then logic bypasses the table scans, which can cause noticeable performance degradation. In the end, the calculation returns the running sum of the sum of sales for the specified window (or frame) and does not repeat the values.

80. SIGN

The SIGN function is used to highlight whether the value of the result is positive, negative, or equal to zero. The returned values are (-1) if the number is negative, (0) if the number is zero, or (1) if the number is positive.

```
SIGN(number)
```

Number = any given number.

Basic:

```
SIGN(-21)
```

The result of this function is (-1) because the expression (-21) is a negative value.

Intermediate:

```
IF SIGN(SUM([Profit]))=1
THEN "Profit"
ELSEIF SIGN(SUM([Profit]))=-1
THEN "Loss"
ELSE "Break-Even"
END
```

The SIGN function is helpful in combination with a logical function. In this example the logical IF function is used, which will return a string to indicate the level of profitability.

81. SIN

The SIN function returns the sine of a given number specified in radians.

`SIN(number)`

Number = any given number, where the number is in radians.

Basic:

`SIN(PI()/4)`

This function calculates the sine of π/4 radians. This function returns 0.707106781186547 radians.

Intermediate:

`SIN(RADIANS(90))`

In this function the number is known in degrees—in this case 90. First the degrees are converted to radians before the sine is calculated. The result is 1.

82. SIZE()

This table calculation function returns the total number of rows in the view/ partition.

`SIZE()`

This function does not require any arguments.

Basic:

`SIZE()`

The function returns the number of rows in the view/partition.

Intermediate:

`WINDOW_SUM(SUM([SALES]))/SIZE()`

This formula first takes the sum of sales for the view or partition and then divides that result by the total number of rows within the partition.

Advanced:

```
IF INDEX()=1 THEN WINDOW_SUM(SUM([SALES]))/SIZE() ELSE NULL END
```

This formula assumes there are a large amount of marks on the view or that the user is dealing with a large data set. Through the use of if/then logic, table scans can be bypassed which can cause noticeable performance degradation. In the end, the calculation takes the sum of sales for the view/partition and then divides by the total rows in the partition. Bonus: Try making the window frames dynamic with a parameter.

83. SPACE

The SPACE function is a simple function allowing the user to create a string of spaces that can then be used within other calculations.

```
SPACE(number)
```

Basic:

```
SPACE(4)
```

The function example simply creates a string of four blank spaces. This string of spaces can now be used in other calculated fields.

Intermediate:

```
[Customer]+SPACE(2)+[City]+SPACE(2)+[Zip Code]
```

The function example output would look like: Andrew Roberts Fresno 93727. Without the SPACE values, the output would look like this: Andrew RobertsFresno93727.

84. SQRT

The SQRT function is the inverse of the SQUARE function. It returns the square root of a number. It gives the same return when using the POWER function when raising the number to the power of 0.5.

```
SQRT(number)
```

Number = any given number greater than zero. If the number is less than or equal to zero the SQRT function returns a NULL.

Basic:

```
SQRT(49)
```

The result of this function is 7. The result can be achieved with the POWER function. In that case the function is POWER (49,0.5), where 49 is raised to the power of 0.5. The ^ symbol can also be used in the calculation instead. The calculation 49^0.5 also returns the same result in this case.

85. SQUARE

The SQUARE function returns the square of the number. In other words it multiplies the expression by itself. It gives the same return when using the POWER function when raising the number to the power of two.

SQUARE(number)

> Number = any given number.

Basic:

SQUARE(7)

> This function multiplies 7 by itself, so 7*7 = 49. Similar to the POWER function, it raises 7 to the power of 2. The ^ symbol can also be used in the calculation instead. The calculation 7^2 returns the same result in this case.

86. STARTSWITH

The STARTSWITH function is similar in its approach to the CONTAINS function; however, it has limits on the way it searches the string. Whereas the CONTAINS function searches the full length of the string for the specified substring, the STARTSWITH function only searches the very beginning of the string.

STARTSWITH(String, Substring)

BASIC:

STARTSWITH([City],"New")

> The function example searches the first 3 characters in the CITY string and will only return a True value if these characters match the substring and are in order. Examples would be New York, New Orleans, New Jersey.

87. STDEV

This function returns the statistical Standard Deviation of the expression using a sample of the population (compared to STDEVP, which uses the entire population to calculate the standard deviation).

Basic:

STDEV([Sales])

> This Formula will return the standard deviation of sales. One possible use would be to use the result for reference lines on a time series chart.

Intermediate:

AVG([Sales])+STDEV([Sales])

> This example shows how you can combine the Standard Deviation calculation with the Average calculation to find the value for the first Standard Deviation.

Advanced:

AVG([Sales])+(([Number of deviations])*STDEV([Sales]))

> This formula uses a parameter to change the number of standard deviations from the mean value you wish to calculate. The number of deviations could be limited to the values (1, 2, and 3).

88. STDEVP

This function returns the statistical Standard Deviation of the expression using the entire population (compared to STDEV, which uses a sample of the population to calculate the standard deviation).

Basic:

STDEVP([Sales])

> This Formula will return the standard deviation of sales. In the example, we can see how spread out each order's sales amount is from the mean for each of the departments.

Intermediate:

AVG([Sales]) + STDEVP([Sales])

> This example shows how you can combine the standard deviation function with the average function to find the value for the first standard deviation.

Advanced:

AVG([Sales])+([number of deviations]*STDEVP([Sales]))

> This formula uses a parameter to change how many standard deviations you wish to see from the average sales value derived from the AVG function.

89. STR

Returns a string for a given expression.

Basic:

STR(5.0)

> The preceding formula changes a number into a string value of 5.0.

Intermediate:

"Total Products = " + STR([Qty])

> The preceding formula returns a string. In this example a custom label is being created using a number field [Qty]. If [Qty] has a value of 10, then this function returns Total Products = 10.

Advanced:

STR([StartDate]) ' to ' + STR([EndDate])

> The preceding formula returns a string describing the period (start to end). This is useful when you'd like to have an annotation, Tooltip, or other label that describes the period of analysis in a custom formatted way. If [StartDate]) is equal to January 1, 2013 and [EndDate] is equal to March 1, 2013, then the function will return January 2013 to March 2013.

90. SUM

This SUM function returns the sum of all the values in the expression. SUM can be used with numeric fields only. NULL values are ignored.

Basic:

SUM([Sales])

> This Formula returns the total sales value for whatever dimension is included in the display.

Intermediate:

SUM([Sales])*[Commission Rate]

> This example shows how to use the SUM of sales and multiply it by a parameter (variable) value to derive a new amount that can be dynamically changed by the parameter control. This example gives us a total amount of commissions for the level of detail displayed in the view.

Advanced:

```
SUM([Sales]) / COUNTD([Customer ID])
```

This formula derives the average sales per unique customer.

91. TAN

The TAN function returns the tangent of a given number specified in radians.

```
TAN(number)
```

Number = Any given number, where the number is in radians.

Basic:

```
TAN(PI()/4)
```

This function calculates the tangent of π/4 radians. This function returns 1 radian.

Intermediate:

```
TAN(RADIANS(45))
```

In this function the number is known in degrees, in this case 45. First the degrees are converted to radians before the sine is calculated. The result is also 1.

92. TODAY

The TODAY function returns the current date. This is similar to NOW() but does not include the time component.

Basic:

```
TODAY()
```

The preceding function works as follows: If today's date is March 12, 2013 at 3:04pm the function will return the date March 12, 2013.

Intermediate:

```
DATEADD('day', -30, TODAY())
```

The preceding formula returns a date 30 days before today's date. If today is March 18, 2013 then this function will return February 16, 2013. This can be very useful in filtering for specific periods (like 30 rolling days) or highlighting a period on a timeline where data may be uncertain.

93. TOTAL

`TOTAL(Expression)`

> **Expression = Any valid aggregate calculation (e.g.,** `SUM ([Sales])`**).**

Basic:

`TOTAL(SUM([Sales]))`

> This formula returns the total across all rows in the database for the window (or pane). It is the same concept as the `SUM(Expression)` function but applies it selectively within the window (or pane).

Intermediate:

`SUM([Sales])/TOTAL(SUM([Sales]))`

> This formula returns the sum of sales and divides it by the total across all rows in the database to get a percent of total. Note: If the values are incorrect or inconsistent, ensure that you are properly using the Compute By portion of the table calculation.

Advanced:

`WINDOW_MAX(SUM([Sales])/TOTAL(SUM([Sales])))=(SUM([Sales])/`
`TOTAL(SUM([Sales])))`

> This formula highlights the *maximum* percent of total value within a partition when it equals the percent of the total portion of the partition. Note: If the values are incorrect or inconsistent, ensure that you are properly using the Compute By portion of the table calculation.

94. TRIM

The `TRIM` function encompasses the logic of both `LTRIM` and `RTRIM` into one function.

`TRIM(String)`
`TRIM("Gemma Palmer")`

> The function example output for this would simply be Gemma Palmer. Best practice would be to use the `TRIM` function if you have any concerns about leading or trailing spaces in imported data.

95. UPPER

This function allows the user to uppercase all characters within a string. The UPPER function will only change the lowercased characters that exist in a string and thus ignore all uppercase characters that already exist.

```
UPPER(String)
```

Basic:

```
UPPER("BatMan")
```

> The function example returns all uppercase letters in the string: BATMAN.

96. USERDOMAIN

This function returns the domain of the person currently logged in to Tableau Server. If the user is not logged on to Server, the function returns the Windows domain. This function can be used in conjunction with other user functions when you desire to create security based on username and domain.

Refer to the assumptions under USERNAME() for the user and domain data used in the examples that follow.

Basic:

```
USERDOMAIN()
```

> If a company had two subsidiaries, Retail and Wholesale that had separate domains (RETAIL.local and WSALE.local), then it would return the domain name for the logged-on user.

Intermediate:

```
CASE USERDOMAIN()
WHEN 'RETAIL' THEN 'Access Granted'
WHEN 'WSALE'  THEN 'Access Denied'
END
```

> The preceding formula would return either access granted or access denied at row level and could be used to drive row level security across two separate domains.

Advanced:

```
IF USERDOMAIN() = 'WSALE' THEN
IF ISMEMBEROF('Report Viewer')Then
'Access Granted'
ELSE
```

```
'Access Denied'
END
ELSEIF USERDOMAIN() = 'RETAIL' THEN
IF ISMEMBEROF('Management') THEN
'Access Granted'
ELSE
IF FULLNAME() = [Sales Person] THEN
'Access Granted'
ELSE
'Access Denied'
END
END
ELSE
'Access Denied'
END
```

> The preceding formula returns either an Access Denied or an Access Granted at row level, which could be used in a filter to apply row-level security. The statement is comparing domains, groups, and users before assigning permissions to access each row of data.

97. USERNAME()

Assumptions used for the examples:

User 1

- Full Name: Malcolm Reynolds

- Active Directory Name: DOMAIN\m.reynolds

User 2

- Full Name: River Tam

- Active Directory Name: DOMAIN\r.tam

User 3

- Full Name: Jayne Cobb

- Active Directory Name: DOMAIN\j.cobb

USERNAME() returns the username of the user logged on to the server. If the user Malcolm was logged on to the server, then USERNAME() would return m.reynolds. Expression = Any valid discrete argument.

Basic:

```
USERNAME()='m.reynolds'
```

> This example returns a Boolean (true/false) value of true if Malcolm Reynolds is logged on the system, and false if he is not.

Intermediate:

```
USERNAME()=[MANAGER]
```

> A row-level security argument that compares the USERNAME() function result with the [MANAGER] field in the data set. This would be useful for data in which users are only permitted to view their own data.

Advanced:

```
IF ISMEMBEROF('Management')then'Access Permitted'
ELSEIF USERNAME()=[Manager]then'Access Permitted'
ELSE'Access Denied'END
```

> This formula returns either Access Permitted or Access Denied at row level. When applied as a filter to show only Access Permitted rows, if the user is a member of the group management, then they can see all rows of data unless the user can only see lines of data, which are tagged with their username as the manager.

98. VAR

This aggregate function returns the statistical variance of the values in the given expression based on a sample of the population. Variance is a measure of dispersion and is calculated using the average of the squared deviations from the mean. Thinking about statistical variance, this function seems like a weigh-station on the journey to arriving at standard deviation—a more commonly used dispersion measure—that is the square root of variance. In normally distributed sets of data, standard deviation implies specific value ranges that are useful for plotting control charts. Variance by itself seems to have less practical use cases. If you have one, please share it.

Basic:

```
VAR(expression)
```

> This function returns statistical variance of the expression—a measure containing a range of values.

99. VARP

This is an aggregate function that returns the statistical variance of the values in the given expression based on a biased sample of the population. Variance is a measure of dispersion and is calculated using the average of the squared deviations from the mean. Thinking about statistical variance, this function seems like a weigh-station on the journey to arriving at standard deviation—a more commonly used dispersion measure—that is the square root of variance. In normally-distributed sets of data, standard deviation implies specific value ranges that are useful for plotting control charts. Variance by itself seems to have less practical use cases. If you have one, please share it.

`VAR(expression)`

> This function returns the statistical variance of the expression based on a biased sample of the population. Expression is a measure containing a range of values.

100. WINDOW_AVG

This function returns the average for a given expression over a window (or pane) specified. Note: Performance is affected with an increase in marks; if the data set is large, using the advanced method will have better performance and scalability.

`WINDOW_AVG(expression,[start],[end])`

> Expression = Any valid aggregate calculation (e.g., `SUM ([Sales])`). `[start]` = Start of window (not required); `[end]` = End of window (not required).

Basic:

`WINDOW_AVG(SUM([SALES]))`

> This formula returns the average of the sum of sales within the window (or pane). Note: When the `[start]` and `[end]` arguments are omitted, the entire frame is used. If the values are incorrect or inconsistent, ensure that you are properly using the Compute By portion of the table calculation.

Intermediate:

`WINDOW_AVG(SUM([SALES]),FIRST(),LAST())`

> This formula returns the average of the sum of sales from the first row to the last row of the window (or pane). Note: If the values are incorrect or inconsistent, ensure that you are properly using the Compute By portion of the table calculation.

Advanced:

```
IF INDEX()=1 THEN WINDOW_AVG(SUM([SALES]),0,IIF(INDEX()=1,LAST(),0)) END
```

> This formula assumes there are a large number of marks on the view or that the user is dealing with a big data set. Through the use of if/then logic, table scans can be bypassed, which can cause noticeable performance degradation. In the end, the calculation takes the average of the sum of sales for the specified window (or pane).

101. WINDOW_COUNT

This table calculation function returns the count for a given expression with a window (or pane) the user specifies. Note: Performance is affected with an increase in marks; if the data set is large, using the advanced method will have better performance and scalability.

```
WINDOW_COUNT(expression,[start],[end])
```

> Expression = Any valid aggregate calculation (e.g., SUM ([Sales])); [start] = start of window (not required); [end] = end of window (not required).

Basic:

```
WINDOW_COUNT(SUM([SALES]))
```

> This formula returns the count of the sum of sales within the window (or pane). Note: When the [start] and [end] arguments are omitted, the entire frame is used. If the values are incorrect or inconsistent, ensure that you are properly using the Compute By portion of the table calculation.

Intermediate:

```
WINDOW_COUNT(SUM([SALES]),FIRST(),LAST())
```

> This formula returns the count of the sum of sales from the first row to the last row of the window (or pane). Note: If the values are incorrect or inconsistent, ensure that you are properly using the Compute By portion of the table calculation.

Advanced:

```
IF INDEX()=1 THEN WINDOW_COUNT(SUM([SALES]),0, IIF(INDEX()=1,LAST(),0)) END
```

> This formula assumes there are a large number of marks on the view or that the user is dealing with a big data set. Through the use of if/then logic, table scans can be bypassed, which can cause noticeable performance degradation. In the end, the calculation takes the count of the sum of sales for the specified window (or frame). Bonus: Try making the window frames dynamic with a parameter.

102. WINDOW_MAX

This table calculation function returns the maximum value for a given expression within the window (or pane) specified. Note: Performance is affected with an increase in marks; if the data set is large, using the advanced method will have better performance and scalability.

```
WINDOW_MAX(expression,[start],[end])
```

> Expression = Any valid aggregate calculation (e.g., SUM ([Sales])); [start] = start of window (not required); [end] = end of window (not required).

Basic:

```
WINDOW_MAX(SUM([SALES]))
```

> This formula returns the maximum of the sum of sales within the window (or pane). Note: When the [start] and [end] arguments are omitted, the entire frame is used. If the values are incorrect or inconsistent, ensure that you are properly using the Compute By portion of the table calculation.

Intermediate:

```
WINDOW_MAX(SUM([SALES]),FIRST(),LAST())
```

> This formula returns the maximum of the sum of sales from the first row to the last row of the window (or pane). Note: If the values are incorrect or inconsistent, ensure that you are properly using the Compute By portion of the table calculation.

Advanced:

```
IF MAX([Ship Date]) = WINDOW_MAX( MAX([Ship Date]))
THEN SUM([Sales]) ELSE NULL END
```

> This function assumes there are a large number of marks in the view or that the user is dealing with a big data set. Through the use of if/then logic, table scans can be bypassed, which can cause noticeable performance degradation. In the end, the calculation takes the maximum of the sum of sales for the specified window (or frame) and does not repeat the values.

103. WINDOW_MEDIAN

This function returns the median for a given expression within a window (or pane) specified by the user. Note: Performance is affected with an increase in marks; if the data set is large, using the advanced method will have better performance and scalability.

```
WINDOW_MEDIAN(expression,[start],[end])
```

> Expression = Any valid aggregate calculation (e.g., SUM ([Sales])); [start] = start of window (not required); [end] = end of window (not required).

Basic:

```
WINDOW_MEDIAN(SUM([SALES]))
```

> This formula returns the median of the sum of sales within the window (or pane). Note: When the [start] and [end] arguments are omitted, the entire frame is used. If the values are incorrect or inconsistent, ensure that you are properly using the Compute By portion of the table calculation.

Intermediate:

```
WINDOW_MEDIAN(SUM([SALES]),FIRST(), LAST())
```

> This formula returns the median of the sum of sales from the first row to the last row of the window (or pane). Note: If the values are incorrect or inconsistent, ensure that you are properly using the Compute By portion of the table calculation.

Advanced:

```
IF INDEX()=1 THEN WINDOW_MEDIAN(SUM([SALES]),0, IIF(INDEX()=1,LAST(),0)) END
```

> This formula assumes there are a large number of marks on the view or that the user is dealing with a big data set. Through the use of if/then logic, table scans can be bypassed, which can cause noticeable performance degradation. In the end, the calculation takes the median of the sum of sales for the specified window (or frame). Bonus: Try making the window frames dynamic with a parameter.

104. WINDOW_MIN

This table calculation function returns the minimum value for a given expression within a window (or pane) that the user specifies. Note: Performance is affected with an increase in marks; if the data set is large, using the advanced method will have better performance and scalability.

```
WINDOW_MIN(expression,[start],[end])
```

> Expression = Any valid aggregate calculation (e.g., SUM ([Sales])); [start] = start of window (not required); [end] = end of window (not required).

Basic:

```
WINDOW_MIN(SUM([SALES]))
```

This formula returns the minimum of the sum of sales within the window (or pane). Note: When the `[start]` and `[end]` arguments are omitted, the entire frame is used. If the values are incorrect or inconsistent, ensure that you are properly using the Compute By portion of the table calculation.

Intermediate:

```
WINDOW_MIN(SUM([SALES]), FIRST(),LAST())
```

This formula returns the minimum of the sum of sales from the first row to the last row of the window (or pane). Note: If the values are incorrect or inconsistent, ensure that you are properly using the Compute By portion of the table calculation.

Advanced:

```
IF INDEX()=1 THEN WINDOW_MIN( SUM([SALES])) ELSE NULL END
```

This formula assumes there are a large number of marks in the view or that the user is dealing with a big data set. Through the use of if/then logic, table scans can be bypassed, which reduces potentially noticeable performance degradation. In the end, the calculation takes the minimum of the sum of sales for the specified window (or frame) and does not repeat the values.

105. WINDOW_STDEV

This table calculation function will return the *sample* standard deviation of a given expression within a window (or pane) that the user has specified. Note: Performance is affected with an increase in marks; if the data set is large, using the advanced method will have better performance and scalability.

```
WINDOW_STDEV(expression,[start],[end])
```

Expression = Any valid aggregate calculation (e.g., `SUM ([Sales])`); `[start]` = start of window (not required); `[end]` = end of window (not required).

Basic:

```
WINDOW_STDEV(SUM([SALES]))
```

This formula returns the sample standard deviation of the sum of sales within the window (or pane). Note: When the `[start]` and `[end]` arguments are omitted, the entire frame is used. If the values are incorrect or inconsistent, ensure that you are properly using the Compute By portion of the table calculation.

Intermediate:

```
WINDOW_STDEV(SUM([SALES]),FIRST(),LAST())
```

This formula returns the sample standard deviation of the sum of sales from the first row to the last row of the window (or pane). Note: If the values are incorrect or inconsistent, ensure that you are properly using the Compute By portion of the table calculation.

Advanced:

```
IF INDEX()=1 THEN WINDOW_ STDEV(SUM([SALES]),0, IIF(INDEX()=1,LAST(),0)) END
```

This formula assumes there are a large number of marks in the view or that the user is dealing with a big data set. Through the use of IF/THEN logic, table scans, which cause noticeable performance degradation, can be bypassed. In the end, the calculation takes the sample standard deviation of the sum of sales for the specified window (or frame). Bonus: Try making the window frames dynamic with a parameter.

106. WINDOW_STDEVP

This function will return the *biased* standard deviation of a given expression over a window (or pane) for which the user specifies. Note: Performance is affected with an increase in marks; if the data set is large, using the advanced method will have better performance and scalability.

```
WINDOW_STDEVP(expression,[start],[end])
```

Expression = Any valid aggregate calculation (e.g., SUM ([Sales])); [start] = start of window (not required); [end] = end of window (not required).

Basic:

```
WINDOW_STDEVP(SUM([SALES]))
```

This formula returns the biased standard deviation of the sum of sales within the window (or pane). Note: When the [start] and [end] arguments are omitted, the entire frame is used. If the values are incorrect or inconsistent, ensure that you are properly using the Compute By portion of the table calculation.

Intermediate:

```
WINDOW_STDEVP(SUM([SALES]), FIRST(),LAST())
```

This formula returns the biased standard deviation of the sum of sales from the first row to the last row of the window (or pane). Note: If the values are incorrect or inconsistent, ensure that you are properly using the Compute By portion of the table calculation.

107. WINDOW_SUM

This table calculation function will return the sum for a given expression over a window (or pane) that the user specifies. Note: Performance is affected with an increase in marks; if the data set is large, using the advanced method will have better performance and scalability.

WINDOW_SUM(expression,[start],[end])

> Expression = Any valid aggregate calculation (e.g., SUM ([Sales])); [start] = start of window (not required); [end] = end of window (not required).

Basic:

WINDOW_SUM(SUM([SALES]))

> This formula returns the sum of sales within the window (or pane). Note: When the [start] and [end] arguments are omitted, the entire frame is used. If the values are incorrect or inconsistent, ensure that you are properly using the Compute By portion of the table calculation.

Intermediate:

WINDOW_SUM(SUM([SALES])),FIRST(),LAST())

> This formula returns the sum of sales from the first row to the last row of the window (or pane). Note: If the values are incorrect or inconsistent, ensure that you are properly using the Compute By portion of the table calculation.

Advanced:

IF INDEX()=1 THEN WINDOW_SUM(SUM([SALES])) ELSE NULL END

> This formula assumes there are a large number of marks in the view or that the user is dealing with a big data set. Through the use of IF/THEN logic, table scans, which cause noticeable performance degradation, can be bypassed. In the end, the calculation takes the sum of sales for the specified window (or frame) and does not repeat the values.

108. WINDOW_VAR

This table calculation function will return the *sample* variance of a given expression over a window (or pane) for which the user specifies. Note: Performance is affected with an increase in marks; if the data set is large, using the advanced method will have better performance and scalability.

`WINDOW_VAR(expression, [start],[end])`

Expression = Any valid aggregate calculation (e.g., `SUM ([Sales])`); `[start]` = start of window (not required); `[end]` = end of window (not required).

Basic:

`WINDOW_VAR(SUM([SALES]))`

This formula returns the sample variance for the sum of sales within the window (or frame). Note: When the `[start]` and `[end]` arguments are omitted, the entire frame is used. If the values are incorrect or inconsistent, ensure that you are properly using the Compute By portion of the table calculation.

Intermediate:

`WINDOW_VAR(SUM([SALES]), FIRST(),LAST())`

This formula returns the sample variance of the sum of sales from the first row to the last row of the window (or frame). Note: If the values are incorrect or inconsistent, ensure that you are properly using the Compute By portion of the table calculation.

Advanced:

`IF INDEX()=1 THEN WINDOW_VAR(SUM([SALES]),0, IIF(INDEX()=1,LAST(),0)) END`

This function assumes there are a large number of marks in the view or that the user is dealing with a big data set. Through the use of `IF/THEN` logic, table scans, which cause noticeable performance degradation, can be bypassed. In the end, the calculation takes the sample variance of the sum of sales for the specified window (or frame). Bonus: Try making the window frames dynamic with a parameter.

109. WINDOW_VARP

This table calculation function returns the *biased* variance of a given expression over a window (or pane) for which the user specifies. Note: Performance is affected with an increase in marks; if the data set is large, using the advanced method will have better performance and scalability.

`WINDOW_VARP(expression, [start],[end])`

Expression = Any valid aggregate calculation (e.g., `SUM ([Sales])`); `[start]` = start of window (not required); `[end]` = end of window (not required).

Basic:

```
WINDOW_VARP(SUM([SALES]))
```

> This formula returns the biased variance for the sum of sales within the window (or frame). Note: When the [start] and [end] arguments are omitted, the entire frame is used. If the values are incorrect or inconsistent, ensure that you are properly using the Compute By portion of the table calculation.

Intermediate:

```
WINDOW_VARP(SUM([SALES]),FIRST(),LAST())
```

> This formula returns the biased variance of the sum of sales from the first row to the last row of the window (or pane). Note: If the values are incorrect or inconsistent, ensure that you are properly using the Compute By portion of the table calculation.

Advanced:

```
IF INDEX()=1 THEN WINDOW_VARP(SUM([SALES]),0,
IIF(INDEX()=1,LAST(),0)) END
```

> This formula assumes there are a large number of marks in the view or that the user is dealing with a big data set. Through the use of if/then logic, table scans, which cause noticeable performance degradation, can be bypassed. In the end, the calculation takes the biased variance of the sum of sales for the specified window (or frame). Bonus: Try making the window frames dynamic with a parameter.

110. YEAR

This date function returns an integer representing the year of any given date. This is a shortened form of DATEPART (year, Date).

```
YEAR(Date)
```

Date is the time period from which the year is extracted.

Basic:

```
YEAR(#March 14, 2013#)
```

> The preceding formal returns 2013.

Intermediate:

```
YEAR(DATEADD('day', [Date], 5 ))
```

> The preceding formula returns the day that [Date] + 5 days lands on. If [Date] is March 14, 2013, then this function will return 2013.

Advanced:

```
CASE [Parameter].[Date Unit]
WHEN 'Day' THEN DAY([Date])
WHEN 'Month' THEN MONTH([Date])
WHEN 'Year' THEN Year([Date])
END
```

The preceding formula returns an integer. A parameter, [Date Unit] is also used to allow the user to control date type that the answer will be expressed in. If the user selects Year, the function will return the year of [Date].

111. ZN

```
ZN (expression)
```

Expression = any given number. The ZN (zero NULL) function is used to return zero values where NULL values exist in the view. If the value is not NULL, then the function returns the expression; otherwise, it returns zero. Use ZN to avert NULL results.

Basic:

```
ZN([Profit])
```

This function will look at all values for Profit that exist in the view and returns Profit value if it is not NULL; otherwise, it will return zero.

Intermediate:

```
ZN(SUM([Profit]))-LOOKUP(ZN(SUM([Profit])),-1)
```

This function returns the difference in profit from the current row to the value in the relative offset of this row; in this case the target row is the previous row. The ZN function is applied twice. In the first calculation the ZN function is applied to return zero if the value is NULL. Then ZN is included in the LOOKUP expression to avoid returning NULL values there as well.

NOTES

1. Tableau User Forum, "4. Re Attribute?", Joe Mako, last modified November 16, 2011, accessed July 20, 2013, http://community.tableausoftware .com/thread/114562?start=0&tstart=0.

Tableau Data Shaper Excel Plug-In

If you rely on spreadsheet or text files as datasources, you'll probably need to reshape the data to facilitate analysis. Reshaping data manually can be time-consuming. Fortunately, Tableau has provided an Excel add-in tool that makes reshaping data fast and easy.

WHY IS RESHAPING DESIRABLE?

Figure B-1 is a typical format for spreadsheet data. The data presented includes revenue categories and time series information.

	A	B	C	D	E	F	G	H	I	J	K	L	M
1	Category	Jan-13	Feb-13	Mar-13	Apr-13	May-13	Jun-13	Jul-13	Aug-13	Sep-13	Oct-13	Nov-13	Dec-13
2	Payroll	1000	1000	1000	1200	1200	1200	1300	1300	1300	1400	1400	1400
3	Rent	800	800	800	800	800	800	800	800	800	900	900	900
4	Supplies	150	150	150	150	150	150	150	150	150	150	150	150
5	Travel	200	500	1000	250	1000	1000	1200	500	500	1500	250	250
6	Other	100	100	100	100	100	100	100	100	100	100	100	100

FIGURE B-1 *Spreadsheet data*

While Figure B-1 is conducive for analyzing data in a spreadsheet, it isn't optimal for analysis using Tableau. Each row below the headings will be interpreted as dimensions:

- Payroll
- Rent
- Supplies
- Travel
- Other

The problem is in how the columns will be interpreted. Each column represents the same measure (expense amounts), but because the expenses are divided by month, Tableau will interpret each column as a separate measure. This isn't how a database would store the information. Attaching Tableau to this datasource won't provide the flexibility you'll require. Figure B-2 shows how Tableau interprets the spreadsheet.

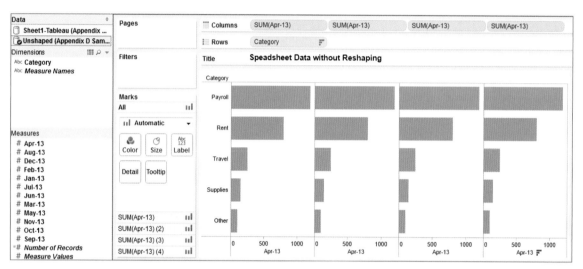

FIGURE B-2 *Tableau connected to original data*

In Figure B-2 you can see that each column of the spreadsheet is interpreted as a separate measure. This makes time series analysis difficult.

USING THE RESHAPER

After running the data reshaper the data will be in a more row-oriented format because the reshaper pivots the data—creating a row for each combination of dimension, date, and amount as you see in Figure B-3.

Adding more descriptive names for columns two (month) and three (expense) can be done in the source spreadsheet, or you can alias the names in Tableau after connecting to the reshaped data. This format is much more conducive to analysis because each row represents a specific dimension for a specific month. Figure B-4 shows a time series chart using the reshaped data.

FIGURE B-3 *Reshaped data*

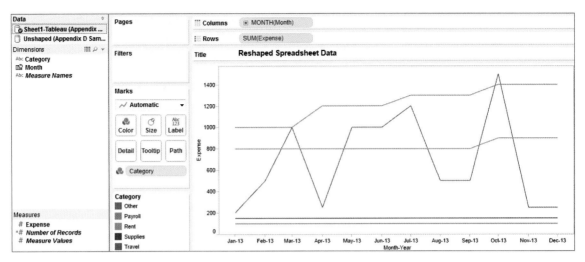

FIGURE B-4 *View using reshaped data*

Tableau interprets the reshaped data, correctly classifying every month of expense as a single measure. The month column is correctly interpreted as a date field, and the expense categories are preserved. The reshaper facilitates more flexible analysis.

INSTALLING THE RESHAPER

Installing Tableau's Excel Data Reshaper is a snap (Excel 2007 and above). An executable file is available on the Tableau website. Find it by searching for Data Reshaper. Tableau also provides installation and operating instructions. Installing the reshaper requires a couple of minutes. Search Tableau's website for a blog post by Ross Perez entitled Reshaping Data Made Easy for clear and concise operating instructions.

InterWorks Book Website

The book's InterWorks book website includes resources to further advance your Tableau knowledge. Point your browser to `http://tableauyourdata.com` and take advantage of free resources including:

- Sample workbooks
- Video training files
- Feature updates for new Tableau releases
- Useful web resources
- Recommended reading

SAMPLE WORKBOOKS

Organized by chapter and annotated with additional instructions, the sample workbook files complement the book by allowing you to follow along with working copies of the material presented in the text.

VIDEO TRAINING FILES

View live demonstrations of techniques included in the book. The videos will be limited to five-minute durations and focus on one or two topics.

FEATURE UPDATES ON NEW TABLEAU RELEASES

Tableau maintains an aggressive upgrade schedule, typically releasing one major update every year with several significant maintenance releases. Read about the new features and how to take advantage of them to enhance your existing dashboards or how to leverage new chart types and datasource connections. These updates will be posted on the InterWorks Book Website. See Figure C-1.

FIGURE C-1 *Website landing page*

USEFUL WEB RESOURCES

The InterWorks team monitors the best websites, blogs, and social media streams on the web related to data visualization and infographics. Find people that love to share their knowledge with the Tableau community.

RECOMMENDED READING

Books about data visualization, infographics, database design, and new open source tools that will add to your Tableau toolset can be found on the Recommended Reading page. Links to blog posts from the InterWorks team and other experienced Tableau practitioners can also be found here.

In addition, updates regarding Tableau conferences, roadshow events, speaking appearances, and other live events in the Tableau ecosystem can also be found under Recommended Reading. Get active in the community by sharing your knowledge at your local user group.

Glossary

The glossary presented is an eclectic mix of Tableau terminology, industry jargon, author jargon, and noteworthy terms, items, and individuals not otherwise covered in the text. Some of these terms have more generic industry definitions. They are presented here in the context of Tableau usage.

32-BIT ARCHITECTURE A computing architecture that is capable of addressing up to four-gigabytes of physical memory without utilizing physical hard disk space.

64-BIT ARCHITECTURE A computer architecture that is capable of addressing over 16 exabytes of physical memory without utilizing physical hard disk space. While theoretically possible in a desktop computer, hardware limitations confine this kind of processing to server environments today.

1000-GIG LAPTOP A mythical vision of the future where a one-thousand dollar laptop can contain one-thousand gigabytes of random access memory that is fully addressable by a sixty-four bit edition of Tableau Desktop. While this is theoretically possible, it will require significant technology advances in hardware and software to achieve.

ACTION Tableau feature that facilitates filtering, highlighting, or invoking a URL call by selecting information contained in a Tableau dashboard or worksheet so that a dashboard or worksheet view is altered by selecting data element(s) from within a pane.

AGGREGATE FUNCTION A function groups together values in a specific way in the resulting view, but the values are presented in the datasource as multiple rows of data. Tableau aggregate functions include AVG (average), COUNT, COUNTD, MAX, MEDIAN, MIN, STDDEV, STDEVP, SUM, VAR, and VARP. See the function reference in Appendix A for specific definitions and examples.

AGGREGATION The level of detail expressed in a view. Highly aggregated data presents less detail. Highly disaggregated data presents more granular (atomic) views of the data.

ANIMATED VISUALIZATION Visualization contained in a dashboard or a workbook that utilizes the Tableau page's shelf to animate the view by automatically incrementing a filter.

ARTISTIC-BENT A person an with artistic-bent values the artistic qualities or esthetics contained within the presentation of data in dashboards and visualizations.

AXIS LABEL An editable part of the axis heading that provides descriptive information regarding the nature of the data being presented by the mark(s) within the view.

BEHFAR JAHANSHAHI Behfar is the CEO and Founder of InterWorks, Inc. Born in Edmond, Oklahoma. He founded InterWorks while attending Oklahoma State University. His last name is pronounced JAH-HAN-SHA-HE.

BETA TESTER Someone who participates in evaluating beta releases of Tableau software and provides valuable, documented feedback on features, functions, and quality issues.

BIG DATA A technology industry buzzword that refers to any particularly large datasource you would like to analyze.

BLUE ICON Refers to the color of the icons used to present discrete entities.

BLUE PILL The blue pill refers to the color used to represent discrete dimensions, measures, and parameters. Discrete entities result in panes (windows) as more granular views of the data are presented within the visualization.

BOOLEAN Boolean refers to Boolean logic—a part of algebra used to derive true or false statements by using logical operators like (AND, BUT, OR, NOT). Formulas that result in true/false or yes/no answers are sometimes referred to as Boolean results.

BOX PLOT A type of visualization typically used to present ranges of disaggregated data for discrete dimensions within Tableau. While this type of chart isn't part of the Tableau's Show Me facility, these charts can be created by disaggregating the data plot and adding a reference distribution and reference lines to the view—creating a box-like appearance around the median value, while also highlighting the minimum and maximum values for each cell in view.

BUBBLE CHART A way to present one-to-many comparisons in Tableau that is generally not favored by data visualization experts because other forms of presenting one-to-many comparisons are more precise.

BULLET GRAPH A chart type invented by Stephen Few that uses the combination of a bar chart, a reference line, and a reference distribution to present actual and comparative data in a space-efficient way. Tableau's Show Me button supports this chart type, although one should verify that the bar reflects the actual value, and the reference line and reference distribution should present comparative budget, historical, or target data.

BUZZED A new Tableau user that is very excited about Tableau's capabilities.

CALCULATED VALUE New measure or dimension created by defining a formula within Tableau's formula editing menu.

CELL The lowest-level of granularity presented within a view.

CENSUS DATA Information that comes from the United States Census Bureau that is also available in Tableau maps expressed as polygon shapes for state, county, zip code, or census block group.

CHOROPLETH MAP (FILLED MAP) Map style in which the shape of a map element (country, state, etc.) is used to depict a value range within the map through the use of color. This chart type is supported by the Show Me feature where it is referred to as a Filled Map.

CLOUD SERVICES Computing services provided to end users via the Internet because they can be economically delivered with adequate performance and security. Tableau Public is an example of a free cloud computing service. Tableau Public Premium is a fee-based cloud computing service.

COLUMN SHELF The place to position dimensions or measures pills so that the data that they represent is expressed horizontally across the view.

COLUMN TOTAL The menu option for expressing the total of a column contained within a Tableau view.

COLUMNAR-ANALYTIC DATABASE A database that is designed to efficiently query and present data from very large data sets very quickly. Tableau has connectors to most of the popular column stores commercially available.

CONTINUOUS DATA TYPE Continuous data types (denoted by green-color pills in Tableau) present data in unbroken, continuous value-streams. For example, dates presented as continuous dimensions within time-series charts will continue to be presented as unbroken lines as time is drilled to more granular levels. Conversely, discrete data types (denoted by blue-color pills) display broken, discrete panes of data as time is presented at more granular levels.

CORE LICENSE Tableau Server licensing model in which the customer licenses Tableau Server in a way that provides for unlimited users but a limited hardware model because the license amount is determined by the number of server core memory microprocessors.

COUNT Database function that is used to count every row from the datasource presented in the view. It is the equivalent to assigning the value of one to each row in the datasource and then summing those values.

COUNT DISTINCT A database function used to count each distinct instance of a value within a set so that repeated entries of the same value are only counted once.

CROSSTAB A visualization style that presents text in grid form, similar to the way numbers are presented in spreadsheets. Crosstabs provide an effective means for looking up specific values.

CUSTOM GEOCODING Tableau provides geographic coordinates of standard geographic entities (state, county, postal code, etc.). If you need to present a specific address on a map you must supply custom geocoding coordinates for the address. Custom geocoding refers to the process of obtaining customized geographic coordinates.

DASHBOARD Dashboards are an assembly of workbooks within a special view within Tableau. Unlike a workbook in which the data shelf presents datasource fields (dimensions and measures), as well as parameter, sets, and groups; the dashboard design page provides a workspace for placing individual work-books within view and enables the resulting panes of information to become interactive.

DATA ANALYST A data analyst is a person responsible for gathering data and turning that data into information that other people can use. Frequently, analysts are required to develop insight and provide analysis of the data so that other staff can act on the information provided.

DATA ARCHITECT A data architect is a technical professional with deep understanding of database schema, extract transform and load logic, and other technical aspects of database design.

DATA BLENDING The act of combining data from dissimilar datasources in Tableau through the use of a common dimension. Data blending joins data from a primary and secondary datasource via a left outer-join-like association of the members of one or more fields.

DATA CUBE A database construct in which data is pre-aggregated in order to achieve improved performance through pre-calculation of the answer set. As a result, data cubes reduce the amount and granularity of data available for the user to query.

DATA EXTRACT Extracting data in Tableau refers to the act of pulling some or all of the data from a datasource into Tableau's proprietary data engine. Extract files provide a compressed (and many times, better performing) alternative versus a direct connection to a datasource.

DATA QUALITY　Data quality refers to the accuracy and completeness of the datasource being analyzed.

DATA SERVICE　Data services offer data for a fee in industry standard data formats. Some data services offer public data without charge. For-fee data services typically provide more accurate and complete data sets in more readily consumable forms than free services.

DATA SHELF　The data shelf is the left side of Tableau's worksheet window that displays the data connections available for the analyst to use to build views. You can connect to as many datasources as you like with Tableau.

DATA VISUALIZATION　Data visualizations in Tableau refer to the worksheet views of the combination of measures and dimensions added to the column and row shelves and the marks card. Combinations of worksheets displayed in dashboard panes are also referred to collectively as data visualizations.

DATE PART　Date part is used to express discrete data types when defining custom date types in Tableau.

DATE VALUE　Date value is used to express continuous data types when defining custom date types in Tableau.

DIMENSION　Dimensions refer to data types that are typically text, a date, or a key value number in a datasource. Number ranges in histograms are also dimensions.

DIRECT CONNECTION　Direct connections in Tableau refer to working directly with a datasource as opposed to using Tableau's data extract engine to store the data.

DISAGGREGATION　Disaggregation refers to exposing progressively more detail contained within the database.

DISCRETE DATA TYPE　Discrete data types (denoted by blue-color pills in Tableau) present data in broken, windowed panes as more granular levels of the data are exposed in a view. For example, dates presented as discrete data types appear as broken lines within data windows (panes) as time is expressed in more granular ways (year, quarter, month, week, etc.). See Continuous Data Type.

DUPLICATE FIELD　A duplicate field in Tableau refers to the act of duplicating a dimension or measure from a datasource within Tableau by right-clicking on the primary field and selecting the Duplicate menu option.

EDWARD TUFTE Edward Tufte is the respected author of books on data visualization.

EXTRACT, TRANSFORM, LOAD (ETL) An ETL process is the act of cleaning suspect source data through computer logic and human intervention.

FACT In a database, a fact refers to a numeric measure to which mathematics may be applied to derive additional insight.

FILMSTRIP VIEW A way of viewing worksheet tabs in Tableau that expresses the information in a small graphic as opposed to text. The filmstrip view can be invoked by selecting the lower right-hand side of the worksheet view (the up and down arrows) and clicking to expose the filmstrip. Alternatively, the upper right section of the worksheet that contains the four grey boxes can be selected to view a Slide Deck style presentation of the filmstrip. Right-clicking on either filmstrip view causes all of the views to be refreshed. This is particularly helpful if you are using Tableau in a presentation because each worksheet will load instantaneously. If you don't refresh all views via the filmstrip, Tableau requires time to render each view individually.

FILTER ACTION An action control that invokes a filter similar to the way a Quick Filter might, but through the use of the data visualization itself. Filter actions restrict the data presented in other panes within a dashboard based on selection(s) made in an individual pane.

FIXED AXIS A fixed axis is an axis that has been specifically restricted to present a predetermined range of values. It is generally not a good idea to fix the axis range within a visualization connected to an active datasource, as the range of values in the data may exceed the range of values in the fixed axis.

FORECAST The act of presenting future estimated values based on historical values. In Tableau this can be done by right-clicking within the view and selecting the Forecast option. Tableau provides a Best Fit forecast that the user can modify by selecting from a menu of available forecast options including Automatic, Automatic With Seasonality, Trend And Season, Trend Only, Season Only, or No Trend Or Season.

GEOCODING Geocoding refers to the act of obtaining longitude and latitude for geographic entities being presented on a map. Tableau automatically geocodes standard geographic entities like country, state, county, and postal code.

GRANULARITY Granularity refers to the level of detail provided within a data set or displayed within a visualization. For example, city is a more granular presentation of geographic data than state.

GREEN ICON Green icons represent dimensions or measures that are continuous.

GREEN PILL Green pills refer to a dimension or measure that is continuous.

GROUP A group is an ad hoc entity in Tableau that is represented by the paper clip icon. Groups refer to combinations of sets of values. Grouping dimension set members is an effective way to deal with many small outlier members of a set.

HADOOP A popular, open source, no-SQL database used to collect and store very large and dynamic data sets without having to pre-define a data schema.

HEAT MAP A data visualization in which up to two measures can be displayed by using size and color to express the values. Heat maps are a good way to express many comparisons of a large number of set members to quickly identify outliers.

HIERARCHY Hierarchies provide the ability to express different values within related dimensions in Tableau by expanding and contracting the hierarchy displayed in a view. Tableau provides automatically-generated data hierarchies for year, quarter, month, and so on. You can manually combine fields to create custom combinations of dimensions in views.

HIGHLIGHT ACTION An action type that provides highlighting of specific selections based on color or shape. Highlight actions can be invoked through color or shape legends or by manual definition through the action menu.

HIGHLIGHT TABLE A crosstab view that uses coloration of the cells to highlight value differences. In Tableau, highlight tables require the selection of one measure only.

HISTOGRAM A visualization type that uses a bar graph to display ranges of values by counting the number of times a particular range of values occurs in the source data.

JEDI A Tableau user that is particularly skilled and knowledgeable.

JOIN A database term used to describe the linking of tables through a common key record. Tableau supports inner, left, and right join types through point-and-click selection. Union join types can be achieved by editing the connection script generated by Tableau within Tableau's connection dialog window.

LEVEL OF DETAIL Level of detail refers to the level of granularity expressed within the view. More granular details of a data set are exposed as more dimensions are placed within the view or within the marks card.

MAINTENANCE RELEASE Maintenance releases are minor releases provided to Tableau customers that fix bugs or provide software upgrades that do not constitute major releases.

MARKS CARD The marks card contains the marks buttons for mark type, color, size, text labels, detail (level of detail), and Tooltips.

MEASURE Measures refer to the numbers contained in the datasource that you may want to apply math toward, geographic coordinates, and the record count calculation supplied automatically by Tableau. Measures can also be created through calculations you define.

NAMED-USER LICENSE Refers to a license type in which the license is determined by the specific username.

ODBC CONNECTION A generic windows connection to an otherwise unsupported database type.

OLAP CUBE See Data Cube.

ONE-TO-MANY COMPARISON A one-to-many comparison refers to any of the chart types used for comparing the different value ranges within the view. Bar charts, bullet graphs, heat maps, highlight tables, histograms, maps, and bubble graphs are typically used for comparing values.

PAGES SHELF The pages shelf in Tableau is a filter type that can be used to animate views. Animated views are only available in Tableau Desktop or Tableau Reader and are not enabled within Tableau Server or Tableau Public.

PANE Panes denote the breaks between discrete entities expressed in the visualization. They are expressed by light grey border lines.

PARAMETER Parameters are formula variables that appear as Quick-Filter-like controls on the desktop. Parameters enable self-service business information by allowing information consumers to change the values or dimensions expressed in views.

PERFORMANCE TUNING Performance tuning refers to the act of improving the load and rendering performance of a visualization or dashboard. Tableau provides performance tuning tools for the desktop (via the Help menu option and the Start Performance Recording selection). The performance recorder analyzes Tableau's log files and creates a Tableau dashboard reflecting the relative speed in which queries are executed and rendering is achieved.

PIE CHART Pie charts are a popular way to visualize one-to-many comparisons that are generally not favored by the Vizerati.

PILL A pill refers to the visual entity used to place a dimension field or measure field on the row shelf, column shelf, or any other shelf within the Tableau worksheet.

POLYGON Polygons are a shape typically used for expressing geographic members on a map. For example, Tableau supplies polygon shapes for country, state, etc.

POWER HELLO The power hello is what happens when you meet Christian Chabot and Kelly Wright of Tableau Software in person. Pure energy and enthusiasm.

QUICK FILTER Quick Filters are filter elements that are exposed on the desktop within a worksheet or a dashboard.

REFERENCE LINE Reference lines are invoked from the axis and are used to express a statistic or value within a cell, pane, or worksheet.

REPLACE DRAG Replace drag refers to the ability to replace a pill by dragging and dropping another pill on top of a pill.

RIGHT-CLICK DRAG Right-click drag refers to the ability to express more granular controls when placing a field into the worksheet.

ROW SHELF The row shelf is used to express the value row-wise in the visualization.

ROW TOTAL The row total is used to express the grand total of the row expressed in the visualization.

SCATTER PLOT The scatter plot is a visualization used to compare two measures. More aspects of the data set can be expressed through the use of shape, color, and size within the scatter plot. Reference lines can be added to express correlation. Scatter plots offer a good way to do ad hoc analysis.

SCHEMA Schema refers to the architectural design of a database.

SET In Tableau, a set can be used to express specific combinations of dimensions and facts within the datasource. Sets can be static (based on manually selected marks) or dynamically defined (based on value ranges).

SHOW ME BUTTON Tableau's Show Me button allows novice users to create data visualizations based on the combination of measures and dimensions selected by the designer without having to understand what shelves to place the pills upon. This facility makes it easy for novices to build data visualizations.

SPARKLINE Sparklines are tiny information graphics first conceived of by Edward Tufte in his book, *Beautiful Evidence*, Graphics Press LLC: 2006.

STAR SCHEMA Star schema refers to a traditional data warehouse design format in which a fact table (consisting of numbers and key records) is surrounded by joined dimension tables (consisting of key records and text).

STEPHEN FEW Seminal thought leader in the data visualization space, Mr. Few is the author of three influential books on data visualization in the computer age.

SYNTAX Syntax refers to the way formulas are expressed including the symbols needed for the computer to correctly interpret the instruction.

TABLE CALCULATION Table calculations are a type of calculated value within Tableau that uses the structure of the view itself to derive the solution set.

TABLE CALCULATION FUNCTION Table calculation functions are function types used to derive solutions using the structure of the visualization express to define the result set.

TABLEAU BOOKMARK (.TBM) Tableau bookmarks are a file type used to copy an individual worksheet visualization from one workbook to another.

TABLEAU DATA EXTRACT (.TDE) Tableau data extract files are files that contain data pulled from the host datasource that has been stored in Tableau's proprietary data engine.

TABLEAU DESKTOP PERSONAL Tableau Desktop personal refers to the desktop license for the personal edition. Personal edition connects to Tableau data extract files, Microsoft Access, Microsoft Excel, or text files.

TABLEAU DESKTOP PROFESSIONAL Tableau Desktop professional refers to the desktop license for the professional edition, which connects to most commercially popular databases or to unsupported databases through ODBC.

TABLEAU ONLINE Tableau Online is a version of Tableau Server that is a cloud-based service managed by Tableau Software. Unlike Tableau Server, Online does not have a minimum user count licensing requirement.

TABLEAU PACKAGED WORKBOOK (.TWBX) Tableau packaged workbooks refer to workbook files that have been saved in a way that bundles the source data with the Tableau visualizations so that both are contained in a single, compressed file. Packaged workbooks can be consumed by Tableau Reader.

TABLEAU PUBLIC A free version of Tableau Desktop that is limited to connecting to data sets with no more than 1,000,000 records. Datasources are also limited to text files, Excel spreadsheets, or Access database files.

TABLEAU PUBLIC PREMIUM A paid version of Tableau public that offers access to unlimited data sizes, more data connection options, and more control over data security.

TABLEAU SERVER Tableau Server is Tableau's data consumption environment for entities that want to share information securely within a defined group of users.

TABLEAU WORKBOOK (.TWB) Tableau workbooks are files in which the design of the data visualizations, the dashboards, and the data connections are saved, but not the data itself. As a result, these files are normally small because the datasource keeps the data, not Tableau.

TDWI (THE DATA WAREHOUSE INSTITUTE) The Data Warehouse Institute is a database industry information service.

TIME SERIES Time series charts are an information visualization type used to display data over time.

TOOLTIPS Tooltips are pop-up windows that display additional details regarding the mark selected within data visualizations in Tableau.

TRANSACTION SCHEMA Transaction schema refers to databases designed to ensure the accuracy of an individual transaction in a database as opposed to a data warehouse schema used to chunk information for analysis.

TREND LINE Trend lines are invoked in Tableau by right-clicking within the worksheet to display a trend line of the data using linear, logarithmic, exponential, or polynomial regression.

TREND MODEL The trend model is used to describe the math employed to create a trend line in Tableau.

UNION A type of join clause used to join two different tables of identical structure, essentially adding them together. Union joins can only be achieved in Tableau by editing the connection script.

URL ACTION An action type that can be used to call webpage URLs to make data from the data visualization interact with a website embedded within a dashboard; or called from a dashboard, and visualized within a web browser.

USER FORUM The Tableau user forum is a place to ask questions and have questions answered about Tableau.

VIEW A view in Tableau refers to an individual data visualization or a pane within a dashboard.

VIZ A viz is an abbreviated way of saying data visualization.

VIZERATI Anyone generally recognized as a member of the data visualization world.

WORKBOOK A workbook is a shorthand way of referring to a Tableau workbook.

WORKSHEET A worksheet is an individual design page within Tableau Desktop.

YODA Yoda is the nickname given by Giedra Aleknonyte (a member of the Vizerati) to the author of this book.

Index